WE ARE THE DEAD

For the children of Carleton Place who gave
their lives during the Great War to end all Wars.

"For Your Tomorrow"

In Memoriam

Here Dead We Lie

Here dead we lie because we did not choose
To live and shame the land from which we sprung.
Life, to be sure, is nothing much to lose;
But young men think it is, and we were young.

A.E. Housman[1]

[1]Brian Gardner, ed., *Up the Line to Death—The War Poets 1914-* Meuthen & Co. Ltd., 1964), p. 170.

Published by

GENERAL STORE
PUBLISHING HOUSE

Box 28, 1694B Burnstown Road
Burnstown, Ontario, Canada K0J 1G0
Telephone (613) 432-7697 or 1-800-465-6072

ISBN 1-894263-24-3
Printed and bound in Canada

Layout and cover design by Leanne Enright
Printing by Custom Printers of Renfrew Ltd.
Illustration by Carole Gagnon, Carleton Place High School

Canadian Cataloguing in Publication Data

Gray, Larry
    We are the dead

ISBN 1-894263-24-3
        1. World War, 1914-1918–Casualties–Ontario–Carleton Place
2. Soldiers–Ontario–Carleton Place–Biography. 3. Carleton Place
(Ont.)–Biography. I. Title

FC3099.C37Z48 2000   940.46'771382   C00-901011-4
F1059.5.C323G74 2000

for Gloria

ACKNOWLEDGEMENTS

It is with gratitude that I acknowledge the contribution by the following persons to this book:

My wife Gloria, who planted the spark for this book and who is the light of my day. Brian Costello, Mayor of Carleton Place, and Ray Paquette who fanned the flames. David Findlay and the Sons of Temperance for their encouragement.

Research played a major role, and without the kind and selfless assistance of Marilyn Caillier, Access to Information Co-ordinator, National Archives, Personnel Records, I would still be muddling around in the dusty stacks of archival records. Janet Baril, Head Librarian of Carleton Place Public Library, offered advice and assistance in finding town records. She was ably assisted by librarians Shirley Jones-Wellman, Lynda Moulton, Judi Simpson, and Donna Currie, who has a special sense of humour.

Martha Knox and her husband, Donnie, graciously granted me time in their home to explain the McDiarmid family and its lost sons. Martha spread the word about this project and that resulted in Mr. Joe Gibben writing from Winnipeg about his uncle Eddie Hockenhull. Dorene Tuff of Ottawa was kind enough to take the time to write and send a picture of her uncle, Fred Trotman, after reading of the search in the *Carleton Place Canadian*. Rosslyn Virtue of Merrickville provided pictures and anecdotal information on her uncles Ralph and Ross Simpson. With their comrades, the names of these veterans appear on the cenotaph. Theirs were the only families to respond with information concerning their warrior ancestors, further emphasizing the cry "Lest We Forget!"

Both Brian Costello and Norm Christie are to be thanked for allowing the use of excerpts from their books. Norm also granted permission for the use, from his publications, of Bill Constable's maps.

I thank Bruce Wilson, who made wonderful use of the Carleton Place High School computer resources (thanks Tom Joron) to help me format the manuscript, copy photographs and maps to disk and who even assisted a techno-peasant install a new computer and ensure that it worked, even if the operator didn't. Without Bruce there were times when I would truly have been "dead in the water."

I also want to thank my editor, Susan Code, whose instruction in English usage and the art of writing has been instrumental in the shaping of this book. Leanne Enright, layout and design, deserves special heartfelt thanks. To Susan and Leanne I owe a great debt. Their role has been tremendously important in the production of this book. Neither ever lost their sense of humour even when the author lost his.

TABLE OF CONTENTS

INTRODUCTION

This did not start as a book. In November 1998, my wife, an English and drama teacher at Carleton Place High School, approached me with a project. She is responsible for the school's Remembrance Day services and was concerned that the list of names from the cenotaph was inadequate. The list, read by students each year during the service, contained only last names and a single initial. The dead had become almost anonymous. She asked me, a retired military type who fancied himself an amateur war historian, to take on the task of putting faces to these names. She wanted identities for all those from Carleton Place who had paid the supreme price in both world wars and Korea.

It occurred to me that this was a terrific idea. If not done soon, these men and women would indeed disappear into the dust of time; 628,736 Canadians served in the Great War and 68,304 were killed. It is important that high school students be aware that the boys who died in the mud of Flanders were just like them; not much older when they died than today's students are when they graduate.

Another influencing factor was the inordinate number of names on the Carleton Place cenotaph. An illuminated Roll of Honour hanging in the town's council chambers lists more than two hundred people who served in this "War to end all Wars." Fifty-one silver stars signify those who died. *The Ottawa Citizen's* columnist, Dave Brown, in his book *Faces of War*, did the math. Brown notes that the town had a population then of about 4,000, half of whom he thought would have been children and a quarter would have been women. That left only one thousand, of whom he estimates two-thirds would have been either too old or would not have met the physical requirements for military service. As Mayor Brian Costello was quoted as saying, "This town has a history of serving."

Mayor Costello is the author of a history of the World War I aviators from Carleton Place who brought fame to this busy Ottawa Valley community. His support and encouragement helped me continue the production of this work.

This book began as a simple list of biographical information about each soldier. However, many questions soon arose. Whose sons were they? What did they do before enlisting? What happened to them during their army service? How did they die and where? I turned first to the records of the Commonwealth War Graves Commission in Canada. Basic information concerning name, rank and serial number surfaced but considerable blanks remained. The number of soldiers with no known grave was striking. Surnames and initials engraved on monuments such as the Ypres (Menin Gate) Memorial and the Canadian National Vimy Memorial are their only commemoration. How sad!

I began researching the war years editions of the local weekly newspaper, the *Carleton Place Herald*. At first I found only small news items about recruiting in the local area and the men going off to war, with mentions in the "local" columns of visits home from training depots. Then I happened upon the published letters Horace Brown had sent home and I was hooked. When I discovered he was a brother of the famous air ace, Roy Brown, it was like eating peanuts or potato chips. You can't stop after just one!

The biographies in this book are those of the people whose names appear on the war memorial. I have tried to follow in the boots of these citizen soldiers. They are in the chronological order in which they either were killed or wounded, or contracted the disease that ended with their untimely deaths due to the effects of the war.

While alive they kept their thoughts to themselves; unable to explain their concepts of service and loyalty to a generation more self-indulgent and liberal than theirs. Their war has been analysed to death, most often with scathing criticism. They never perceived themselves as heroes, nor even as particularly brave. Most of the time they were scared absolutely stiff. But they endured, achieved, and remain convinced of the rightness of their actions.

For each name there is a history. Tragically, some are all too short. They need telling and recording. Hopefully this volume does that, and interests readers enough to further explore their heritage. Most of all I hope this writing does honour to a remarkable generation. A similar publication of the World War II names will follow.

Chapter One

ONCE UPON A TIME

People will not look forward to posterity,
who never look backward to their ancestors.
Edmund Burke, 1790

The military history of the town of Carleton Place precedes its birth. During the War of 1812–1814, British troops stationed in the colony held American forces to their own side of the St. Lawrence. However, this military threat made evident to the colonial authorities that it would be advantageous to have a more permanent military presence in the "back counties" of Upper Canada. Many of the settlers had distinct sympathies for American aims. What better means to establish a loyal population than to integrate recently discharged soldiers into the colonial civilian populace? Soldiers released from regiments that fought in Europe against Napoleon, and those who had fought in Upper and Lower Canada to repel the Americans, provided a good source of loyal, trained militiamen should any danger to the British crown arise.

The townships of Bathurst, Drummond and Beckwith were surveyed. Demobilized soldiers and emigrants from Scotland and Ireland arrived in 1816 and 1817. One of these settlers was Mr. James Kent who, in 1817, was given a land grant in Beckwith Township as a reward for his nine years' British military service. There he took up teaching school. He had been a private soldier in the Glengarry Light Infantry Fencible Regiment and had fought during the 1812–1814 war against the United States. The settlement of Morphy's Falls (later Carleton Place) was established in 1819 where the Mississippi River empties into a substantial lake. William Morphy and William Moore, both from Ireland, were granted rights that year to much of the present townsite of Carleton Place. The land was cleared and homes were built. The little falls provided power for grist and lumber mills.

The early settlement was known as either Morphy's Falls or Carlton Place. It took on its present spelling, Carleton Place, when

Caleb Bellows, a merchant who owned a licensed distillery, became the first postmaster in 1830. Rumour has it that the changed spelling was simply an error by Canadian postal bureaucrats. The Scottish community near Glasgow, whose name Alexander Morris took for his Canadian community, is still spelled "Carlton Place." Transportation routes opened with the railway arriving from Brockville in 1859 and from Ottawa in 1870. Carleton Place was incorporated as a village in 1870 and as a town on January 6, 1890. Its population was 4,200.

Evidence of early, military activity is found in the accounts of the Ballygiblin Riots which occurred following the annual militia muster in 1824. Men of military age were required to gather once a year for a head count and to have their names enrolled, reminding them that they were members of the King's militia. The unit of militiamen of Beckwith and Ramsay townships had been designated the 4th Regiment of Carleton Militia, which later became known as the 3rd Lanark Regiment. In 1824, a series of disturbances between the early Scots arrivals, mainly in Beckwith township, and the recent Irish settlers in Ramsay, flared up following the April 23 militia muster. They had met at Alexander Morris's Mill Road Inn. Fighting broke out and the tumult continued during two weeks of reprisals by each faction, exchanges of gunfire and the loss of one life. Only intervention by district officials from Perth quelled the inflamed tempers.

During the Upper Canada Rebellion of 1837–38, Robert Bell, a lieutenant colonel in the reserve militia, organized the volunteer Loyal Village Guards. A rebel attack near Prescott in 1838 caused the call to active service of some seventy-five members of the Beckwith and Ramsay militia based in Carleton Place. Under the command of Captain Glendenning, they readied themselves, but the rapid defeat of the rebels negated their call to arms.

The Carleton Place Rifle Company, numbering more than fifty men, was formed in 1862 to protect Canada during the Fenian Raids. They replaced the ill-equipped and untrained militia to become part of the first active service military unit composed entirely of volunteer soldiers. In December 1862, the unit was officially designated the Carleton Place Volunteer Militia Rifle Company. Captain James Poole and Lieutenant John Brown commanded. The company was called up in March 1866. They travelled by special train to Brockville, in uniform with their guns and bayonets, ready to respond to threatened Fenian incursions from across the river.

This force was also available to quell Canadian fears should the Union Army of the United States realize an early victory over Confederate troops and turn an expansive eye toward the north.

Further strengthening of the militia in 1866 resulted in the formation of the 41st Battalion, Brockville Rifles, composed of six companies, one each from Brockville, Carleton Place, Gananoque, Merrickville, Pakenham and Perth. Carleton Place also provided the battalion's brass band.

In May 1870, Fenian raids took place in the Eastern Townships of Quebec. In Eastern Ontario, the local threat appeared to be from Malone, New York, probably against Cornwall and Prescott. All six companies of the 41st Battalion and the band travelled by steamboat from Brockville to take up posts along the river. The Carleton Place Company, No. 5 of the 41st Battalion, numbered fifty-three officers and men. Commanding was Captain John Brown (James Poole had been promoted to the rank of major and assigned to battalion duties) and Ensign David MacPherson. Earlier in May the lieutenant, Josiah Jones Bell, had left the company to volunteer for service in the Red River Rebellion. Perhaps this military might proved too intimidating, for the anticipated Fenian campaign across the St. Lawrence never materialized. The Canadian militiamen were released from duty.

In the *Carleton Place Herald* of December 12, 1916, note was taken that Captain J. Jones Bell, son of the late Robert Bell of Carleton Place, now on the military retired list, had been granted the rank of honorary major in the Canadian militia. Captain Bell had served as an officer in The Royal Canadian Regiment with Lord Wolseley on the Red River expedition.

In 1900, Canadian soldiers from Carleton Place volunteered for active service and duty in South Africa against the Boers. William H.V. Hooper, who was to lead the first contingent of Carleton Place boys overseas in 1914 was a Boer War veteran. His military service began at age fourteen when he joined the 43rd Militia Regiment in Ottawa as a bugler. After serving with The Royal Canadian Regiment in the South African War, he came to Carleton Place at age twenty-one, buying the photography business of Charles Pelton. By 1901, he was a captain with the 42nd Lanark and Renfrew militia regiment. In 1914, this regiment provided troops to the 2nd Battalion of the Canadian Expeditionary Force.

Boer War contracts benefiting the town included one to the Gilles and Hawthorn mills of the Canadian Woollen Mills for the supply of serge cloth to be used in British army uniforms. To meet the demand the local mill expanded its operation. But in 1903, with the loss of their market to British millers, the company went bankrupt and closed.

The town slowly progressed into the twentieth century. The first Carleton Place motor vehicle fatality occurred in 1906. An automobile driven by Samuel Torrance collided with a railroad locomotive and a passenger in the car was killed. In 1910, the first Boy Scout troop was formed by William Moore, a veteran of the South Africa war who had served with Lord Baden-Powell during the siege at Ladysmith. This was the second Scout troop in Canada, the first having been formed in Merrickville by Mr. Hammond, a Boer War comrade of Mr. Moore. In 1913, plans were made to form the first Carleton Place High School Cadet Corps after the principal, Mr. E.J. Wethey, and nine high and public school students attended a cadet camp of more than twelve hundred boys at Barriefield, near Kingston.

World events intruded upon the peace of Carleton Place in August 1914. War was declared in Europe. Within two weeks a dozen volunteers from the local militia battalion, under the command of Capt. William H. Hooper, boarded a train for Perth and their "great adventure." The August 15 parade to the railway station was led by town officials, the Carleton Place brass band and a pipe band from Renfrew. Hundreds of citizens joined the throng. As the train pulled away from the station with the first men to answer Empire's call, strains of *Auld Lang Syne* wafted over the melancholy stillness of the afternoon. Everyone truly expected the war to be won and the boys back home before Christmas.

Chapter Two

THE FIRST CONTINGENT

During the summer of 1914, France, Russia and Great Britain faced off against Germany and Austria-Hungary. On June 28, the Archduke Franz Ferdinand of Austria was shot and killed by a Serbian nationalist while on a state visit to Sarajevo in Bosnia. This gave Austria, bent on conquest, its excuse to declare war on Serbia and the escalation began. Russia mobilized; Germany declared war on Russia on August 1 and on France two days later. On August 4, en route to France, the German army trampled neutral Belgium. When a British ultimatum demanding Germany withdraw from Belgium expired at midnight on August 4, Britain was at war. Canada, the dutiful dominion, followed suit. Prime Minister Sir Wilfred Laurier had stated on January 12, 1910, "When Britain is at war, Canada is at war. There is no distinction."

In its issue of August 18, 1914, the *Carleton Place Herald* reported that Capt. William H. Hooper marched the Carleton Place members of "B" Company, the 42nd Regiment, to the train. They departed for Perth for reorganisation with the rest of the regiment before proceeding to the army's largest, and newest, training base in Canada— Valcartier. There they became part of the 2nd Battalion, Eastern Ontario Regiment. Among the soldiers destined never to return alive were Ptes. Robert Boreland, Lockhart Campbell, Joseph Hamilton, Arthur J. Simons and Neil McPhee. Sgt. J. Horace Brown was wounded and repatriated home, only to be commissioned and returned to England where he perished. Surviving those first years of trench warfare were Sgts. James McGill and George New, and Ptes. Leonard Halsey, Harry McLaren and Ernest Reynolds. But both their psyches and their bodies were deeply scarred.

Why did they go? The answer to that mystery lies buried with each veteran of the war. It must be remembered that in young Canada there were few white natives, and fewer still of an age to be in military service. Most young men were immigrants or the sons of immigrants. Many were involved in the local militia unit. In the best British tradition this was a very socially acceptable activity for young bloods. Were they motivated by a desire to return to the British Isles, for personal or patriotic reasons? They scrambled to get tickets early because few thought this war would last more than a couple of months. Were they "doing the right thing"? Some knew previous active service in the Boer War. Was it just the prospect of adventure for men and boys in rural colonial Canada? Farm life and factory employment was dull, monotonous and labourious. Those with militia service were confident that war would be fun. Wearing a uniform with bright flashes of colour, marching together with friends behind brass bands before the adoring eyes of young ladies, collecting medals attesting to their personal valour—Oh, it would be such great fun!

The German army wheeled south from Belgium into France. A small British expeditionary force made a stand at Mons, but the task was impossible. The first British soldier killed in World War I, Pte. J. Parr of the Middlesex Regiment, shot on August 4, lies buried in Saint-Symphorien Cemetery outside Mons. Nearby lies the body of the last fatality, a Canadian, Pte. George Lawrence Price of the 28th North West Battalion, 6th Canadian Infantry Division. Price was killed near the canal at Mons by a sniper's bullet through the chest. It happened two minutes before 11:00 a.m. on November 11, 1918, less than a kilometre in distance but four dreadful years in time from where the first man fell. The First World War ended where it had begun. Those eager and idealistic boys who departed Carleton Place with such fanfares on that warm August afternoon could never have imagined the horror they would face.

The Eastern Ontario Battalion was transported from Valcartier to Quebec City, where they boarded the steamship S.S. *Cassandra*. Anyone who thought he would have a fast trip to Europe quickly had that illusion dashed. For two days they were cooped up aboard the ship as it lay at anchor opposite the Citadel of Quebec, in full view of Dufferin Terrace and the twinkling lights of the Château Frontenac. The ship lay close enough to shore that its passengers could hear the music and observe the civilians promenade.

They steamed up the St. Lawrence but two days later dropped anchor again, in the Gaspé basin, to await the rest of the armada. At three o'clock on the afternoon of October 3, *Cassandra* sailed out into the gulf to join the great convoy carrying 32,000 Canadians to the battlefields of Europe. Thirty-one makeshift troopships were led by three Royal Navy warships.

The crossing was uneventful, even idyllic. Due to reported German submarine activity in the English Channel, the convoy made for Plymouth Sound rather than Liverpool, as originally scheduled. They arrived on October 14, but again the soldiers faced a tedious wait afloat. It was ten long days until, on the 25th, they disembarked at 9:45 p.m. Plymouth was the ancestral home of Capt. Hooper, who now had command of the Carleton Place boys in "H" Company. He had not been back to the city for nineteen years. He was given the proud honour and privilege of leading the battalion, at the head of his own company, through the streets of his hometown.[1]

[1] Col. W.W. Murray, The History of the 2nd Battalion (Ottawa: The Historical Committee, 1919), p.11.

Chapter Three

ARMY LIFE

The battalion, in a bivouac at Bustard Camp, was under canvas for the winter of 1914–15. They had the misfortune to experience the heaviest winter rainfall in years. The main priorities were training, equipping and organizing the troops. The company of Carleton Place men in the 2nd (Eastern Ontario) Battalion was assigned to the 1st Brigade of the 1st Canadian Division. All companies were renumbered and command was given to officers holding the rank of major. The company was now called No. 4 Company under command of Maj. H.G. Bolster, with Capt. Hooper as second in command.

Training during the deplorable weather conditions turned into drudgery. Yet the Canadian troops maintained a high state of morale, even though they had no way to dry their clothes and the entire camp turned into one giant sea of mud. Regulations dating back to 1893 prohibited alcoholic beverages from camp. Valcartier had been dry, but General Alderson, wisely it turned out, established "wet canteens" in Bustard Camp where the officials could at least control the quality and the quantity of liquor. This move also put a stop to quarrelsome soldiers causing disturbances in nearby villages. All such localities were placed "out of bounds" to all military persons except to those with special passes. A help to morale, however, was the policy of granting all ranks up to six days' leave and providing them with a free rail ticket to anywhere in the British Isles.

Letter writing was very much in vogue and the only means of long distance communication. Correspondence home provides fine detail of the lives of these citizen soldiers. Horace Brown, who had relinquished his militia sergeant's stripes for those of a corporal in the regular army, was a prolific writer. Brown was billeted in the town of

Amesbury near the Salisbury Plain. The Plain became infamous to Canadian soldiers of both world wars for its cold, wet weather. Horace wrote on November 13, 1914, that they had been "given two shillings a day for food allowance and were living like kings." Responding to a question from his father about the canteens, he criticized the decision to allow wet canteens in the camp. Horace felt that the extra money the soldiers now had, and the availability of alcohol, was "the worst thing possible." He was quick to establish, however, that "the boys from Carleton Place are well behaved." He reported that all the Carleton Place men were still in the United Kingdom.[1]

Another letter writer, identified in the December 2, 1914, *Carleton Place Central Canadian* only as "one of the boys," under the date of November 14, covers all the faces:

> All from town are well and seem not to mind the weather, although it rains almost every day and we are still in tents. We are pretty well scattered to-day, for Corporal Brown is down to Amesbury [seven miles away] on picquet; Corporal George New is on guard; Jim McGill and J. McPhee are in Salisbury for a visit; Bobby Boreland is over to Ireland on furlough; S. Campbell and J. Hamilton have returned from a trip to Portsmouth to see the latter's brother, who is leaving again for the front; Len Halsey is settling down again after his trip to County Wicklow; Harry McLaren and Ernie Reynolds are on duty; so you see we are all accounted for.

On October 29, 1914, the German army made one last effort to reach the Channel ports of Belgium. The British Expeditionary Force, against overwhelming odds, held them off in the First Battle of Ypres, a country town in that little corner of Belgium known as Flanders. However, these early campaigns cost Britain the greater part of her professional regular army. Very soon the lives lost to all nations in the fight over the Ypres Salient would escalate beyond imagination. In the winter of 1914, movement halted and two great armies filled virtually impenetrable trenches along a seven-hundred kilometre front. The line of ditches stretched from the Belgian seacoast to the border with Switzerland. For the next four years little would change.

[1] The entire text of letters quoted may be found in the Appendix.

Horace Brown continued his correspondence. On January 31, 1915, after a brief stay in hospital for an undisclosed illness, he predicted the Canadians would soon move to the south of France. He cited the weather and an outbreak of spinal meningitis that had killed some dozen soldiers as factors determining their move. Brown presented the soldier's view of the controversy over the Canadian Ross rifle (a sporting weapon unfit for warfare) and the British Lee-Enfield. ". . . I guess we are keeping the same rifle. Some of the Canadians have the Lee-Enfield, but if we cannot get it we can get along quite well with what we have. Although we have all run down the Ross it is not a bad rifle, at least not so bad as some try to make out." The Ross rifle was the result of the Canadian government's decision to make its own rifles. Sam Hughes, Canadian Minister of Militia and a friend of Sir Charles Ross, the designer, had the Ross rifle issued to his army. As a target weapon it was very good, as Canadian marksmen discovered in competition. But in the trenches Canadian soldiers would die trying to manipulate their jammed weapons.

Horace wrote on February 4 that the Canadians had been inspected by the King preparatory to going to the continent. They had been issued with their web equipment that included "knapsack, haversack, waterbottle, sidearms, ball pouches and intrenching [sic] tool." No. 4 Company was transported across the English Channel on the S.S. *Blackwell.* They were aboard from midnight on February 8 until noon on the11th. Quarters were very cramped and the seas rough in stormy weather. The first night at sea, horses and vehicles below decks broke loose. The men had the unenviable task of trying to control scrambling, kicking, frightened horses and vagrant wagons, all deep in the darkened hold. However, a card mailed from Capt. Hooper by February 15 reported that they were all in France, in billets, and fine.

Canadian troops were soon introduced to the realities of trench warfare. After brief training, the 1st Canadian Division relieved veteran British troops over a distance of four miles of front line in the Armentières sector. On February 19 the Canadians entered the trenches at La Chapelle d'Armentières. Thoughts of military glory were quickly dispelled by dirt, disease, despair and death. As well as confronting the enemy they had to learn to fight lice and rats.

INTO THE BREACH

Horace Brown described life in the trenches in a letter of March 11, 1915, to his mother. He found them "pretty dry and I have built and fixed it up so it is quite good now." He told of a "sham attack to draw up the German reserves . . . [during which] two of the old 42nd answered their final roll call in it. Two good lives for King and Country." His words are surprisingly sanguine after only a month's exposure to war.

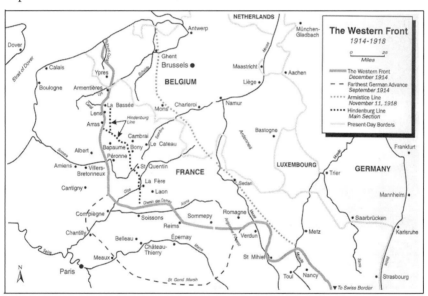

He had discarded much of his heavier equipment to carry food and commented that:

> . . . we had fresh meat to-day. We do all our own cooking in the trenches over open fires in old pails and have to hunt up the fuel. The worst of it is the hot fire melts the solder on our canteens and they leak. I wish we had the seamless ones. Do you think you could get me one and send it to me.

> . . . The Germans fire at our parapet and knock mud into our food when we are cooking, but we do likewise.

The Germans and our side yell back and forth at each other. They speak perfect English and we often jolly each other. They ask are our jobs kept for us in Canada, how much pay we are drawing off our jobs, etc.

The pseudo-civility ended in April. Canadian troops were moved from their relatively quiet sector into the line in front of the town of Ypres. The Second Battalion moved to Vlamertinghe on April 20. To their right were two British divisions and on their left the French 45th Algerian Division. On April 22 the Germans introduced their newest weapon—poison gas.

Following an intensive artillery bombardment, 160 tons of the vile and wicked chlorine gas was released into a light northeast wind. Thick clouds of the yellow-green chlorine drifted over the trenches. French defences crumbled as their troops, unprotected, their lungs seared, died or broke and fled, leaving a gaping four-mile hole in the Allied line. German forces pressed forward, threatening to sweep behind the Canadian trenches and put fifty thousand Canadian and British soldiers in deadly jeopardy. In the face of the massed German infantry, Canadians soon learned the terrible disadvantage of the Ross rifle. It frequently jammed after only a few rounds were fired. Frantic and desperate soldiers had to hammer the bolt back with their boots or shovels in order to reload. Their initiation to war was brutal. But where other troops fled, the Canadians stayed and fought.

> . . . the whole horizon burst into flames. To the north, outlined against the sky, countless fires were burning. It was if hordes of fiends had suddenly been released, and dropping on the distant plain, were burning every town and village. A chill of horror came over us. War seemed suddenly to have assumed a merciless, ruthless aspect that we had not realized till then. Hitherto it had been war as we conceived it, hard blows, straight dealing, but now for the first time we felt as if some horrible Thing, utterly merciless, were advancing to grip us. It might have been a plague or an invasion of rats whose burning eyes were fixing us from right away beyond the river, and we understood, as our hearts missed a beat, that our people would have to fight, not to win a war, not for laurels and honours, but for the right to

exist. Those fires over there told us something indescribably evil. The enemy who lit them would show no mercy. It came over us that each man would have to fight for something more precious than life, for what each of us called home; remote things, far away and precious beings, were suddenly very near, very unprotected, almost in contact with this horror that had suddenly arisen. A peaceful river flowing between tall trees in a distant land, a group picnicking on the bank, pretty faces, laughter, what a frail barrier we were between what that stood for and this . . .

It suddenly became very clear that to survive it would be necessary to go on beyond exhaustion, to march when the body clamoured to be allowed to drop and die, to shoot when eyes were too tired to see, to remain awake when a man would have given his chance of salvation to sleep. And we realized also that so to drive the body beyond its physical powers, to force the mind to act long after it had surrendered its power of thought, only despair and the strength of despair could furnish the motive force.[1]

All through the night, the Canadians fought to close the gap. They mounted a counterattack to drive the enemy out of Kitchener's Wood, an oak plantation near St. Julien. In the morning two more disastrous attacks were made against enemy positions. Little ground was gained and casualties were extremely heavy, but these battles bought some precious time to close the flank.

Darker days yet lay ahead near St. Julien. On April 24, the Germans attacked in an attempt to obliterate the Ypres Salient once and for all. A violent bombardment was followed by another gas attack in the same pattern as before. This time the target was the Canadian line. Here, through terrible fighting, peppered with shrapnel and machine-gun fire, hampered by the frequently jammed Ross rifles, violently ill and gasping for air through mud- and urine-soaked handkerchiefs, they held on until reinforcements arrived.[2]

[1] Maj. Gen. Sir Edward Spears, *Liaison 1914* (London:Eyre & Spottiswoode Ltd., 1930), pp.106-107.

[2] Captain Scrimger, a medical officer with the 14th (Montreal) Battalion, developed an effective antidote to mustard gas. He had the men urinate on their handkerchiefs and tie them around their mouths. This caused the chlorine to crystallize and saved many lives. Jim Lotz, *Canadians At War* (London: Bison Books, 1990), p. 32.

The three brigades of Canadians, in their first appearance on a European battlefield, established a reputation as a formidable fighting force. But the cost was high. In these forty-eight hours, 6,035 Canadians, one man in three, were lost from the country's little force of hastily trained civilians—a grim foreshadowing of what was still to come.[3]

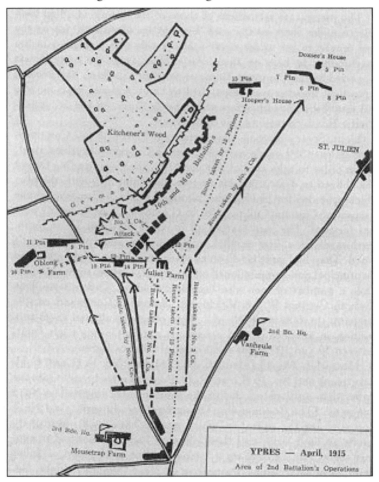

The Ontario boys of the 2nd Battalion had been seconded to the 3rd Brigade commanded by Brig.-Gen. R.E.W. Turner, V.C. He used them to attack a German strong point on the southwest corner of Kitchener's Wood. That first contingent of Carleton Place boys figured prominently in this battle. Their action became known as "the farmhouse fight." They were involved in capturing and trying to hold a

[3] Patricia Giesler, *Valour Remembered–Canada and the First World War* (Ottawa: The Department of Veterans Affairs, 1982), p. 5.

farmhouse near St. Julien. One company seized Oblong Farm while the other cleared trenches and farmhouses east of the wood.

Capt. William Hooper's No. 15 platoon advanced at 5:30 a.m. on April 23 to Alberta Farm, which became known as "Hooper's House." The buildings were sited on a gentle slope in a commanding position. The Germans attached some importance to them. Twice between six and eight o'clock they delivered determined counterattacks. Fighting was intense and bloody, but 15 Platoon beat the enemy back each time. Several prisoners were taken, including an officer carrying a German flare pistol together with some shells. Employing the flares generously in the course of the night, Hooper surprised the enemy on a number of occasions as they prepared to rush the position. Hooper had asked for, and received, a machine-gun, which came with the order that the farm must be "held to the last." How gallantly that order was carried out was only to be revealed the next afternoon.

Saturday, April 24, turned hellish. No. 15 Platoon was alternately digging and fighting. A number of brisk local actions developed in which the bayonet was freely used. From all of them the platoon emerged with honour, but the Germans maintained a relentless attack. The Canadian defenders' chief need was for small arms ammunition, particularly of the type suitable for the machine-gun. This lack seriously threatened their ability to hold on, but after replenishment by runners, Hooper advised headquarters that he "could hold out for two more days." [4]

Only a score of Hooper's men remained by 4:00 p.m. He had succeeded in getting the majority of the group to a trench near the edge of Kitchener's Wood, and from there they maintained their heroic resistance. The machine gun was still in action but Hooper, like nearly all his men, was severely wounded and practically helpless. Withdrawal would be difficult as every escape route came under heavy enemy fire. To get back to the trench, the defenders would have to cross seventy-five yards of ground swept by enemy bullets.

A neighbouring farmhouse was held by a platoon under Lt. William Doxsee, who was killed in the fighting along with most of his men. A handful managed to escape but those in Hooper's House, their

[4] Daniel G. Dancocks, *Welcome To Flanders Fields–The First Canadian Battle of the Great War: Ypres, 1915* (Toronto: McClelland and Stewart, 1988), p. 169.

valiant spirit undaunted, had waited too long to evacuate. They were overwhelmed by the advancing German infantry. Musketry continued as a faint and irregular rattle, becoming fainter and more irregular as the resolute men from Lanark County fell, one by one. Gradually it diminished to a few sporadic bursts. Then the firing ceased. A few men struggled back to the safety of the Canadian lines; Capt. Hooper and Sgt. New began a three-year ordeal in German prison camps.

When the remnants of the platoon withdrew they left behind:

Pte. Robert Boreland—Killed, age 24

Pte. Lockhard Campbell—Killed, age 18

Pte. John Hamilton—Killed, age 24

Pte. Neil McPhee—Killed, age 24

Pte. Arthur Simons—Killed, age 19

Capt. William Hooper—Prisoner of War

Sgt. George New—Prisoner of War

Two weeks later, Pte. James McGill wrote to his mother. His letter, with details of the action at the farmhouse, was published in the *Carleton Place Herald* on May 25, 1915. Excerpts:

We were ordered up to relieve an English regiment who were holding the trenches near St. Julien . . . Capt. Hooper took twenty five of his own boys ahead into a house at the right of the bush along with a machine-gun for the purpose of sniping at the enemy. It was a brick building, so was bullet proof, and we made holes through the walls to shoot through.

The enemy's artillery . . . could not get the right range so we were left there for two days without any person being hurt . . .

In the afternoon of the third day I was sent out again for ammunition when the enemy broke through the French lines on our right leaving us open to a heavy flanking fire, so we had to retire to keep in contact with the French. In the meantime the enemy flocked into the bush on our left in great numbers almost cutting us off in this house. While I was coming up through the reserve trenches with ammunition the Major gave me an order for Capt Hooper to retire. I got through with it to him, and he sent me back again to tell the Major to hold the trenches till we got into them, which he did, but the enemy was too close to us so as soon as the boys came out of the house they cut them down leaving only seven out of the bunch that went in . . .

L. Halsey and E. Reynolds from home were with the stretcher-bearers . . . Halsey afterwards got wounded with a piece of shrapnel. Harry McLaren was in the house, but he says he was one of the first to leave it, so he got through all right. I cannot account for the rest, as we're not sure of what happened to them. Some think they were taken prisoners or were suffocated by that awful gas . . .

It was a great day for the Canadians, but it cost a great many lives. I don't know how I got through, but I never got a scratch, but had to throw away all my personal property and kit bag as it was too heavy, and my life was more valuable.

The battalion that had come into being at Valcartier, that had griped impatiently over disembarking delays at Plymouth Sound, that had for months endured the exposures and privations of Salisbury Plain, was now destroyed. The fine impressions the men had made on imperial troops by their keenness and diligence, and on high-ranking commanders by their soldierly demeanour, were things of the past. Once they reached the fighting front, a life of only nine weeks had been allotted to the 2nd Battalion. The small surviving nucleus was woefully deficient in officers and NCOs. Col. Watson, by necessity, was compelled to build his new 2nd Battalion around this motley group of survivors.

In the edition of August 15, 1916, the *Carleton Place Herald* marked the second anniversary of the departure of the first contingent.

Two years ago today, it does not seem so long, since our first contingent were given a send-off at the station for overseas service. Little did we think the war would last so long or assume such great proportions. The following are the names of our heroes who left on August 15, 1914:

Capt. W.H. Hooper—prisoner in Germany

Sergt. J. Horace Brown, lately discharged from hospital and again awaiting orders at the base

Sergt. Geo. New—prisoner in Germany

Sergt. Jas. McGill incapacitated

Pte R. Boreland, dead

Pte L. Campbell, dead

Pte J. Hamilton, dead

Pte L. Halsey, wounded

Pte A.J. Simons, dead

Pte N. McPhee, dead

Pte H. McLaren in hospital

Pte E. Reynolds in hospital

At the feet of those who have paid the supreme penalty we lay a laurel wreath; to those in confinement we say do not cease to hope; to those unfit we pray your health may shortly be fully restored. Heroes all, we can but honour you as such. You have done your best for King and Country. God bless you all.

Chapter Five

NEVER TO RETURN

Nulla dies umquam memori vos eximet aevo.
"Nothing shall ever erase you from the memory of the ages."

Virgil

ROBERT JOHN BORELAND

Robert, sometimes known as Bobby, Boreland was born in Belfast, County Antrim, Ireland. He was the son of Robert and Margaret Boreland, who brought him to Canada as a lad. He had served in the 42nd Regiment—Lanark and Renfrew Militia in Carleton Place from August 12 to September 22, 1914. He, like his militiamen friends, converted to active service when war with Germany was declared. They formed the first local contingent, Company "B", to respond to the call to arms. The unit became "H" Company of the 2nd Battalion, Eastern Ontario Regiment.

The 2nd Battalion was organized on August 6, 1914. Its motto was *Semper Paratus* (Always Ready) and it served in France and Flanders with the 1st Infantry Brigade of the 1st Canadian Division from September 12, 1915, until the armistice. The battalion is perpetuated by the Governor General's Foot Guards.

Robert Boreland was twenty-two years old when he joined the army. He was a man of a fair complexion with blue eyes and fair hair. Standing 5' 3", he was only a half inch over the minimum height requirement.[1] He had previously been employed as a labourer. After training in Valcartier, he sailed with his battalion on October 4, 1914, aboard the S.S. *Cassandra* from Quebec City. Shortly after arriving in England, Robert took advantage of the gener-

[1] In July 1915, the minimum height requirement was lowered from 5'3" to 5'2" for infantrymen and from 5'7" to 5'4" for artillerymen.

ous leave provisions and a free travel ticket to visit his sister Elizabeth (Lizzie) who still lived in the Balliskillan area of Belfast, Ireland. His military records name her as his next of kin.

Robert was with the unit when they went to France as part of the 1st Canadian Division and moved up into the trenches early in 1915. The Germans advanced in the Second Battle for Ypres and fighting near Langemarck and St. Julien was very heavy. He was in No. 15 Platoon led by Capt. Hooper to the little farmhouse beyond the trench line. There, he met his death. The official army record shows him as "missing" sometime between April 22 and 26, 1915.

The *Carleton Place Herald* of May 25 reported Pte. Boreland as wounded and badly crippled, having lost both a leg and an eye. There is no attribution of this report. Harry MacLaren wrote home that Boreland was missing, while Leonard Halsey wrote, in July 1915, that "R. Bowland" was listed as dead.

Three years later to the day, more was learned of Robert's last few minutes. Capt. Hooper was released from German captivity and had arrived in Murren, Switzerland.[2] He wrote to his wife on March 25, 1917, in regard to the death of Archie Sinclair of Perth, who was also in the farmhouse fight and who also was killed on April 24. Capt. Hooper's letter was published in the *Herald* of April 24, 1917:

> About twelve of those boys fought like demons, and although I could do nothing [he had been badly wounded] but lay there they kept me informed of what was going on. I remember Archie, McIntyre and Boreland getting ammunition off the dead boys in order to keep up their stock. We had a regular hell all our own for a while, and then quietness.
>
> We then found out that Archie and I were almost gone, Boreland, McIntyre and Ormsby were gone, . . .
>
> [Hooper passed out and when he regained consciousness] . . . we heard shots and sometimes crys. Archie said; "My God they are shooting down our wounded boys."

[2] Under the Hague Convention, Britain established an agreement with Germany on October 27, 1915, for prisoner exchanges. Only those sufficiently sick or disabled to be of no further service would qualify for release and officers and NCOs also had to be useless for training or headquarters duties. Desmond Morris, *Silent Battle* (Toronto: Lester Publishing Ltd., 1992), pp. 119-120

The army, for official purposes, in May 1915 considered Robert Boreland killed in action, on or since April 26, 1915. He was twenty-four years old. His body was lost without a trace in the mud of Flanders, southeast of the village of Brieland. His name is etched on the Menin Gate, the Ypres Memorial, in Ypres (now Ieper), Belgium. It is under this gate, over a main road into the city of Ypres, that traffic is stopped every evening at eight o'clock. Two buglers of the city fire department, playing silver bugles provided by Britain, sound the *Last Post* and observe two minutes of silence for the fallen whose names adorn the gate and who have no known graves.

WILLIAM LOCKHARD CAMPBELL

Lockhard Campbell was born in Owen Sound on May 10, 1896, the son of Mr. and Mrs. William James Campbell. His family eventually moved to Carleton Place and lived on Flora Street. He joined his friends in the 42nd Militia Regiment but was employed as a farmhand by Mr. W.J. Bailey. Lockhard's father owned a prosperous farm just outside Carleton Place, near Boyd's Settlement. Campbell was eighteen years, five months old when he joined the regular army. He stood 5' 8" tall and was a young man of a medium complexion with blue eyes and brown hair. He belonged to the Wesleyan Church.

Lockhard enlisted on September 23, 1914, and was with that first contingent to go by train to Perth with Company "B" of the 42nd Regiment. From there they travelled to Valcartier for more intense army training. The group of boys from Carleton Place remained a cohesive unit, sailing together for England and training on the Salisbury Plain. They all became part of "H" Company of the 2nd Battalion, Eastern Ontario Regiment. Just before going to France, Lockhard's feet blistered and he spent March 5–9, 1915, having them treated at the 1st Canadian Field Ambulance medical facility. The affliction was probably the result of a combination of poorly fitted boots and extensive route marches. Most of their training seemed to consist of shouldering their heavy packs and rifles and trudging off for miles across the English countryside.

Lockhard went into the trenches at Ypres. With the forward party of No. 15 Platoon Capt. Hooper ordered him into the farmhouse. Something of the circumstances of this young man's last moments was learned from Harry MacLaren's letter to his father on May 14, 1915: "Campbell is reported missing but I saw him fall when we rushed through the woods. He was hit on the head." Sergeant James McGill, himself wounded, wrote from a hospital in England:

> . . . poor Lockhard is gone to a better land; dying the death of a brave soldier without stain on his conscience.
>
> He was always a good soldier and did all his work willingly and few ever heard him grumble.
>
> As he was counted a good shot . . . he was one of the picked men to go into this house between the two firing lines for sniping purposes . . . We held this house for three days till the enemy made his big advance on April 25th.
>
> . . . A number of the boys being wounded we were obliged to get back to our trenches as quickly as possible so the Captain sent six of us out at first and watched results. That was where Lockhart [sic] met his death by a bullet in the head. It was instant death, causing no pain . . .

Campbell was obviously very well thought of by his comrades in arms. Undoubtedly his youth endeared him to his mates making his loss more heavily felt by those who survived. His was the first notice of the death of a Carleton Place soldier in World War I to appear in the *Carleton Place Herald*, printed in the issue of May 11, 1915. He was one of the youngest boys in that group that had marched so confidently off to war on a warm August 1914 afternoon. He died just two weeks short of his nineteenth birthday.

A measure of Lockhard Campbell's humanity, and regard for the plight of others, is found in the last letter home. He wrote it the day before the battle for Langemarck and his mother received it the same day that she received the report of his death:

> . . . we are just beginning to realize what this war means to the Belgium people . . . chased out of house and home . . . old women . . . carrying larger and heavier packs than we carry . . .

farmers . . . with their horses and waggons loaded to the limit. It makes a person vow vengeance on those who are causing their suffering. The last week we have been through a part of Belgium which has not been touched by the Germans and it is certainly a nice country. But still it isn't like it would be in peacetime for there are refugees all through the country.

Leonard Halsey wrote to his parents on July 27, 1915, "Lockhart [sic] Campbell is dead."

In spite of the fact that he was seen to fall, the body of eighteen-year-old Lockhard was lost at St. Julien without a trace. His name is immortalized on the walls of the Menin Gate at Ypres, Belgium, along with other Canadians who have no known last resting place.

JOHN (AKA JOSEPH) HAMILTON

There is some confusion as to this young man's name. It appears as "John" on his army records but the Commonwealth War Graves record uses the name "Joseph." Hamilton joined the army under the name "John." He gave his birthdate as May 24, 1891, and his parents' names as Joseph and Ada Hamilton of Greet, Birmingham, England. However, in one of Leonard Halsey's letters home, after the Langemarck battle, Hamilton is referred to as "Joe." His military service number and record confirms that "John" and "Joseph" were one and the same.

Hamilton's pre-war occupation was recorded as a "metal polisher"working in Findlay's Foundry. When war broke out, he joined the Canadian Expeditionary Force to fight for Mother England. John was an older soldier, enlisting at age twenty-three years, five months. He was of a dark complex-ion, with blue eyes and black hair, standing 5' 7" tall. Identifying marks included a tattoo of a girl's face on his left forearm. He was an adherent of the Methodist Church.

Pte J. Hamilton was part of the first contingent of "B" Company, 42nd Regiment, which left Carleton Place by train that bright August afternoon in 1914 for Perth en route for training in Valcartier. With the other Carleton Place men, he was taken into "H" Company of the

2nd Battalion. Together they sailed for England on October 4, 1914, aboard the steamship S.S. *Cassandra*. The normal destination was Liverpool, but fear of submarine activity drove this first convoy to the port at Plymouth, where they arrived at dawn on October 15. One of Hamilton's first furloughs in England was spent in Portsmouth with his brother, a soldier in the British Army who had already seen action and was due to return to the front.

After the battle at Hooper's House, Hamilton was first listed as missing on operations. He was named in the *Carleton Place Herald* of May 18, 1915, as one of the four local men unaccounted for after the battle at Langemarck. When his name never appeared in the German records of prisoners, and he himself never appeared, for official purposes the army presumed him to have died on or after April 26, 1915, in the vicinity of St. Julien.

John (Joseph) Hamilton's name is, like all those who perished without a trace in the Ypres Salient, engraved on the Ypres (Menin Gate) Memorial along with 6,994 other Commonwealth war dead. From James McGill's letter it can be concluded that all the missing Carleton Place soldiers were killed on April 25.

NEIL JOHN MCPHEE

Neil McPhee, the youngest son of Angus and Jane McPhee, was born in Carleton Place on June 9, 1890. After completing his schooling he went west in search of work. At one point he was reported as having returned back east, and employed in Boston. Neil was a very athletic young man and participated in a variety of sports. He achieved some success at paddling with the Carleton Place Canoe Club, along with his brother Archie. He was a very popular young fellow in town.

Neil was working as a labourer when he answered the call to duty. He left with the first contingent of the 42nd Regiment and in Valcartier was enrolled into "H" Company of the 2nd Battalion on September 22, 1914. He stood 5' 8" tall and was described as having a dark complexion, brown eyes and black hair. His family attended St. Mary's Roman

Catholic Church. Neil sailed to England with the other townsmen aboard the S.S. *Cassandra*. Capt. Hooper singled him out for tribute as ". . . one of his best boys, a conscientious and reliable soldier."

The group of Carleton Place men at the farmhouse fight included Neil. He was lost when the unit was forced to retreat. For some time he was listed as missing, and one report—a letter from Leonard Halsey written on July 27, 1915—speculated that McPhee was a prisoner of war in Germany. But no trace of him was ever found.

A casualties list, published in the *Carleton Place Herald* on May 9, 1916, stated that:

> The latest word received from those who survive, when the house that Capt. W.H. Hooper and his noble boys defended until blown up, is to the effect that Pte. Neil McPhee . . . lost his life in the explosion . . .

His elderly parents never gave up hope. Angus walked every day to the post office in hopes of receiving a letter or some other news of his son. Nothing could be learned of his whereabouts. In July 1916, a letter arrived from the Department of Militia advising the sorrowing parents that, since Neil was not among the prisoners of war, nor with any other unit, "he is presumed to have died on or after April 22, 1915" at St. Julien. Accompanying an official certificate was a letter to his mother, Jane, from Maj.-Gen. Sam Hughes, Minister of Militia and Defence for Canada:

Dear Mrs. McPhee—

Will you kindly accept my sincere sympathy and condolence in the decease of that worthy citizen and heroic soldier, Private Neil John McPhee, previously reported missing now for official purposes presumed to have died on or since April 22nd, 1915?

While one cannot too deeply mourn the loss of such a brave comrade, there is a consolation in knowing that he did his duty fearlessly and well, and gave his life for the cause of liberty and the upbuilding of the Empire.

Again extending to you my heartfelt sympathy.

Faithfully
Sam Hughes

His mother did not survive long afterwards. Neil's service records show her as next of kin and he had assigned a portion of his pay to her. But when his medals, and the silver Memorial Cross,[3] were delivered, only his father was alive to receive them. She had died on May 4, 1919. Neil's war pension stopped when Angus died on July 15, 1920.

ARTHUR JOHN SIMONS

Arthur Simons was working for Findlay's Foundry in Carleton Place as a stove mounter when war was declared. His name was on the militia personnel records of the 42nd Regiment (Lanark and Renfrew) from August to October 1914. He was eighteen-and-a-half years old

 when he joined the young men of "B" Company for the train trip to Valcartier where he enlisted in the regular army. Part of his motivation probably was that his parents still lived in England, at Combe, Florey, Somerset. He had ventured out to Canada alone to find work in a new, young country.

Arthur was born in Kingston, Somerset, on May 3, 1896, the son of Mr. and Mrs. Harry Simons. He was a good-looking young man, 5' 7" tall with brown eyes and brown hair. He officially enlisted in the regular army on September 22, 1914, when the battalion was in Valcartier. He was with "H" Company of the 2nd Battalion when it sailed to England on October 4, 1914, aboard the S.S. *Cassandra*.

Training on the Salisbury Plain that damp, cold winter afforded Arthur some time to get away and visit his parents. Soon enough he found himself in the mud of Flanders and the front lines outside Ypres. He was part of Capt. Hooper's hand-picked group to occupy the farmhouse. After the German attack of April 22–26, he was listed among the missing. He had been in the army seven months and still had two weeks before he could celebrate his nineteenth birthday.

As late as June 1915, Harry MacLaren wrote home that Simons was still missing, but Leonard Halsey wrote on July 27, 1915, that "Poor Arthur Simons, I am afraid, is dead."

---

[3] The Memorial Cross, known in Canada as the Silver Cross, was issued to the widows or mothers of all who were killed or died on active service. Hung from a ribbon of purple satin, the cross is of dull silver, surmounted by a crown. The monarch's royal cypher is in the centre and a wreath of laurel appears between the arms of the cross. The cross is registered and bears a serial number.

His body was never found. The army, since he went missing during the attack in the vicinity of St. Julien, "for official purposes" declared him "presumed to have died on or since April 22, 1915." Arthur Simons is commemorated on the Ypres (Menin Gate) Memorial in Ieper, Belgium. His medals, the 1914–15 Star, a Victory Medal and the British War Medal were mailed to his parents.

There is no World War I medal, other than the 1914–15 Star, recognizing service during a specific time or in a specific theatre of operations. Those killed from 1916 onwards received no campaign star and were eligible only for the two standard-issue service medals.

The War Medal

The Victory Medal

I speak to you from beyond the grave,
I once was a warrior brave,
I fought for this country 'til my blood ran red,
Now I lie with heroes, all of them dead.

The fighting was fierce and the guns were loud,
Young men scared but young men proud,
We tried to rest in the damp and cold,
And dreamed of having a hand to hold,
Silent thoughts of a place called home,
Far away, over the ocean foam.

Still we fought on for freedom for all,
In victory and death we now stand tall,
This is my story, remember it well,
Freedom is sweet, and war is hell.[4]

Peter Torreson

[4] This poem is the creation of thirteen-year-old Peter Torreson of Nepean, the 1999 Ontario winner of the Royal Canadian Legion annual poetry contest. It was printed in the Friday, May 14, 1999 edition of *The Ottawa Citizen*, page D4.

Chapter Six

THE WAR OF ATTRITION

The second Carleton Place contingent, the reconstituted "B" Company of the 42nd Regiment, departed by train for Kingston. *The Carleton Place Herald,* on November 3, 1914, reported that they left with no uniforms, weapons or luggage; they were to be equipped in Kingston. The mayor gave each man a box of "the finest Havanas." This second group would leave on the battlefields of Europe Ptes. S. Hamilton and Dan O'Donovan, two more who rest forever in France.

But first they cooled their heels in Canada until May 1915; training with the 21st (Kingston) Battalion of the Eastern Ontario Regiment until recruiting brought the battalion up to strength. They sailed from Montreal on May 6 aboard R.M.S. (Royal Mail Steamship) *Metagama* and landed in England on May 15. By mid-June they had disembarked in France. For these men who had left home seven months before without even uniforms, there was no time for any extensive training in England.

The 21st Canadian Infantry Battalion (Kingston) was organized on March 15, 1915. It served in France and Flanders with the 4th Infantry Brigade of the 2nd Canadian Division from September 15, 1915, until the armistice. Their mascot was a white and black goat named "Nan," who received an honorary discharge when the battalion returned to Canada after the war. The battalion is perpetuated by The Princess of Wales' Own Regiment.

The Battle of Ypres continued for another three weeks. The only Canadian troops remaining in the area were with the Princess Patricia's Canadian Light Infantry. Before leaving the line, however, three Canadian battalions, with the 2nd (Eastern Ontario) Battalion acting as a covering unit, dug a 1200–yard trench from Hampshire to Turco Farms. This work gained important ground without a single casualty.[1]

[1] Colonel G.W.L. Nicholson, *Canadian Expeditionary Force 1914-1919* (Ottawa: Queen's Printer, 1962), p. 88.

The decimated units of the 1st Canadian Division were moved from the Ypres Salient south to join other offensives. British troops were repulsed at Aubers Ridge. French forces were notably unsuccessful in an attack on Vimy Ridge. A ghastly pattern evolved. Army commanders on both sides relied on outdated traditions of fighting that called for massive head-on assaults against trenches, the greatest advantage of which was defence.

Attacking infantry went "over the top" into land churned to muck by artillery and tangled with that terrible new invention, barbed wire, only to be cut down in ordered ranks by the latest killing engine—the machine-gun. Planned breakthroughs didn't happen and the front line ebbed to and fro. Attacks stalemated. Sporadic fighting dragged on for weeks and months as the casualty lists steadily rose. More men, more guns, more ammunition were thrown into the fray.

By the summer of 1915, the army was no longer keeping a recruiting officer stationed in Carleton Place; instead, in September, an office was set up in the Masonic Block with Mr. D.C. MacRostie in charge. To further stimulate enlistments the Militia Department had also decided that it was no longer necessary for a recruit to have his wife's permission or, if he were a single man aged eighteen to twenty-one, the consent of his parents, to enlist. It was announced in September that the entire 2nd Canadian

Carleton Place went about its normal autumn activities. Rural agricultural fairs abounded. Carleton Place High School, "The Old Stone School" on the northwest corner of High and Moffatt Streets, opened on September 14, 1915, with an enrollment of 148 young men and women. The public (today known as an elementary) school housed a student population of 594. Public school teachers who held a Second Class Certificate were paid $500 a year. The local Red Cross unit was raising funds to purchase a machine gun for the troops. In June of 1915, they had supplied a mobile ambulance with the name "Carleton Place" boldly emblazoned in prominent white letters on the side. If you were visiting Carleton Place and wanted to stay at the Mississippi Hotel, a night would cost $2.

In November, the Methodist Church celebrated its anniversary services with guest speaker, Sam Hughes, Minister of Militia and the Defence of Canada. He couldn't tarry after his speech to chit-chat with the congregation as he had to hurry to catch the last train back to Ottawa and attend to affairs of the nation. The same month, the high school received its last consignment of thirty specimens of stuffed birds and animals from Geneva, Illinois. Apparently the school had a well-stocked nature museum.

Division was to be supplied with the controversial Ross rifle. Financiers in London were predicting that Germany could prolong the war no longer than six more months. At the end of September, the death toll was listed as 5,575,000 killed; 1,800,000 of those were sons of Germany.

A Canadian enlisted soldier received $1.10 a day with clothing and equipment, board and lodging and, if married, a separation allowance of $20 a month. In comparison, the English troops received 25 cents, the Italians 20 cents, the French five cents and the Germans 10 cents for each day of service.

The 130th Lanark and Renfrew Overseas Battalion of the Canadian Expeditionary Force was authorized on November 14, 1915. While affiliated with the local 42nd Regiment of the Canadian Militia, officially it was called the 130th Canadian Infantry Battalion (Perth) and had as its motto *Fac et Spera* (Do and Hope). In England the battalion was absorbed by the 12th Reserve Battalion to provide reinforcements for the Canadian Corps in the field. It is perpetuated by the Lanark and Renfrew Scottish Regiment. One hundred recruits were billeted in Carleton Place for the winter months. The Department of Militia estimated that it cost $1,000 to equip and keep a soldier in the field for a year. Overseas, in December, the first British pattern steel helmets, similar to those introduced by the French, were issued to Canadian soldiers in the trenches.

On February 3, 1916, fire wiped out the Parliament Buildings in Ottawa, including, it was reported, the House of Commons' bar, which was not to be reestablished in the temporary quarters of the Victoria Museum, and was likely to be abolished for good. William Thorburn, the member of Parliament for Lanark North and who hailed from Almonte, lost his hat, overcoat and overshoes in the fire. With the innocence of ignorance, the Carleton Place Herald also printed a story that stated, "Twenty Indians, all crack marksmen, from the Walpole Island Indian reserve have enlisted in the 149th (County of Lambton) Overseas Battalion." On April 16, the first motorcar to make the trip from Perth to Carleton Place arrived. And, finally, four white bull terriers, official mascots for the 130th Battalion, became the latest recruits. When on parade, they marched four abreast in front of the men.

During the winter of 1915–16, soldiers added much "colour" to the social life of the town. In January, "C" Company took a route march to Almonte to lend their support to a 130th Battalion band concert.

All in all, the winter of 1915–16 passed rather serenely in Carleton Place, except for those families mourning the loss of the boys who fell at Langemarck. The horror of the European killing ground seemed very remote indeed. But the start of the spring offensives brought local names again to the news. In May word arrived of the death of William Tyrie, followed in June by William Wright and Sydney Hamilton.

Chapter Seven

BACK INTO THE BREACH

When the 2nd Canadian Division arrived in France the Canadian Corps was formed (the nation's leaders had stoutly resisted any division of Canadian troops). Lt.-Gen. E.A.H. Alderson, who had commanded Canadian troops in the Boer War, took command of the corps, with Maj.-Gen. R.E.W. Turner, V.C., commanding the newly formed 2nd Division and Maj.-Gen. Arthur Currie commanding the 1st. Turner was a slight man whose eyesight demanded the wearing of spectacles. His appearance gave no hint of the heroism that had earned him the Victoria Cross in South Africa. Currie was a real estate broker from Victoria and a former militia gunner.

The corps spent a dreary winter in the lines between Ploegsteert Wood and St. Eloi. They were joined by the Princess Patricia's Canadian Light Infantry (PPCLI), retiring from near Ypres, and the Royal Canadian Regiment (RCR), fresh from garrison duty in Bermuda. The 3rd Canadian Division was formed in December under the command of Maj.-Gen. M.S. Mercer. Thus, early in 1916, the Carleton Place men in the 2nd Battalion (Eastern Ontario Regiment) found themselves on a new front with the 1st Infantry Brigade of the 1st Division. The fresh troops of the 21st Battalion were in the same area with the 4th Infantry Brigade of the 2nd Division. A few also served with the PPCLI and the RCR in the 7th Infantry Brigade of the 3rd Division. Tyrie and Hamilton were with the 21st Battalion and Wright was with the 2nd Canadian Infantry Battalion (Eastern Ontario).

Winter at the front was not as comfortable as winter in Carleton Place. Units would spend, in six-day shifts, time in the support trenches, on the front lines and in reserve. It rained incessantly. The trenches simply dissolved and men stood for days in thigh-high water. High rubber boots did not arrive until much later that spring so they had no means of protection from the penetrating wet and cold. In the area to the rear, roofs of billets leaked and coke and charcoal fires produced little more than noxious smoke. Influenza and respiratory ailments were prevalent. The only relief in the trenches was the daily rum ration of a half gill (1/64th of a gallon) to help ward off the effects of cold and always wet clothing. Little did the Women's Institute realize the value of their gift of warm socks to the departing Carleton Place boys! Trench foot was particularly difficult to control or cure and, if not contained, soon resulted in gangrene.

Rum was used by both sides to motivate their troops to action. In the British forces, the tradition of a daily rum ration had begun centuries earlier in the Royal Navy. The Canadian army in Europe in 1915 quickly adopted the custom. It was known to be powerful stuff, giving even meek soldiers the will to fight. Rum helped the men to sleep at night, making them oblivious to noise and their abominable surroundings, it boosted morale and sometimes was withheld as a punishment. Its primary purpose, ladled out just before an attack, was to suppress the fear of ordinary men and remove any hesitation to their taking extraordinary actions. Special Red Demerara, 186-proof Jamaican rum, encouraged a man's will to fight and was an essential motivator to the First World War trench soldier from Canada.

Christmas Day, 1915, was quiet. Artillery remained silent and in at least one location the infantry on both sides walked openly without a shot being fired. But in 1916, there was none of the open fraternization that characterized the previous year. Memories of Ypres and gas attacks stayed fresh. Front line troops were instructed that, should the enemy attempt "to bring about a temporary cessation of hostilities," such measures were to be met with small arms and, if necessary, artillery fire.[1]

The 2nd Division got its "baptism of fire" in the water-filled mine craters at St. Eloi. Mine warfare was an important tactic in the static operations of trench warfare. Both sides did extensive tunnelling under the other's front line trenches and planted thousands of tons of explosives. None was so dramatic as those that were exploded on March 27, 1916, at St. Eloi. The 2nd Division was to relieve a British division scheduled to attack in conjunction with the mine explosions. But the eruptions were so horrendous that entire companies of the enemy were annihilated, landmarks disappeared, trenches collapsed. Such was the confusion that the British troops could not achieve their objective and could not be relieved. Finally, they were so

[1] War Diary, 5th Infantry Brigade, December 25, 1915.

exhausted that the Canadian Corps, on the night of April 3–4, changed places with them.

The Canadian 2nd Division, including Eastern Ontario's 21st Battalion, formed part of that relief force. For the first time they were wearing steel helmets, or at least half of them were. Each company of 100 men received only fifty helmets.

On the morning of April 4, the 6th Brigade took positions in front of the St Eloi craters. There were four huge holes and three smaller ones, all of which quickly became small lakes. The entire Canadian front line came under constant heavy bombardment and intense German counterattacks. Occupation of the craters changed often and quickly. By the night of April 6–7, the 6th Brigade had suffered 617 casualties; they were relieved by the 4th Canadian Brigade.

The 21st Battalion tried, during the night of April 8–9, to regain Numbers 2 and 3 craters, but were repulsed by German rifle and machine-gun fire. The following night, attacks by three battalions— the 18th, 20th and 21st—also failed. Counterattacks by the enemy were driven off. The 5th Brigade relieved the 4th on the night of April 13–14 and shortly thereafter both sides reverted to static warfare, occupying their troops with the task of making improvements to their front lines.

St. Eloi was the first fight for the 2nd Division. They emerged quite frustrated, having made no gains. The thirteen days of attacks and counterattacks over six waterlogged mine craters cost 1,373 Canadian lives, including that of William Tyrie. And the Battle of the Somme loomed yet ahead.

WILLIAM TYRIE

William Tyrie was born in Dunoon, Scotland, on June 13, 1894. He and his sister, Jessie, emigrated together to Lanark County. He was employed, prior to joining the army, as a farm labourer with a Mr. Leslie, while his sister worked as a domestic for Mrs. Rodger, who lived in Carleton Place across the street from the newspaper office. William was a somewhat short man, standing only 5' 4 ", with a fair complexion, blue eyes and light brown hair.

He enlisted in the 21st Battalion of the Eastern Ontario Regiment on November 12, 1914, at Kingston, joining the second contingent of Carleton Place men to go to war. The large bunion on his right foot was no barrier to being accepted. He was all of twenty years, six months old.

The battalion embarked on May 6, 1915, aboard the R.M.S. *Metagama,* at Montreal, bound for Liverpool. The voyage was most pleasant. What little idle time the troops may have had was taken up by organized sports programmes for both the officers and men. They arrived in England on May 15th and spent an unusually warm, dry summer training on the Salisbury Plain. Prominent at all battalion activities was its mascot—a beautiful white goat.

A sure sign that the division was ready for overseas service was a royal inspection. On September 2, the 2nd Canadian Division marched past their king, Lord Kitchener and a beaming Maj.-Gen. Sam Hughes. The 21st Battalion had been given their colours before leaving Kingston and these were deposited with the Canadian high commissioner in London pending the battalion's return from the continent.

They went to France on September 14, 1915, landing at Boulogne, and were immediately sent to the front. The 21st Battalion was the first unit of troops of the 2nd Canadian Division to enter the firing line. They went into "C" Trenches in front of Messines on September 19, 1915, and stayed there until September 28. This was the first of the battalion's fifty-eight tours of duty in the front line. William Tyrie spent a wet, cold winter guarding the southern flank of the sacred, and cursed, Ypres Salient. The division occupied the line at Hazebrouck near the Ypres-Comines canal by St. Eloi.

Tyrie carried the Mark III Ross rifle that had been issued in December 1914, even though most of the 1st Division had, without authority from Canada, replaced it with the British Lee-Enfield. This weapon was shorter, lighter and much more reliable in adverse conditions. Maj.-Gen. Richard Turner, newly promoted and a favourite of Sam Hughes, had alone spoken well of the Ross rifle. Now in command of the 2nd Division he threatened harsh punishment to any man found with the Lee-Enfield.

The *Carleton Place Herald* of April 18, 1916, reported the wounding of Pte. Wm. Tyril (sic), sadly misspelling his name. He had in fact been admitted to the No. 8 Casualty Clearing Station on April 3 with penetrating gunshot wounds to the head, neck, arm and chest. The historical calendar of the 21st Battalion lists the following events for April 1916:

> 2—Two officers and 22 other ranks, volunteers, assisted 1st Gordons at posts 44 and 45 to attack Post 65.
>
> 3—One officer and 8 other ranks, volunteers, assisted 1st Gordons and captured Post 65.[2]
>
> 5—Relieved by a battalion of the Border Regiment. Moved to La Clytte, southern sector of Ypres Salient.
>
> 8—Relieved 27th Battalion in "P" Trenches St. Eloi.
>
> 9 to 11—Each night was a series of crater fights and finally ended with the capture of Nos 1 and 2 craters.
>
> 11—Relieved by 20th Battalion.

Describing the same action in "N" and "O" Trenches near La Clytte, the battalion's war diary records:

> 2/4/16—Enemy artillery active—200 rounds— mostly Whiz Bangs being fired; our artillery reply was not very effective . . .
>
> At 11:15 pm last night a Bombing Party composed of 1st Gordons and 21st Canadians attacked post 65 and repeatedly assaulted it till daylight but was unable to dislodge the enemy, and our Bombers retired to posts 44 and 45.
>
> Enemy machine-gun fire very active. Casualties 14 and one fatal.
>
> 3/4/16—Enemy was very active with Bombs sending over 87 Fish tail grenades and such like . . . Artillery not very active only 83 rounds being fired. Our artillery was very active especially with H.E.s.[3] Enemy machine guns very active from 7 pm till 10 pm. Lieut. Davidson and 8 of our Bombers left at 10 pm to assist the 1st Gordons in another attack on post 65 which this time was successful—Casualties five (one fatal).[4]

[2] It was during this action that Pte. William Tyrie received the wounds that would prove fatal.
[3] High Explosives.
[4] William Tyrie was one of the five wounded.

William died of his wounds on April 13, ten days after he was shot. He was buried in the Hazebrouck Communal Cemetery in France where his remains still lie. He was just two months short of his twenty-second birthday.

The Commonwealth War Graves Commission commemoration:

In Memory of
W. TYRIE
Private
60014
21st Bn., Canadian Infantry (Eastern Ontario Regt.)
who died on
Thursday, 13th April 1916.

From October 1914 to September 1917, Casualty Clearing Stations were located at Hazebrouck. The British began burials in October 1914. The soldiers were first buried among the civilian graves, but after the Armistice they were moved to the main British enclosure. There are more than 950 1914–18 war graves at this site, of which nearly thirty are of unidentified remains. The Graves Registration Commission erected the original wooden cross over William's grave.

On the last Sunday in April 1917, the Carleton Place Methodist Church honoured four dead soldiers with a memorial service. The pastor, Rev. Gould, used the opportunity to call for an annual memorial day as a reminder of those who had fallen. William Tyrie's photograph rested on the altar, "peacefully within the folds of the Union Jack."

Chapter Eight

A NEW WEAPON—THE MACHINE-GUN

In the summer of 1914, at militia camps sweltering under the sun, there was talk of war. But that talk rarely included the new machine gun. Infantry battalions had enough troubles trying to disentangle section and platoon foot drills. In musketry, what the Canadian militia lacked in smartness and discipline they more than adequately made up in shooting. Few soldiers spoke of the machine gun and fewer officers or men had ever seen one. There was one on the inventory, with the 43rd Battalion in Ottawa, and officers who had taken courses there had been shown the gun.

In fact "machine-guns" had already played an important role in Canadian military history. In 1885, at the battles of Cut Knife Hill and Batoche, concentrated fire from Gatling guns, under the command of United States Army Capt. Howard, had provided critical covering fire allowing movement of the militia forces advancing against, and retreating from, Métis and Indian opposition.

When the Great War began in 1914, the German army was the only European power to recognize the importance of the weapon and incorporate machine-gun battalions into its military organization. In Canada, a French army reserve major and millionaire living in Montreal, Raymond Brutinel, and a prominent Canadian lawyer, Clifford Sifton, conceived the idea of mounting machine-guns on armoured cars. Such a vehicle would be a double threat—firepower with mobility. They took the idea to Sam Hughes, Minister of Militia and the Defence of Canada, who enthusiastically authorized the organization of the 1st Canadian Automobile Machine-Gun Brigade.

The brigade was privately financed with a strength of ten officers and 124 other ranks. They were equipped with twenty-four Colt machine-guns, eight armoured cars (to be built to Brutinel's specifications), eight trucks and four cars. While recruiting was carried out at the Château Laurier in Ottawa, Brutinel went to the United States to acquire the guns and armoured cars. They all arrived one month from the day they were ordered, despite a sabotage attempt by German sympathizers.[1]

Two Carleton Place soldiers whose names endure on the war memorial served as machine-gunners: Harold William McDiarmid and Henry Utman.

HENRY UTMAN

Henry Utman must have desperately wanted to be a soldier, or else he had a highly defined sense of patriotism. He was a veteran of the Boer War, having served in South Africa for a year with the 3rd Canadian Mounted Rifles. Then, on September 19, 1914, he walked into the Château Laurier hotel in Ottawa and joined the fledgling Automobile Machine-Gun Brigade. This was only the first of four enlistments in the army he made during World War I.

At this enlistment, Henry gave his date of birth as September 21, 1883, which would have made him seventeen when he went to the South African war. He attested that he was born in Carlsbad Springs and gave as his next of kin his wife, Julia. He stated that his occupation was an artist—a portrait painter. He belonged to the Wesleyan Church. At his physical examination he was described as thirty-one years old, 5' 7" tall, of a dark complexion with brown eyes and brown hair.

The men recruited for the Machine-Gun Brigade were chauffeurs, mechanics, ex-regular soldiers and militiamen. Precise analysis of the reasons men joined the machine-gunners defies any common thread, including mechanical aptitude. After hours of practice, even the mechanically ignorant could assemble piles of ill-assorted gadgets into an operating weapon. Their only "perk" was that they served no guard or fatigue duties which, in time, did become an envied distinction.

On September 29, 1914, the unit embarked for England on the S.S. *Corinthian*. They preceded the vast armada of thirty-three ships that left the Gaspé Basin on October 3 carrying the first contingent of Canadian troops to the Mother Country. However,

[1] Charles H. Stewart, "Overseas": The Lineages and Insignia of the Canadian Expeditionary Force 1914-1919 (Toronto: Little and Stewart, 1970), p. 119.

upon arriving in the United Kingdom, on October 20, 1914, the brigade met only indifference and opposition from English senior officers. Consequently, it was not until June 17, 1915, that Henry Utman and the Automobile-Machine-Gun Brigade No.1, re-christened the 1st Canadian Motor Machine-Gun Brigade, arrived in France. The brigade had been employed on home defence duties at Ashford, Kent, and Henry had not quite been a model soldier in England. On March 1, he was fined £2 and the next day awarded five days "#1 Field punishment" (confined to barracks). Just before going across the Channel, on June 6, he was fined $5.[2] His record does not detail the infractions.

From June 1915 to August 1916, the brigade served with the 1st Canadian Division. They arrived just as the war appeared to be entering a stalemate in trenches stretching from the Swiss border to the North Sea. The newly formed machine-gun companies, attached to the various brigades of the 1st Division, participated in the battles at St. Eloi, Sanctuary Wood and Hooge. The Canadian Corps spent a dismal winter in the front between Ploegsteert Wood and St. Eloi while routine trench warfare exacted its daily toll of casualties. On March 27, seven mines were blown and enormous geysers of earth, stones, trees, men and equipment left the enormous craters near St. Eloi.

On April 14, 1916, Henry was admitted to No. 14 General Hospital, near Wimereux, France, diagnosed with "tabes dorsalis," a severe degeneration of the bones and joints of the lower spine causing intense pain, and "scabies," a contagious skin disease caused by a small mite boring furrows in the skin with attendant itching and eczema. He was serving with Lt. Col. R. Brutinel's 1st Brigade near Poperinghe. Battalion records show that every day during this tour in the line there were "gas alerts" issued for varying lengths of time and various times of day. Hardly a day went by that the troops were not exposed to some amount of poison gas.

On April 20, Utman was transferred to the Canadian Casualty Assembly Centre suffering from shell shock. He was invalided to England where he spent time in various military hospitals. On May 2 he was admitted to King's Canadian Red Cross Hospital in Bushey Park, diagnosed with shell shock, and on May 4 was "struck off

<hr>

[2] British pounds and Canadian dollars were used interchangeably by the Canadian army, even though the British pound was worth about $2.50 Canadian.

strength" on discharge to be returned to Canada. Unfortunately, his equipment did not seem to keep up with him. On April 30, while still in the hospital, he was fined a stoppage of pay of 9p[3] for losing his satchel. After he was released, on May 7, he was penalized by further stoppage of pay of 7p for a lost knife, 4p for his fork, 11p for a spoon and 6 p for his mess tin. Army discipline could not condone the loss of equipment even while a soldier was in or travelling between hospitals!

In a statement made on May 9, 1916, while in the Canadian Convalescent Hospital at Epsom, Henry stated he "was near Ypres on April 13th when a shell exploded near to me lifting me into the air, but not wounding me but I was very weak and my nerves were very shaky. Was sent to No. 11 British General. Stayed 3 or 4 days when I was sent to Huddersfield War Hospital." Another report while at the hospital in Epsom, dated May 26, recorded that he "feels good and fit except for slight pains in head at times.—Fit."

He was sent back to Canada. On July 13, 1916, Henry was admitted to a convalescent home in Kingston. The *Carleton Place Herald*, on July 18, 1916, carried the following news item:

> Among the invalid soldiers who arrived at Quebec on Saturday from overseas we observe the name of H. Utman . . . of Carleton Place . . . an Englishman whose wife resides here.

On June 29, 1916, the Pensions and Claims Board granted Henry a pension for a period of six months at $96 a year. A Medical History on an Invalid, dated October 30, 1916, records Henry's medical assessment:

> Blurring vision due to Tabes Dorsalis, which has been precipitated by shock. History of infection 8 years ago, disability dates from shock while in trenches, April 17th/16.
>
> By trade a portrait painter. Finds he cannot blend colours. Condition has greatly improved. When condition was precipitated by shock could not recognize a person three feet away. At present, able to read without glasses—but finds his eyes tire and blur on reading a while. Unable to return to previous occupation, however, as sight not good enough for colours.

---

[3] A "p" is the sign for a British penny. There are 12 pennies in a shilling ("s") and 16 shillings in a pound ("£").

The town of Carleton Place honoured two soldiers who were at home recuperating. On September 19, 1916, a reception was held for Gunner H. Utman and Lt. J.H. Brown. A motorcade that had already picked up Brown travelled to George Street to get Gunner Utman before proceeding to the town hall. A large crowd greeted them with "three cheers." In an address, Mayor Smythe said:

> Pte. Utman, it is our sincere hope that your recovery may be as complete as possible and that you may be long spared to enjoy the high esteem that your conduct has merited. Your family and your fellow citizens will remember you as one to whose courage the acid test of battle was applied and who was found to be pure gold.

Each soldier was presented with a chain and locket by the town. In response to the mayor's words, Utman said that while he was not a native of the town, and had not enlisted there, he assumed the honour paid him was due to his wife. However, he stated that their wishes were very much appreciated and he most graciously thanked the citizenry. Recruiting officers of the 240th Battalion used the occasion to make a strong bid for more bodies to enlist.

On November 1, 1916, Henry Utman was discharged in Kingston from the Motor Machine-Gun Brigade of the Canadian Expeditionary Force as medically unfit for further service.

But Henry had no intention of going back to being an artist, nor did he let his defective vision stop him from applying once again to serve King and Country. Barely two weeks after his discharge, on November 16, Henry re-enlisted with the 240th Battalion, which was recruiting in Renfrew for overseas duty. He freely gave his previous service in the Boer War and in France and Belgium with the Machine-Gun Brigade. It didn't take much checking for the unit to discover his background and to discharge thirty-three-year-old Henry Utman, on January 29, 1917, as medically unfit. On December 22, 1916, the Pension Commissioners of Canada had found Henry entitled to a gratuity of $25 for the defective vision in both his eyes.

Henry went back to civilian life. But world events would once again give him an opening. In 1917, the Bolshevik Revolution erupted and quickly spread throughout Russia. By March 3, 1918, the Bolsheviks had overthrown the Russian government and signed the peace treaty of Brest-Litovsk with Germany and Austria. At the invitation of the Soviet government, and to forestall German incursions, Britain landed 150 marines at Murmansk in April 1918. In mid-May, the War Office suggested a tiny Canadian contribution of five officers and eleven NCOs, but by July, with a need to reinforce the British on the ground, Canada was asked to contribute an infantry battalion, " . . . since troops with experience of a rigorous climate were required." [4]

This invitation was declined, but in July, a special force, consisting of a brigade headquarters, two battalions of infantry, a machine-gun company and a battery of artillery raised primarily from discharged soldiers, formed the Canadian Siberian Expeditionary Force. They left for Murmansk in September and by November 11, 1918, which marked the cessation of hostilities on the Western Front, Canadian artillerymen were engaged in a bitter fight on the Dvina River.

Henry heard the clarion call to action. On October 3, 1918, he enlisted as a sapper in the Signal Training Depot of the Siberia Signallers. The rank of sapper, normally only used in the Engineers, was employed because in the First World War the Signal Corps was part of the Canadian Engineers. This time he gave his name as Harry Edward Utman and listed his wife as Mrs. J. Annie Utman and his address as Gloucester Street in Ottawa. He changed his birth date to September 21, 1885, and claimed no previous service. At age thirty-three he weighed 142 pounds and was described as having a dark complexion, brown eyes and black hair. He was a regular attendee at the Methodist Church.

Utman could escape neither his past nor his health. From October 24 to 26 he was in Flemming Hospital in Ottawa suffering from influenza and neurasthenia (an anxiety condition marked by chronic weakness and fatigue). Three days after the Armistice, on November 14, 1918, he was again discharged as medically unfit. His medical case sheet records:

---

[4] Colonel G.W.L. Nicholson, C.D., *Canadian Expeditionary Force 1914-1919* (Ottawa: Queen's Printer, 1962) p. 512.

Discharged from Army Nov 1916—Since then has done clerical work, and lately has been conductor on street cars. At the latter work, there was cause of excitement and patient became more nervous.

But Henry still wanted to be a soldier and the lack of war did not deter him. Perhaps there were simply no civilian jobs available for an aging artist with a nervous disorder and vision problems. He tried once again. On February 5, 1919, he enlisted at the Headquarters Detachment into the Canadian Ordnance Corps, which had the huge task of supplying, equipping and outfitting the entire Canadian army. He and his wife were now living on Botelar Street in Ottawa. He gave his correct date of birth and owned up to having "slight nervousness." He was given a medical category of BII, indicating that he was fit for service only in Canada. Henry lasted forty-five days and was discharged, on demobilization of the unit, on March 21, 1919.

Henry Utman died on September 15, 1923, a week before his fortieth birthday. The pension authorities ruled that his death was "due to service," so his widow, Julia, who stood by him from their wedding on June 15, 1913, was entitled to a meagre pension for her husband's war service and subsequent disabilities.

Chapter Nine

TOWARDS THE SOMME

A change of command for the Canadian Corps occurred at the end of May 1916. Alderson was replaced by Lt.-Gen. the Hon. Sir Julian Byng, who would later become governor general of Canada. The Canadians remained in the Ypres Salient while Sir Douglas Haig began concentrating troops in anticipation of an offensive on the Somme. The 2nd Division remained in the line at St. Eloi, and took the brunt of some of the heaviest German artillery bombardments and infantry attacks during the first weeks of June.

In Canada, on May 1, 1916, the 130th Battalion held a farewell band concert in Carleton Place Town Hall. It was ordered mobilized on May 20. In preparation for their departure, the Carleton Place Women's Institute presented each man of the Carleton Place company with a pair of socks and each of the "town boys" with a "housewife" valued at $1.50 each.[1] On May 25, the Perth Independent Order Daughters of the Empire presented the battalion with its Colours, heavy embroidered ceremonial regimental flags with golden fringes, which were deposited for safekeeping for the duration of the war in St. James Anglican Church in Perth. (They are still there).

Barriefield camp, near Kingston, was opened on May 22, 1916, and the 130th (Perth) had the distinction of being one of the first to arrive. The men had spent the winter billeted in Carleton Place and area homes. Early in June, the railroad began running excursions for friends and family to visit "the brave defenders and their training camp" at a cost of $2.65 round trip from Carleton Place to Kingston. Then, on June 27, the *Carleton Place Herald* announced that an advance party of 100 men from the 130th had arrived at Valcartier. They joined 11,000 men already there awaiting transport to England. On July 11, two officers, Capt. J. Gates and Lt. Kemp, travelled from Valcartier to Carleton Place to accept the gift of a Savage-Lewis machine-gun, valued at $1,000, from Beckwith Township. After a summer's training, the

[1] Presentation of a "housewife" always caused considerable mirth among the troops. In fact, it was a well-stocked sewing kit containing needles, thread, buttons, thimbles and all those necessities a man may need to repair his clothing when left to fend for himself. The issue of a housewife to Canadian servicemen, and women, continued well into the 1970s.

battalion embarked from Halifax aboard the S.S. Lapland, a White Star Line steamer. The voyage passed without incident and they landed in Liverpool on October 5, 1916. Sent to the camp at West Sandling, in Kent, they were transferred to the 12th Reserve Battalion, and within a month all eligible men were drafted to France.

Recruiting efforts were increased to feed the insatiable need for troops. On June 2, 1916, authorization to organize another battalion was received, the 240th, into which Lanark and Renfrew men enlisted. Maj. Edgar John Watt, who, from November 1915 to June 1, 1916, had been the second in command of the 130th , was promoted to lieutenant-colonel and given command of the new battalion.

In England, the 240th Canadian Infantry Battalion (Renfrew) "Lanark and Renfrew Battalion" was absorbed by the 6th Reserve Battalion to provide reinforcements for the Canadian Corps in the field. It, too, is perpetuated by the Lanark and Renfrew Scottish Regiment.

During June 1916, the Canadian section of the Ypres line held by the 2nd Division was hardly quiet. Skirmishes raged back and forth; no quarter given nor taken and no particular gains made or lost—the ebb and flow of war. During ten days in early June, German artillery, machine-guns and exploding mines slaughtered Canadian troops at Hooge and Mount Sorel. The fiercest bombardment on June 12–13 obliterated entire sections of the 3rd Division's trench, hurling bits of mud, trees, weapons, equipment and bodies into the air. On June 13, the 1st Canadian Division mounted a successful counterattack at Mount Sorel—Sanctuary Wood. By the time firing died away on June 14, the Canadians had suffered 8,430 casualties, the Germans–5,765. One of those lost was Sid Hamilton.

SYDNEY HAMILTON

Sid Hamilton left his job as a metal-polisher with Findlay Foundry to go with the men of "B" Company, the 42nd Regiment, into active service. They left with the mayor's gift of cigars, but no uniforms or weapons.

Hamilton was born on July 8, 1894, in Birmingham, England, coming out to Canada for work in his trade. He was one of the few married men, leaving his wife, Ruby Alberta (Janoe) behind. He was officially enrolled into the Regular Army, "D" Company of the 21st Battalion, in Kingston on November 6, 1914,  after arriving with his militia comrades. In spite of his slightly flat feet and short stature (he stood 5' 3" tall), he passed the physical examination. He was of a fair complexion, with grey eyes and brown hair.

After training in Valcartier, he sailed with the unit on the *R.M.S. Metagama* and arrived in England on May 15, 1915. His only son, Sydney, was born later that year. Pte. Hamilton was a nonsmoker and a total abstainer from alcoholic beverages, but minor health problems beleaguered him. In late July, after eating some canned pineapple, he was admitted to hospital for five days with stomach pains and severe diarrhea. In September, complaining of chest pain, he was again hospitalized. When released, he was sent on furlough to his parents' home in Sparkhill, Birmingham. He returned to duty but still suffered from stomach pains. Doctors considered him neurotic and sent him back to the depot for further evaluation.

His recovery must have been satisfactory, at least for army purposes, because he was sent overseas, landing in France on November 13. With the 21st Battalion of the 2nd Canadian Division, Sid was on the march and in the trenches throughout the spring of 1916. On May 20, Charlie Walford wrote from Flanders that the only Carleton Place boys in the 21st Battalion were himself, Sid Hamilton, Rex Sibbitt, Bert Henry and Alf Rowledge. The letter stated that they had been in the trenches for the last three months:

> . . . life is full of excitement, and we take no heed of the bullets and shells, as we are among them all the time, and it seems a wonder how we get tame to them. But it is all in the way you look after yourself.

Charlie wrote that he, Rex Sibbitt and Sid had gone, two weeks ago, to visit Carleton Place boys in other units. He mentioned Ralph Simpson, Art Maguire, Cecil Brice (sic), Sam McLaren, Horace Brown and Ed Stoddard. Charlie wrote that, if they were sending him anything, cigarettes would be nice.

On July 11, from a location "In the Field," Frank Teale, of the 21st Battalion, 4th Brigade, wrote to the Carleton Place Women's Institute thanking them for their parcels and "comforts." He continued:

> I regret to say up to the time of writing this letter one of our Carleton Place boys has fallen. Pte. Sid Hamilton. He was in my section, No. 12 of 2 Coy (Company), 21st Batt. He died game. He was always smiling and joking with one or another of us. Poor Sid, I feel his loss very much. We slept together all the time during our training in England.

Sydney Hamilton was killed in action by a shell explosion on June 14, 1916. Although he had given his age as twenty-two years at enlistment, when he was killed, according to his recorded birthdate, he was three weeks away from his twentieth birthday.

The 21st Battalion's Historical Calendar contains the following:

June 1916:

2—At night moved to position in G.H.Q. Line on account of enemy attack at Sanctuary Wood on 3rd Canadian Division.

10—Relieved 19th Battalion in Front Line Nos 33–38 Trenches.

13—Successful counter-attack by 1st Canadian Division at Mount Sorrel— Sanctuary Wood.

17—Relieved by 19th Battalion, moved to reserve, Bedford House area.

The War Diary of the 21st Battalion for June 14 records:

> Enemy machine-gun fire during the night from Opposite Trench 36 was very active. Flashes could not be located. The

enemy had been successful during the night in placing about 40 yards of coiled wire upon parapet at I.34.d.3..8. [map co-ordinates of the position]. Also about 15 yards of new sandbags on parapet at [more co-ordinates]. Our artillery were successful in firing on a working party at [more map co-ordinates].

Enemy artillery during the day was very active sending over 865 rounds most of which in the vicinity of the Railway Cutting and the DUMP and in our supports.[2]

Enemy was active with 'Rum Jars'[3] in afternoon and between 1:30 pm and 3:30 pm sent over about 20. We retaliated effectively with trench Mortars (60 lbs) and artillery.

Between 5 pm and 6 pm about 20 shells which seemed to be 4.5's Howitzer fell short and damaged our support and front line at right of 35 Trench. These proved to be from our own artillery. One of these Heavies hit on Dugout in our front line smashing same in and killing one signaller and wounding several others. Casualties 1 officer, 16 other ranks wounded and 7 killed.

Pte. Sid Hamilton was killed in action in the trenches near Ypres, in an area called "The Bluff."

He is buried in Bedford House Cemetery, Zillebeke, Ieper, Belgium, one of 350 Canadians, out of a total of 5,120 burials in this cemetery. Bedford House was the name the army gave to Château Rosendal, a country house with moats in a small wooded park. It never fell into enemy hands, but the house and trees were gradually destroyed by shell-fire. Sid is buried in Enclosure No. 4, the largest in the cemetery, used from June 1916 to February 1918, and containing 3,324 graves, almost two-thirds of which are unidentified.

In Memory of
SYDNEY HAMILTON
Private
59416
21st Bn., Canadian Infantry (Eastern Ontario Regt.)
who died on
Wednesday, 14th June 1916

[2] Support trenches. The second line of trenches containing men and material for reinforcement of the front line.

[3] A particular type of artillery explosive.

In one of those curious happenstances of war, Sid Hamilton's serial number was 59416; 59415 was allotted to R.L. Hamilton, who died on September 17, 1916, and 59414 was G. Hamilton's number, who was killed on the same day as Sid. All were members of the 21st Battalion but none was related.

On the last Sunday in April 1917, a memorial service was held in the Carleton Place Methodist Church. There, ". . . peacefully within the folds of the Union Jack," rested photographs of four fallen heroes, including that of Sydney Hamilton.

The Canadian Corps was spared the horror of the first days on the Somme by remaining in the Ypres Salient until the beginning of September. They continually harassed the enemy with raids, bombardments and mining. On August 14, King George V and the Prince of Wales visited the corps to witness an artillery barrage of the St. Eloi craters. Four days later, the recently knighted Sir Sam Hughes, Minister of Militia and the Defence of Canada, visited the 3rd Division. Units withdrew into reserve and their activities shifted to advanced training and practising new techniques.

A lesson learned at St. Eloi was further emphasized at Mount Sorel. Canadian soldiers, armed with the Ross rifle, could not fight effectively. On June 21, the War Office authorized the exchange for Lee-Enfields. By mid-August, the 2nd and 3rd Divisions had the new weapon, which the 1st Division had adopted, without authorization, the year before.

Chapter Ten

THE SOMME

On July 1, 1916, in broad daylight, one hundred thousand men climbed out of their trenches in the valley between the Ancre and the Somme Rivers and marched, shoulder to shoulder, in line, toward the waiting German guns. The day ultimately provided the heaviest loss ever suffered by a British Army—57,500 British and Commonwealth men killed, wounded or missing in a single day. The Newfoundland Regiment advanced into point blank fire at Beaumont Hamel. Of the 801 Newfoundlanders who stood up and marched into battle, only sixty-eight answered the next day's roll call. July 1, rather than November 11, remains in Newfoundland the day of commemoration and mourning.

Before Action

By all the glories of the day
And the cool evening's benison,
By that last sunset touch that lay
Upon the hills when day was done,
By beauty lavishly outpoured
And blessings carelessly received,
By all the days that I have lived,
Make me a soldier, Lord.

By all of man's hopes and fears,
And all the wonders poets sing,
The laughter of unclouded years,
And every sad and lovely thing;
By the romantic ages stored
With high endeavour that was his,
By all his mad catastrophes,
Make me a man, O Lord.

I, that on my familiar hill
Saw with uncomprehending eyes
A hundred of Thy sunsets spill
Their fresh and sanguine sacrifice,
Ere the sun swings his noonday sword
Must say goodbye to all of this;—

> *By all delights that I shall miss,*
> *Help me to die, O Lord.*

W.N. Hodgson
Written two days before his death on July 1, 1916.[1]

At the end of July, the 2nd Battalion of the 1st Canadian Division was back in the Ypres Salient. They had enjoyed a well-earned rest early in the month, but by July 11 were back in the line near Mount Sorel. During the night of July 26, the battalion went forward into the front line for what was to be their last tour of duty in the Ypres Salient. They were back at Hill 60, a spot notorious to the battalion from their fighting there on April 26.

The trenches on Hill 60 received violent bombardment from the Germans placed higher on the hill. The only shelter the shallow dugouts offered came from sheets of corrugated iron. The weather was warm and breezes brought a nauseating stench from decomposing bodies lying in No Man's Land, along with millions of blowflies carrying diseases hatched in the rotting corpses.

Heavy shelling from enemy artillery and minor patrol skirmishes were the main activities during this tour. A reconnaissance patrol, on the night of July 27, found the enemy well within bomb-throwing distance and the Canadians attacked. A local action developed. Trench mortars were used as well as machine-guns, which swept the land in front of the trenches to good effect. The next day, concentrated fire from the enemy almost obliterated the front line trench system. No. 2 Company's signallers took a direct hit from a *minenwerfer* and a shell exploded near the battalion headquarters, mortally wounding the medical officer.

During this period, the battalion suffered fifty-two casualties, including sixteen NCOs and men killed. Among them were Sgt. E.T. Handyside, one of three brothers serving in the same battalion, and Pte. William J. Wright. The Handyside brothers—Cecil Bryce, Ralph Simpson and William Wright—had all been drafted to the 2nd Battalion from the 38th (Ottawa) Battalion, and all had joined 2nd Battalion in the field on August 28, 1915, when the unit was at Ploegsteert, known to Canadians as "Plug Street."

[1] Brian Gardner, ed., *Up the Line to Death, The War Poets 1914-1918* (Oxford, Eng.: Meuthen & Co. Ltd., 1964), pp. 32-33.

On the evening of July 31, the 16th (Canadian Scottish) Battalion relieved the 2nd. Two days later, Sir Julian Byng, the newly appointed Commander of the Canadian Corps, inspected 2nd Battalion, accompanied by Maj.-Gen. Arthur W. Currie, the division commander. Along with others, William Wright's position in the formation was vacant.

WILLIAM JOHN WRIGHT

Born in Pakenham, Lanark County, on February 2, 1884, the son of Mr. and Mrs. Robert Wright, William joined "A" Company of the 38th (Ottawa) Infantry Battalion on February 24, 1915. He was living in Riverside Park, Ottawa West, with his wife, Maria Eliza. He had no previous militia service and was working as a clerk.

William was given regimental number A10255, which later became 410255. At thirty-one years of age, he was described as 5' 4" tall, weighing 140 pounds with a ruddy complexion, hazel eyes and black hair. He was a member of the Roman Catholic faith.

He went to England that summer and on July 4 was taken on strength by the 12th (Reserve) Battalion, in Shorncliffe, a holding unit providing reinforcements to the Canadian Corps overseas. William was drafted to the 2nd Battalion in France on August 25, 1915, and, along with many other Ottawa men from the 38th, he joined the battalion in the field at Ploegsteert on August 28. This was just in time to be on the parade inspected by Lt.-Gen. Sir Herbert Plumer, army commander.

Pte. Wright spent a month in the 1st Canadian Field Ambulance medical facility, from September 9 to October 6, 1915, with trench fever.

William rejoined the battalion from the hospital. He participated with the entire battalion, indeed the entire Canadian front line, in demonstrations to make the Germans think a tremendous offensive was about to begin:

> Men were instructed to show scaling ladders above the parapets, fire off their rifles, shout 'hurray,' make war-like noises with tin-cans, burn wet straw and thus create a thick smoke. In

point of fact they were required to do almost everything that no army ever does, or is ever likely to do, when about to launch an attack. How the thought could ever be entertained by full-grown men, graduates, no doubt of the Staff College and such like institutions, that this childish nonsense had any relation-ship to the waging of war is one of the minor mysteries of the campaign.

The 2nd Battalion dutifully did as they were instructed . . . the only effect of which was to irritate an obviously bored antago-nist and prompt him to put a stop to that sort of thing. This they did by dropping several heavy shells in and around the front-line. The cure was quite effective.[2]

Pte. Wright experienced the torrential rain, blustery wind, sleet and cold of the Flanders' winter. Trench warfare gave the men no shelter. The trenches themselves simply dissolved as the ground filled with water. However, for their first wartime Christmas in France, battalion officers staged a largely successful Christmas dinner at the town of Bailleul. In reserve billets, the entire battalion attended en masse. By the new year, they resumed trench warfare. The weather had not improved.

William was with the battalion when it returned to the Ypres Salient and he went into the trenches on Hill 60. There, on July 29, 1916, Private William Wright was killed in action.

In 1920, William's widow, Marion, received a gratuity of $116; a $64 bonus had already been paid to her. By this time, she had married a Mr. H.B. Spence and was living in New Edinburgh, near Ottawa. During his time in service, William had dutifully sent her a monthly assignment of $25; however, on May 1, 1916, he reduced it to $20, the amount most soldiers allotted their dependents or next of kin. Marion also received his medals, but the Memorial Cross (the Silver Cross of Valour) was delivered to his mother, Mrs. Robert Wright, in Carleton Place.

---

[2] Colonel W.W. Murray, *The History of the 2nd Canadian Battalion* (Ottawa: The Historical Committee, 2nd Battalion, 1947), pp. 74-75.

The *Carleton Place Herald* of August 15, 1916, carried the following notice:

> The casualty lists of last week contained the name of William J. Wright, son of Mrs. Robert Wright of Carleton Place and a brother of the Misses Wright. Pte. Wright enlisted in Ottawa with a contingent of recruits for the Princess Patricia's Light Infantry[3] and was killed in action on the 22nd of June.[4] He is survived by his wife and two children, his mother, three sisters and a brother, all of whom have the deepest sympathy of many friends in their hour of bereavement.

Pte. William John Wright is buried in Woods Cemetery, Zillebeke, four kilometres southeast of Ieper, West-Vlaanderen, Belgium. His body rests in the hallowed ground behind a low brick wall. He is amongst 300 others from the 2nd, 3rd and 10th Canadian Battalions. Thirty graves are those of unidentified soldiers.

[3] An error—he joined the 38th Battalion.
[4] Another error.

Chapter Eleven

POZIÈRES RIDGE

Late in August 1916, the Canadian Corps, "Byng's Boys," were moved along dusty roads from the muddy fields of Flanders. They were to take over part of the line at the Somme in front of the village of Courcelette. The 2nd and 3rd Divisions were ordered to prepare for a strong attack about mid September. The 1st Division took over 3,000 yards of battered trenches from a weary 1st Anzac (Australia/New Zealand) Corps.

Turner's 2nd Division had the task of seizing Courcelette. They were to attack over the higher ground of Pozières Ridge and take a German trench just south of the Pozières windmill. On September 9, at about 2:00 a.m., the company and unit commanders were notified that Zero Hour was 4:45 p.m. At 9:20 a.m. they began to move out, leaving 200 yards between platoons. During the warm and quiet afternoon, under a brilliant sun, Cecil Bryce moved up with his platoon, a small part of the 2nd Battalion. Overhead, aeroplanes droned lazily in the seemingly endless canvas of unbroken blue.

Sir Max Aiken (later Lord Beaverbrook), in assembling war records, had decreed that motion pictures would be taken to aid recruiting. These proved so successful that he expanded operations to film actual battle operations. The first such assignment was to "shoot" this day's attack by the 2nd Battalion. When the men clambered over the trench parapet, the camera operator, a Lt. Bovil, set up his camera and, in the middle of a hail of bullets and exploding shells sending shrapnel every which way, calmly reeled off many feet of film.

The 2nd Battalion of the 1st Canadian Division was up against the 212th Reserve Infantry Regiment of the 90th Brigade of the 45th Reserve Division of the German Army. They, too, were new to the battle zone, having only arrived in the sector that morning.

At precisely 4:45 p.m. the artillery opened fire. The men climbed out of their trenches and moved forward. For three minutes they tried to get as close to the barrage as possible. Unhappily, they either misjudged the impact areas of the shells, or the number of rounds landing short was unusually great. Canadian casualties from this friendly fire were many. Progress temporarily halted as the German riflemen picked up the range and the enemy artillery laid down its own heavy bombardment. Company and platoon commanders, urging the men to proceed, were especially hard hit. In a particularly fierce fight in an enemy trench, Cpl. Leo Clarke single-handedly killed two officers and eighteen German soldiers and captured the sole survivor. He was recommended for the Victoria Cross. He knew of the recommendation but was killed two weeks later and the Cross was awarded posthumously.

Thirty-two minutes after the opening artillery barrage, the 2nd Battalion reported that they had captured the enemy's positions. Casualties were heavy. Hampered by a lack of ammunition, water and personnel, and no support or reserves to call upon, the battalion's position became tenuous. Front-line officers advised the commander that their own artillery shells continued to land short, causing many unnecessary casualties. Early in the evening, reinforcements from the 3rd and 1st Battalions arrived. With them came a heavy mist which helped veil the men in their attempts to build protective barricades. Early the next morning, under intense shelling, groups of enemy soldiers appeared, but concentrated heavy fire drove them to ground. Nothing more was seen of them. During the afternoon of September 10, the 2nd was relieved by the 19th (Central Ontario) Battalion.

The 2nd Battalion's attack on Pozières Ridge was successful, but at a high price. Five officers and eighty-seven other ranks had been killed and five officers and 138 other ranks wounded. Cecil Bryce would never know of his comrades' success. He lay dead on the ridge, killed by the blast of a shell.

CECIL ELMAS BRYCE

Cecil was born in Rockland, Ontario, on May 20, 1896. Since he listed only his father, Mr. Thomas Bryce, as "next of kin," and sent a pay allotment to him, and the department issued no Memorial Cross, it must be concluded that his mother had died some years earlier. Along with Percy Moore and Thomas Flegg, Cecil was an active Boy Scout in the first troop organized in Carleton Place.

He enlisted at Smiths Falls on January 14, 1915, into the 42nd Regiment of the local militia. He gave his occupation as a "spinner," probably with Bates and Innes, the largest woollen mill in Carleton Place. When he joined the army he was eighteen years old, weighing 142 pounds and standing 5' 7" tall. He was described as having a florid complexion, grey eyes and brown hair. He carried a burn scar on the elbow of his right arm and his right hip and calf from an accident with fire. On March 27, Cecil was sent to Ottawa and the 38th Battalion. After a few days' leave at home, on June 23, 1915, he was sent overseas to the 12th Reserve Battalion of the Canadian Expeditionary Force.

Late that summer, Cecil went to France as a reinforcement and joined the 2nd Battalion in the field on August 29. He was with the battalion throughout the campaign in Flanders. Charlie Wolford's letter of May 20, 1916, mentions that he had seen Cecil. At the age of twenty years, three months, Cecil Bryce was killed at Pozières Ridge, near Courcelette, on September 9, 1916, from the effects of an exploding artillery shell. He is buried in Pozières British Cemetery, Ovilliers-La Boiselle, Somme, France.

In the *Carleton Place Herald* of October 17, 1916, under a photograph of the young soldier is the epitaph:

Cecil Elmas Bryce

son of Mr. Thomas Bryce of Carleton Place, aged 20 years, who enlisted at Smiths Falls with the 38th Batt. in the fall of 1914. Went overseas in August 1915 and a month later went to France, and was at the front until September 9, 1916, when he was killed in action at the Battle of the Somme.

Ralph Simpson was also with the 2nd Battalion at the Battle of the Somme. In fact, he had been with the battalion since joining it in the field in France on August 28, 1915. When the battalion came out of the line on September 10, after achieving their entire objective, they marched back to Albert along the Albert-Baupaume Road. The battalion band joined them and as it led the dirty, weary, bloodied soldiers back to billets, the gaps in the formation told the tale of men left behind. Their achievement on the ridge preceded them. Hearts swelled and steps became jaunty as other troops lining the roadway applauded and cheered the "Good Old Second!"

The development of that intangible spirit of brotherhood of the Great War was taking shape. Valour in battle is rarely, if ever, inspired by King and Country. Bravery is what a man believes he owes his friends in his platoon, company or battalion. He takes personal ownership of such units. A soldier does what he must to keep faith in front of his friends and pride in his own being and accomplishments.

The battalion would have welcomed a period of rest in the billets of Albert. But it was not to be. The vast number of troops and equipment engaged in the Battle of the Somme demanded that Albert and all surrounding villages be used as staging points. Units had little time to spare and were moved every day to accommodate other incoming troops.

Chapter Twelve

THE BATTLE FOR COURCELETTE

Two innovations of war made their appearance on the Somme: rolling barrages by the artillery, which were designed to lead the infantry across No Man's Land and deny the enemy any opportunity to use their deadly machine-guns; and the tank—tracked, armoured monsters that should flatten any opposing machine-guns and the crews that manned them.

The 2nd Battalion was ordered to seize Courcelette in mid-September 1916. Here, for the first time in history, they would see the newest weapon of war—the tank. These "land cruisers" were 26 feet long, 14 feet wide and about 7 feet high. The tank weighed twenty-eight tons and was powered with a six-cylinder, 105-horsepower Daimler engine. Designated the Mark I, it had a speed of 3.7 miles an hour but, over shell torn ground, it did well to advance at about half a mile an hour. The normal armament was two six-pounder guns and four machine-guns. The crews were taken from the Machine Gun Corps and each tank required one officer and seven men. The first tanks arrived in France in mid-August and they were to go into action with the 2nd Division against Courcelette on September 15.

Pte. Ralph Simpson was denied the privilege of witnessing the first appearance of these war machines in action. On September 12, the 2nd Battalion, with reinforcements filling the gaps in their ranks made on the Pozières Ridge, left Albert to march into position for the attack on Courcelette. However, being out of the trenches did not mean being safe from enemy bombardment. Whenever troops moved, the opposing artillery and infantry marksmen were sure to mark their progress. On September 12, Ralph Simpson received the wound that removed him from further action on the Somme.

RALPH PATTERSON SIMPSON

Ralph was the first of the two Simpson brothers to enlist. He joined the 42nd Regiment in Smiths Falls on March 6, 1915. He served in the militia for three weeks before he transferred to the 38th

Battalion in Ottawa on March 28. He was enrolled in the regular army on June 23 and was sent overseas. He arrived at Shorncliffe, England, on July 4, 1915.

The 38th Canadian Infantry Battalion (Ottawa) was organized on July 1, 1915. Its motto was "Advance." The battalion served in Bermuda as a protective garrison from August 12, 1915, to May 30, 1916. It went to France and Flanders to serve

with the 12th Infantry Brigade of the 4th Canadian Division from August 14, 1916, until the armistice. It is perpetuated by the Cameron Highlanders of Ottawa.

Ralph was born in Carleton Place on April 10, 1895, the oldest son of William and Minnie Simpson. He spent his boyhood in the town and pursued his avocation as a butcher. His profession probably gave him the scar on the inside of the little finger of his right hand that was found at his enlistment medical examination. Ralph and his family regularly attended the Presbyterian Church. When he joined the army, he was twenty-one years old, stood a relatively tall 5' 11", and had a fair complexion, blue eyes and fair hair.

From July 15 to 29, he was in St. Martin's Tent Hospital in England for a minor ailment. Then on August 25 he was drafted to France and the 2nd Battalion. He joined the unit in the field. On Christmas Eve, 1915, Ralph celebrated. He was absent from 4:00 p.m. on December 25 to 9:00 a.m. on the 26th. That night of revelry cost him the forfeit of two days' pay.

In Charlie Wolford's letter of May 20, 1916, he wrote, "Well, I have seen Ralph Simpson (and others) . . . That is all the C.P. boys . . . if you see any of their folks you may tell them for me they are fine." On September 12, Ralph was wounded by a rifle bullet hitting his right thigh. He was evacuated to #3 General Hospital. The *Carleton Place Herald* of September 19 reported Ralph's name as appearing on the latest casualty list. On October 13, his wound had "practically healed," and he was discharged from the hospital but returned to England to recuperate. After convalescing he rejoined the 2nd Battalion in the field on November 17, 1917.

His brother, Ross, who was to be seriously wounded near the Canal du Nord in September 1918, joined the 2nd Battalion in January, 1918. Ralph survived the rest of the war unscathed. After the armistice he stayed in Europe with the Occupation Forces until January 6, 1919, when he was transferred to England. He left for Canada on February 8 and arrived aboard the S.S. *Princess Juliana* in Halifax on February 17. He was discharged from the army on March 3, 1919. Ralph lived out the rest of his life in Carleton Place, dying at the relatively young age of thirty-six years, eleven months on March 5, 1932. His death was deemed by military authorities to have been attributable to his war wound.

DESIRE TRENCH ON THE ANCRE RIDGE

The 21st Battalion, engaged in heavy fighting to break through the German line and, with the help of the newfangled tanks and other battalions of the 2nd and 3rd Divisions, advanced on Courcelette. After fierce hand-to-hand fighting they took the village. The enemy retreated to Regina Trench, a line northwest of Courcelette.

On October 1, 1916, the 2nd Division made the first attempt to take Regina Trench. The attack failed. On October 8, the largest Canadian attack, with eight battalions, took place. Again they failed because the operation was not properly planned. The artillery barrage left the German barbed wire undamaged and the infantry exposed to machinegun fire. After their successes of September 25, the Canadian Corps was unable to follow up. It withdrew from the Battle on the Somme.

WILLIAM JOHN GRIFFITH

During the second attempt on Regina Trench, the Canadians suffered 1,364 casualties. One of those severely wounded was Pte. W.J. Griffith. He lay dying in a battalion dressing station near Rouen.

William John Griffith was born in Beckwith Township, outside Carleton Place, on June 18, 1892, the son of John and Mary Anne Griffith. The family moved to Norwood (Winnipeg), Manitoba, where he worked as a teamster before joining the 61st Battalion on June 9, 1915. The medical examiner described a fit, twenty-two-year, eleven-month-old recruit with a dark complexion, brown eyes and dark hair. He was 5' 9" tall and weighed 145 pounds. He had previous service with the 106th Regiment of the Canadian Militia.

The 61st sailed with the first draft from Montreal on September 11, 1915, aboard S.S. *Metagama*. They arrived in England on September 20 where the battalion was broken up to provide reinforcements in the field. Many, including William Griffith, went to the 17th Reserve Battalion to await posting to a unit fighting in France. During the wait, on November 20, 1915, Pte. Griffith was punished with two days' confinement to barracks for being in bed after reveille and not complying with an order—to get up! On December 13 he was posted to the 8th Battalion and on the 14th went to France.

The 8th (Winnipeg "The Black Devils") Canadian Infantry Battalion served in the 2nd Brigade of the 1st Canadian Division in France and Flanders. Their motto was *Hostie Acie Nominati* (Named by the Enemy) due to the battalion's nickname, "The Black Devils," that a befuddled group of German soldiers who had opposed them bestowed upon them. The battalion is perpetuated by the Royal Winnipeg Rifles.

On Christmas Eve, 1915, Griffith left the holding unit in France, joining the 8th Battalion in the field on December 27. The 2nd Brigade was in the line facing the German 117th Division, which was occupying Messines, but fortunately there was little activity in the trenches. Battling the weather was enough adversity for both sides. Influenza, paratyphoid and trench foot took their toll.

Early in 1916 Canadian soldiers were busy "wearing down" the enemy with sniping, raiding and surprise artillery shoots. During the operations at St. Eloi in March of 1916, when six mines were exploded with astonishing results "like the sudden outburst of a volcano," the 1st Division occupied trenches near the ruins of the town. It was here, in early April, that Canadians began wearing steel helmets for the first time, although there were not enough to issue one to every soldier. For nearly two weeks the fighting went back and forth over the mine craters, both sides enduring continuous heavy bombardment. Generally, the Canadian operation was unsuccessful. It was the 2nd Division's first fight and it left the troops frustrated as the Canadian forces withdrew from the front for other positions in the Ypres Salient.

In September, the Canadian Corps moved toward the killing fields of the Somme. The summer was relatively uneventful, but Griffith managed to get himself sentenced to five days' Field Punishment # 2 (confinement) for "Not complying with an order—i.e.—smoking on parade." Regina Trench had been unsuccessfully assaulted by Canadian soldiers on October 1. On October 8, the 1st and 2nd Divisions made a second attack. The preliminary bombardment failed to cut the maze of barbed wire and the weather steadily worsened with snow, sleet and rain thickening the mud. In spite of all the adverse conditions, the attack went on as ordered.

Three Canadian battalions actually made it into Regina Trench, but without support and, in the face of merciless counterattacks, were unable to hold. They retreated. By October 9 there were no attacking troops left in the trench. This last Canadian action on the Somme cost 1,364 casualties. Pte. W.J. Griffith lay mortally wounded. He died the next day, October 10, from the wounds received in action.

Although Griffith died at a dressing station, somehow his body disappeared and his only trace is his name engraved on the Vimy Memorial. The Commonwealth War Graves commemorative information reads:

In Memory of
WILLIAM JOHN GRIFFITH

Private
460142
8th Bn., Canadian Infantry (Manitoba Regt.)
Who died on
Tuesday, 10th October 1916. Age 21.
Son of John Griffith, of Hilbre, Manitoba.

His parents had moved to the small farming community of Hilbre, Manitoba, and it was to that address that his medals, a Memorial Cross and a $180 gratuity, were delivered on July 26, 1920.

The 4th Canadian Division came back into the line in October and launched its first attack on Regina Trench on October 21. Improper planning and uncut wire again resulted in heavy losses and no gains. On November 11, three battalions charged the by now nearly obliterated trench. They finally succeeded. After forty-two days of

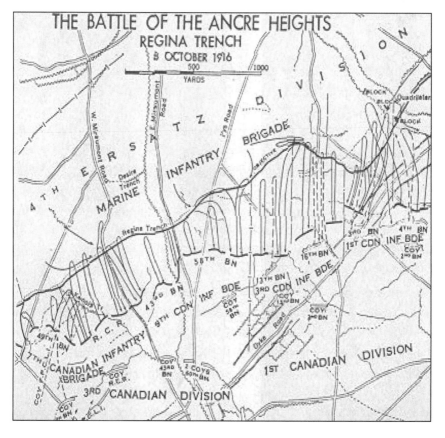

hard fighting, the Canadians captured Regina, the longest trench constructed by German troops on the Western Front.

On the home front, the *Carleton Place Herald* continued its chatter on military matters. In the issue of September 26, it reported, "There is good news for the young subalterns (second lieutenants) who have struggled to meet the militia requirements which calls for a moustache. A new order has been issued to the effect that in future, military men will not be required to wear moustaches." Perhaps tongue in cheek, the *Herald* noted that no reason was given for the new order.

On October 10, the paper carried the notice that the 130th Ontario Battalion had landed safely in England. The following week, October 17, residents of Carleton Place and area woke to the first snowfall of the season—nearly three weeks earlier than the year before. On October 24, a laudatory story about Murray Galbraith, who was serving as a pilot in the British Royal Naval Air Service, noted:

> Sub-Lieut Murray Galbraith . . . is adding glory to his name by his excellent work in the Royal Naval Aeriel [*sic*] Service. His first achievement was made by looping the loop and striking his enemy in a vital spot and sending him to the earth.
>
> His second encounter was with an enemy seaplane at an altitude of 11,000 feet over two banks of clouds, when he had a very close call indeed, the sight of his gun being struck by a bullet from the enemy before he got a shot that struck the Teuton's tank and exploded the machine, sending it into the sea. The fight was witnessed by a French aeronaut who congratulated our brave young townsman upon his success. We are proud of our gallant boys at the front, and especially pleased to hear of their success under the most difficult circumstances.[1]

The next week's news noted that "Flight Lieutenant Galbraith was awarded the French Croix de Guerre after downing his third German aircraft—a Fauker [*sic*]."

On the Western Front, the first snowfall of the winter happened during the night of November 17–18. The battle for Desire Support Trench, located some 400 metres north of Regina Trench, was fought in the worst possible conditions. Starting at six in the morning, the

---

[1] His mother and sister had only returned from visiting him in England three weeks earlier.

Canadians advanced in blinding sleet that later turned to rain. They groped forward in freezing mud, frequently becoming lost because of the inability to identify their objectives, which were now covered in snow. On November 18, the 38th Battalion (Eastern Ontario), 87th, 54th (Kootenay), 75th (Mississauga Horse), and 50th (Alberta) captured Desire Trench. The Battle of the Somme was over. This last engagement cost 8,000 Canadian lives for two-and-a-half kilometres of ground-up chalky farmland. Left in the obliterated trench was Pte.Fred Trotman, lost without a trace in the churned-up muck.

FREDERICK GILBERT TROTMAN

Fred Trotman joined the 42nd Regiment (Lanark and Renfrew) in Smiths Falls on October 5, 1915. He transferred to the Active Force and the 80th Battalion on October 12th. Fred  was born in Carleton Place on June 15, 1893, the son of Mr. and Mrs. Harry Trotman. At 5' 7 " tall, weighing 155 lbs, he had a fair complexion, blue eyes and fair hair with a light-coloured mustache.

He was twenty-two years, five months old when he left his job as a "moulder" with Findlay Foundry to go to war. The moulder of molten metal was one of the elite of the foundry workforce, receiving the highest rate of pay.

The Trotman family had five sons: Albert, Fred, Ernest, Austin and Wilfred. There were also two daughters, Pearl and Gertrude

Pte. Trotman sailed for England on the S.S. *Baltic*, leaving from Halifax on May 16, 1916, and arriving in Liverpool on May 30. Just before he sailed the news arrived of the death of his uncle, David Trotman, killed in action with the 21st (Kingston) Battalion. David was a Permanent Force veteran of the Boer War who left a wife and two children in Kingston.

The 80th Battalion was broken up and absorbed by other battalions to provide reinforcements for the Canadian Corps in the field. Fred went to the 74th (Toronto) Battalion for training in England. He was transferred to the 11th Brigade Machine Gun Company on July 22, but

ten days later, on August 2, he was transferred to the 75th (Toronto) Battalion. The battalion was better known as the Mississauga Horse serving as a unit of the 1st Central Ontario Regiment. On August 12, Pte. Trotman disembarked in Le Havre, France.

On November 18, 1916, the 75th Canadian Infantry Battalion, on the far right side of the 11th Brigade, was ordered into the attack on Desire Trench during the final phases of the Battle of the Somme. Fred had been fighting with the battalion for three months.

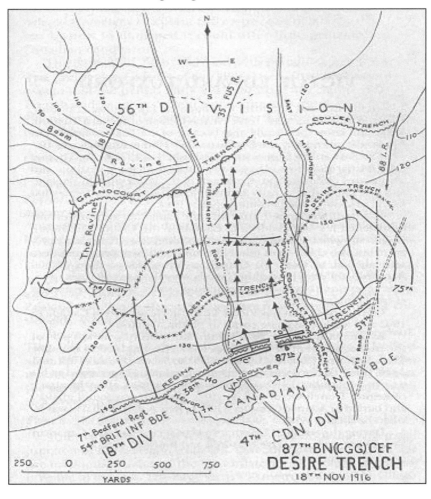

18/11/16 On the morning of the 18th at 6:10 a.m. a successful attack was made on DESIRE TRENCH by this battalion[2] with the 54th on the left and the 50th on the right. The 50th Battalion on the right failed to capture their objective and consequently our Battalion was exposed to a heavy enfilade fire and continuous sniping from enemy trench on our right. We established a block in DESIRE TRENCH a few yards west of PYS ROAD and dug a new trench parallel to and about 100 yards north of DESIRE TRENCH. This position was held by us until relieved at 5 a.m. on the 20th November by the 102nd Bn.

Casualties during this attack:

220015 Trotman F.G.

(Several pages of additional names)

In this, the final battle of the Somme operation, the 75th played a prominent part.

Objective (4th Division) Desire Support trench and to consolidate a new trench about 150 yards in advance. Objective extended from Regina Apex along spur westward to ravine junction.

Zero Hour 6:10 A.M.

The Attack As a whole the attack was a brilliant success, all objectives being captured except on the left, where the 10th Brigade encountered a stiff resistance and had to fall back from their objective. In consequence the 75th Bn. suffered heavily from enfilading machine-gun fire from the right. Nevertheless the battalion established a block in Desire Trench a few yards west of Pys Road and dug a new trench parallel to road about 100 yards north of desire Trench. The position was held until the battalion was relieved at about 5 a.m. on the 20th by the 102nd Bn. (Victoria, British Columbia) . . .

The 75th Battalion suffered heavily; Major Alexander Milne, Lieut. B. Wright and 65 other ranks were killed.[3]

Fred was killed during the attack on Desire Trench on November 18, 1916. The *Carleton Place Herald* printed the following article in its December 12 edition:

[2] 75th Battalion War Diary

[3] 75th Battalion, Historical Records, Public Archives, Ottawa.

Fred Trotman Pays the Extreme Penalty

The sad news reached Mr. and Mrs. Harry Trotman last week of the death of their son, Pte. Fred G. Trotman, who was killed in action somewhere in France on November 18th, whilst taking a German trench. Fred was one of our best boys. He went overseas with the 80th Batt., did his part nobly and met with a soldier's fate. His parents have the deepest sympathy of the whole town in their hour of bereavement. Pte. Trotman was 23 years of age, and was highly esteemed by all who knew him. He was an employee of the Findlay foundry, a member of the Sons of England, an Oddfellow and a member of the Can. Order of Foresters. He was a faithful member of the Baptist Church, an usher, and secretary of the Sunday School. Next Sunday morning a memorial service in his honor will be conducted by Rev. Mr. Newton.

Fred Trotman, killed in action on the Somme, has no known grave. His name is commemorated on the Canadian National Vimy Memorial at Pas de Calais, France.

Before joining the army, Fred had been a very religious young man, spending a good part of his life in church activities. In the *Herald* of November 19, 1918, his family placed a memorial:

In Memoriam

Trotman—In loving memory of Private Fred G. Trotman, who died for King and Country, Saturday, November 18, 1916.

Nobly he did his duty
Bravely he fought and fell,
But the sorrow of those who mourn him
Only aching hearts can tell.

It may be a soldier's honor
For his country's cause to fall,
But we cannot think of the Glory
For the pain it has caused us all.

Mother and Father

The Almonte Gazette, in its issue dated December 28, 1917, noted that "A brass tablet to the memory of the late Pte. Fred Trotman was unveiled in the Baptist church a week ago Sunday evening."

The Memorial Cross (Silver Cross) issued to his mother is now in the Carleton Place Victoria School Museum.

Grief lingered long for the Trotman family. The Spanish Influenza epidemic gripped Canada during the winter of 1918–1919. In five days during the first week of February 1919, the Trotmans of Carleton Place lost five family members to this scourge. Taken was Fred's older brother, Albert; Albert's wife, Else, and their daughter Doreen; the family patriarch, Harry; and Fred's sister Pearl. The *Herald* of February 2, 1919, reported, "Bert Trotman and his sister Pearl both died today from the flu and Harry Trotman died on the 4th from flu and Mrs. Bert and her baby both died of flu on the 6th."

Overall, Canada paid the price of 24,029 casualties at the Somme. This was mass butchery ordered by anonymous, yet omnipotent, general officers. However, it did establish the Canadians' reputation as hard-hitting shock troops. The 2nd Division could remember proudly the Battle for Courcelette, and the 4th Division the attack and capture of Regina and Desire Trenches. For the rest of the war, they were more often than not brought to the head of an assault. But there was no further advance that year. The rains of autumn turned the battlefield into a boggy marsh halting any notion of offensive operations.

> . . . merely to maintain themselves made severe physical demands upon the men in the trenches. For the soldier in the front line existence was a continual struggle against cold and wet, as he crouched all day in the rain and the mud, gaining what protection he could from a rubber groundsheet wrapped around him. Hip boots were issued to help guard against 'trench feet,' but often these had to be abandoned when the wearer became mired in the clay. For health's sake frequent reliefs were necessary, even though affecting these was an exhausting process. Towards the end of the Canadians' tour on the Somme infantry battalions had as much as eight miles to march to the trenches from their billets in Albert, and at least four miles from the nearest bivouacs at Tara Hill. 'With the bad weather,' reported General Watson to Canadian Corps Headquarters, 'the men's clothing became so coated with mud, great coat, trousers, puttees and boots sometimes weighing 120 pounds, that many could not carry out relief.'[4]

Truly, the winter of 1916–1917 was a Winter of Despair on the Western Front.

[4] Colonel G.W.L. Nicholson, C.D., Canadian Expeditionary Force 1914-1919 (Ottawa: Queen's printer, 1962), p.197.

Chapter Thirteen

AFTER THE SOMME

The winter of 1916–1917 presented the harshest weather in Europe since 1881. Veterans who wintered at the Front remembered frozen hands and feet. Hot food froze in their mess tins before it could be eaten. There were no major operations during the early months of the year but limited hostilities never ceased. The Canadian Corps, when relieved from the Somme, had replaced a British Corps holding a ten-mile line from a little north of Arras to just short of Lens. They were facing the German 6th Bavarian and the 12th Reserve Divisions. All winter they exchanged mortar fire, did extensive patrolling and occasionally mounted trench raids. The object was to inflict casualties, take prisoners, gather intelligence and destroy enemy dugouts.

The Canadian Corps was intact for the very first time. When they came out of the Somme, the officers no longer spoke with British accents. Each Division also put up distinguishing shoulder flashes, great rectangles of coloured flannel: red for the 1st Division, blue for the 2nd, grey for the 3rd and green for the 4th. As well, each battalion now wore a distinguishing patch above the divisional identifier.

In the Ottawa Valley, the 240th—the new "Counties Battalion"—made a four-week march in October. They tramped cross-country from Renfrew, battalion headquarters, to Perth, Smiths Falls, Franktown, and around into Carleton Place. In each town they held evening meetings and attended Sunday church services. In Carleton Place, the last weekend of October, squads were detailed to each of the churches. An afternoon meeting was held in the town hall for the women and an evening public meeting was also held in the town hall, after church services. The presence on the streets of so many men in khaki gave the town, according to the *Carleton Place Herald* of October 31, 1916, "a busy appearance." The whole object of the exercise was to fill the ranks with recruits. At each halt the soldiers held public meetings to make the need of the battalion known to the townsfolk.

Recruiting in Canada had become extremely problematic and many line officers overseas were appalled at the ill-disciplined and poorly-trained reinforcements they received. This public exposure tactic by the 240th must have worked. While recruiting elsewhere in Canada was reaching crisis proportions and fuelling the calls for conscription, the *Herald* reported in December:

> The 240th Battalion . . . has established what is believed to be a record for county battalions in Canada in the third year of the war by recruiting 213 men during the month of November. The battalion finished the month of November with an even 500 men enrolled.

The personals columns of the newspaper carried many notices of mothers and daughters, wives and fiancées, and many others, mostly women, travelling to England. This in spite of the government's plea that such travel was undesirable, except in cases of necessity, because "every additional person in England now who is not doing some real national service becomes a drain upon the food supply." Travellers were warned that transportation limitations could make it very difficult for them to return to Canada if they waited until the return of troops began. That this war would continue another two years was still unfathomable.

Historically, wives, sweethearts, and even mothers had often followed their men into battle. One hundred years before, during the Peninsular War of 1809–1815 between France and England, wives, children and other camp followers walked with the supply wagons behind their men's battalions. They were actually included as part of the battalion's marching orders and counted for the requisition of supplies.

In January 1917, orders were issued prohibiting little children from wearing khaki uniforms, "or any attire similar to the soldiers' uniforms." Capt. Hooper, who had been taken a prisoner in April 1915, was released to Swiss authorities as a first step to repatriation. In February all soldiers, whether of the legal age of twenty-one or not, were given the right to vote. This had been promised in the Liberal Speech from the Throne the previous autumn. Lack of manpower overseas remained so acute that, as noted in the *Herald* of February 20, 1917, new measures were needed:

> All members of the 130th Battalion brass band, who have been at Sandling camp with the 12th Reserve Battalion since arriving in England, have been permitted to go to France, according to a letter received from Bandsman Murray Walker this week. Heretofore the band was obliged to stay in England awaiting orders.

In Europe the killing continued.

Chapter Fourteen

APPROACHING VIMY

For the Canadian Corps, the winter of 1916–1917 was free of any major operations. Limited hostilities continued throughout the winter with the opposing troops exchanging periodic mortar fire, doing extensive patrolling and occasionally raiding each other's trenches. A number of these attacks were carried out in January. The object was to inflict casualties, take prisoners, capture weapons and destroy enemy dugouts. The infantry was supported by artillery, machine-guns, and often by smoke screens provided by the Engineers. Following one of these forays, on January 24, 1917, Pte. Thomas Cummings was helped into No. 23 Casualty Clearing Station with "dangerous wounds."

THOMAS CUMMINGS

The *Carleton Place Herald* of January 4, 1916, reported an additional recruit to the 130th Battalion, Thomas Cummings. When he enlisted, on December 30, 1915, a week after the battalion was orga-

nized, Thomas stated that he had had two weeks' volunteer training with the 42nd Regiment. He joined other Carleton Place men, such as Leo Corr, Herb Dowdall, Percy Moore and L.J. McDiarmid in "C" Company. He gave his date of birth as October 9, 1887, his birthplace as Ramsay Township, and listed his father, David, as his next of kin, even though he had a wife.

Thomas was described as twenty-eight years old, weighing 140 pounds and standing 5' 7" tall. He had a dark complexion, brown eyes and black hair. He was an adherent to the Church of England. He listed his civilian employment as doing bridgework for the Canadian Pacific Railroad.

The post office issued a new 3-cent stamp in January 1916, increasing the cost of mailing a letter by a whole cent. In June special train excursions were advertised for friends and relatives who wished to visit the boys in camp.

On January 25, "C" Company did a route march to Almonte. By May the men of the 130th were preparing to move to Barriefield, the newest Army training camp. On September 23, the battalion embarked on the S.S. *Lapland* in Halifax to sail for England. They arrived in Liverpool on October 6. By November 12, many of the men, including Thomas Cummings, were transferred as reinforcements to the 3rd Battalion overseas. He arrived in France on November 14 and joined the battalion on December 8.

The 3rd Canadian Infantry Battalion (Toronto) was organized on August 6, 1914, and served in France and Flanders with the 1st Infantry Brigade of the 1st Canadian Division from February 12, 1915, to the armistice. It is perpetuated by the Queen's Own Rifles of Canada and The Royal Regiment of Canada.

Cummings was only with the 3rd Battalion a few weeks. He joined the unit after it had left the Somme and while it was in the trench system before Vimy Ridge. On January 23, 1917, Thomas was seriously wounded in the thigh by an enemy rifle grenade. He was attended and evacuated to No. 23 Casualty Clearing Station where he succumbed to his wounds three days later, on January 26. The War Diary of the 3rd Battalion lists the number of casualties for January 1917 as one officer and 18 other ranks. On January 25, they recorded one other rank wounded and one other rank wounded accidentally.

The *Herald,* in successive papers, carried the following notices:

> January 30, 1917—Pte Thomas Cummings of Carleton Place has been reported as dangerously wounded. Pte Cummings is a son of Mr. David Cummings, High St., and is about 25 years of age and married. He enlisted with the 130th Batt.

> February 6, 1917—The sad news reached the relatives here on Friday of the death of Pte. Thos. Cummings, mentioned last week as seriously wounded. The sympathy of the whole community flows to the young wife and the relatives in their bereavement.

> February 13, 1917—Pte. Cummings, whose death in France of wounds was mentioned last week, was 29 years of age. He is survived by his wife, formerly Miss Munson; his father Mr.

David Cummings; one brother, William; and four sisters: Mrs. John R. Lewis and Miss Viola of Carleton Place; Mrs. Clarence Hunter of Smiths Falls; and Mrs. J. Woreal [*sic: correct name is Worrall*] of Montreal. Before enlisting Pte. Cummings was an employee of the C.P.R. in the bridge department.

Thomas was buried in the La Pugnoy par Marles-des-Mines cemetery. The official Commonwealth War Graves Directory has the following entry:

Thomas Cummings (787642 Private) son of William David and Sarah Ann Cummings, husband of Mrs. F.M. Lackey (formerly Cummings) Carleton Place. "A" Company, 3rd Battalion, 1st Central Ontario Regiment. Killed January 26, 1917, age 29. Buried LaPugnoy Military Cemetery, Pas de Calais, France.

LaPugnoy Military Cemetery was established in 1915 for burials from the nearby casualty clearing stations. It contains 349 Canadian graves, only one of which has a body of an unknown soldier.

By the time the Department of Militia got around to granting a widow's pension and delivering his medals to his wife Phyllis, she had married Mr. F.M. Lackey. The last Sunday in April 1917, a memorial service was held in the Methodist Church that was full to capacity. On the altar was a photograph "of the fallen hero . . . Pte Cummings (and others) . . . resting peacefully within the folds of the Union Jack."

In the fall of 1917 an officer of the 240th Battalion visited the schools in Carleton Place. He asked "all those who have relatives in khaki, please stand up." He was quite surprised when every scholar in the room took to his or her feet. He felt that nowhere else in the Empire was such sacrifice being made by the splendid men and women who parented such loyal citizens.

It was about this time that the Government of Canada realized they must recognize the status of those men who were at home. A system of war badges was devised that men in civilian clothing could wear in the lapel of their jackets to show that they had served, or at least had tried to serve, in the armed forces. There were four distinct classes of war badges:

Class A—for those who had seen actual service at the front.

Class B—for those who had served in the present war and had been discharged: a metal button, in the centre of which was the Tudor crown with the inside red enamel and the word "Canada" below and "For Honourable Service" in a circle around the crown.

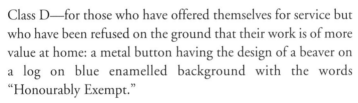

Class C—for those rejected as medically unfit: a metal badge with the Canadian coat of arms surrounded by the words "Honourably Exempted" and, at the base, "Canada."

Class D—for those who have offered themselves for service but who have been refused on the ground that their work is of more value at home: a metal button having the design of a beaver on a log on blue enamelled background with the words "Honourably Exempt."

No badge was to be issued to those who had accepted their discharge by reason of the stoppage of working pay if they were still medically fit.

One of the most elaborately planned Canadian raids, prior to the assault on Vimy, was carried out on the night of February 28–March 1.

Hill 145[1] was the highest point on Vimy Ridge. It was the most important feature because it afforded the German defenders, the 16th Bavarian Infantry Division and the 79th Reserve Division, a commanding view of the Ridge, the Souchez and Zouave Valleys, and the Douai Plain beyond. The German trench system and fortifications were particularly strong. This raid by the 4th Division, of which the 75th Battalion was a part, was aimed to gather information and inflict damage on the defences. Tear gas and chlorine cylinders were in place to aid the attackers but preliminary bombardment and wire cutting was not done in order to achieve surprise. The chlorine could not be used due to a changing wind, but German shelling set some cylinders off causing casualties amongst the Canadians.

---

[1] The number designating a hill was taken from its height measured in metres. These heights were marked on the contour lines on the topographical maps used by army planners.

The entire effort failed completely. The Canadians captured thirty-seven of the enemy, but lost 687 of their own, including machine gunner Pte. Arthur Tufts. For the next two days, Canadian troops were allowed to move freely, and were even assisted in recovering their dead by the German defenders.

The 75th Battalion (Mississauga) was ordered mobilized in Toronto on June 30, 1915. It was initially raised entirely from the 9th Mississauga Horse Regiment, which explains why the name "Mississaugas" was adopted. They were known by that name until the regiment went overseas where, for purposes of uniformity, it became the 75th Canadian Infantry Battalion.

The 75th mobilized in three weeks and by July 31, 1915 was in training camp at Niagara-on-the-Lake. The soldiers spent the winter and spring at Exhibition Park in Toronto. Their arming and equipping was practically completed by the time they left on March 26, 1916. They sailed from Halifax aboard the *Empress of Britain* on April 1 and arrived in Liverpool on April 9, 1916, going into camp at Bramshott the next day for training prior to deployment in France.

The battalion spent the winter months of 1916–1917 preparing for the great Vimy offensive. Pte. Arthur Tufts left the 130th Battalion and joined the 75th in the field in December. The unit spent January and February alternating their time between training and uneventful tours in the line. On March 1, raiding parties of the 75th joined the elaborate raid carried out by the 4th Division on Hill 145.

The raiders attempted to enter the enemy's trenches in seven parties, but were only partially successful. Three parties under command of Lts. Wallace, Molyneux and Swinnerton penetrated to a depth of 300 to 400 yards, but then had to retire. Lt. Swinnerton was wounded and captured. The battalion officer-commanding, Lt.-Col. S.G. Beckett, was killed while in the open trying to steady the right side of the attack. Maj. L.M. Langstaff, the officer commanding the raid, was also killed. The battalion suffered heavy casualties; seven other officers were wounded, and amongst the other ranks, sixty-eight were killed, thirty-one went missing and 112 were wounded.[2]

The 11th Field Company of Canadian Engineers provided demolition parties for the destruction of dugouts, strong points and trench mortars. One sapper (the rank of an engineer equivalent to the rank of private in the infantry) was assigned to the 75th Battalion. These engineers provided written "Reports on Co-operation" following the raid:

> At ZERO hour the wind was blowing from the west about 12 miles per hour. Within ten minutes after ZERO hour the wind swung around to North West approximately, and the GAS CLOUD appeared to drift South east along No Man's Land.
>
> *Sapper Camp*—I was with #7 Party on the Right Flank of the 75th Battalion. Our objective was Crater 'F'. At plus 2:15, we went forward into No Man's Land. We advanced slowly with short pauses until we got about 100 yards out. We then saw the 54th party on our right retiring while the 75th party on our left continued to advance. Our party started out 3 sappers and 18 infantry and at this stage it was reduced to 2 sappers and 1 infantry as the enemy machine gun was continually working us. We (Sapper Dallas and I) decided to withdraw and we picked up and helped in 12 wounded on our way.
>
> *Sapper Thomas*—I was with number 3 party of the 75th Battalion and our objective was Crater 'I'. Everything went exactly to schedule with our party, and all waves reached their objectives. There was nothing in the crater so we hunted about and found a few small dugouts partly blown in. I spent a lot of time searching for a deep dugout or shaft without success and when I saw the first and second wave returning I threw my charge into a small dugout and destroyed it. On my way back I travelled along the enemy front line and came to an H.Q. dugout a little south of the sap. I had no explosive so I threw some Mills Grenades down it and some German grenades which were near the entrance. They were ineffective. We all returned together but missed our infantry party on the way back. The enemy trench is only a muddy ditch with a few bath-mats there was no gas in the enemy lines.

[2] 75th Battalion Historical Records, March 1, 1917.

Sapper Nason— . . . Sgt. McNaughton of the 75th behaved in the most gallant manner when the enemy attacked us and on the way back he carried in a wounded man from the enemy lines . . .

514165 Spr. Hatton—No. 3 Gap. Objective Crater I—Arrived OK. Thomas and Bryan and 4 infantry. No occupation in crater, no dugouts. Went to next crater right and did not find anything there. Came back brought in a wounded man from no man's land . . . I put my 20 lb. charge down a dugout outside of which were several rifles clean and ready for use. There was gas in the enemy dugouts which blew out when the charges went off. Enemy trenches are only muddy ditches.[3]

ARTHUR ZIMMERMAN TUFTS

In the *Carleton Place Herald* of April 4, 1916, a small notice reports that A.Z. Tufts signed up the previous week with the 130th Battalion. Arthur enlisted in Carleton Place on March 28, 1916, during the 130th's recruiting campaign in the area.

He was born in Hungerford, Tweed, Hastings County on June 13, 1887. He listed his next of kin as his father, Robert Tufts, of Tweed and his occupation as an engineer. Arthur was twenty-eight years, nine months old when he enlisted. He stood 5' 8" tall and weighed 152 pounds. He was described as having a fair complexion, blue eyes and light hair. The only distinguishing mark was a scar on his left breast. He was an adherent of the Methodist Church. He had moved to Carleton Place to work at the Findlay Foundry.

After a summer's training, including several route marches through the surrounding area to drum up recruiting, Arthur embarked on September 23, 1916, with his regiment at Halifax aboard the S.S. *Lapland.* They landed in Liverpool on October 6 and he was transferred to the 12th Battalion, the holding battalion for overseas reinforcements at West Sandling. On December 5 he was transferred to the 75th Battalion overseas and on December 9 he joined the unit in the field.

During the 75th Battalion's training in the early months of 1917, leading up to the attack on Vimy Ridge, Arthur took a four day training course, from February 14 to 18, as a Lewis machine-gunner. He took part in the raid on Hill 145 of March 1.

[3] Report on Co-operation by 11th Field Company, C.E. in Operation #G52-9.

1/3/17—Raid on Hun trenches in which 481 (all ranks) took part.

The first part of the night of Feby 28/March 1st was normal; the usual number of flares being fired by the enemy.

The raiding party, temporarily divided into seven columns each corresponding to a gap in the wire, was assembled in the Zouave Valley . . . moved at 10 minute intervals into position in the jumping-off trench . . . The last party was in position at 2:50 a.m. and the movements had been carried out quietly and without confusion.

The first gas wave was released at 3 a.m. and at 3:03 several red lights [flares] were put up by the enemy and a few rifle shots were fired. At 3:06 the machine guns opened up . . . at 3:09 a desultory artillery bombardment opened up . . . only one shell striking the jumping-off trench killed two and wounded three. Respirators were worn for 35 minutes. By about 4:15 a.m. things had quietened down to normal again except that flares were fairly numerous. At 4:45 a.m. the wind had changed . . . consequently no second gas wave was discharged on the 11th Infantry Brigade front . . .

At 5:15 the assault moved forward into No Man's Land and lay down. Double bath-mat bridges were used in seven places; by means of tapes previously laid from jumping-off trench, through the gaps in both lines of wire. The movement over the broken ground was easily accomplished.

At 5:40 our barrage opened on enemy F.L.T. [front line trench] with fairly good bursts and immediately the enemy machine guns started their full volume. Fairly heavy enemy artillery fire opened mostly well behind the assaulting troops.

At 5:47 the barrage moved forward and the assault advanced and tried to enter the enemy Front line. This was found very heavily manned and severe casualties were inflicted on our troops by enemy bombs, rifle and machine gun fire, particularly on the right of our battalion frontage.

In a few isolated instances was the enemy line entered except on the left where three parties . . . although under heavy machine gun fire from the right, succeeded in penetrating on a depth of from 300 to 400 yards . . . When they arrived at the craters the Germans were found manning the further lips and a stiff fight ensued. the enemy tried to rush our parties through the craters but were bombed back with severe casualties.

These parties being unsupported . . . retired.

It is reported from several sources that enemy exploded small land mines in the gaps in their wire while our men were passing through.

No evidence of gas casualties were observed in enemy's line.

The enemy gathered in many of our casualties from his wire, both immediately following the action and in the fog of the morning.

Killed 68 other ranks, missing 31, wounded 112.[4]

On March 27, the *Carleton Place Herald* noted "Private Arthur Tufts, reported missing last week, is now reported Killed in Action on March 1st." As well as his parents, Arthur was survived by a sister, Mary, and a brother, William.

In the Commonwealth War Graves Register is the following entry:

ARTHUR ZIMMERMAN TUFTS

(787678 Private) 75th Battalion, 1st Central Ontario Regiment. Killed in Action March 1, 1917. Buried in Zouave Valley Cemetery, Souchez, Pas de Calais, France.

The War Graves Registration Commission, which recorded all of the soldiers' last known resting places, reported in 1919 that a memorial had been erected in the Zouave Valley Cemetery inscribed with Tufts' name and the words "Buried near this spot."

[4] 75th Battalion War Diary.

Chapter Fifteen

DEATH DUE TO ACTIVE SERVICE

Not all Canadian military heroes died "with their boots on." Many soldiers on active service did not die as a result of gunfire, shelling, gas or explosions. Many went to the front, faced the abominable conditions in the trenches, became ill and had their lives snuffed out years before their natural time. One such was Thomas Flegg.

THOMAS REYNOLDS FLEGG

Thomas Flegg was born in Carleton Place on December 18, 1891. When he joined the army, he listed as his next of kin his father, Thomas Flegg of Lloyd Street in Ottawa. Nowhere in the records is there any mention of his mother and when his medals were delivered to his father there was no Memorial Cross, the Silver Cross that is issued only to mothers and/or wives. From this it is assumed that his mother must have died earlier. As a young lad Thomas was active in the first Boy Scout troop formed in Carleton Place.

Thomas joined the 42nd Regiment (Militia) on October 8, 1915. He transferred to active service and the 80th Battalion on October 12, 1915. The 80th was organized in August 1915 in Belleville, Ontario, but was broken up after it arrived in England to provide reinforcements for other battalions in the field. The battalion motto is *Paratus* (Ready) and the unit is now perpetuated in the Hastings and Prince Edward Regiment.

When he enlisted in Smiths Falls, he was twenty-four years, ten months old. He gave his previous trade as labourer. Thomas was described as having a medium complexion, blue eyes and dark hair. He barely met the height requirement at 5' 3". He weighed 130 lbs and his physical examination revealed that he had lost a finger from his right hand; not enough disability to keep him from military service.

After basic training in Canada, the soldiers embarked aboard the S.S. *Baltic* on May 16 and arrived in England on May 29, 1916. On June 13, Pte. Flegg was transferred to a holding battalion, the 74th, and on July 18 he was transferred to his fighting unit, the 46th Canadian Infantry Battalion (Regina, Saskatchewan).

The 46th Battalion was a Highland battalion which marched past to *Scotland the Brave*. They wore kilts in the Royal Stewart tartan and a headdress made of dark blue Glengarry with black cock's feathers. The battalion was reputed to have a fine pipe band. It was organized in Regina on July 1, 1915, and served in France and Flanders with the 10th Infantry Brigade of the 4th Canadian Division from August 11, 1916, until the armistice. The battalion is perpetuated by the Saskatchewan Dragoons.

When the 46th went overseas, disembarking at Le Havre on August 11, 1916, Pte. Thomas Flegg was in the ranks. Almost immediately they were sent into action. Twelve days later, on August 23, Thomas was wounded by a gun shot to his face. The wound appeared minor; he was treated at a casualty clearing station and returned to his unit on August 27.

Thomas's health started to deteriorate. On October 29 he was sick enough with diarrhea to be seen at the aid station. Although he was returned to the unit on November 4, he was then sent, because of his diarrhea, to a convalescent hospital in Rouen. There he stayed until November 23 when he was discharged to the base depot to await orders for return to full duty. Three days later, on November 26, he was sent to No. 7 (Dalhousie University) Canadian Stationary Hospital in Le Havre. This time the diagnosis was bronchitis. He seemed to recover and on December 9 was transferred to the convalescent depot. With continued improvement, Pte. Flegg was discharged to the base depot on December 12.

Thomas spent the next two-and-a-half months back with the 46th, training for the 4th Division's planned assault on Vimy Ridge. But he could not shake his medical problem. He was admitted on March 5, 1917, to No. 11 Canadian General Hospital in Dannes, Camiers, France, again diagnosed with bronchitis. His condition rapidly worsened. He was sent back to England and admitted as seriously ill to the military hospital at Frensham Hill in Farnham.

A case history sheet, completed for Thomas on March 22, 1917, has the diagnosis "bronchitis" stroked out by pen and "Bright's Disease" written in. Although Bright's Disease can no longer be found in current medical literature, it is an inflammatory disease of the kidney associated with dropsy and blood in the urine. Treatment at the time consisted of keeping the patient completely at rest, with a diet that put as little strain as possible on the kidneys, helping the patient to expel waste matters through the bowel and glands of the skin. In this time long before antibiotics, and even penicillin, the only effective drugs were sulphanilamide and mandelic acid,[1] drugs long since surpassed with more effective treatments.

The medical officer wrote on the case sheet:

> Gives a history of failing health for these last three months. During this time he has lost weight, been troubled constantly with a cough with expectoration, has had night sweats most of the time, and swelling about face and eyes . . . in my opinion this is a case of trench nephritis caused by Active Service.[2]

Pte. Thomas Flegg died on Sunday, April 8 at 3:00 a.m. He had been in the army eighteen months, overseas for eleven months and was twenty-five years, three-and-a-half months old. His body is interred in Bramshott (St. Mary) Churchyard, Hampshire, England.

From the autumn of 1915 to October 1919, a Canadian training centre was placed in the open country on both sides of the road to Portsmouth, near Bramshott. Soldiers who died in No. 12 Canadian General Hospital, which served the camp, were buried in Bramshott Churchyard.

In the Commonwealth War Graves Commission Register is the commemoration:

In Memory of
PRIVATE T R FLEGG
219969
46th Bn., Canadian Infantry (Saskatchewan Regt.)
who died on Sunday, 8th April 1917.
Remembered with honour.

[1] Franklin J. Meine, Ph.B, M.A., Editor-in-Chief, *The Consolidated-Webster Encyclopedic Dictionary* (Chicago: Consolidated Book Publishers, 1953), p. 267.

[2] Nephritis is an inflammatory kidney disease.

Chapter Sixteen

VIMY RIDGE

Early in 1917, the Canadian Corps was given the formidable task of seizing Vimy Ridge. It was a vital key in the German defensive system, and well fortified. The tunnels even had electric lights, a telephone exchange and a light railway to maintain supplies to the trenches and dugouts. All previous attempts by French and English forces to take the ridge had failed. This time Canadian commanders were confident that elaborate preparation and planning would determine success. They had models of the area built. Every man could rehearse his role and know exactly what was expected of him when the attack occurred.

As they had been in every theatre of this war, Carleton Place men were well represented in this action, which has since been credited with contributing a great deal to the formation of a Canadian identity and nationalism. For the first time, all four divisions of the Canadian Corps, under the direct command of Canadian officers, would attack

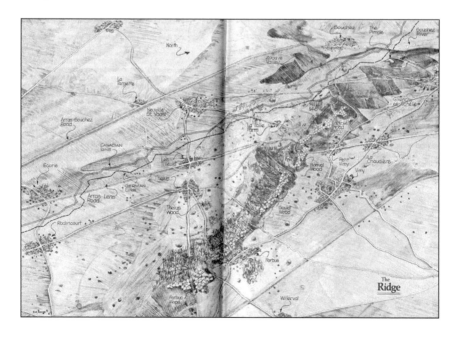

together. In two days of fighting, April 9 and 10, the Canadian Corps suffered 7,707 casualties; 2,967 were fatal. The terrible weather continued . The attack was mounted in the midst of a wet snowstorm in the face of blinding sleet.

Five Carleton Place boys would never walk off the ridge. At least two more would die of the wounds they received there. Three of the four McDiarmid brothers in uniform lost their lives in connection with the assault on Vimy Ridge. Two men, Ed Hockenhull and Vic McDiarmid, served together in the 75th Battalion. It had been badly hurt when it lost its commanding officer in the raid on Hill 145 only the month before. The loss of experienced officers and men in that raid would cost the 4th Division, of which the 75th Battalion was a part, dearly at Vimy Ridge.

The objective of the 4th Division was again Hill 145 and its eastern slopes, the highest and most heavily defended point on the ridge. The slope was very steep and previous battles had ground the terrain into a lunar nightmare of craters and shell-holes. The attack started well but the centre of the 4th Division advance soon became a disaster. Men of the 87th Battalion, which was followed closely by the 75th, were caught in the open and killed instantly. The artillery barrage had failed to destroy the German front line trenches. Unaware of the failure, the 75th advanced on schedule and was caught in a hailstorm of bullets. Losses were huge. No Man's Land was covered with dead and wounded Canadians.

Both Ed and Victor McDiarmid initially joined the 80th Battalion. Victor joined "C" Company with his brother Arthur in August 1915 while Ed Hockenhull joined later in the year, in October, after the 80th had gone to Barriefield for training.

VICTOR LIONEL MCDIARMID

Victor travelled to Smiths Falls to join the Canadian Expeditionary Force. Victor was the second son in the family and joined the active force one day earlier than his younger brother, Arthur. When Arthur joined the next day, the recruiter simply took Victor's application, which had been typewritten, and wrote over it with Arthur's information. While probably saving a sheet of paper, he remained completely

ignorant of the fact that he could easily have caused considerable confusion in identity.

Victor was born on February 24, 1897. He was one of four sons who served in World War I born to William and Mary McDiarmid. The eldest, Leo James, was the only one to survive. Frank Carleton, the second son, stayed home to help his father run the family general merchant business in Carleton Place. Harold, Victor and Arthur lost their lives. The youngest son, Donald, attended McGill University in Montreal. There were also four daughters—Jane, Evangeline, Natalie and Frances.[1]

When Victor joined, at age eighteen years, six months, he gave his prior occupation as student. With his family he attended the Presbyterian Church in Carleton Place. He was described as 5' 7" tall, weighing 124 lbs with a medium complexion, black eyes and black hair.

Growing up in Carleton Place, Victor played hockey with a great deal of skill. He was a forward on the "Ragged Seven" team that won the Dunbar Shield during the winter of 1914–1915. The trophy was presented to the champions of the Carleton Place Hockey League. His brother Frank tended goal. Every player played the entire game. With only seven players, there was no three-line system as today.

Private V.L. McDiarmid, regimental number 219202, with his brother Arthur accompanied the 80th battalion to Barriefield for basic training. The *Carleton Place Herald* reported that he and his brother Arthur visited home over the Christmas/New Year's holiday of 1915–1916 and again for a few days during the beginning of April 1916.

The battalion trooped aboard the S.S. *Baltic* on May 16, 1916, and arrived in England on June 9. The battalion was broken up in England to provide reinforcements to the Canadian Corps in France. Victor was assigned to a holding unit, the 74th Battalion. On July 18,

---

[1] Much family information was obtained in an interview with Mrs. Martha Knox, a daughter of Leo. Martha still attends the service at the Carleton Place Cenotaph every November 11th to lay the McDiarmid family wreath in honour of her three uncles. The tradition began when, as a very little girl, she would accompany her grandmother, Mary. After Mary's death, one of Martha's aunts would take her every year. Now the honour is Martha's alone. Grandmother Mary was given the privilege of unveiling the Carleton Place War Memorial in 1924; she walked up the path on the arm of her only surviving soldier son, Leo.

he was transferred to the 54th Infantry Battalion but, on July 30, he was posted to the 11th Brigade Trench Mortar Battery. After training he was transferred back to the infantry, to the 75th Battalion, and it was with this unit that he went to France on August 12, 1916.

Pte. McDiarmid was but one soldier in the 4th Division that went to France that August. They trained in trench fighting at Ypres, traded in their Ross rifles for Lee-Enfields, then marched south to the Somme. The 4th Division went into the line on October 17 for a horrible introduction to war. Sharp winds prevailed and icy rains turned the trenches into ditches knee-deep with water.

In November, a week after the 4th Division won Regina Trench, in the first driving snow of the winter, the 11th Brigade attacked Desire Trench. They advanced well but had to retire when the units on either side failed. This was the last battle of the Somme for these Canadians. The 4th Division had spent nearly seven continuous weeks in the front line. It was not relieved until November 26–28, and Victor, still not twenty years old, had already seen more than his share of war.

Limited hostilities continued throughout the winter. Periodic exchanges of mortar fire, occasional trench raids and extensive patrolling occupied the troops. On Christmas Eve, 1916, Victor was admitted to No. 22 Casualty Clearing Station with gunshot wounds to his left leg and right shoulder. He returned to duty on January 12 and continued the extensive training and preparations for the assault on Vimy Ridge.

For this attack, Zero Hour for the 11th Brigade was 5:30 a.m. on April 9. Every man in the Canadian Corps had received a hot meal and a ration of rum before they went into the assembly positions by 4:00 a.m. Very strong opposition was encountered from the outset of the attack. Considerable success was attained by the 102nd (North British Columbians) and 54th (British Columbia) Battalions, on the right of the brigade's line of advance. But the failure of the 87th (Grenadier Guards of Montreal) and 75th (Mississauga Horse) lost much of the other battalions' success. The 87th were stopped dead, losing sixty per cent of its effective fighting strength, and the 75th faltered. That night, the 85th Battalion (Nova Scotia Highlanders) came up from reserve and went through to the further side of the hill. This was the 85th's

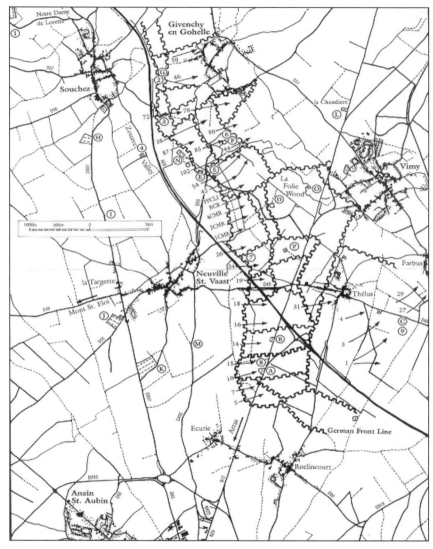

first action. The men surged across the fields of fire finally dislodging the German defenders from Hill 145.

On the night of April 10, 1917, the 75th Battalion was relieved and withdrew to Bertonval Wood. It left behind ninety-six other ranks killed, 159 wounded and fifty-nine missing.

At first, Victor was listed as "missing." The *Herald*, on May 8, 1917, printed a casualty list that included the following:

More Carleton Place boys Reported from the Vimy Ridge battle

Pte. Victor Lionel McDiarmid, 219202, son of Mr. and Mrs. Wm. McDiarmid, was also reported as 'missing' yesterday to his parents, from April 9th. Victor was a crack shot and was with an infantry brigade.

Finally, on December 12, 1917, the army recorded that "Pte. McDiarmid, previously reported missing, now for official purposes, was presumed to have died on or since 9.4.17 [9 April 1917]." Victor's body was never found. He was last seen during the attack northwest of Vimy. His commemoration is on the Vimy Memorial and his name is also in the Commonwealth War Graves Register:

VICTOR LIONEL MCDIARMID

(219202 Private) 75th Battalion, 1st Central Ontario Regiment. Missing, presumed dead, April 9, 1917. No known grave, commemorated on the Vimy Memorial, Pas de Calais, France.

The victory of Canadian soldiers at Vimy Ridge sealed the reputation of the Canadian Corps as a fighting machine to be reckoned with. But the toll was immense. More than 3,600 Canadians died between April 9 and 12. The most impressive memorial of World War I is the Canadian National Memorial to the Great War rising majestically above Hill 145. Engraved on its sides are the 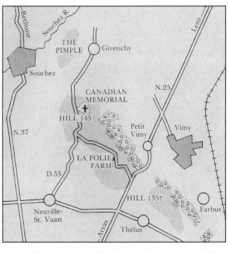 names of 11,285 Canadian soldiers who were killed in France and lie beneath its soil in no known grave. It sits amid the Canadian Memorial Park, an area of dilapidated trenches, eroded shell holes and mine craters. Some trenches and tunnels have been reconstructed providing an eerie link to the surrounding military cemeteries. Vimy stands as the best preserved Canadian battlefield of the First World War.

JOSEPH EDWARD HOCKENHULL

Edward Hockenhull was working as an express clerk with the Dominion Express Company when war broke out. He had been active in the militia with the 42nd Lanark and Renfrew Regiment, including ten months' training and home defence duties at Petawawa. He enlist-

ed with the 80th (Belleville) Battalion when they were in camp at Barriefield, near Kingston, on October 18, 1915.

Pte. Hockenhull was born in Carleton Place on March 4, 1894, the son of George and Matilda Hockenhull. George and Matilda had four sons and four daughters. Except for the eldest, John, who was born at home on Munroe Street, all of the children were born at the family home located at 13 Mary Street. The family consisted of John, George Henry (Harry), Mary Ellen (Nellie), Gertrude, Edward, Bessie, Leo and Carmel.

Eddie grew up in the Ottawa Valley town. He and his brothers, John and Leo, were active in the Carleton Place Canoe Club. They were especially successful in local and Canadian regattas in the war canoe events. John also served in World War I with the Canadian Engineers. The patriarch, George, had emigrated from England and had spent his entire working life in Carleton Place as a machinist with the Canadian Pacific Railway, as did his surviving sons and at least one grandson.[2]

A physical examination at enlistment recorded that Hockenhull was twenty-one years, five months of age. He stood 5' 7" tall and weighed 160 lbs. He was described as having a dark complexion with brown eyes and dark hair. A small dark moustache graced his upper lip. He was found to have scars on his left knee, no doubt a remnant of his active participation in sports. He professed to be a member of the Roman Catholic faith.

[2] This information was provided by Mr. Joseph (Joe) Gribben of Winnipeg, son of Carmel and nephew of Eddie.

During his militia days, Eddie had been made a sergeant but once he joined the regular army his rank became that of a private soldier. There were a number of boys from Carleton Place with Eddie Hockenhull aboard the S.S. *Baltic* when it slipped its lines on May 21, arriving in England on May 30, 1916. Before he left, however, he received leave to visit home. The *Herald* reported on April 11, 1916, that "Sergt. E. Hockenhull of the 80th Battalion returned to Picton on Saturday after spending a few days at his home here." He left for Halifax on May 16.

When he was transferred to the 75th Battalion on June 5, 1916, he was appointed acting sergeant. However, he was reduced in rank to corporal on June 25.[3] He went to France, disembarking at Le Havre, when the entire 4th Division went overseas on August 12, 1916. Like Victor McDiarmid, he was with the 11th Brigade during the attack on Desire Trench in the last battle on the Somme. It was undoubtedly with some relief that he marched away after seven weeks of fighting in the yellow, slimy mud of the Somme battle-field. He was promoted to sergeant on November 18 to replace a Sgt. Rowley, who had been evacuated wound-ed following the attack on Desire Trench.

On March 24, 1917, Sgt. Eddie Hockenhull went to the rear area for a service course of instruction, rejoining the battalion on April 7. On Vimy Ridge, Easter Monday, April 9, at 5:30 a.m., he stood dry-mouthed, waiting to lead his section of 75th Battalion men following the lead of the 87th Battalion. The Germans resisted in this portion of the line much more fiercely than elsewhere. The 87th was stonewalled with heavy casualties. The 4th Division diary states that the 87th and 75th Battalions formed up, each in two lines, the 87th leading. The 75th could not proceed and in the open became easy targets for the German machine-gunners.

The 4th Division was the youngest in the Canadian Corps, yet at Vimy Ridge they had by far the hardest fight. The new tactic of

---

[3] Acting sergeant is an appointment "whilst so employed." He kept the substantive rank of corporal and when the battalion went to France reverted to it as they obviously had no need for another acting sergeant. He got sergeant rank back as soon as a vacancy opened when Sgt. Rowley was evacuated.

artillery "rolling barrages," followed closely by attacking infantry, was believed to allow them to walk over the German trenches with near-impunity. One colonel thought that the assault on Hill 145 would be helped if the artillery left a key German trench intact as cover for his men. The Canadians found it full of hard-fighting Germans. They were then so close to the enemy line that their artillery could not blast it without killing their own infantry. It was after dark that a raw battalion of Nova Scotians went up and took the hill. The 4th Division was exhausted.[4] The 75th Battalion withdrew during the night of April 10, leaving niney-six other ranks lying dead, including Sgt. E. Hockenhull.

The *Carleton Place Herald* of May 1, 1917 carried this item:

> Mr. Geo. Hockenhull had received this morning the official announcement of the death of his son Pte. Edward Hockenhull, killed in action.

Eddie Hockenhull had been a regular attendee at St. Mary's Roman Catholic church. He was very well known in town and described as one of the community's most promising young men. He left three sisters, Gertrude, Nellie and Carmel, all of Carleton Place, and three brothers, Harry, at Winnipeg, John at Joliette, and Leo, at home. Bessie had yet to be born.

In the Commonwealth War Graves Register is found:

> *JOSEPH EDWARD HOCKENHULL*
>
> *(220039 Sergeant) son of Mr. and Mrs. George Hockenhull, Carleton Place. 75th Battalion, 1st Central Ontario Regiment. Killed April 9, 1917, age 23. Buried in Canadian Cemetery No. 2, Neuville-St Vaast, Pas de Calais, France.*

Canadian Cemetery No. 2 lies approximately where the attack of the 87th and 75th Battalions failed. It is in the Vimy Memorial Park and was established by the Canadian Corps in April 1917. The original burials consist of men from the 4th Division, particularly the 75th Battalion and the 87th Battalion who were killed on April 9. The cemetery contains 693 Canadian bodies, 226 of which are unidentified.[5]

---

[4] Desmond Morton, "Vimy Remembered", *The Ottawa Citizen*, April 9, 1997, p. A17.

[5] Norm Christie, *For King and Empire, The Canadians at Vimy* (Winnipeg: Bunker to Bunker Books, 1996), p.73.

Attack

At dawn the ridge emerges massed and dun
In the wild purple of the glow'ring sun,
Smouldering through spouts of drifting smoke
that shroud

The menacing scarred slope; and, one by one,
Tanks creep and topple forward to the wire.
The barrage roars and lifts. Then, clumsily bowed
With bombs and guns and shovels and battle-gear,
Men jostle and climb to meet the bristling fire.

Lines of grey, muttering faces, masked with fear,
They leave their trenches, going over the top,
While time ticks blank and busy on their wrists,
And hope, with furtive eyes and grappling fists,
Flounders in mud. O Jesus, make it stop!

Siegfried Sassoon[6]

Pte. Percy Moore served at Vimy Ridge with the 38th (Eastern Ontario) Battalion, also a part of the 4th Division but in the 12th Infantry Brigade.

PERCIVAL MOORE

Undoubtedly inspired by his father's service in the Boer War, Percy Moore lied about his age so he could join the army. When he enlisted in the 130th (Perth) Battalion at Carleton Place, on January 4, 1916, he gave his birthdate as June 21, 1897. That made him eighteen years old, sufficient for enrollment into the Canadian Expeditionary Force.

Percy was born in Miles Platten, Manchester, England, to William and Elizabeth Moore. The family emigrated to Canada in 1903 and settled on Prince Street in Carleton Place. Young Percy participated, as reported in the *Carleton Place Herald* of August 10, 1915, in "A company of Boy Scouts organized some time ago—Mr. Wm. Moore being the District Warrant Officer, were drilling on behalf of the recruiting campaign." Percy, it seems, took the recruiting rhetoric to heart.

[6] Brian Gardner, ed., *Up the Line to Death: The War Poets 1914-1918* (Oxford, Eng.: Methuen & Co. Ltd., 1962), pp. 160-161.

The citation for Percy's award read:

On July 14th, 1915, Scout Percival Moore, of Carleton Place, went to the assistance of a man who was struggling in the water and later with the assistance of another boy got the man safely to shore. From the evidence of eye witnesses of the deed it would appear that the man was under the influence of liquor and was in about four feet of water.

The local Board of Honour recommended the awarding of a Silver Cross to the scout in question but the Executive of the Provincial Council held the opinion that the Medal of Merit should be awarded in this case. This was concurred in by the members of the Medal Board of the Canadian General Council.

The Medal of Merit is awarded to a scout who does his duty exceptionally well though without grave risks to himself.

The rescued man's name was "Nero," a local labourer; the eye-witnesses were Walter Lewis, Carl Jones and James Pendergast. The boy who assisted Percy was Fred Purdy. Percy received his honour at Rideau Hall on September 20, 1915, from the Duke of Connaught, Governor General of Canada and Chief Scout for Canada. (Courtesy of Toni Marcon-Stewart, Scouts Canada)

Percy's father, inspired by Lord Baden-Powell under whom he had served in South Africa, started one of the first Scouting groups in Canada in 1910. Other members of that first Boy Scout troop included Cecil Bryce and Thomas Flegg. Percy, for an act of selfless courage, was awarded the Boy Scout Life Saving Award, one of scouting's highest honours. Heedless of his own safety, he had plunged into the Mississippi River to save the life of an elderly gentleman who had fallen in and was quite helpless. Percy was invested with his award at Rideau Hall by the governor general, the Duke of Connaught.

On joining the army, Percy gave his previous trade as factory hand. He passed the physical examination and was described as 5' 4" tall and 125 lbs. He had a medium complexion, brown eyes and dark brown hair. He made the minimum height requirement with two inches to spare. The previous July, army authorities had reduced the required height from 5' 3" to 5' 2". Percy professed his faith to be that of the Church of England.

The *Herald* reported on January 18, 1916, that the "members of Coy 'C', 130th Bn, C.E.F. included Pte. P. Moore." He spent the summer training in Canada and embarked from Halifax on September 23, 1916, with the battalion aboard the S.S. *Lapland.* They arrived in Liverpool on October 6. In England, the 130th was broken up and its troops distributed throughout the 12th Reserve Battalion to provide reinforcements to the Canadian Corps in France. Percy volunteered for transfer to the 38th (Ottawa, Ontario) Battalion on November 14 and joined it in the field on November 21.

The 38th Battalion, whose motto is "Advance," was organized in Ottawa on July 1, 1915. It first saw service as a protective garrison in Bermuda between August 1915 and May 29, 1916. It was then sent directly to Europe and served in France and Flanders in the 12th Infantry Brigade of the 4th Canadian Division from August 14, 1916, to the armistice. The battalion is perpetuated by the Cameron Highlanders of Ottawa.

Percy missed the 12th Brigade's limited action on Desire Trench on November 17–18. He joined the battalion in France just as the 4th Division left the Somme to rejoin the Canadian Corps on the Lens-Arras front. A bright spot in his early service was when the corps commander, Gen. Sir Julian Byng, inspected the battalion on December 14.

They moved into the trenches before Vimy Ridge on December 30, having marched from their billets at Petit Servius. Percy would not miss the miserable conditions of that terrible winter in the lines. His medical records show that he only reported ill once, on January 31, 1917, when he was treated at No. 12 Canadian Field Ambulance Station for diarrhea before being discharged back to duty.

The historical records of the 38th Battalion present a very good picture of a soldier's life while training and preparing for the offensive:

> During the weeks of labourious preparation for the attack upon Vimy Ridge the Canadian Corps maintained an unexampled policy of local aggression. Raid after raid was carried into the German lines until the opposing garrisons appeared nervous to the point of hysteria. All sorts of petty annoyances and exasperating tricks were practised by our men. As soon as the enemy changed the type of his SOS signals rockets our engineers would carefully construct excellent imitations and, choosing some quiet sector with a broad strip of No Man's Land, set them off and await the reply of the German batteries. The hostile guns would throw a ton or so of shells into the barren ground, or shell their

own front line trenches, and everybody would be pleased. It was amusing, also, to send up SOS rockets on a wide front, and while the German gunners were attempting to cover this with their fire, raid an unsuspecting enemy to the left or right.

March 1917 was an exciting time for the regiment. Not only were the preparations for the big offensive nearing completion, but the enemy seemed aware of it, and hostile gunners developed an easy accuracy from Vimy Heights that threatened all Canadian communications and caused numerous casualties to the Corps. The enemy's bombardment was unusually heavy . . . minor patrol engagements . . . mining activity . . . On the 28th every gun of every calibre fired from both the Canadian and German lines and 'was most unpleasant for the unfortunate infantry between the guns, who suffered for the outburst of hate.'

The regiment returned to the line on April 4th relieved the 78th Bn. in the trenches . . . Several days of heavy shellfire followed, for the enemy was aware that an offensive was pending, and on the 8th, every man was busy preparing for the next day's fighting. The battalion strength consisted of 44 officers and 1135 men, of whom 12 officers and 550 men were to form the main attacking waves.[7]

It was an exciting time for a young Carleton Place youth, but the dreadful weather, acres of bottomless, sticky mud, and the constant collection of casualties must have convinced him that war was a very serious business indeed; definitely injurious to one's health.

The operations order for the attack on Vimy included the following:

Firing Instructions:

Leading waves to fire on the move, from the shoulder, if a target presents itself, Rifle Grenadiers should fire over and cover riflemen. Ammunition and bombs must not be wasted.

Lewis guns should be wrapped loosely in a rubber sheet which may be dropped at any time. Lewis guns may be fired from the hip if possible. Care must be taken to keep Lewis guns and rifles free from mud.

Bayonets to be fixed at ZERO minus 15 minutes. They must not be exposed before advance is commenced.[8]

[7] Historical Records–38th Battalion, The National Archives of Canada.
[8] 48th Battalion Operation Order No. 64, in reference to the attack on Vimy Ridge.

For the attack, the 38th was designated as an assault battalion, which meant that it would "go over the top" first. The 4th Division's northern attack by the 73rd (Royal Highlanders of Montreal), 72nd (Seaforth Highlanders of Vancouver) and 38th Battalions started well and they advanced according to plan. But with the collapse of the advance of the 87th in the centre, German machine-gunners were able to focus on the flanks of the 12th Brigade. The 38th Battalion was suffering severely and was slowly being forced back from its hard-won gains.[9]

The historical record continues:

The main objective of the 38th Bn lay well over the crest of the Ridge . . . this was termed the main line of resistance and beyond it lay craters and strong points which were to be captured also.[10]

The men went forward at half past five on the morning of the 9th and found the enemy's front line practically deserted. There was a great deal of shrapnel and high explosive about, but little machine-gun fire, and our fellows were able to make fairly good progress, though the state of the ground prevented them from keeping close to the barrage. The mud was really appalling, and many wounded men were suffocated or drowned in shell-holes. However, just before six o'clock Colonel Edwards reported the successful occupation of the first and second objectives.

Now the third and fourth waves pressed forward to attack the craters and it became difficult to secure information of the isolated actions that ensued. the sky had been overcast and dull since dawn, and now a strong North westerly wind began to blow snow and sleet into the faces of the Germans. This was very satisfactory from the point of view of the action, but it tendered the condition of the wounded even more pitiable.

Shortly after six o'clock Colonel Edwards reported that the craters and strong points had been occupied on the left and center of the attacking front, but that no word had been received from the right. Stiff fighting was going on here, and already our men were hampered by the slow advance of the 11th Brigade on the right flank. This failure to gain ground exposed the 38th to

[9] N.M. Christie, Winning The Ridge (Nepean: CEF Books, 1998), p. 29.
[10] The battalion attacked in four waves with "A" and "D" Companies in the first wave. War Diary–38th Battalion.

enfilading fire from the South-East, and greatly increased the resistance of the craters the regiment had to occupy.

Capt. Thain MacDowell, officer commanding "B" Company, reported to Battalion headquarters at 8:00 a.m. that a runner he had sent to "A" Company with a message had just returned and he had been unable to find any of "A" Company's officers. The runner reported "The men's rifles are a mass of mud but they are cleaning them."

. . . half past eight . . . "A" Company was suffering heavy rifle and machine-gun fire from the right.[11] At this point Capt. MacDowell took the initiative and led a small group forward, capturing the two machine guns that were causing all the havoc, entered a major subterranean complex and captured 77 German soldiers, greatly contributing to pushing forward the 4th Division's stalled attack. His courageous actions earned him the Victoria Cross.[12]

By 11 a.m. all objectives had been consolidated, except on the right, where the difficult situation was not cleared up until the evening. The expected counter-attack did not materialize, and our fellows had time to strengthen and fortify their new positions. throughout the night the enemy shelled the captured ground, but already he was moving back his batteries and the bombardment was not heavy . . .[13]

. . . On the 13th the regiment was relieved, withdrawing to billets at Coupigy. Seven hundred and forty men of the regiment took part in the fighting between April 9th and 13th, and of these some three hundred and twenty-five were casualties. On the 24th the battalion returned to the trenches.[14]

The *Carleton Place Herald* of May 8, 1917, printed the following:

Pte. Percival Moore, son of Mr. and Mrs. Wm. Moore, town, was officially reported to the parents on Saturday as 'Missing' from the 9th of April. Pte. Moore was but 18 years of age. He

---

[11] Pte. Percy Moore was in "A" Company.

[12] At 9:30 a.m. there was still no report from "A" Company but a wounded man had brought to battalion headquarters the news that the captain and one lieutenant had been killed and that the company was being led by another lieutenant. War Diary–38th Battalion.

[13] On April 10th, at 4:25 p.m., "A" Company, the most disorganized, was brought in to Blue Bull Tunnel for rest and re-organization. Two officers who had been brought up with the reinforcements from Chateau de la Haie were put in charge.

[14] Historical Records–38th Battalion.

enlisted with the 130th and went overseas. He was only a few days in England when he was transferred to the 38th Royal Battalion of Ottawa.

On December 12, the War Department declared Percy "previously reported missing now for official purposes presumed to have died on or since 9.4.17. [April 9, 1917]" in the attack southeast of Souchez. When Percy went missing on Vimy Ridge, he was only sixteen-years-old. He had lied by four years when he gave his birthdate on enlistment. Had he lived, he would have been seventeen in June.

Percy's body was later identified and interred in the Canadian Cemetery at Neuville-St Vaast. The entry for him in the Commonwealth War Graves Register reads:

PERCIVAL MOORE

(787646 Private) son of William and Elizabeth Moore of Carleton Place. "A" Company, 38th Battalion, Eastern Ontario Regiment. Killed April 9, 1917, age 16. Buried in Canadian Cemetery No. 2, Neuville-St Vaast. Pas de Calais, France.

DANIEL O'DONOVAN

Dan O'Donovan was in his early thirties, older than most of his comrades, when he joined the 21st Battalion in Carleton Place. He had emigrated from Ireland to work at Findlay's but for a time was employed with the Canadian Pacific Railroad as a locomotive fireman. In the *Carleton Place Herald* of November 3, 1914, was the news item that stated:

> Among the 2nd contingent of "B" Company, 42nd Regiment, that left for Kingston was Pte. Dan O'Donovan. The mayor gave each man a box of the 'finest Havanas'. They had no arms or luggage and were not in uniform; they are to be equipped in Kingston.

Daniel O'Donovan was born the son of John and Mary Ann O'Donovan, in Killarney, Ireland, on July 10, 1883. It is not known when the family moved to Carleton Place, but at the time Dan enlisted his widowed mother was living in town. Undoubtedly, Dan was one of the Irish tradesmen actively recruited for work in Canada by the managers of the Findlay Foundry.

Dan was responsible for at least one exciting event during his time in Carleton Place. On May 15, 1914, at work in the foundry, he lit a smoke and discarded the match into a pail of dynamite and blasting caps. The explosion smashed every window in the foundry office and some 200 to 300 windows in the foundry itself. It had sufficient force to break twenty-one windows in the nearby Findlay home. Fortunately no one was hurt.[15] There is no record of how Dan escaped.

Dan left Carleton Place with the 42nd Militia Regiment, but in Kingston he formally enlisted into the 21st (Eastern Ontario) Battalion on November 6, 1914. His physical examination revealed a man thirty-one years, four months, standing 5' 9" tall. He was of a dark complexion had blue eyes and light brown hair. He had two tattoo marks on his right arm and three marks on his left arm. No specifics of the "marks" were recorded. He was Irish Roman Catholic. He listed his next of kin as Pat O'Donovan, probably a brother who lived on Cambridge Street in Ottawa.

While in training in Kingston, Dan had a bout of inflamed tonsils and spent two days before Christmas, 1914, in the hospital. He was hospitalized again, for another minor infection, for the entire month of January 1915. Basic training completed, Dan, along with other 21st Battalion soldiers from Carleton Place, such as William Tyrie and Sid Hamilton, boarded the R.M.S. Metagama on May 6, 1915, and sailed for England. They arrived in Liverpool on May 15.

Dan was not too impressed with army life, its discipline, rules and regulations. Maybe he was just reacting to the proud Irish tradition of having nothing to do with an English army that had invaded his native land so many years before. Irish antagonism to the English is rooted in the ancient histories of both nations. But often the only escape from Irish poverty was to take the king's shilling by joining the English army.

A long string of misdemeanours began while Dan was in camp on the Salisbury Plain. He went absent without leave (AWL) May 28 to 31, which cost him a fine of $2, five days in detention and four days'

[15] Under the date of May 15, 1914, from the unpublished diaries of George H. Findlay, fourth child of David and Margaret Findlay, written sporadically from 1884 to early 1945. David Findlay established the well-known foundry in Carleton Place.

pay. (That would have been another $4). From July 4 to 8, he was again AWL and this time forfeited five days' pay and spent ten days in detention. He was listed as AWL for the day of September 24, 1915.

The battalion was sent to France in November and into the Ypres Salient. On November 30, in the field, Dan went absent from his platoon after they had been warned for duty in the trench. He was sentenced to fourteen days Field Punishment No. 2 (detention) and to fifteen hours extra fatigue duty. He had been absent for two days so he forfeited another two days' pay.

The army was able to keep track of Dan for the first few months of 1916 and even promoted him to the rank of Corporal. In January he was treated for influenza at No. 5 Canadian Field Ambulance. On February 3 he again became ill while in the field near Etaples. He was so seriously sick that he was invalided to England. He was admitted to the Duchess of Connaught Canadian Red Cross Hospital at Taplow, Bucks, where he stayed from March 1 to May 4, 1916. Upon admission to the hospital a medical case history made the following observation:

> Born 1881 [sic], lived in England when 9 or 10. Lived here 17 years. Went to Canada 9 years ago. Has lived in Carleton Place. Habits—tobacco good deal in his time; alcohol—Whiskey a good deal. Lost weight—normal 189 lbs.

On recovery, Dan was transferred on May 8, 1916, to the 39th (Belleville) Battalion to await orders to return to France. He was only two days out of the hospital when he disappeared again. He was gone from May 10 to 15 and for this absence was awarded Field Punishment No. 2 (detention) for six days with the loss of six days' pay plus three more days' pay and allowances (the allowance would have been the ten cents a day he got for being overseas). He was also demoted back to Private.

From May 1 to May 29 he was gone again. This time the army had had enough. Pte. Daniel O'Donovan stood a Divisional Court Martial at East Sandling. He was accused of "when under orders for embarkation for active service absenting himself without leave with intent to avoid embarkation." This was serious stuff. This was desertion. The company sergeant-major testified that on May 21 he had warned O'Donovan, who had been assigned to "C" Company, that he would soon be going on a draft to France, but that very night he was reported absent from "tattoo."[16] Dan was also warned not to leave camp.

At 8:00 p.m. on May 29, Dan was picked up by a member of the regimental police in the bar of the Prince of Wales Inn in nearby Hythe. He was arrested and taken to the battalion guard room. At his court martial, an officer from the 21st Battalion testified in Dan's defence that he was an excellent soldier while training in Canada, but had to admit that Dan's conduct had dropped off considerably in England.

In his own defence, Dan told the court he had had no leave since the previous August and that he had spent six months in France. He did not mean to get off the draft but, he said, he had asked for a pass and was refused. He stated that he had only been with the 39th eleven days when warned for the draft. He wanted to go to Hythe to get a watch and say goodbye to some friends. He said that he had stayed in Hythe all the time he was away and that he had seen men from the 39th, but no one had told him the draft was gone or that he was wanted. He testified: "I had no intention of missing the draft. I have brothers in the 21st Battalion to which the draft was going.[17] I was passed by a Medical Board on the 9th May as fit for duty . . . I intended to come back to camp the night I was arrested. I was a locomotive fireman in civilian life."

Dan was found guilty on June 8 and sentenced to undergo detention for six months. The sentence was confirmed by higher authority, the general staff. But there was a war to fight and Maj.-Gen. Steele, commanding the troops at Shorncliffe, commuted it to forty-two days detention, "in order that the accused may be sent out with an early draft."

On release from prison, Dan was sent to France and assigned to a Canadian entrenching battalion. These units had been formed in early August. Each division was allotted an entrenching battalion to serve as an advanced reinforcement unit to which infantry and engineer reinforcements were posted pending their assignment to a battalion or

---

[16] Evening roll call.

[17] Dan's brothers were Private Denis O'Donovan in the 21st Battalion, Private Con O'Donovan in the 38th Battalion and Sergeant Patrick O'Donovan in the 130th Battalion. Brother Con (Cornelious) was killed in September 1918 near Cambrai.

field company. During their stay in the entrenching battalion, personnel were employed in the construction and repair of trenches and roads, and in similar maintenance duties.[18]

On October 6, 1916, Daniel O'Donovan returned to the 21st Battalion of the 4th Brigade of the 2nd Canadian Division, just in time to join the Canadian troops arriving in the Vimy sector from the Somme battlefields in the south. The previous main offensives were over but Vimy was far from quiet. The fighting simply went underground. During 1916–1917 mining warfare was a continuous threat to both sides. Large craters were blown out of the earth. In March 1917, when mining battles were not going well, the British relieved French troops in the Vimy area. The Canadians were positioned on the northern flank, which included Vimy Ridge. Previous failures by the French and British aside, it simply had to be captured.

The 2nd Division, with the 1st Division on their right and the 3rd on their left, would attack and seize the main German trench line before the town of Thélus. The first battalions across the line were the 18th (Western Ontario), 19th (Central Ontario), 24th (Victoria Rifles of Montreal) and 26th (New Brunswick). After the 18th and 19th reached the main German trench, the 21st continued the attack toward the village of Thélus. The distance was significant but the slope was gentle and defences thought to be minimal.

The 21st Battalion moved, on April 8, 1917, to Bois des Alleux near Mont St. Eloy. On the morning of the 9th, they moved into the assembly positions in support of the 18th and 19th Battalions. They watched the attack commence at 5:30 a.m. and by 6:30 they passed through as planned and captured Les Tilleuls. The attack went according to plan and the advance of the 21st to positions north of the village went smoothly. By dusk, the division had reached its planned objectives with the least number of casualties of all the attackers. But one of those down was Pte. Daniel O'Donovan.

[18] Colonel G.W.L. Nicholson, Canadian Expeditionary Force 1914-1919 (Ottawa: Queen's Printer, 1962), p. 155.

In this area of the ridge, the Germans seemed very complacent in their belief that their positions were impregnable. The 31st (Alberta) Battalion, which had passed through the 21st's positions in the final thrust to Thélus, captured a large dugout, just over a kilometre from the front line, that contained an officers' bar, five uniformed waiters and a table laid for lunch! The speed of the assault gave the German officers no time to enjoy their meal.[19] It was Easter Monday on Vimy Ridge.

The *Herald*, in its edition of May 1, 1917, announced that "Mrs. O'Donovan received a message last Thursday advising her of the death of her son Pte. Daniel O'Donovan, who was killed in action in France." Dan met his death during the attack from southeast of Neuville-St. Vaast toward the west of Thélus. His body was first buried where he fell, one mile east of Neuville-St. Vaast, four-and-a-half miles north of Arras, then exhumed for placement in a military cemetery.

DANIEL O'DONOVAN

(59755 Private) son of John and Mary Ann O'Donovan,
Carleton Place. 21st Battalion, Eastern Ontario Regiment.
Killed April 9, 1917, age 33. Buried in Nine Elms Military
Cemetery, Thélus, France.

Nine Elms Cemetery is six kilometres north of Arras. It was constructed by the Canadian Corps after the Battle of Vimy Ridge originally for the burial of eighty men killed from the 14th Battalion (Royal Montreal Regiment). After the war, battlefield clearance teams brought in the dead from many small cemeteries established by individual fighting units immediately after the battle. The cemetery holds 539 Canadians, ninety-nine of whom are known only unto God.

EUGENE ARTHUR MCDIARMID

Not all the soldiers whose deaths can be attributed to the battle for Vimy Ridge were the victims of gunfire or shell explosions. Arthur, the youngest McDiarmid brother to serve, fell victim to the effects of exposure to poison gas.

In June 1915, Arthur was living at home in the large house still standing at the end of McArthur Avenue. He was in high school, then

---

[19] N.M. Christie, *Winning the Ridge* (Nepean: CEF Books, 1998), p.17.

located at the corner of Moffatt and High Streets, and a member of the High School Cadet Corps. After a rifle competition that month it was reported in the *Herald* that he had shot a score of ten out of a possible twenty (not an impressive score). All his brothers were good shots, includ-  ing Arthur in their enjoyment of hunting and skeet shooting. Arthur apparently couldn't wait to leave school and join the army. He was in uniform by August.

On August 28, 1915, Arthur, with his brother Victor, joined the 80th Battalion in Smiths Falls. Arthur gave his birth date as April 17, 1898, and claimed to be seventeen years old. He listed his mother, Mary, as his next of kin. Arthur was a healthy young man and had no difficulty passing the medical examination. He stood 5' 7" tall and was described as of a medium complexion with black eyes and black hair. He had no visible marks or scars. He claimed his religious affiliation as Presbyterian.

The battalion went to Barriefield for equipping and training. Arthur and Victor got home for the Christmas holidays in December 1915 to early January 1916. They were home again in April just before the battalion left for Europe. They boarded the S.S. *Baltic* on May 16 and landed in England on May 30.

Troopship: Mid-Atlantic

And staring at the magic with eyes adream
That never till now have looked upon the sea,
Boys from the Middle West lounge listlessly

In the unlanterned darkness, boys who go,
Beckoned by some unchallengeable dream,
To unknown lands to fight an unknown foe.

Wilfrid Gibson
on the S.S. *Baltic*, July 1917[20]

Both McDiarmid boys went to a holding battalion, the 74th, in June. That was the last time they would serve in the same unit. Arthur was transferred to the 73rd (Montreal "Royal Highlanders") Battalion on July 18, but then went overseas to France, on August 8, 1916, with

[20] Brian Gardner, ed., *Up the Line to Death: The War Poets 1914-1918* (Oxford, Eng.: Meuthen & Co., 1964), p. 74. Gibson served in the ranks from 1914 but spent only a short time at the front.

the 4th Divisional Salvage Company of the Canadian Army Service Corps. The Service Corps had the tremendous task of supplying the entire Canadian Corps with every necessity required to maintain a fighting army in the field. Soldiers of all ranks—a total of 619,636—passed through the Canadian Expeditionary Force during World War I, all their needs supplied by the brains, sweat and brawn of the Canadian Army Service Corps.

He was treated at the 13th Canadian Field Ambulance, December 15–18, 1916, for sore feet and on March 26, 1917, for an abscess on his right thigh. Otherwise, he soldiered on with the Service Corps until just after the assault on Vimy Ridge. On April 19, he was transferred back to the infantry, and to the 42nd Battalion, which was still in the line at Vimy Ridge, having attacked as part of the 7th Brigade of the 3rd Canadian Division.

Both the 42nd and the 73rd, to which Arthur had been posted in England, were from Montreal and were "Royal Highlanders." The 73rd, serving with the 12th Infantry Brigade of the 4th Division, was withdrawn from the battle zone on April 14, 1917, after suffering heavy casualties in the attack on Vimy Ridge. Since he could not return to his original unit, Arthur was transferred to the 42nd. It served with the 7th Brigade in the 3rd Division and stayed in the line until the armistice. Their motto was *Nemo me Impune Lacessit* (Let No One Touch Me with Impunity), and the battalion wore the Black Watch tartan. Both battalions have been perpetuated by the Black Watch of Canada (Royal Highland Regiment).

The action at Vimy Ridge ended for the 42nd Highlanders at 7:45 p.m. on April 11, 1917. The battalion entered the battle with an effective strength of 722 all ranks. It suffered 302 casualties —eleven officers and 291 other ranks. Five officers and forty-nine other ranks had been killed. The 42nd Battalion suffered more severely than any other unit in the 7th Brigade.

On June 30, Arthur was sent to No. 18 General Hospital, located in Camiers. He left the trenches complaining of a slight cold and cough. His treatment was provided by physician/soldier Lt.-Col. John McCrae, the doctor who wrote *In Flanders' Fields*, and who died at that hospital on January 28, 1918, of pneumonia. Dr. McCrae had Arthur admitted on July 7 with a diagnosis of nephritis (a kidney inflammation) and a tubercle of the lung. On July 19 he was invalided sick to England and the Ontario Military Hospital in Orpington, Kent, which had been established by the Ontario government.

Arthur spent the summer in the hospital in England. During his recuperation, he had time to gather souvenirs to send home to his youngest brother. *The Almonte Gazette*, in its issue of June 8, 1917, carried the following story:

> Master Donald McDiarmid of Carleton Place has received a soldier's khaki belt from his brother Arthur, who is in the trenches in France. The belt was literally covered with crests picked up in the field—36 in all—some from Australia, France, Germany and different parts of Canada.

On October 17, 1917, he was invalided home to Canada aboard the Hospital Ship *Araguaya*. Arthur was sent to a sanatorium at Quebec City for further treatment. He had been diagnosed as having contracted pulmonary tuberculosis at Vimy Ridge during March of 1917. Administratively, he was still on the strength of the 42nd Battalion, but on November 24, he was sent to the Mowat Memorial Sanatorium[21] in Portsmouth, Ontario, on Lake Ontario near Kingston. On February 25, 1918, the doctors recommended that Arthur have six more months of treatment. He refused! He told them he was sick of institutions and that his people wanted him home. The medical officers considered Arthur's refusal to be unreasonable but acquiesced and recommended his discharge from the army.

On April 11, 1918, Arthur McDiarmid was discharged as medically unfit for further service. At his Medical Board for Discharge, he was described as nineteen years old, 5' 8" in height, with a scar on his

[21] *The Almonte Gazette* of June 29th, 1917 reported that, "A vocational and recreational building for returned soldiers on the Mowat Memorial Hospital grounds was opened on Friday and is regarded as one of the best equipped in Canada. Art and craft work will be taught and instruction will be given in stenography, bookkeeping, telegraphy, commercial law, civil service qualifications, elementary work, and when a fully equipped garage is completed motor mechanics will round out the list."

forehead. He told the board that he had worked in a woollen mill before service. He was deemed to be 100 per cent disabled and recommended for special sanatorium treatment that may lessen his incapacity. Arthur had picked up, somewhere overseas, a tattoo on his left forearm of a bird, a lizard and a flag (the Canadian Red Ensign with the word "Canada"), and another on his right forearm of a horseshoe with clasped hands.

He came home to Carleton Place to recuperate. *The Almonte Gazette*, of November 9 reported:

> Pte. Arthur McDiarmid, fifth son of Mr. and Mrs. Wm. McDiarmid, arrived home Monday morning, having come back with the recent disabled ones from France. Arthur does not look too bad after his war experiences and long journey back. Monday afternoon his school mates thought it becoming that they should afford him a welcome, and sent an auto up and brought him to the high school, where he was heartily welcomed, Principal Wethey making an appropriate speech and the class presenting him with a signet ring. The entire class with their hero had a trip around town in autos, some eight or ten cars being put in commission by the owners for the occasion. It was a very nice thought of the school boys, and as Arthur is the first of the boys to return whilst his comrades are still in classes the appropriateness of the reception will be more fully appreciated.

Being the second youngest son, and a very handsome young man, the girls of this close-knit family doted on "young Art." But during the evening of January 19, Arthur told his sisters, "I'll be leaving tonight!"

The *Carleton Place Herald* of January 28, 1919, carried the following news item:

> Pte. Arthur McDiarmid at Rest
>
> The sympathy of the entire town goes out to Mr. Wm. McDiarmid and family, who have been sorely bereaved as a result of the war. Four of their sons enlisted. Harold died of wounds, Victor was lost and is still missing, presumed to have been killed, Arthur came home 15 mos ago after being in hospital for some time in England, suffering from poison gas, and finally succumbed on Sunday evening. Arthur was the fifth son

of Mr. and Mrs. McDiarmid, and was only 16 when he enlisted with his brother Victor in the 80th Batt. in 1915. Being a big boy for his age he passed the inspection and went overseas in the spring of 1916. After getting to France his first mishap was to be buried by a shell burst, getting out of that he remained at the front until he fell victim to the pernicious poison gas of the enemy. From this attack he never came back, although he seemed to rally for a time after getting to his native Canada. He was a very modest young man and died a hero. The funeral took place this afternoon, and by request of the deceased was private. The remains were placed in St. James Vault.

In the same edition was the death notice:

In Carleton Place, January 20th, Eugene Arthur McDiarmid, fifth son of Mr. and Mrs. Wm. McDiarmid, aged 19 years and 9 mos.

The 8th Infantry Brigade of the 3rd Canadian Division was composed entirely of battalions from the Canadian Mounted Rifles. In World War I, the Mounted Rifles were, in fact, dismounted and saw service as infantry. Thus the 1st (Saskatchewan), 2nd (British Columbia), 4th (Central Ontario) and 5th (Quebec) Mounted Rifles formed the 8th Infantry Brigade.

The 3rd Division was assigned to attack opposite La Folie Wood. Their target was the eastern slope of the ridge, an advance of about one kilometre. The attacking battalions were the 1st, 2nd and 4th Mounted Rifles, the Royal Canadian Regiment, the Princess Patricia's Canadian Light Infantry and the 42nd (Black Watch of Montreal). The ground they had to cross had been well dug up in the fighting of 1915 and was full of shell holes, mine craters, old and new trenches. It was well suited for defence. One of the young lieutenants with the 2nd Canadian Mounted Rifles was John H. Christie.

In December 1914, the 30th British Columbia Horse and the Victoria Squadron of Horse mobilized and formed the 2nd Canadian Mounted Rifles. They were organized into the Canadian Expeditionary Force, as an infantry battalion, on March 15, 1915. The unit served in France and Flanders with the 1st Canadian Mounted Rifle Brigade from September 1915 until January 1916, when it was reorganized and assigned to the 8th Infantry Brigade, 3rd Canadian Division, where they remained for the rest of the war. They are perpetuated by the British Columbia Dragoons.

JOHN HATCHELL HALLIDAY CHRISTIE

John Christie was born in Glenavy, Ireland, the son of William and Emma Jane Halliday Christie. William was a minister and John followed in his footsteps. At the time he joined the army, John was attending to the spiritual needs of the Methodists of Appleton and Carleton Place. In the *Carleton Place Herald* of June 8, 1915, it was noted:

> Rev. J.H. Christie returned to Carleton Place for a farewell service.
>
> Mr. J.H.H. Christie, acting pastor of the Methodist Church, is leaving to join the Overseas Ambulance Corps. The village of Appleton gave him a well-filled purse, the Carleton Place Ladies Aid presented a purse and the Epwoth League gave a gift of gold.

The Rev. Mr. Christie enlisted on June 4 in Montreal as a private soldier in "A" Section, No. 2 Field Ambulance Depot of the Canadian Army Medical Corps. He gave his date of birth as October 28, 1891. His father was listed as his next of kin and the address given for the parents was Drumshambo, County Letrim, Ireland. John was twenty-three years, seven months old. He was described as 5' 8" tall, weighing 163 lbs. He had a fair complexion with blue eyes and brown hair and a small burn scar on his right hand. He gave his occupation as minister and his affiliation as the Methodist Church. He was given a regimental number of 400269.[22]

While training in Valcartier John fell victim to influenza, "la grippe," and was treated for pharyngitis by his own field ambulance unit from June 10 to 15, 1915, and again from the 22nd to the 28th. John went to England, arriving on November 4, 1915. Shortly thereafter he

[22] During World War I, only the other ranks were identified by regimental numbers. The officers were identified by their ranks. Those officers with regimental numbers were men who had been promoted from the ranks, and they were plentiful as the war wore on and the officers fell in increasing numbers.

was promoted to the rank of lance corporal. On February 12–13, 1916, he embarked for overseas and the battlefields of France. His unit, No. 7 Canadian (Cavalry) Field Ambulance, along with Nos. 8, 9 and 10 Field Ambulances, went over with the 3rd Canadian Division.

Except for the wounded, the gassed, and the victims of non-battle accidents, the Canadian troops' health remained fairly good. The medical people had to deal with some cases of influenza, paratyphoid and a new condition—trench feet. The Canadian Army Medical Corps earned a well-deserved reputation for efficiency and excellent care of their troops. The Canadian army was the only Great War national force to inoculate all of its troops against typhoid fever, a disease rampant in the other armies.

The 3rd Division participated in the battles for the craters of St. Eloi in April 1916 and at Mount Sorel in June. For the rest of the summer they remained semi-stationary in the Ypres Salient. At the end of August, the Canadian Corps moved to the Somme and took part in the battles there until November when they were drawn back and sent to the Vimy Ridge area to get ready for that major offensive.

From November 17, 1916, until January 21, 1917, L/Cpl. Christie was attached to the Artists' Rifles.[23] On February 16, 1917, he was granted a temporary commission as a lieutenant and posted to the 2nd Canadian Mounted Rifles (CMR). On February 24, he was taken on strength of the unit as a supernumerary officer. The nominal roll of the battalion shows Lt. J.H.H. Christie taken on strength on February 19, 1917, having been commissioned from the ranks of the 7th Canadian Field Ambulance.

The attack on Vimy Ridge by the 3rd Division went very well. The Mounted Rifles overcame the defenders and captured La Folie Farm. The 2nd CMR took the first large number of prisoners, 150 surprised Germans of the 263rd Reserve Regiment. The enemy trenches had been obliterated, causing some confusion as soldiers failed to recognize landmarks and advanced into their own barrage. But overall the attack went very well and by 6:25 a.m. both the 7th and 8th Brigades had met with success at their planned objectives.

---

[23] This unit was initially recruited entirely from performing artists in London, England.

The army was critically short of junior officers and NCOs because the casualties in these men, who lead from the forefront of the ranks, was proportionately greater than those of the troops. Units were scoured for men of experience and education who were worthy of elevation to the status of "temporary gentlemen." Officer-cadet battalions were holding units to which these men were temporarily posted for the few months it took to complete officer training. Most experienced infantrymen found the practical side of the training a breeze, but had more difficulty with the paperwork. However, any opportunity to get out of the misery of trench warfare was seized and the opportunity to gain a king's commission with the appropriate respect and deference outweighed the short life-expectancy.

The division reached the crest at 7:30 a.m. and occupied part of the Bois de la Folie. The centre battalion, the 2nd CMR, had made it to La Folie Farm, which they found to be nothing but rubble. With almost no opposition they had no problem overrunning it. On April 10, the 3rd Division reached its second objective: a line running through Vimy, Petit Vimy and La Chaudière.

April 10 (Stormy with snow)
All night and in the morning of the 10th the work of consolidation proceeded steadily, and from time to time additional prisoners were taken out of our dug-out and sent back.

At 4 p.m. during a heavy snowstorm, strong patrols were sent out by Brigade instructions to work in conjunction with patrols from right and left Battalions in order to [indecipherable] enemy positions. Lieut Hennesy [sic] and Spinks taking charge of the patrol from this Battalion which reconnoitred PETIT VIMY and BLOATER trench system. These defenses were heavily manned and severe casualties ensued from rifle and machine gun fire. Lieut Spinks who had already rendered splendid service as Scout and Sniping Officer being killed, and Lieut Hennesy seriously wounded, in spite of the heavy enemy fire both killed and wounded were brought in.

Towards dusk the weather improved . . . the work of front line consolidation [continued].

At 11 p.m. a [indecipherable] with five other prisoners was brought in by the RCMP and he confirmed the information observed by patrol during the afternoon as to the Bloater and Petit Vimy defenses

Throughout the night work continued, which our artillery kept up an intermittent fire upon defensive targets reported in front of our position.[24]

April 10, 1917—Consolidation carried on steadily. At 4:00 p.m. strong patrol sent out to reconnoiter [*sic*] Petit Vimy and Bloater Trench system—found them heavily manned. We suffered many casualties.

Between 1:00 and 3:30 some of our 6" howitzers dropped a large number of rounds in and around our forward positions, forcing us to withdraw and causing casualties.

The Battalion attacked with 23 officers and 664 other ranks and its strength upon relief was 14 officers and 353 other ranks.[25]

One of the officers left behind was the newly promoted Lt. John Hatchell Halliday Christie. He had been with the battalion all of three weeks. Christie was reported missing on April 14, then reported killed in action on April 16. The date of death was later corrected to April 10, 1917. Lt. Christie was buried where his body was found, one-and-a-half miles south of Givenchy-en-Gohelle, five miles south of Lens, then exhumed to be interred with other dead Canadians.

March 1917—officers on duty during tour of trenches: "C" Company—Lt. J.H. Christie

5 Apr—"A" and "C" Companies left huts, Villiers au Bois and went under canvas about 1 kilometre south of Villiers au Bois.

7 Apr–8 pm—"A" and "C" Companies left Villiers au Bois for front line. Weather very stormy and continued rain.

List of officers in attack:

. . . "C" Company . . .

Lt. J.H. Christie (Killed)

At 5:55 a.m. Maj T. Godfrey (officer commanding "C" Company) reported the capture of the SWISCHEN STELLUNG (their objective) and that FICKLE TRENCH (their second objective) was absolutely obliterated, the SWISCHEN would be consolidated as a defensive trench.[26]

---

[24] Handwritten narrative found in the 2nd Canadian Mounted Rifles War Records.

[25] War Diary–2nd Canadian Mounted Rifles.

[26] War Diary–2nd Canadian Mounted Rifles.

In the *Carleton Place Herald* of May 1, 1917, under a photograph of Lt. (Rev) J.H.H. Christie, was the following account:

Memorial Service in the Methodist Church in Honour of Mr. Christie and Others.

Last Sunday evening's service in the Methodist Church will long be remembered by those fortunate enough to secure an entrance. Long before the hour the church was filled as all were anxious to hear something about the actions of Rev. J.H.H. Christie and others who fell somewhere in France in defence of the Empire . . .

The pastor, Rev. W. Gould Henderson was in excellent form . . . strongly urged the congregation to continue the memorial day from year to year as a reminder of the bravery and heroism of those who have fallen already and those who still may fall . . .

Photographs of the four fallen heroes Lieut. Rev Christie, Pte. Cummings, Pte. Hamilton and Pte. Tyrie were placed at the altar, and rested peacefully within the folds of the Union Jack.

The Almonte Gazette,[27] in its newspaper dated Friday, May 4, 1917, carried a similar report regarding this ceremony:

Memorial Service for Rev. Mr. Christie

A memorial service was conducted in the Carleton Place Methodist Church last Sunday evening for the late Rev. (Lieut.) J. Halliday Christie, who fell at the battle of Vimy Ridge. He went overseas with the Medical Corps but won promotion and accepted his commission in the Canadian Mounted Rifles, which regiment he was serving at the memorable battle of Vimy Ridge. Mr. Christie entertained the hope of return to work in Canada. The war office advised Mr. and Mrs. Hiram McFadden of Carleton Place of the casualty. The effects of the lamented student were in their care and will be forwarded to the parents in Ireland.

The late soldier clergyman was a student of the Methodist ministry, having come to Canada about two years ago. His father is the Rev. W.J. Christie of Drumshambo County, Leitrim, Ireland.

[27] Unfortunately, the newspapers of the *Carleton Place Herald* for the period, approximately June 1917 to fall 1918, have been lost and no archival record exists. *The Central Canadian* issues of the entire period are reported to have been destroyed years ago. Happily, *The Almonte Gazette* carried articles of interest regarding Carleton Place soldiers serving in World War I.

Much sympathy is felt for the bereaved parents and family. The late Mr. Christie supplied the pulpit of Carleton Place church for upwards of a year after the death of the late Dr. Sparling. He was in his 23rd year then, but for his gifts and graces won a foremost place in the affections and respect of the entire community. He was a gifted musician, and had a rich tenor voice well calculated. His rendering of classic selections and ballad songs will long be remembered by all who had the pleasure of hearing him. He is one of the Empire's fine young men who have offered a precious sacrifice upon the altar of liberty.

The service on Sunday evening was conducted by the Rev. W. Gould Henderson of Carleton Place.[28] . . . The choir sang a hymn that the fallen soldier minister had joined in singing on the evening of his departure from Carleton Place with a few friends gathered at the home of Capt. Hooper, who is a prisoner recently transferred from Germany to Switzerland. It was a favourite of the Lieutenant's entitled 'When the Roll is called up Yonder'. . .

JOHN HATCHELL HALLIDAY CHRISTIE

(Lieutenant) son of Rev. William John Christie and Emma Jane Halliday Christie of Barnbridge, Ireland. Enlisted Montreal, 2nd Canadian Mounted Rifles, 1st Central Ontario Regiment. Killed April 10, 1917, age 25. Buried in La Chaudière Military Cemetery, Vimy, Pas de Calais, France.

La Chaudière Cemetery is just east of Vimy, built next to a German gun position. It contains 638 Canadian graves, of which 132 are unidentified. The burials are from the Battle of Vimy Ridge and Canadian actions following Vimy.

Machine-Guns

The first modern machine-gun was invented in 1862 by Dr. R.J. Gatling of Chicago. It was operated by manually turning a crank and offered continuous fire. A strong turner could reach as high as 1200 rounds a minute fired. It was brought out just in time for use in the Civil War of the United States. A Gatling machine-gun had also been used in the Canadian Northwest Rebellion of 1885. But the technology

---

[28] Rev. Henderson was himself a veteran of the United States Civil War.

of machine-guns was so new that they were relatively unused during the Boer War in South Africa. By the time the Great War began there was little experience and even less interest. The gun was not widely accepted because general officers still thought the secret to winning wars was not machines but manpower.

Then events moved with incredible speed. Driven by Sam Hughes, Minister of Militia and the Defence of Canada, men and material were soon on their way to Europe and newer weapons of destruction gained consideration by the relatively hidebound brass. Sponsored by a few militia officers, and paid for by voluntary donations, battalions of  machine-gunners were slowly raised. By September 1914 the first unit had sailed for England, where they were generally ignored by senior officers who had not the slightest idea, nor interest, in how best to utilize the weapon.

Sections of machine-guns were attached to twelve battalions of the 1st Canadian Division. The number of machine-guns per battalion was set at four, but some battalions had as many as eight, contributed by communities or individuals. In Carleton Place, the Red Cross ladies held fund-raising events in order to purchase a gun to send overseas with their soldiers. The Canadian Division went to France in February 1915, all units having been landed at St. Nazaire by February 15. The machine-gun sections belonged to the battalions but a brigade machine-gun officer was now employed to assist in co-ordination and training. At first the gravest error made by the battalions was to deploy their machine-guns entirely to the front line instead of in supporting positions.

HAROLD WILLIAM MCDIARMID

The last Carleton Place casualty from Vimy Ridge was the third McDiarmid brother, machine-gunner Pte. Harold William McDiarmid..

Harold was the eldest of the McDiarmid boys to die in the Battle for Vimy Ridge. He was born to William and Mary McDiarmid in

Carleton Place on January 30, 1895. Harold had been educated as an engineer and was working in New Glasgow, Nova Scotia, when he heard the call to enlist in the Canadian Expeditionary Force. He had followed his sister, Evangeline, to Nova Scotia. Evangeline was married to Harry Ruhl, a construction engineer with the railroad who had been sent to New Glasgow for a particular project. Harold joined them to work on the same job.

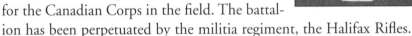

On March 30, 1915, Harold joined the 40th Battalion. It was officially organized on July 1, 1915, as the 40th Canadian Infantry Battalion (Halifax). Pte. H.W. McDiarmid went overseas with the 40th and was then transferred to the 17th Reserve Battalion when the 40th was broken up to provide reinforcements for the Canadian Corps in the field. The battalion has been perpetuated by the militia regiment, the Halifax Rifles.

At enlistment, Harold was twenty years, two months old. He stood 5' 7" tall and was described as having a dark complexion, hazel eyes and dark brown hair. He was a member of the Presbyterian Church. After basic infantry training at Valcartier, Harold left Canada on the S.S. *Missanabie*. The unit, with the third contingent of Canadian troops bound for Europe, boarded the ship in Montreal on October 8, 1915, and arrived in England on October 25. While training on the Salisbury Plain, Harold was not above some frivolous actions. In Folkstone, on December 21, he celebrated the Yuletide season early and was fined $3 for drunkenness.

To get to France, Harold accepted a transfer to the 6th Brigade Machine-Gun Company on March 16, 1916. He sailed for Le Havre, France, on March 17 and joined his new unit in the field on the 24th. The previous autumn, on October 29, 1915, the formation of brigade machine-gun companies had been authorized. This was an important step in the road to recognition of machine-gunnery as a separate arm of the service, with its own peculiar tactics, fitting between the artillery and the infantry. The companies took their names (numbers) from the brigades to which they were attached. Thus, as a member of the 6th Brigade, 2nd Canadian Division, Harold's company was supporting the 27th (Winnipeg), 28th (Saskatchewan), 29th (British Columbia) and 31st (Alberta) Infantry Battalions. The guns used until July 1916 were Colts, but in the transition from battalion sections to brigade companies, and with the arming of infantry battalions with Lewis guns, a shortage of machine-guns occurred.

Harold was in time for the 2nd Division's initiation to the battle-field. The 2nd relieved a British division near St. Eloi where the craters caused by the German mine explosions of March 27 had become small lakes of mud and water. The sector at St. Eloi fell to the 6th Brigade. They moved in on April 3–4 during a German artillery saturation bombardment. By noon on the 4th, half the men of the 27th Battalion were dead or wounded. The 29th Battalion was sent up to relieve them and arrived just as the enemy launched a counterattack. It was a disas-ter. The trenches, full of mud and water, were now also filled with men. Command was confused between the two battalions and in the pitch dark the Germans won back all they had previously lost. The 31st Battalion took back Craters 6 and 7 but an error in command caused a crushing bombardment by their own artillery that buried the defenders in the mud. The few survivors surrendered. The 2nd Division lost 1,373 men before withdrawing. The Canadian division-al commander, Turner, and the brigade commander, Ketchen, were fired.

During the summer, the Canadians stayed in the Ypres salient and were not involved in the beginning offensives of the Battle of the Somme. But in late August they marched south along dusty roads to participate in a combined Allied assault, timed for September 15. The target was Courcelette. Men of the 2nd Division attacked at 6:20 a.m. The 27th and 28th Battalions of the 6th Brigade overran the enemy trench and advanced toward the village. Such was their success that they broke into the village of Courcelette at 6:00 p.m. The fighting was bloody. The Canadians had to capture each farm, building and cellar one by one. With great courage they succeeded, but the village was not cleared of Germans until the next day.[29] The 6th Machine-Gun Company reports this action:

> Weather fine. Attack by 27th and 28th Battalions on German lines. No. 2 section advanced and took up defensive positions in support. No. 3 and 4 sections, conducted indirect fire. Approximately 45,000 [rounds of ammunition] were fired during the course of the attack.[30]

On September 26, the 31st and 29th Battalions attacked north from Courcelette toward Thiepval Ridge and Regina Trench. The fighting was continuous and death prevailed without letup.[31] The 6th Company had six guns with the 28th, 29th and 31st Battalions. On September 28, the rare, fine weather allowed use of mounted cavalry. That day the foot soldiers witnessed the strange sight of Canadian cavalry patrols being pushed forward to make contact with the enemy. While waiting for relief by the 4th Company, Harold McDiarmid took his first wound, but remained on duty. His unidentified wounds were recorded as slight. He wrote to his parents, in a letter that was paraphrased in the *Herald* on October 24, 1916:

> Pte. Harold McDiarmid, son of Mr. and Mrs. William McDiarmid in a letter to his parents written after the mishap, brought assurance to them that his injury was not serious.

By remaining with his unit, Harold participated in several of the four attempts to take Regina Trench from October 1 to November 11, 1916.

[29] N.M. Christie, *Futility and Sacrifice—The Canadians on the Somme, 1916* (Nepean: CEF Books, 1998), p. 17.

[30] C.S. Grafton, Lt. Col., *The Canadian "Emma Gees"—A History of the Canadian Machine Gun Corps* (London, Ont.: The Canadian Machine Gun Corps Association, 1938), p. 51

[31] "The air was seething with shells. Immediately above, the atmosphere was cracking with a myriad of machine-gun bullets, startling and disconcerting in the extreme. Bullets from the enemy rifles were whistling and swishing around my ears in hundreds, that to this day I cannot understand how anyone crossed that inferno alive. . . . As I pressed forward with eyes strained, to the extent of being half closed, I expected and almost felt being shot in the stomach. All around our men were falling, their rifles loosening from their grasp. The wounded, writhing in their agonies, struggled and toppled into shell holes for safety from rifle and machine-gun fire. . . . Rifle fire, however, was taking its toll, and on my front and flanks, soldier after soldier was tumbling to disablement or death, and I expected my turn every moment. The transition from life to death was terribly swift."

Donald Fraser, 31st (Alberta) Battalion.

N.M. Christie, *Futility & Sacrifice—The Canadians on the Somme, 1916* (Nepean: CEF Books, 1998), pp. 15-17.

The Canadians then moved to Vimy to prepare for that assault. Artillery barrages were now joined by the "ringing chatter" of machine-gun fire as they took on the role of light artillery, filling in the gaps left by the "heavies." As the gunners became more efficient in the use of indirect fire, infantry confidence increased and they began to trust machine-gun covering fire.

For the attack on Vimy, the Canadian Corps had 358 machine guns. Each of the sixteen Canadian Machine-Gun Companies had sixteen Vickers guns, as did the four supporting companies of the 5th British Division. The 1st Canadian Motor Machine-Gun Brigade had thirty-eight guns. One hundred and four mobile guns were detailed to the attacking infantry, plus a liberal supply of Lewis guns.

At 5:30 a.m, every gun on the twelve-mile front opened up, including the 230 machine-guns participating in their first large-scale barrage. Each machine gun had fifty yards to cover with fire. The 2nd Division's mobile guns swept forward with the attack. The 6th Company augmented their firepower with two captured German machine-guns and a large store of ammunition. They had numerous targets on the reverse slope and found the captured weapons very useful. In the afternoon, German artillery shelling increased. The 6th Company lost two of their three officers. The 1st and 2nd Division used infantry carriers, two per gun, to bring up ammunition. By nightfall, the 1st, 2nd and 3rd Divisions were at their objectives on the ridge and the 4th was fighting a stubborn enemy on Hill 145.

By 11:00 a.m., the 29th Battalion had overrun Thélus Trench and the 26th and 31st cleared the ruins of the village of Thélus. A halt of ninety minutes allowed time to bring the machine-guns forward to support the advance to their final objective. A night attack on April 9–10 took Hill 145. Further assaults, on a hill known as "The Pimple" and down the reverse slope, took place in a blinding snowstorm. The Germans were pushed back until they were forced to withdraw beyond Vimy village on the April 13.

Up the slopes of Vimy, on its crest and down the other side, the Canadian Corps became a cohesive entity and the machine guns played no small part. They lost nine officers and 191 other ranks killed or wounded. Fifty-one other ranks were killed. The machine-gun companies had acquitted themselves well. Vimy took on special significance for them as, just a week later, on April 16, 1917, the Canadian Machine-Guns Corps was authorized as its own service. But Harold McDiarmid would never learn of this success.

On April 12, 1917, Pte. Harold McDiarmid suffered his second wound in action. This time it proved fatal. He took gunshot wounds to the leg (thighs) and to the left pelvic area and was admitted to No. 18 General Hospital, Camiers, France, as dangerously ill. He died on April 14, 1917, of gas gangrene in his wounds. This was one of the pervasive effects and a double danger of mustard gas. A soldier who survived an initial attack by wearing a respirator would still have the gas permeate his clothing. Any subsequent bullet wound carried shreds of gas-impregnated clothing into the wound causing painful and mortal poisoning. The tissues became gas infected. Gangrene resulted, often with fatal results.

The *Carleton Place Herald* carried the following items:

April 14, 1917—No less than five Carleton Place men were reported yesterday in the Casualty List.

Pte. Harold McDiarmid, son of Mr. and Mrs. Wm. McDiarmid, from shot wound, in the thigh and suffering from gas poison.

We trust that in no case will the disability be of lengthy or serious duration.

May 1, 1917—[under a photograph of Harold McDiarmid]
Son of Mr. and Mrs. Wm. McDiarmid who enlisted with the 40th Batt. in Nova Scotia. reported wounded for the second time. Harold is one of four sons of Mr. McDiarmid who are at the front.

May 8, 1917—[under a notice about Victor being reported missing] Pte. Harold McDiarmid Succumbs to his Wounds

The sympathy of the entire town goes out to Mr. and Mrs. William McDiarmid and family in their hour of trouble and bereavement. Yesterday morning they received word of their son Victor being 'missing' from the Vimy Ridge fight and in the evening a letter came to Mrs. McDiarmid from the matron of the hospital in France where Harold had been taken for treatment, telling of his death on 14th April. From the letter it would appear that Harold had been badly hit with bullets in the thighs [probably machine-gun shower] and he passed away the same day he entered the hospital. He was buried in the military cemetery at Etaples, France.

Notice: Died of Wounds

McDIARMID—At No. 18 General Hospital, Camiers, France, April 14th, 1917. Harold William McDiarmid, third son of Mr. and Mrs. Wm. McDiarmid, Carleton Place, Ontario, aged 22 years, 2 months and 14 days.

The register with the Commonwealth War Graves Commission records:

HAROLD WILLIAM MCDIARMID
(414605 Private) son of William and Mary McDiarmid,
Carleton Place, 6th Company, Canadian Machine Gun Corps.
Died of wounds received at Vimy Ridge, April 14, 1917, age 22.
Buried in Etaples Military Cemetery, Pas de Calais, France.

The Etaples Cemetery is about three kilometres north of the town of Etaples. It holds 1,123 Canadians, mainly from the major actions at Mount Sorrel, the Somme, Vimy and Passchendaele.

The Almonte Gazette of September 21, 1917 had the story:

Mrs. Wm. McDiarmid has just received a letter from one of the chaplains in France which stated that the Canadian nurses at Nos. 1 and 7 General hospitals decorated the graves of the soldier martyrs on Dominion Day. Among the graves remembered was that of her son, Harold. The chaplain states that the cemetery is like a large park and is nicely taken care of, flowers being cultivated there in great profusion. Mrs McDiarmid also received the flag which had covered the grave of her departed son, together with a copy of the program used at the decoration ceremonies . . .

It is interesting to note that, after two years of warfare, not all Canadians were eager to rally around the flag. Those who would not, or could not, themselves enlist sought others to go in their place. The *Herald* of April 10, 1917 carried this story:

> W.A. Cole, an Ottawa auctioneer, ineligible for militia service, has secured a substitute in a young mechanic, hitherto prevented by family obligations from enlisting, whom he will insure, and pay $24.00 a month.

Special Order of the Day:

by Field Marshall Sir Douglas Haig, GCB, GCVO, KCI, Commander-in-Chief British Armies in France.

From His Majesty The King to Field Marshall Sir Douglas Haig, dated April 10, 1917:

"The whole Empire will rejoice at the news of yesterday's successful operations—Canada will be proud that the taking of the coveted Vimy Ridge has fallen to the lot of her troops. I heartily congratulate you and all who have taken part in this splendid achievement."

Message from Sir Henry Horne, Commanding First Army to General Officer Commanding Canadian Corps—10 April 1917:

". . . the army Commander wishes to express to the GOC Canadian Corps, the Divisional Commanders, and all ranks, his high appreciation of the splendid work carried out during the last three days by the troops of the First Army.

The VIMY Ridge has been regarded as a position of very great strength; the Germans have considered it impregnable. To have carried this position with so little loss testifies to the soundness of plan, thoroughness of preparation, dash and determination in execution, and devotion to duty on the part of all concerned. The 9th April, 1917, will be an historic day in the annals of the British Empire."

Message from Sir Edward Kemp, Minister of Militia:

"The troops still in Canada awaiting their opportunity to join their comrades at the front; the young Canadians who are about to enlist and the officers and men who have been deprived of the privilege of participating in active operations at the front but who have devoted themselves to the task of raising and organizing the Canadian Expeditionary Force; on behalf of all these I extend to yourself [Gen. Byng, corps commander] and the officers and men under your command their warmest congratulations, in which I heartily concur, upon the splendid and inspiring victory of Canadians at Vimy Ridge."

Message from Sir William Hearst, Prime Minister of Ontario:

"Government and people of Ontario heartily congratulate Canadians on their glorious achievement and thank them for their magnificent service to the Empire and to Civilization. Ontario rejoices that her sons have again proved worthy of the best traditions of our race. Our country is thrilled by the story of great victory which will be an immortal inspiration to noble deeds and is assurance of final overthrow of tyranny."[32]

---

[32] The messages from Sir Edward Kemp and Sir William Hearst were found recorded in the April 1917 War Diary of the 2nd Canadian Mounted Rifles

Chapter Seventeen

BACK TO FLANDERS

After their great victory at Vimy, the Canadian Corps continued operations in the area of Arras, partly to divert German attention away from the hard-pressed French front, and partly to conceal their planned offensive in Flanders.

The Second Battle of the Scarpe—The Battle of the Arleux Loop, April 23 to 28

THOMAS REYNOLDS

Thomas Reynolds was born in Birmingham, England, on March 29, 1887. He was the son of Richard and Amelia Reynolds. He emigrated to Canada to pursue his vocation as an iron-maker in the Findlay Foundry. In England he had several years service with the Fifth Worcestershire regiment. A brother, Ernest, also emigrated and began his business as a builder and contractor on Herriott Street in Carleton Place. Thomas helped his brother by doing some carpentry. Thomas enlisted in Ottawa on August 13, 1915, into the 77th Overseas Battalion.

The 77th became known as the Governor General's Foot Guards, but on August 15, two days after Thomas enlisted, it was officially organized as the 77th Canadian Infantry Battalion (Ottawa). It was a Highland battalion, with a pipe band, and marched past to *Bonnie Dundee.* The battalion was broken

up in England and absorbed mainly by the 51st Battalion to provide reinforcements for the Canadian Corps in France.

On enrolment, Thomas was described as twenty-eight years, five months old, weighing 156 lbs at 5' 8" tall. He was an adherent of the Church of England. He had a medium complexion, blue eyes and brown hair. He listed his brother Ernest as his next of kin. He was hospitalized during training in Valcartier from the 8th to the 15th of February 1916, with tonsillitis. Thomas embarked from Halifax on June 19, 1916, on the S.S. *Missinabie*, and landed in Liverpool on June 29.

Thomas Reynolds and Arthur McDiarmid were transferred together to the 73rd Battalion, "Royal Highlanders of Canada," in July; Thomas on the 3rd and Arthur on the 18th. They both went to France on August 12 with the 12th Brigade of the newly formed 4th Division, landing at Le Havre on August 13.

The 4th Division, instead of going to the Somme with the rest of the Canadian Corps, was sent into the line against the German 26th Division at the Ypres-Comines Canal. They went into reserve on September 21 where they received their new Lee-Enfield rifles, learned to advance behind a creeping barrage at the rate of 100 yards in three minutes and tested their new gas masks against tear gas. During the night of October 2–3 they went by train to the Somme.

The 4th Division participated in the last battles of the Somme at Regina and Desire Trenches. The primary brigades in the line were the 19th and 11th, with the 12th in reserve. Thus, the 73rd Battalion was spared some of the dreadful casualties caused by these battles. For the 4th Division, the Battle of the Somme, one of the most bloody battles in the history of modern warfare, ended on November 18. From November 26 to 28, the 4th Division rejoined the other three Canadian Divisions at the Lens-Arras front in anticipation of the Battle for Vimy Ridge.

During the first assault on the ridge it was the job of the 73rd Battalion to protect the 4th Division's northern flank. The attack started well with the 73rd, 72nd and 38th Battalions advancing satisfactorily on the northern fringe. But the centre battalion's attack proved a disaster. Artillery had not destroyed the German trench system; faced with unrelenting machine-gun and rifle fire, the Canadian assault was doomed to failure. The northern flank then came under heavy machine-gun fire from two sides. The pivot point was Hill 145, which was finally taken by the inexperienced 85th (Nova Scotia Highlanders) Battalion during the night of April 9–10.

The official history of the 42nd Battalion, also called "Royal Highlanders of Canada," notes the transfer of the remnants of the devastated 73rd to their battalion:

> A notable event of the week [of the April 12] was the arrival of an officer and 240 other ranks from the 73rd Battalion, The Royal Highlanders of Canada, which was broken up as it was felt that it would be difficult to maintain three service battalions from the home regiment in the field . . . The splendid draft received by the 42nd from the 73rd was a valuable addition to the strength of the Battalion and everything possible was done to make the men feel at home in their new environment . . . From this date forward former members of the 73rd had an important part in the activities of the Battalion.[1]

Both Arthur McDiarmid and Thomas Reynolds were among the troops of the 73rd to join the 42nd in the 7th Brigade of the 3rd Division. They were both able to maintain their connections with a Highland battalion throughout the rest of their service.

Thomas's time with the 42nd was to be awfully short. The battalion history records:

> On April 21st the battalion moved into Corps reserve and was quartered in dugouts and tunnels in the old La Folie section of the front line as it was before April 9th. From here numerous working parties were supplied chiefly in connection with road building. Before the end of the month the battalion moved up in close support of Vimy village where the men were nightly employed upon the construction of a new trench line. The area was under heavy shell fire from time to time and the tour was extremely unfortunate in the matter of casualties.
>
> This thoroughly unpleasant tour came to an end on the night of April 29th–30th. During the night Vimy village was steadily bombarded with gas shells for six hours and the relief was completed under conditions of the utmost difficulty and discomfort.[2]

[1] Lt. Col. C. Beresford Topp, *The 42nd Battalion C.E.F. The Royal Highlanders of Canada in the Great War* (Montreal: Gazette Printing, 1931), pp. 135-136.

[2] Ibid., pp. 136-137.

Pte. Thomas Reynolds was reported as killed in action on April 25. The date was later corrected to the 26th. The *Carleton Place Herald* reported on May 15, 1917:

> Mr. Ernest Reynolds, received a cable on Saturday notifying him of the death of his brother Pte. Thomas Reynolds, who was killed in action on April 24th somewhere in France. Pte Reynolds enlisted in Ottawa with the 77th Batt. and was transferred in England. He was 30 years of age, and was a man of splendid physique.

On May 22, the *Herald* ran a photograph of Thomas identifying him as "Brother of Mr. Ernest Reynolds, whose death on April 27th was recorded last week." Thomas Reynolds was killed in action while in a dugout in Vimy village, on the early morning of April 26. He was instantly destroyed by the explosion of an enemy shell which made a direct hit on the dugout. His remains were first buried in Vimy, then exhumed to be placed in a Canadian grave in the Bois-Carré.

The Commonwealth War Graves commemoration reads:

In Memory of
THOMAS REYNOLDS
Private
144756
42nd Bn., Canadian Infantry (Quebec Regt.)
who died on
Thursday, 26th April 1917. Age 30.
Son of Richard and Amelia Reynolds.
Native of Smethwick, England.

Remembered with Honour
Buried in the Bois-Carré British Cemetery, Thélus,
Pas de Calais, France.

This cemetery was begun in April 1917 by the Canadian Corps. It now contains 382 Canadian graves, forty-four with unidentified remains. They are men from all four Canadian Divisions that fought at Vimy Ridge and in later battles when the Canadians moved out into the Douai Plain.

The Battle of Fresnoy—May 3, 1917

After the final battle for Arleux on April 28, the Canadians' next objective as they pushed east from Vimy was the line at the hamlet of Fresnoy. This fight became known as the Third Battle of the Scarpe, part of a British offensive that had little success except that of the 3rd Canadian Battalion at Fresnoy. The Germans needed to hold the position and they were ready for an attack.

Early on May 3, the Canadians moved into position. The 3rd Battalion was to attack through the woods just on the northern edge of the village. German shelling killed many of the gathering attackers as a full moon silhouetted the troops moving into assembly positions. At 3:45 a.m. the Canadian artillery began its barrage and the infantry advanced. They captured the wood and by 6:00 a.m. had possession of Fresnoy.

The enemy tried two counterattacks but both failed in the face of heavy artillery and small-arms fire. The German artillery continued a heavy pounding throughout the day, causing many Canadian casualties. They lost 1,259 killed, wounded or missing, and their success could not be held by the British troops that relieved them on May 5. A devastating counterattack by German forces lost Fresnoy and pushed the defenders back toward Arleux.

JOHN LEO CORR

John Leo Corr survived the assault on Vimy Ridge, only to fall during the battle for Fresnoy.

Leo Corr was born in Carleton Place on July 12, 1886, the son of Mr. and Mrs. W.L. Corr. After his schooling he went to work for Findlay Foundry and learned the trade of a stove mounter. In 1915 he joined the militia and spent eight months in the 42nd (Lanark and Renfrew) Regiment. He enlisted into the active force on November 27, 1915, during the 130th Battalion's recruiting campaign in Lanark County. The *Carleton Place Herald* of December 7, 1915, listed on the roll of Captain J.H. Bates's (previously a superintendent of the Bates and Innes Mill) "C" Company of the 130th Battalion, one Corr, J.L.

At enlistment, Leo recorded his mother, Hannah, as his next of kin. The medical examiner found him, at thirty years of age, to be 5'

7" tall and weighing 160 lbs. He was described as having a birthmark on his right side and being of a fair complexion with blue eyes and light brown hair. He was a member of the Roman Catholic faith. His attestation was certified correct by the 130th Battalion's Commanding Officer, Lt.-Col. J.E. de Hertel.

Pte. John Leo Corr spent almost a year in Canada, training at Barriefield and Valcartier. The *Herald* of January 18, 1916, listed Cpl. L. Corr in Company "C" of the 130th Battalion, C.E.F., and the February 22 issue noted that "Cpl. L. Corr is attending NCO class at Perth." He departed for England with the battalion on the S.S. *Lapland* from Halifax on September 23, 1916. The battalion arrived in Liverpool on October 6. On November 12, as the 130th was broken up, Leo was transferred to the 3rd Battalion of the 1st Canadian Division. He went to France on November 14, but it was not until March 24, 1917, that he joined his unit. He was in training and doing various fatigue duties in the rear areas. He was in plenty of time to participate in the battalion's attack on Vimy Ridge.

The 3rd Battalion recorded the events of May 3–4:

2:41 a.m.—"D" Coy has had a very hard time, suffering many casualties.

3:00—Word received from Assembly Area that casualties are: "A" Coy—1; "B" Coy—6; "C" Coy—nil.

3:05— Enemy artillery fairly active, his barrage line seems to fall on about "C" Coy's line in Assembly Area.

3:45—Attack commenced, enemy artillery active especially on back area.

4:40—German machine-guns appear active.

5:20—Word received from "D" Coy that they are in position but that they have only 25 men left.

12 noon—Word received that the Germans are advancing on our newly won positions. SOS sent up and a protective barrage laid down.

1:40 pm— Platoons which left at 12:30 pm returned . . . report it is absolutely impossible to get across to the BLUE objective, the enemy laying down a very heavy barrage and also a very heavy direct machine-gun fire . . .

5:00—Brigade Major advises relief for tonight impossible.

6:00—Enemy artillery shelling quite heavy.

The end of action report contained the following:

Observation:

One Lewis gun per platoon found to be of immense value throughout days of May 3 and 4 when many of the enemy were caught moving forward en masse [*sic*] and mowed down.

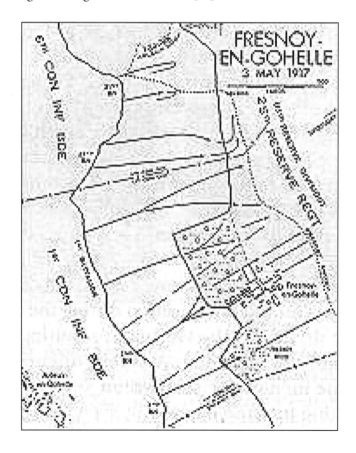

Enemy Positions:

The enemy was found to have many dugouts etc. in the wood, many of these were passed over in the first assault, the enemy hiding in them and causing a few casualties by sniping, during the morning of the 3rd. These were cleared out on the night of May 3/4 when 75 other ranks were found in them. A number of wooden huts were also found in FRESNOY WOOD.

Enemy Morale:

Fair, a trifle better than prisoners captured on April 9th.

Our Morale:

Excellent, especially in "A" and "B" Coys [front line companies] on account of the excellent targets the enemy offered to our Lewis Gun and rifle fire.

May 1–May 4—Fresnoy Engagement

May 1—Very heavy strafe along whole front at 9:00 p.m.

May 2—10:00 a.m.— morning quiet.

     5:20 p.m.—Zero Hour changed from 4:20 to 3:45 much to disappointment; seems too early.

     9:00 p.m.—very heavy artillery along our front.

May 2/3— Battalion in company positions by midnight; area well forward just inside enemy barrage therefore entailing numerous casualties throughout ZERO day. Attacking force— "A" and "B" Companies.

May 3—1:30 a.m.—"D" Company were considerably disorganized by a shell causing them some casualties including their guide and a platoon commander. When last seen their Company seemed to have been heading away over to right.

     1:40—very heavy enemy straefe [*sic*] opened on our front and to our right.

     2:00 —straefe [*sic*] dying down.

     2:20—everything quiet.[3]

---

[3] War Diary–3rd Canadian Infantry Battalion

A history of the battalion tells that they were, on May 3, 1917, at Fresnoy in the front line on the right flank of the Canadian Corps. For the month of May, the battalion suffered casualties of eleven officers and 222 other ranks, of which, John Leo Corr, was but one. His personal record shows that he was killed in action "In the Field" in France.

On May 22, the *Herald* ran the following item:

> The wires continue to bring the sad information day by day of casualties to our boys at the front, and during the last week . . . more have been added to the list of those from Carleton Place who have paid the supreme penalty.
>
> Pte. Leo Corr, son of Mr. Wm. Corr, who enlisted with the 130th, reported killed in action May 3rd.

The commemorative information in Canadian Expeditionary Force records lists Leo as "Missing, presumed dead, May 3, 1917. No known grave, commemorated on Vimy Memorial." Leo's body was never recovered. It is quite possible that his remains, like those of many other Canadians, were burned by the Germans, a standard method of disposing of enemy dead employed by both sides.[4] He was last seen during the attack east of Arleux-en-Gohelle.

The Commonwealth War Graves Commission has this commemoration:

In Memory of
JOHN LEO CORR
Private
787603
3rd Bn., Canadian Infantry (Central Ontario Regt.)
who died on
Thursday, 3rd May 1917. Age 30
Son of Mr. and Mrs. W.J. Corr, of Carleton Place, Ontario.

Early in May 1917, the government announced that all members of the Canadian Expeditionary Force who have been overseas, and who have given at least six months' continuous service, would receive a grant of three months pay and allowances when they were honourably discharged. This grant would apply to all those already discharged and it was expected to add $50 million to the cost of the war.

---

[4] N.M. Christie, *For King and Empire: The Canadians at Vimy* (Winnipeg: Bunker to Bunker Books, 1996), footnote 13 on p. 64.

The Vimy Memorial at Pas de Calais, France, is Canada's most impressive tribute to those who fought and died in the Great War. The majestic and inspiring Memorial rises from Hill 145, the highest point of Vimy Ridge. Inscribed on its ramparts are the names of 11,285 Canadian soldiers posted as "Missing, presumed dead" in France. Construction of the massive sculpture began in 1925 and on July 26, 1936, King Edward VIII unveiled it before 8,000 Canadian veterans and their families. Canadian trees and shrubs are planted in the ninety-one hectares "the free gift in perpetuity of the French nation to the people of Canada."

Chapter Eighteen

ARTILLERY

The role of the artillery in any type of warfare is to give maximum support to the infantry, thus allowing infantrymen the ability to carry out their tasks more effectively and to reach objectives with minimum loss of life. The bottom line in any action is that only an infantryman can hold ground. All other units support him. The Canadian artillery in the Great War certainly achieved its mandate.

The Canadian Artillery motto is *Quo Fas et Gloria Duncunt* (Wherever Right and Glory Lead). Their guns are their only Colours.

Artillery has little glamour attached to its tedious work. In World War I, as in every conflict, brand-new tactics were developed for the supporting role of the guns. They had to do preparatory fire prior to a mass infantry assault, spend tedious hours of work involved in siege gunnery, and study and develop more effective ways of protecting the infantry. In this war, the preparatory barrage usually only created an almost impassable morass of mud for the assault waves of infantry to cover. It did cut enemy wire to facilitate infantry access in some places, but its major fault was that it simply alerted the enemy to the impending attack. Defenders could protect themselves in bunkers and, as soon as the barrage lifted, crawl out and fire into the unprotected mass of approaching infantrymen. A Canadian artilleryman, Lt.-Col. (later Lt.-Gen.) Andrew McNaughton, perfected the creeping, or rolling, type of barrage. Advancing infantry could follow as closely as thirty yards behind their own exploding shells. McNaughton coupled this with a system of indirect fire from artillery and machine guns which allowed further protection to the advancing infantry's flanks.[1]

Divisional ammunition columns were responsible for the delivery of ammunition to the gun batteries and other units from the ammunition refilling points. Two Carleton Place gunners lost their lives with

[1] Charles H. Stewart, *"Overseas" The Lineages and Insignia of the Canadian Expeditionary Force 1914-1919* (Toronto: Little & Stewart, 1970), p. 130.

ammunition columns—Herb Robertson with the 2nd Division, and Herb Dowdall with the 3rd Division.

After winning Fresnoy, the 1st Canadian Division went into reserve, replaced by a British division. The 2nd Division stayed in the line north of the village. The 5th Bavarian Division received orders on May 5 to recapture Fresnoy. German artillery launched unusually extensive firing—well over 100,000 shells were fired between the evening of May 6 and the morning of May 8. At 4:00 a.m. on the 8th, advancing German troops stumbled into the 2nd Division's lines, just as the 4th Brigade was relieving the 6th. The incoming 19th (Toronto) Battalion joined forces with the outgoing 29th (Vancouver—nicknamed Tobin's Tigers), and quickly ejected the intruders. The German main attack, launched two hours later, was supported by massive artillery that could not be answered. Some of the defending guns had been damaged by incoming shell-fire, some crews were suffering the effects of gas shelling and a dense mist prevented rapid identification of possible targets. By nightfall, the entire salient, and the 2nd Division's right flank had been pushed back almost to Arleux. Heavy German shelling was maintained on the 9th and a counterattack had to be abandoned. Fresnoy was lost after having been held for three days.

HERBERT ARNOLD ROBERTSON

Herb Robertson was born on January 7, 1898, in Carleton Place, the son of Alexander and Florence Robertson. He left his job as a knitter in one of the mills in Carleton Place and travelled to Ottawa to enlist in the 51st Battery, 13th Brigade, Canadian Field Artillery. At his enlistment proceedings, on February 24, 1916, Herb was described as eighteen years, one month old, 5' 4" tall, weighing 130 lbs. He was of a medium complexion with brown eyes and brown hair. He gave his religious affiliation as Presbyterian.

After a few days' leave to get his affairs in order, he arrived in Kingston on March 1, 1916, for basic training. On May 30, he began his advanced artillery training. Herb embarked from Halifax on September 18 and landed in Liverpool on the 25th. He was admitted to the Whitley Camp hospital for a day, September 28, to recover from the effects of the voyage.

Gunner Herb Robertson proceeded overseas to France on March 17, 1917, with the 83rd Howitzer Battery of the 15th Brigade. Immediately upon arrival, however, he was transferred to the 2nd Division Ammunition Column. This unit was tasked with providing all artillery ammunition to the 2nd Division's 5th and 6th Brigades' Field Artillery. Each brigade had four batteries, three field batteries and a howitzer battery. Herb helped provide artillery support for the 2nd Division's assault in April on Vimy Ridge, and stayed for the attacks beyond the ridge. During the German counterattack, under an umbrella of very heavy artillery fire, Herb lost his life near Fresnoy. He was killed in the performance of his duties, packing ammunition to the gun positions in Willerval.

The *Carleton Place Herald*, in the issue dated May 22, 1917, reported the news of Herb's death along with that of Leo Corr:

> The wires continue to bring the sad information day by day of casualties to our boys at the front, and during the last week two more have been added to the list of those from Carleton Place who have paid the supreme penalty.
>
> Driver Herbert Arnold Robertson, son of Mr. and Mrs. A.T. Robertson, enlisted a year ago with a Battery at Ottawa; killed in action on May 10th. Herbert was only 19 years of age.

In the newspaper of June 5, under a photograph of "Gunner Herbert Arnold Robertson," was the additional information: "Son of Mr. and Mrs. A.T. Robertson, enlisted in Ottawa last summer with a Field Battery, trained at Petewawa [*sic*] and Kingston and went overseas. He was 19 years of age. He was killed in action on the 10th of May."

The Commonwealth War Graves record has the entry:

Herbert (Herb) Arnold Robertson

(319948 Gunner) son of Alexander T. and Florence Gertrude Robertson, Carleton Place. 2nd Division Ammunition

Column, Canadian Field Artillery. Killed in Action May 10, 1917, age 19. Buried in La Targette British Cemetery, Neuville-St Vaast, Pas de Calais, France.

The *Herald* on June 5 reported on a special memorial service held at Zion Church:

> A special service in honor of Pte. David McLaren, son of D.B. McLaren, reeve of Beckwith and Gunner Herbert Arnold Robertson, son of Mr. and Mrs. A.T. Robertson, and Pte. Leslie Foulds, who enlisted here last summer whilst on the staff of the Bank of Ottawa, was held in Zion Church on Sunday evening last.
>
> The pulpit was draped with a Union Jack and small Dominion flags adorned the choir rail, and also marked the pews in the church where the deceased young men used to sit . . .
>
> At the conclusion of the service the congregation stood whilst the Dead March was played by the organist.
>
> Photographs of the two home boys were upon the communion table, and many of those present took a look at them as the congregation passed out.

The following week, June 12, a Card of Thanks appeared:

> Mr. and Mrs A.T. Robertson desire to acknowledge their most sincere thanks to the friends who have been so kind and sympathetic to them since the death of their son Gunner Herbert A. Robertson. The many kind expressions of sympathy have done much to alleviate the pangs of sorrow and encourage us in the hour of bereavement.

The commemorative information in the Commonwealth War Graves directory follows:

In Memory of
HERBERT ARNOLD ROBERTSON
Gunner
319948
2nd Div. Ammunition Col., Canadian Field Artillery
who died on
Thursday, 10th May 1917. Age 19
Son of Alexander T. and Florence Gertrude Robertson, of
Carleton Place, Ontario.

Neuville-St Vaast is a village 6.5 kilometres north of Arras. The British Cemetery was begun the end of April 1917, and was used by field ambulances and fighting units until September 1918. There are nearly 650 1914–18 graves in which over forty are unidentified. Nearly a third of the graves are those of the officers and men belonging, or attached, to artillery units. It is enclosed by a stone curb on two sides and on the other two by a low rubble wall. In March–April 1917, the artillery of the 2nd Canadian and 5th Divisions and certain heavy artillery units had their headquarters in a deep cave at nearby Aux-Rietz.

On the home front in Carleton Place life continued, during the month of May 1917, at a fairly constant pace. Unless, of course one had relatives overseas or at the front, in which case they hung on every snippet of war news. On May 1, the *Herald* reported that members of the 240th Battalion passed through town the previous Wednesday afternoon and were given a "hearty send-off" by crowds gathered at the train depot. Along with the casualty lists, containing the names of Victor McDiarmid and Thomas Reynolds, the May 15 edition informed townsfolk that the Bank of Ottawa (situated in the same building now occupied by the Royal Bank) had a supply of French paper money available in small denominations should relatives wish to send small amounts to the boys at the front. An editorial comment in that same paper:

It would seem that most of the Carleton Place boys were in the Vimy Ridge battle, judging from the letters received by the

"Orders in the Field" provide some insight into the regulations imposed on Canadian soldiers even while in the front lines of a battle zone:

Daily Routine in the Field—
2.5.17 [2 May 1917]:

Reveille	6:30 a.m.
Sick Parade	7:00
Breakfast	7:30
Company Parades	9:00 to noon
Dinner	12.30 p.m.
Company parades	2:00 to 4:00
Orderly Room	4:30
Supper	5:00
First Post	9:00
Last Post	9:30
Lights Out	9:45

Battalion Orders—4 June 1917:

In the case of an OR being wounded, Platoon Commanders will write next of kin, and in the case of an OR being Killed in Action, both Platoon and Company Commanders will write next of kin.

relatives at home. And we venture to say that they did their part as bravely as the rest, some having paid the supreme penalty.

An item to gladden the hearts of those boys who left high school to join the army was news of their principal:

> Principal Wethey, of the High School, has enlisted with the 41st Regiment, Canadian Defence Force, headquartered at Brockville and received the title of Sergt. Major. He was formally accepted by Capt. Botsford having passed the necessary examinations, and is now the official recruiting officer for Carleton Place for the company to be raised here in connection with this regiment.

The wearing of an identity disc in two parts originated in World War I due to the great number of casualties to be accounted for. The identity discs carried by all ranks were instituted. Canadian army orders for the wearing and use of the discs were, as with the British army:

Identity Discs:

Several bodies have been found lately by Burial Parties from which both the Green (No. 1) and the Red (No. 2) Identity Discs have been removed.

Although it may be necessary to remove the Red (No. 2) Identity Disc for identification purposes before burial, the Green (No.1) Identity Disc is on no account to be removed, as the object of it is to safeguard against loss of identity when the bodies are buried.

In future each officer and soldier will be supplied with two identity discs which will be worn as shown on the diagram below:—

The upper disc will be known as 'Disc, identity, No.1, green'; the lower one as 'Disc, identity, No. 2, red'.

In case of the death of an officer or soldier in the field, the lower disc, known as 'Disc, identity, No. 2, red,' will be removed and disposed of in the same manner as heretofore.

The upper disc, known as 'Disc, identity, No.1, green,' will not be removed but will be buried with the body.

Consequently, in cases where a body can be reached and identified but cannot be brought back for burial, the lower disc will be removed, to ensure proper notification of death, while the upper disc will remain as a safeguard against loss of identity when it becomes possible to bury.

The two discs will be worn around the neck, as directed in Army Order 987 of 1916, by all officers and soldiers on active service, and neglect to wear the discs will be regarded as a breach of discipline.

Chapter Nineteen

RAIDS

In May 1917, the 4th Division was holding a section of the Canadian Corps' line across the road between Lens and Arras, from the hamlet of La Coulotte to the Souchez River. During the night of June 3–4, the 3rd and 4th Canadian Divisions, after a successful gas bombardment of the German positions, advanced and were able to take La Coulotte and a brewery slightly north of it. However, the majority of the heavy artillery had been transferred to Flanders and, without supporting guns, the Canadians had difficulty holding the newly won trenches. The commanders decided that, instead of trying to hold on at great cost, they would instead take on large scale raids.

A British attack astride the Souchez River during the night of June 24–25 caused the German defenders to fall back. The 3rd and 4th Canadian Divisions immediately advanced and secured a continuous line from the river to the town of Avion, just north of La Coulotte.

The 1st Brigade of the 1st Division came out of the line early in the summer of 1917 for a month of rest, relaxation and refitting. The brigade was composed of the 1st, 2nd, 3rd and 4th Battalions. A member of the 3rd (Toronto Regiment) Battalion was Frank Fumerton. The four battalions exercised their competitive spirit in various sports events and parades during which they endeavoured to outshine each other.

Early in June, the brigade moved to the Bois des Alleux, near Mont. St. Eloy. This area was a target of German high-velocity shelling during the day and extensive aerial bombing at night. Before moving into the line, the four battalions paraded to bid farewell to the corps commander, Sir Julian Byng. During his eighteen months leading the Canadians, Byng had endeared himself to all ranks. The only consolation in his departure was the promotion of Sir Arthur W. Currie, the 1st Division commander, to lieutenant-general and his assumption of command of the Canadian Corps.

For much of the rest of June and July, battalion activities revolved around holding the trenches in the front line between Acheville and Fresnoy. They rotated between the line in front of the village of Vimy and to reserve and support positions at La Targette and Mont. St. Eloy. On Dominion Day, 1917, a Sunday, the brigade held a special church service attended by the entire brigade and General Sir Arthur Currie. Back in the trenches the following Thursday, July 5, Frank Fumerton was killed during an artillery bombardment.

FRANK FUMERTON

Militia service ran through Frank Fumerton's blood. He was a descendant of John Fumerton, who was attending the militia muster in 1824 at Morris's tavern when the Ballygiblin Riots erupted. Responding to the threats of the Irish, John fired his gun through an end window. Although no one was hit, John was later charged with "malicious shooting at Bartholomew Murphy." He, Captain Thomas Glendinning, James Richey  and John McGinnis, were all acquitted by the assizes court in Perth.

Frank was born on November 30, 1896, the son of Mr. and Mrs. Robert A. Fumerton. He claimed the trade of "railroader" when he joined the 42nd Lanark and Renfrew (Militia) Regiment in Smiths Falls on October 18, 1915. He transferred to the active force, 130th Battalion, on his nineteenth birthday, November 30, 1915. He listed his next of kin as his father, Mr. R.A. Fumerton.

On his enlistment, Frank was described as nineteen years, eleven months of age (in fact he was only eighteen), weighing 157 pounds and standing 5' 6" tall. He was of a fair complexion, having blue eyes and brown hair. He had a burn scar on his left leg. His religious affiliation was to the Church of England.

After almost a year of training and organizing in Perth (during which most of the local soldiers were billeted at home), and Barriefield, the battalion embarked on the S.S. *Lapland* and sailed from Halifax on September 23, 1916. Before leaving, on August 24, 1916, Frank married Miss Irene Galvin, daughter of Mr. and Mrs. Patrick Galvin of Smiths Falls. His pay assignment to her, of $20 a month, was started November 1. After his death his medals and a Memorial Cross were delivered to his widow, Mrs. Irene May of Smiths Falls.[1]

[1] These items were not delivered to the mothers or widows until some years after the war, by which time many of the young widows had remarried.

The battalion arrived in Liverpool on October 6 and moved to Bramshott Camp on the Salisbury Plain where it was broken up and the men reassigned for duties with other units. On October 9, Frank was sent to the 12th Battalion, a holding battalion. On November 12, 1916, Pte. Fumerton was transferred to the 3rd Battalion for service overseas. He arrived in France on November 14.

Thomas Cummings and Leo Corr both sailed with Frank to England. All three were sent to the 3rd Battalion and all landed in France on November 14. Cummings went directly to the battalion and was killed on January 26, 1917. Corr and Fumerton were both sent to the 1st Canadian Entrenching Battalion[2] from November 14 to March 22, 1917, when they both joined the 3rd Battalion in the field. Leo Corr was killed on May 3.

Frank joined the 3rd Battalion on March 24, 1917. He was in time for the last minute preparations and participation in the Battle for Vimy

Ridge. He was with the battalion when it moved onto the Douai Plain and into the trenches facing the slowly retreating Germans. On Thursday, July 5, 1917, during an intense artillery volley, Frank Fumerton was killed by shell-fire. He had not yet reached his twentieth birthday. His body was recovered from the trenches at the Mont Forêt Quarries where he died, and laid to rest in the Aux Rietz cemetery. It was later moved to La Targette Military Cemetery

The Almonte Gazette in its issue of July 27, 1917, had the following item in its "Carleton Place News" section:

> The casualty list of Saturday last contained the name of Pte. Frank Fumerton, son of Mr. R.A. Fumerton, Carleton Place. Frank enlisted with the 130th, and went overseas with that battalion. In England he was transferred to the 75th and went over to France. He made the supreme sacrifice on July 5th, being killed in action.

[2] Each division was allotted an "entrenching battalion" as an advanced reinforcement unit to which infantry and engineer reinforcements were posted pending their assignment to their respective battalions or field companies. During their stay in the entrenching battalion, personnel were employed in the construction and repair of trenches and roads and similar maintenance duties.

Col. G.W.L. Nicholson, Canadian Expeditionary Force 1914-1919 (Ottawa: Queen's Printer, 1962).

Pte. Frank Fumerton, regimental number 787323, of the 3rd Battalion, 1st Central Ontario Regiment, is buried in La Targette British Cemetery, Neuville-St Vaast, Pas de Calais, France. The cemetery was begun at the end of April 1917 and used by field ambulances and fighting units until September 1918. There are 650 World War I graves, of which more than forty contain unidentified bodies.

The *Carleton Place Herald* contains the following notice in its July 2, 1918, edition:

In Memoriam

Fumerton—In loving memory of Pte. Frank Fumerton. Killed in action at St. Eloi, France, July 5, 1917.

He sleeps not in his native land,
But 'neath a foreign sky.
Far from the mother who loved him dear,
In a hero's grave he lies.

Sweet be your rest, my son so dear,
'Tis sweet to breathe your name;
In life I loved you very dear
In death I do the same.

Sister Belle

In its edition of March 4, 1919, The *Herald* reported:

Memorial Service at St. James

Last Sunday evening the Honor Roll presented by Mr. W.A. Nichols to St. James Church was hung in the church, and a memorial service for those members of the congregation who had given their lives for the Empire, Justice and Freedom, was held. The Honor Roll contains 74 names, of whom four are Nursing Sisters. Nine were Killed in Action viz. Cecil Bryce, T. Cummings, H. Dowdall, Geo. Fanning, F. Fumerton, Geo. Hudson, Percy Moore, T. Reynolds and A. Simons. One died of injuries, Capt. Sterne T. Edwards. One died of wounds, H. Eastwood. One is missing, W. Lewis, and one was a prisoner of war, now repatriated, Walter Rogers. Returned soldiers paraded in a body to the church . . .

Chapter Twenty

MEDIC!!

Members of the Canadian Army Medical Corps went overseas with the First Contingent and were among the first into battle. Medical staff with No. 2 Stationary Hospital were the only Canadian troops who became eligible for the 1914 Star, sometimes called the Mons Star. To receive it a person had to serve in France or Belgium between August 5, 1914, and midnight on November 23, 1914. The 1st Canadian Division did not arrive in France until February 16, 1915. Those medical troops beat the infantry into the war zone.

The Medical Corps served wherever Canadian troops were sent—England, northwest Europe, the Middle East, Dardanelles, Siberia and northern Russia. They maintained their own identity even when under British command. Their efficiencies in the treatment of wounds and their strict attention to preventive medicine against epidemic diseases were the envy of the Allies. The Canadian Army was the only force during the Great War to be 100 per cent inoculated against typhoid fever, a disease that ran rampant throughout other armies. In comparison, only a handful of Canadian soldiers ever came down with it. The Corps employed 1,351 medical officers, 1,886 Nursing Sisters and 12,243 field medics and orderlies. One of these field medics, serving overseas with the No. 3 Canadian Field Ambulance, was Pte. Wesley Albert Peever of Carleton Place.

C.A.M.C

WESLEY ALBERT PEEVER

After leaving school, Wesley Peever was trained as a spinner with one of the noted Carleton Place woollen mills. He enlisted in Carleton Place on July 19, 1916, and was sent to Barriefield for training and enrollment into the Queen's Ambulance Corps, sponsored by Queen's University. As his next of kin, he gave the name of his aunt, Mrs. M.R. Green of Carleton Place.

At his physical examination he was recorded as eighteen years, four months old, swearing to being born on March 10, 1898, in Carp, Ontario. He was a member of the Methodist Church and he was described as having a medium complexion, blue eyes and brown hair. His height was not recorded but his weight of 126 lbs was. He had a linear scar on the right side of his forehead that he said was the result of an accident in childhood.

A month after Wesley's enrolment, the *Carleton Place Herald* noted, in its August 15, 1916, paper:

> Ptes. H. Menzies, A. McFarlane, W. Coyles. H. Sinclair, D. Emerson, W. Peevers [*sic*], W. Morphy, A. Houston and S. Houston of the Queen's Ambulance Corps, Barriefield, spent a few days at their respective homes here last week.

It was one of his last visits home before shipping out. The Queen's Ambulance left Halifax aboard the S.S. *Grampian* on October 26, 1916, and arrived in the United Kingdom, at Liverpool, on November 5. Having already been trained, they were immediately sent to France on November 29 and Wesley was transferred to the No. 3 Canadian Field Ambulance on December 12. Before going overseas, Wesley made a pay allotment of $20 a month to Mrs. Jennie Dulmage which was later changed to Eliza Peever in care of the Inspector of Public Charities and Prisons, Toronto, as guardian.

Wesley was too late for the Battle of the Somme, but he was in plenty of time to provide medical services for the 1st Brigade of the 1st Division at Vimy Ridge. A memorandum in the unit's historical record outlines its mission immediately after the battle. The memorandum is dated April 12, 1917, and orders:

> . . . No. 3 Field Ambulance clearing the left sector, composed of the 1st, 4th, 7th and 5th Canadian Battalions.

The clearing will be done from the Battalion Aid Posts to the Advanced Dressing Stations of the respective Field Ambulances. From the Advanced Dressing Stations the clearing will be done along the Tram Line to ARIAN.

The M.O.s of the various battalions have been informed as to these arrangements.

About 50 yards from the ADS of No. 3 Fd Amb a well has been found in a deep dug-out which gives an adequate supply of water for this station.

Capt. Kenny, M.O. 10th Cdn Bn reports this water fit for use.

The nominal roll of the 3rd Field Ambulance, which was kept up to date monthly, shows 535033 Pte. Peever, W.A., written in for the first time on December 12, 1916. His name was recorded every month thereafter until July 31, 1918. On August 31, 1917, he was reported as "evac gassed," and on October 1, 1917, he was listed as "evac wounded." The unit records show his service: "B" Section, former trade—spinner; date of birth—1898; joined the unit on 13.12.16 [December 13, 1916] from Base Depot; next of kin—Mrs. E.J. Peever, Carleton Place; Methodist. This was all the front line unit needed to know if he became a casualty.

Hill 70

The Canadian assault on Hill 70, where Wesley Peever was gassed, was supposed to be a "killing by artillery."[1] Nine field brigades of artillery supported the infantry assault of the 1st and 2nd Canadian Divisions. Supplementing the barrage was 160 machine-guns. At 4:25 a.m. on August 15, just as dawn was breaking, the artillery began pounding away with a very effective rolling barrage. Careful planning paid off and the Canadian forces captured this strategic position located on the northern approaches to the city of Lens. They also captured the western part of the city, gaining considerable ground and denying the enemy free transport of fresh troops to Flanders. They were responsible for 9,198 casualties.

On the night of August 17–18, the Germans shelled the Canadian artillery batteries of the 1st and 2nd Field Brigades with the newly

---

[1] Comment attributed to Gen. A.G.L. McNaughton in British Official History.

acquired "Yellow Cross" (mustard gas)—a blistering agent they had first used in July. The Canadian Field Artillery gunners suffered heavily. When the droplets of gas fogged the goggles of their respirators some removed the face-pieces. They quickly became casualties. Soldiers whose clothes had been sprinkled with the liquid sought shelter, contaminating others in gas-proof shelters. In some cases it took a day or more for the gas to take effect, but by noon on August 21 the two artillery brigades had suffered 183 casualties.

Wesley Peever's personal records show that he was admitted to No. 7 General Hospital, the Queen's University Hospital, on August 21, diagnosed as "having been shelled and gassed—severe."

The historical records of No. 3 Canadian Field Ambulance contain the following narrative concerning the action in which the unit was involved during the night of August 17–18. It was written by the doctor commanding the medical station:

> Gas Shell Attack on Night of 17th–18th Aug 1917
>
> At 11 p.m. on 17th August the enemy launched a gas-shell attack bombardment on the area comprising the village of LOOS, thence southward 1500 yards and eastward as far as the Double Crassier.
>
> The bombardment was of great intensity, and so rapidly did the thousands of shells come whirling over that it gave one the impression that they were being fired from automatic machines.
>
> The Gas Shells were of the new Yellow Cross variety, about which so much literature had recently been circulated and for which we had been fully prepared, and these were mixed with a good proportion of 5.g H.E.[high explosive] Shells.
>
> The bombardment lasted from 11 p.m. (17th inst.) to 3 a.m. (18th inst.) and again from 3:30 a.m. in slightly less violence to 5 a.m.
>
> No. 3 Post came in for a good deal of attention from these Gas Shells, as well as the A.D.S. ST PATRICKS, a report from the officer in charge of which station is worthy of publication:—

' . . . The early evening was quiet and I lay down at about 10:45 p.m. At 11 p.m., a furious enemy bombardment opened, followed quickly by our own. I went out twice in the next half-hour and watched the shelling. I noticed no gas shells at this time.

Orders were issued that if Gas Shells were thrown all men in surrounding dug-outs were to come in to the A.D.S. which we knew to be gas-proof, from previous bombardment. Our gas blankets were wet and adjusted, and I lay down.

Was awakened by sentry at 2:30 a.m. who said that gas shells were raining in, and had been for some time. All the men at the A.D.S. were inside . . .

I went outside and could hear plenty of gas shells bursting, but could detect no "mustard odor" and concluded that only Phosgene Gas was being thrown. At 3 a.m. a squad brought in a case from 1st Bn. R.A.P. (Regimental Aid Post) . . . These bearers were showing effects of gas—nausea and shortness of breath only—and there was no "mustard odor" detected. The patient had worn his mask down and was alright. The bearers reported that there was so much heavy shelling and gas around the R.A.P. that they decided to come right through. They wore their masks part way but wires were down in the trench and the alternate flashes and intense darkness made it impossible to see so they took off their masks. They reported that three other cases were on their way and that the Pioneers said more were coming in.

At 3:30 a.m. I went with a runner to the tunnel. We wore our masks on starting but after falling into a new hole in trench and several times getting tangled in loose wires, we took the masks off our eyes and went as quickly as we could. We waited in a culvert as the shelling was increasing and heard many gas shells and smelt an odor resembling the odor emitted from an old root cellar. Our eyes smarted a little. I found 7 cases [wounded men] lying in the tunnel.

At the 1st Bn R.A.P. there were 5 cases and only 1 squad of bearers, so I sent a request to the O.C. No. 3 Field Amb. to turn out all bearers to clear these cases, which was done. I then returned to ST PATRICKS at about 8 a.m. after having advised the M.O. 1st Cdn Bn to move his Aid Post forward to the old Aid Post vacated by the 7th Cdn Bn.

About 9:30 a.m. a report came from 107th Pioneer Bn. that men were suffering intensely with their eyes, and at the same time a runner came over from No. 3 Post to say that there were a lot of men lying on the road blinded and vomiting, including our relay squad. I took a car and went to No. 3 Post and found 36 cases (34 gassed, including O.C. 1st Bn. C.F.A.). I cleared these cases direct to MAROC. It was from the clothing of the men of the 1st Batt. that I got a first, strong, mustard odor—nipping the eyes. I then returned to ST PATRICKS, which I found full of 107th Pioneers gassed and a rather strong odor of gas pervaded.

I made all patients undress in the trench and come in naked. All orderlies washed their arms and heads with strong soda sol. and took 30 grs of Soda. Each patient was then washed from head to foot in soda, including eyes. He was then given 30 grs Soda internally and sent out in pyjamas on a stretcher.

During the afternoon about 60 cases, gunners chiefly, were cleared from No. 3 Post. Two orderlies of the A.D.S. were evacuated on the 19th—one rather badly blistered. The first blistering I saw was late in the afternoon. Intense pain in the eyes and nausea were the most prominent symptoms—so marked injection of the ocular conjunctivae and increased swelling of lids.

The system of treatment to which the gassed cases were subjected at the A.D.S., preparations for which had previously been carried out in expectation of an attack by these shells, proved of exceptional value in the later treatment of the cases, and called forth considerable comment from the Os.C. [officers commanding] Casualty Clearing Stations, at which they arrived in comparative comfort and showed a minimum of blistering.

Nearly all the bearers of the Ambulance suffered from the effects of the gas shells, as they had to keep the posts clear of cases and in order to carry in the pitch darkness over [an] exceptionally obstructive piece [of] ground it was found imperative to remove the Respirator from the eyes, the nose-clip and mouth-piece only being used. In all 66 bearers were gassed, necessitating the evacuation of 54 of them—including the Sergt-Major. The Commanding officer also suffered considerably from the effects of the gas—'My eyes by this time [2 p.m. 18th inst] were severely inflamed and the pain was intense; the eye-lids were very edematous, and the pain compelled me to go bed.'

It was found that a man could live in the gas without noticing any effects whatever for several hours—and then the effects would come on very suddenly, with violent pain in the eyes.

No deaths occurred in the cases of gassing whilst in the hands of the Ambulance.

> A. Donaldson
> LtCol. C.A.M.C.
> O.C. No. 3 Canadian Field Ambulance

Pte. Wesley Peever was admitted on October 6, 1917, to No. 12 Convalescent Depot at Aubengue and from there, on October 19, to a rest camp at Boulogne. He was discharged Class "A" on October 21 and sent back to his unit on October 30, arriving back with No. 3 Field Ambulance the next day, October 31. He saw action at Passchendaele during November 1917, but in December, starting on the 14th, he was given fourteen days leave in England. Returning to the unit before the new year, Wesley stayed with them for the rest of the war, earning the Good Conduct Badge on July 19, 1918.

The need for medical facilities did not abruptly cease with the armistice. Wesley Peever did not get back to England until March 19, 1919, leaving for Canada aboard R.M.S. *Baltic* on April 29. His arrival in Canada on May 7 was noted by the *Herald,* issue of May 13, in the list of returned men that was by then printed weekly.

Wesley was discharged in Barriefield on May 9, but the effects of his gassing remained. At his discharge medical examination, it was recorded that "gas resulted in chronic bronchitis/received wound August 18, 1917, at Hill 70." He was having some trouble taking a deep breath. His birth date was now listed as March 10, 1899; he had obviously lied about his age when he enlisted in order to be accepted, at age seventeen.

Pervasive mustard gas does not let its victims off easily. The *Carleton Place Herald*, in the edition of January 19, 1921, reported the deaths of Wesley Peever and Ross Simpson, attributing their premature passing to the Great War:

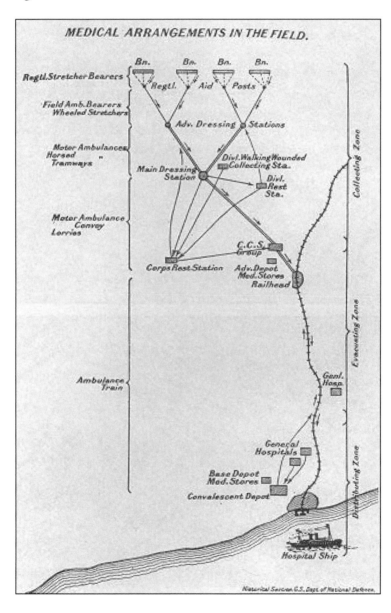

Two Young Soldiers Pass Away

Pte. Wesley Peever

Among our Christmas visitors was Wesley Peever, who took an office job in Montreal in the fall after spending the summer on a farm in this neighbourhood; he being a graduate of the Taber Business College; having taken a commercial course after returning from France, and no one would think who saw him then that the last call would sound so soon for him. But so it was. A kidney infection necessitated an operation in the hospital and the result did not prove a success and collapse followed. The remains were brought here for burial, his latter home, although his father, John Peever, is deceased, and his mother is an invalid in Brockville. The members of Stella Lodge took charge of the body and conveyed it to the home of Mr. Samuel Dulmage, Mr. Peever having allied himself with the Oddfellows only last spring. The funeral took place Saturday afternoon to the Methodist Church, the Oddfellows, the O.Y.B. and the members of the G.W.V.A. turning out in a body forming quite a large procession. The pallbearers were all triple-link vets—Jas. Williams, Lorne Fraser, Herb. Bennett, Geo. Burnie, Herb. Sinclair and Roy Saunders—and at the church door the casket was received by four members of the young men's class, of which Wesley was a member when here . . . The church was filled to the doors . . . The remains were placed in the vault at the 8th Line Ramsay cemetery.

The army sent Wesley's medals to his mother, Eliza J. Peever, in care of Mrs Mary A. Green, 214 Union Street, Kingston. It was noted that he was the only son of his widowed mother.

Chapter Twenty-One

RAILROADERS

In 1914, Canada, foreseeing problems in the transport of supplies over a broad front, offered to raise railway units for service in France. The offer was rebuffed by the Imperial General Staff. However, when they learned, slowly, that their motor transport was not capable of the job, they condescended to let Canada raise two railway battalions complete with rails for service in France.

The Canadian Overseas Railway Construction Corps was composed of 540 selected volunteers from the Canadian Pacific Railway. Recruiting was completed by May 15, 1915. All the men were experienced construction workers. Each had to pass a test as to his technical ability. This nucleus was to grow to thirteen battalions of Canadian Railway Troops, three battalions of Skilled Railway Employees, Railway Bridging Companies and Railway Company drafts and depots. In the last year of the war, there were 8,000 men in active construction work and another 4,000 on repair duties. These soldiers were responsible for the construction and maintenance of railways of all gauges, including light railways, in France and Belgium. Some were formed as Royal Engineer units but after the formation of the Corps of Canadian Railway, they became the responsibility of the Officer Commanding the Royal Canadian Engineers, although they were never a part of the Canadian Engineers military structure.

The equipment these troops brought with them had never been seen in Europe. Steam shovels, graders, cement mixers and thousands of specialized construction implements helped the corps lay 1,169 miles of heavy track and 1,404 miles of light track during one six-month period. They also built cement gun emplacements that could not have been con-  structed with manual labour. They expedited the delivery of supplies and manpower and eventually controlled all railway marshalling yards in France and Flanders.[1]

[1] Charles H. Stewart, *Overseas* (Toronto: Little & Stewart, 1970), p. 149.

One of these railroaders, a man from Carleton Place, was Sapper William Fraser. The railroad troops adopted the rank structure of the Canadian Engineers, hence the rank of sapper.

WILLIAM FRASER

William Fraser joined No. 1 Section of the Skilled Railway Employees (SRE) in Ottawa on January 4, 1917. This was a railway

 construction battalion. He gave his trade as "roundhouseman" and his qualification as a machinist's helper. On enlistment he gave his address as Pakenham and his next of kin his wife, Laura Elizabeth. He was assigned the regimental number of 2124809.

William was born in Dundee, Scotland, on September 2, 1872. At age forty-four, like most of the SRE, he was considerably older than the infantry enlistees. Being Scottish, he was also a staunch Presbyterian. At his enrolment medical examination he was found to weigh 121 lbs, stand 5' 6" tall with a dark complexion, light brown eyes and dark hair. He wore a full mustache.

These specialized troops needed no trades training. Nor was there a requirement for them to practise or perform rifle drill. They needed only to endure some military foot drill. They were paid their normal civilian working pay plus military pay of one dollar a day for engineers and yardmasters, 80 cents for firemen, 90 cents for conductors and mechanics and 70 cents for brakemen. The men of No. 1 Section SRE were transferred to No. 2 Section and on March 1, 1917, Spr. William Fraser was given a credit balance of $10 as a uniform allowance for the months of January and February.

No. 2 Section of the SRE, along with No. 13 Light Railway Operating Company which had been mobilized in Montreal on January 27, 1917, boarded His Majesty's Troopship, the S.S. *Grampian* in Halifax on April 16, 1917. They sailed two days later, and arrived in Liverpool on April 29. They were sent to Burfleet but, by May 7, 1917, were residents in the camp at Aldershot. The entire unit was sent on leave from 4:00 p.m. on May 11, 1917, to 9:00 p.m.

on May 17. When they returned for duty with the Royal Engineers of the British Expeditionary Force, they were credited with six days allowance of one shilling, nine pence, in lieu of rations.

At home, William's wife moved. On June 1, he officially changed her address to Carleton Place. On June 9, the Operating Company went to France aboard the S.S. *Viper*, but William was transferred to the Railway Troops Depot to take instruction in the operation, maintenance and repair of petrol-electric locomotives and petrol tractors. These courses were conducted at the school in Apple Pie Camp, Longmoor, Hants. Fraser went to France on July 9 and caught up with his unit on the 10th.

To follow William's activities in Flanders, reference is made to the War Diary of the No. 13 Light Railway Operating Company. They were at Coxyde, Belgium at the time of writing in August 1917:

> 23.8.17—Things running smooth. A game of baseball was played today between our boys and the 1st Canadian Casualty Clearing Station and we lost to the tune of 15 to 3. The first game of amusements since landing in France.
>
> 25.8—track blown up
>
> 26.8—Engine 1276 derailed. track in bad condition . . . shelled very badly this date. 14 cars ammunition moved up to Coxyde for safety.
>
> 27.8—heavy shelling at Coxyde. Track blown up.
>
> 29.8—Enemy shelling Coxyde very badly at 10 p.m.
>
> 30.8—Everything very quiet.
>
> 31.8—Still no broad gauge train in. Engine 1214 over on its side near aerodrome . . . shelled. Derailed one repair car and Engine 1300—one shell dropped in front of the tents.
>
> 1.9.17—1:30 a.m—Month started very badly for this unit. A shell struck a dug-out at Oost Dunkirk where there was four of our men in. Killing three and the fourth was badly shell shocked . . . Rained during the day. The three men were buried in the afternoon at Coxyde.
>
> 2.9—Fine day. Quiet as regards work.

9.9—125 men sent to XV Corps rest station and they need it for there wasn't much sleep to be had in the last camp owing to the continual bombardment each night.

10.9—Men ordered back from rest camp owing to us having orders to remove out to another area.

The Almonte Gazette of September 21 noted that, "Mrs. J.A. McIntosh received word last week that her brother, Pte. Wm. Fraser, had been killed in action. Pte Fraser was living at Packenham [*sic*] previous to enlistment."

In September several items of interest were printed in the Almonte Gazette, on the 21st:

> Messrs Bates and Innes are building a dam across the rapids just below the old one at Carleton Place. It will cost at least ten thousand dollars. The former dam which dates from the earliest Gilles period has become leaky and gives but lukewarm aid to the machinery of the factories.

And in the paper of September 28:

> The dining room of the Queen's Hotel building, Carleton Place, is being made into a school room, the accommodation in the public school building being insufficient.

> Lieut. Horace Brown of Carleton Place has been accepted in the R.N.A.S.

> A number of Masonic Lodges in Canada are providing each of its members who serve in the war with a Masonic passport, commending to the brotherly care of all Masons who find him in need of help. The passport will be printed in English, French and German, and will be carried in a folder attached to a belt to be worn next to the body.[2]

Spr. William Fraser was listed as killed in action on Saturday, September 1, 1917, at Rouen. The official commemoration has him belonging to the 13th Canadian Light Railway Operating Company, Canadian Railway Troops. He would not have recognized the name since the unit was reorganised in September, after his death, and the word "Canadian" was added only in November 1917. Fraser died while asleep in a dugout at Oost Dunkirk. He and two comrades were instantly killed when an enemy shell made a direct hit on the dugout.

Coxyde was about ten kilometres behind the front line. The cemetery had already been begun by French troops when they were relieved by the British in June

[2] A copy of one of these passports may be seen in the history of the Carleton Place Lodge written by Alexander (Sandy) Docker.

1917. The village was used for rest billets and was occasionally shelled, but the cemetery was found to be reasonably safe. It was used at night for the burial of the dead from the front line. There are over 1,500 1914–18 war dead commemorated at this site.

After his death, William's widow and five of their six children moved to 171 Frank Street in Ottawa and it was to that address his medals were sent. By then the oldest boy, Lawrence, was in England with a signals regiment training for action at the front. Laura received a special pension bonus of $80 and a gratuity of $100 for the loss of her husband.

Chapter Twenty-Two

PASSCHENDAELE

Passchendaele. For years after the Great War the very name struck shivers up the spines of the Canadian veterans who survived its particular horror.

I died in hell—
(They called it Passchendaele); my wound was slight
And I was hobbling back and a shell
Burst slick upon the duck-board; so I fell
Into the bottomless mud, and lost the light.
                                         Siegfried Sassoon

Passchendaele was just a small crossroads village in Flanders. The military operation that began in July 1917 was in fact known as Third Ypres.[1] The major involvement by Canadian Corps consisted of four attacks that took place from October 26 to November 10 and which became known as the Second Battle of Passchendaele.[2] Allied politicians decided that they could not end the war in 1917, but that they must keep the pressure on the Germans on the Western Front. The United States joined the fray on April 6 because of Germany's ruthless use of unrestricted submarine warfare. But there was little hope of any effective military help from the Americans before 1918. Then the Russian Revolution in mid-March introduced the strong possibility that Germany would mount a major offensive on the Eastern Front while Russia remained disorganized. Thus the Allies were faced with the realization that they must prosecute the war on the Western Front quite vigorously.

By the autumn of 1917, no other name was as synonymous with gruelling, bloody and bizarre battles as Passchendaele. Rain and artillery shells fell equally for four months straight. The killing ground rapidly disintegrated into a swampy quagmire. As the infantry struggled just to remain upright, let alone advance, tanks and horse-drawn artillery pieces simply disappeared into the quicksand-like muck. Even

[1] It was the third time that the same ground had been contested in a major offensive.

[2] The "first" battle had been waged by British, Australian and New Zealand troops during August. They were fought to a standstill by the German opposition.

the air was poisoned with the smell of the corpses of animals and men, and the permeating odour of mustard gas.

> Passchendaele was indeed a scene of strange and terrible happenings and strange anomalies. You might see men in full equipment sitting on the duckboards in the rain, fast asleep under shell fire. Many during the attacks were mired and drowned in swamps filled with barbed wire. On one occasion Hun prisoners loaded belts for us voluntarily, while waiting for escort to the rear area. A Canadian M.G. officer, severely wounded, was carried for miles on the slippery mule tracks by 6 German prisoners without escort. No one would have been any the wiser had they left him to die in the mud and they would have had an easier and safer trip back to the prison cage. One feature of the Passchendaele campaign was the absence of cover. Except for immediate need or when possible as a shelter from the rain, cover was forgotten and everybody stumbled in the open. The bad footing lent a sort of aimlessness to one's gait and added to the general inanity of the scene. In no other campaign of the war was one so conscious of an insistent undertone of helplessness.[3]

Historians and political scholars now argue that Passchendaele need never have happened. But it did! And after it was over the territorial gains won in those four desperate months, solidified by Canadian troops in October and November, had cost 275,000 Allied and 200,000 German casualties. In three days in March 1918, the gained ground was all taken back by the Germans.

Following their success at Vimy Ridge, the Canadians remained in the area of Arras. They continued operations designed to keep the Germans occupied there and away from the planned offensive in Flanders.

But there was Canadian involvement in Third Ypres from its start. The battle opened on June 7 with the explosion of nineteen huge mines under Messines Ridge. A total of nearly one million pounds of high explosive was used to blow up eight-and-a-half miles of front line trenches. The explosion was reportedly heard in London. The 1st

---

[3] Captain Walter Moorhouse, 4th CMR/Cdn. M. Gun Corp., in *Poor Bloody Murder*, ed. by Gordon Reid (Oakville, Ontario: Mosaic Press, 1980), p. 169.

Canadian Tunnelling Company fired one mine and the 3rd Company fired four others. The Germans were shocked and overwhelmed. British infantry held the entire ridge within a few hours.

After weeks of delay, a second attack was launched in July. The initial artillery barrage not only warned the enemy that the British were coming, but it also ground the battlefield into vehicle-eating potholes, filling the air with dust. That very night the summer rains started and the infantry began their struggle through an impassable swamp. German riflemen and machine gunners, firing from fortified concrete pillboxes, inflicted terrible casualties.

In this morass, the British forces bogged down. For the next four months negligible advances were made. Early in October, with the British near exhaustion, Field-Marshall Sir Douglas Haig, the British commander-in-chief, was determined to make at least one more drive. The Canadian Corps was brought up and ordered to relieve the decimated 2nd Anzac Corps in the sector near Ypres. The front trenches that the Canadians occupied on October 16 ran from the Valley of the Stroombeek to between Gravenstafel Ridge and the heights about Passchendaele. It was virtually the same front line the Canadians had held in April 1915 before the gas attack and fight at Hooper's House that cost the first of so many Carleton Place lives. But hardly a trace of villages, woods or farmhouse remained in the unrecognizable ridges and hollows.

The Canadians were ordered to prepare to attack and capture Passchendaele. Lt.-Gen. Sir Arthur Currie, commanding the Canadian Corps, inspected the sodden battlefield. It was littered with thousands of rotting corpses and had become a sea of yellow mud that would drown any soldier who strayed off the duckboards leading forward. He reported that the intended operation could not be successful without enormous cost. His protestations were overruled. After all, the Canadian Corps owned the only successes of the dismal Allied war in 1917. Vimy, Arleux, Fresnoy and Hill 70 had all fallen to Canadian attackers. Their reputation of success was due to efficiency and excellent planning.

Currie's meticulous preparations began with a massive road-building programme. Canadian Engineers and Pioneer Battalions, working just a little faster than the German artillery could destroy each day's progress, set off to establish artillery battery positions and repair and extend plank roads. They suffered some 1,500 casualties even before the fighting began. Currie realized that the men could not, as was traditional, move up to "jumping off" positions just before the battle was to begin. They would be exhausted after struggling through knee-deep mud and, besides, there was no real area for rest in the entire sector. So he had his infantry move into position a couple of days before the attack to get as much rest as possible before "Zero Hour."

Originally planned for October 24, Currie postponed the initial attack until the 29th. Haig, however, insisted that they be ready for October 26. At 5:40 a.m. on the 26th, the Canadians went over the top. The 3rd Canadian Division attacked Bellevue Spur and advanced some 1200 yards toward Passchendaele. The 4th Division attacked the Passchendaele Ridge. Despite many individual acts of heroism and bravery, the 3rd Division could not achieve its objective. They dug in to consolidate the little gain they had and await the next phase of the battle. The attacking battalions had lost 2,481 men.[4]

The 4th Canadian Mounted Rifles of the 8th Brigade was one of the assaulting battalions of the 3rd Division and the only one to achieve its desired objective for the day. In bitter fighting, they captured Wolf Copse and secured that part of the line for the 8th Brigade. The battalion's narrative of events for this action begins on October 15:

> For a period of about three weeks previous to the 15th of October, the Battalion had been in training at Cambligneul for the attack on Mericourt. The success in Flanders caused the training to be cancelled on October 4th and the Battalion was warned to become mobile on the 10th Inst.
>
> On Oct. 15th the Battalion moved by train from Savy Station to Caestre. The battalion for this move was 34 officers and 910 other ranks strong. From Caestre the battalion marched to the Koorten Loop area and commenced the special training required by the fighting in store. A general warning order and 'Instructions for the Offensive' were received on October 18th.
>
> On October 19th, Lieut. Col. Patterson went forward with the

[4] Desmond Morton and J.L. Granatstein, *Marching to Armageddon–Canadians and the Great War 1914-1919* (Toronto: Lester & Orpen Dennys Limited, 1989), p. 168.

Brigade Major to Abraham Heights where the 2nd Anzac Corps was holding, and examined the position in front of Passchendaele, which the Battalion was to take. The following day, Lieut. A. Clarke went forward with six observers, for the purpose of cutting wire in preparation for the battalion's attack. On October the 20th the Company Commanders and senior N.V.Os [*sic*: NCOs) also went forward and took a preliminary view of the ground. Plans were received and maps made.

On the 18th, a warning order was received from the 8th C.I.B. [Canadian Infantry Brigade], which stated that the 3rd Canadian Division would relieve the 1st New Zealand Division, commencing October 21st. On October the 20th, at 6.00 p.m., Operation Order of the 9th C.I.B., under whose administration the Battalion was placed for a phase of the forward move, was received. At 1.30 a.m., Oct. 21st, the battalion marched out from its billets at Koorten Loop and arrived at Caestre at 3.30 a.m. they did not entrain until 7.40 a.m.

Blankets were stored under Brigade supervision at Hondeghem, the men carrying fighting kit, greatcoats and packs.

The Battalion proceeded by train to Ypres, the Transport by march route to Salvation Corner, North of Ypres. The Battalion marched from Ypres to the Wieltje Area. On arriving, they found that the units they were to relieve were apparently to be relieved the following day. After considerable difficulty and delay, the battalion was accommodated towards evening in tents and bivouacs east of St Jean. Just at nightfall enemy planes bombed the area and wounded Lieut. Waddell, the Signal Officer, Sgt. Morris, the Signal Sergeant and killed one runner.

The following day, Oct. 22nd, the battalion moved in the morning under Operation Order received from the 9th C.I.B. to California Trench, with headquarters in Pommern Castle, and relieved the 2nd Otago battalion and the 2nd Auklands. Carrying parties reported to Bilge Dump. On the 23rd, under further Operation Order of the 9th C.I.B. the battalion moved to the Support Area with headquarters in Cluster House. The Battalion underwent rather severe enemy shelling and casualties were suffered. On the night of the 23rd the battalion came under the administration of the 8th C.I.B.

On October the 24th, the battalion moved from the support area, under orders of the 8th C.I.B., to the front line relieving the 1st C.M.R. Bn. and with headquarters in Kronprinz Farm. A heavy rain had fallen throughout the day and was still falling when the Battalion commenced to move forward. The ground was almost impassable, owing to the shell holes, filled with water, the swamps and the sticky mud. The guides from the 1st C.M.R. Bn. lost their way in many cases and the relief was not completed until 5.00 a.m. of Oct. 25th. Rations were got up, but no water.

Casualties occurred during the relief, including Lieut. J.R. Woods (killed), Lieut. J.D. Campbell, (killed) and Lieut. A.D. McDonald (wounded) and 15 other ranks.

On Oct. 25th the battalion in the line had their first opportunity of seing [sic] their front and objectives. The weather having cleared, the men had a chance to dry out. Operation Order of the 8th C.I.B. was received this night for the attack the following morning. The battalion issued its Operation Order . . . Rations were late in arriving but no water arrived in time for the attack[5]

Oct. 26—Zero hour was set for 5.40 a.m. The Battalion was assembled in front and in the rear of the original line by 5.45 a.m. . . . with each company advancing with one platoon extended as a screen and the other two platoons in a rough column of sections.

At Zero hour the barrage was laid down sharp on time, but was erratic and not uniform, causing a number of casualties in our left leading company. Simultaneously with the barrage, a heavy rain commenced to fall, which greatly enhanced the difficult conditions of the ground.

At Zero hour the enemy opened a light barrage on our front line and supports and a heavy machine gun fire on the front. Four officers and a number of other ranks became casualties almost at the outset.

[5] This meant that the men went forward with empty water bottles.

The leading waves suffered severely from rifle and machine gun fire but after desperate fighting, secured the first line of 'pill boxes'.

Then developed a hard fight for the Wallemonen-Bellevue line of 'pill boxes'. The supporting companies with two Vickers Machine Gun teams, pushed forward and our Intermediate Objective was reached sharp on the time with the barrage. At this point it was found that the Battalions on both our flanks had been held up, exposing us to devastating fire from enemy 'pill boxes' on both our flanks, especially our right. One company of the Royal Naval Division on our left side-slipped behind our left companies, thus leaving their own objective 'pill boxes' unengaged. This Company later assisted in the consolidation and junction on left and then rejoined their unit.

One company of the 1st C.M.R. Bn. moved into the front line when it was vacated by our troops at Zero (hour).

Portions of two platoons of our Battalion penetrated as far as Woodland Copse but were so exposed to enemy fire and so reduced by casualties that it was found necessary to withdraw. The Battalion, after many fine efforts to gain a footing in spite of enfilade fire it was exposed to, was forced to commence consolidation on the high ground in the immediate vicinity of our intermediate objective. The enemy here made desperate efforts to dislodge and prevent us from consolidating on the ridge. He opened a heavy barrage on this position, which gradually died down and the position was made good at approximately 11.00 a.m. A deep, continuous trench was successfully laid, junctions being made with our flanks. Major Hart, commanding 'B' Co., reported to Bn. Headquarters that it was impossible to advance further without reinforcements. 'C' Company was without officers, five officers only of the sixteen who entered the action remaining and a large proportion of the N.C.Os. had become casualties. One of the Vickers guns attached to us had also been put out of action . . . The location of the right flank was somewhat obscure, as the 43rd battalion had met with a serious check . . .

At 2.00 p.m., the 52nd Bn., passing through the 43rd Bn., developed an attack on our right flank and succeeded in dislodging the enemy from the 'pill boxes' which had been causing us serious losses, and the position on the right was made good. When this action was completed, a junction of our right flank with the 52nd Bn. was made.

About 2.00 p.m. two companies of the 1st C.M.R. Bn. moved into position in our original front and support trenches and four guns of the 8th M.G. Coy, under Sgt. Rook, were sent to our new position. At 8.00 p.m., the three companies of the 1st C.M.R. Bn. were relieved by three companies of the 2nd C.M.R. Bn. Scattered shelling and harassing fire persisted throughout the day and night but through the splendid efforts of the Battalion Chaplain, Capt. W.H. Davis, and the Stretcher Bearers, our ground was cleared of the wounded.[6]

Although several counter attacks were attempted during the day, none of which were permitted to develop, none were attempted during the night, our patrols which covered the ground in advance of our outposts succeeded in capturing an enemy patrol of four men.

Oct. 27—The Battalion remained throughout the day secure in its position. A number of casualties were suffered through enemy shell fire but the work of rescuing the wounded and burying the dead was proceeded with and completed by nightfall of this date. The 2nd C.M.R. Bn. arrived for relief at 9.00 p.m. and in spite of the severe losses in the battalion, a strong and well organized position was handed over.

[6] Another, more complete account of this event.

"Late in the afternoon by common, uncommunicated consent, without notification or sanction, both sides suddenly decided on a temporary armistice to look after their wounded and dead. It was one of those things, arranged without agreement. It just happened. It suited both sides. And illustrates the curious turn of events. Padre W.H. Davis was searching in No Man's Land for Canadian casualties when suddenly large numbers of Germans got out of their trenches and commenced to search for wounded. When they found a wounded Canadian they would mark his position by sticking his rifle in the mud and placing his helmet on it; or carry him to a pill-box which soon became a clearing station where the troops of both sides forgathered and exchanged the wounded. Since sunrise the fighting had been bitter; each side trying to create as much havoc as possible among the men whom they now were trying to succour. It was a rational paradox for the men in the line. But the unofficial truce did not last long. Some young, enthusiastic forward-observing officer of the gunners could not resist reporting the existence of so many targets and soon the guns opened on the weary missionaries who had to postpone their rescuing."

Captain S.G. Bennett, M.C., *The 4th Canadian Mounted Rifles 1914-1919* (Toronto: Murray Printing Company, 1926), p. 85.

The casualties up to and including this date totalled as follows:

	Killed	Wounded	D of W	Missing	Wd & Miss	Total
Officers	8	9	0	—	—	17
Other Ranks	58	194	1	18	3	274

In the action, 175 unwounded prisoners and 25 wounded prisoners were taken by us. Seven heavy and five light machine guns were captured, but owing to the conditions of ground, were not brought out.[7]

One of the seriously wounded by machine-gun fire was Cpl. Herb Eastwood.

HERBERT JOHN EASTWOOD

Herbert Eastwood was the son of Mr. and Mrs. J.N. Eastwood and the husband of May Rachael of Cache Bay. He was born in Pembroke on December 27, 1889. He worked as a telegraph operator for the Canadian Pacific Railroad before he joined the 130th Battalion in Carleton Place on December 7, 1915.

At enlistment, Herb was described as twenty-six years old, 5' 6 " tall weighing 138 pounds. He was clean-shaven with a fair complexion, blue eyes and medium brown hair. He was an adherent to the Church of England.

The 130th recruits did most of their basic training locally, primarily doing route marches through Valley communities, while the battalion sought volunteers to bring the unit up to overseas strength. It was noted in the *Carleton Place Herald* of May 9, 1916, that:

> Sergeant Herb. Eastwood arrived home from Montreal Sunday morning, where he has been attending the Physical Training and Bayonet Fighting class. In the final examinations held on May 3 and 4, he qualified with good percentage.

And in the edition of May 23 was the following item:

> On Thursday evening, May 18th, the officers and members of L.O.B.A. Mississippi Lodge 122 waited upon Sergt. Herb. Eastwood at his mother's home and presented him with a magnificent wrist watch and the following address:

[7] Historical Records, The 4th Canadian Mounted Rifles, National Archives.

Sergt Herb Eastwood.

Dear Friend—It is with feelings of deepest regret we meet tonight to bid you 'farewell' and 'God speed' on your journey from us and this your home town. Still we cannot but feel pride in your unselfishness and heroism in answering the call of your Empire, and enlisting to serve your King and country and right. We are reminded so often of the inscription on the South African monument, 'Take up the sword of Justice now,' and it is in the holy cause of Justice that so many young men like yourself throughout Canada are challenged to take up the sword of Justice. They do not love war, they revolt at it; but Justice was violated when Germany invaded Belgium and warred against every other law-abiding nation. There was nothing for Britain to do but take up the challenge. Britain's lead was Canada's excuse. In going away from us we shall miss you. Oh so much; miss your cheery willingness to be of service in all our doings. But we are proud of your friendship and your great courage to leave so much that is dear and make life worth while, and take your stand in defence of right. We wish you, dear friend, to take with you this wrist watch as a slight token of our appreciation and a remembrance from the Ladies Orange association, your dear mother's particular friends, and you may feel assured we shall do all we can to cheer and comfort her, also your father and your own family. We hope and pray you may be spared to return to them and to us in the near future. Until then all we can say is 'God Be With You Till We Meet Again.'

Signed on behalf of
the Ladies Orange Association

On July 18, the *Herald* noted that, "Bombardier Eastwood is making a home call at present"; and then on August 29:

Sergt Eastwood of the 130th Batt. is making a farewell visit to relatives in Carleton Place, and incidentally looking for a dozen or more recruits from the vicinity to bring the company up to full strength. The Battalion will leave shortly for overseas, and as the men are in fine fettle they are anxious that the ranks be full. Anyone desirous of enlisting may see Sergt. Eastwood at any time or find him at the home of his parents near the station.

Eastwood and the 130th Battalion embarked aboard the S.S. *Lapland* for Britain on September 23, 1916, and arrived in Liverpool on October 6. The battalion was broken up and Herb went to the 12th Battalion to await orders as a reinforcement to some other Canadian Expeditionary Force infantry battalion at the front. He was made an acting sergeant with pay on October 6, but then reduced to the ranks again on October 10. He was appointed to the rank of corporal on January 5, 1917, and then went to France with the 4th Canadian Mounted Rifles on January 20. The 4th C.M.R. urgently required reinforcements. On June 2, 1916, they had held their position under a bombardment of four-and-a-half hours until the battalion was virtually wiped out. They lost twenty-one officers and 619 other ranks that had to be replaced to restore them as an effective fighting unit.

On July 10, 1917, the Canadian Corps, under their new commander, newly knighted Sir Arthur Currie, replaced a British Corps in trenches looking across No Man's Land to Lens and the hills of Sallaumines and Hill 70. Corporal Eastwood missed the battle for Hill 70 that August because on July 14 he received by a shell wound to the forehead. He was not released from No.6 Casualty Clearing Station until August 30, rejoining the Mounted Rifles on September 1. In the absence of conscription, and an adequate supply of reinforcements, Canadian wounded soldiers were sent back to the front time and again until the medical officers determined that they were too mutilated to be cannon fodder any longer.

Although they retained the name "Mounted Rifles," the thirteen World War I battalions with that name were organized as infantry units. They hardly ever saw a horse that wasn't pulling an artillery gun, let alone ride one into battle.

By the middle of the afternoon of October 26, the battalion was holding its position on Passchendaele Ridge. They signalled to aeroplanes by waving helmets, since it was too wet to light their water-soaked flares. By this time, the battle seemed over for both sides. There was spasmodic shelling for the remainder of the day, then the line settled down, ready for the anticipated counterattacks. At dusk, out-posts were established and, at 10:00 p.m., one of the posts reported a body of troops gathering in the vicinity of Source Trench, 500 yards to the east of Wallemolen and on the battalion's immediate left front. Remaining cool and calculating, the Canadian defenders trained their Lewis guns on the intruders. The men were ordered to stand fast until the party was within 100 yards. Then the command to fire was given. Shooting thus, over ranged rifle-sights, resembled musketry drill. This unusual reception so completely disorganized the enemy that they withdrew leaving behind their dead and wounded. The rest of the night was fairly quiet.

The battalion paid heavily for its part in this first stage of the cap-ture of Passchendaele; an enormous sacrifice for so little ground gained. There were seventeen casualties among the officers; eight were killed and nine wounded. There were only four of the attacking troops who escaped untouched, and some of them had most uncanny escapes. Three-hundred-and-four other ranks were killed, wounded or missing, or evacuated suffering from exposure. The four hours of fighting accounted for half the total strength of officers and a third of all the men. Again the battalion gave more than its share of man power.

One frail delicate youth with a contagious smile, Pte. Tom W. Holmes, won a Victoria Cross for valour and bravery on October 26. Single-handedly he ran forward and bombed two machine-guns, killing the crew. He then returned to his companions, got another bomb and again ran forward, throwing that bomb into the entrance of a pillbox causing the nineteen occupants to surrender.[8]

There were many others who did more than their duty. Cpl. Herbert Eastwood, injured by gunshot wounds to the left thigh and groin area, died of those wounds on October 31, 1917, at No. 44 Casualty Clearing Station. His body lies in Nine Elms British Cemetery near Poperinghe, Belgium. Nine Elms was a hospital centre specifically set up for the Third Battle of Ypres. The burial ground con-tains 1,556 Commonwealth burials, of which 289 are Canadians. They are all Passchendaele casualties.[9]

[8] Bennett, op. cit., pp. 82-84.

[9] Norm Christie, *For King and Empire, vol. IV, The Canadians at Passchendaele, October to November 1917* (Winnipeg: Bunker to Bunker Books, 1996), p. 63.

The "Carleton Place News" section of *The Almonte Gazette* of August 3 reports the following:

> The casualty list of yesterday contains the name of A. Corp. Herbert J. Eastwood of Carleton Place. Corp. Eastwood is a son of Mrs. J.N. Eastwood, and is married, his wife and children residing here. He is reported as seriously wounded.

In the *Carleton Place Herald* of November 5, 1918, the Eastwood family placed the following notice:

In Memoriam

Eastwood—In loving memory of Herbert J. Eastwood, who died for his King and Country Oct 28th, 1917.

Servant of God well done
Thy glorious warfare past,
Thy battle fought, the victory won
And thou art crowned at last.

Soldier of Christ well done
Praise be thy new employ,
And while eternal ages run,
rest in your Saviour's joy.

On September 4, 1920, the grateful Canadian government sent a Memorial Cross (Silver Cross) to Herb's widow, and paid her a $180 gratuity.

With The Patricia's

At 5:50 a.m. on October 30, fresh battalions tried to further the advance on Passchendaele. This time the Princess Patricia's Canadian Light Infantry (PPCLI) attacked into the Valley of the Ravebeek. Volume I of the history of the Patricia's tells the tale:

> The attacking companies wallowed through the marsh over the cross-road and up the valley toward Duck Lodge, under very heavy fire from every arm. The artillery barrage first caught them; then the rifles and machine guns in Duck Lodge, from a pill-box on the Meetcheele Ridge and from the defenses of Graf Farm, swept them like a storm of hail . . . The Patricia's suffered . . . heavily, and it was among their officers that the early losses were most severe . . . By the end of an hour almost every sub-

altern with the companies was gone: Lieutenants J.R. Riddell and M.W. Williams were killed outright . . . [all other officers were either killed or wounded, leaving] Captain Ten Broeke the only officer left in the front line.

By 7 a.m. it was only vaguely known that the Patricia's were at Duck Lodge, [then communications broke down completely and] for several hours thereafter the[se] regiments vanished into the mud and the unknown.

. . . the very low-lying ground over which the attack began was so completely commanded from the Passchendaele height of land, and it was in their first advance that the Patricia's suffered their worst losses. Nos. 2 and 4 Companies approaching Duck Lodge from Snipe Hall, encountered violent fire from rifles and light machine guns in isolated German posts— not pill-boxes . . . Bombs were used by the attackers to clear the ground. There was little bayoneting by either side, but it was a great day for snipers, and most of the Regiment's losses came from this source.[10]

Also in that history is the summary of the regiment's war diary:

Oct 30—General Action: The Third Battle of Ypres (Passchendaele). The regiment attacked at 5:50 A.M.[sic] beside the 49th Battalion and captured the Meetcheele Ridge, advancing from Snipe Hall and Bellevue. The condition of the ground was terrible and the advance was met by heavy fire which caused very severe losses, especially among officers. Duck Lodge was captured by the right companies [2 and 4] which then advanced to the Meetcheele Spur; while the left [1 and 3], led by Lieut. H. McKenzie, D.C.M., and Sgt G.H. Mullin, M.M., rushed a pill-box on the spur and completed the capture of the ridge, which was consolidated by 3 P.M [sic]. Three counterattacks were beaten off.[11]

At the start of this attack, Maj. Talbot Papineau, a young man from Montebello, Quebec, turned to the adjutant of the regiment,

[10] Ralph Hodder-Williams, *Princess Patricia's Canadian Light Infantry 1914-1919*, Vol. I (London: Hodder and Stroughton Ltd., 1923), pp. 258-260.

[11] Ibid., vol. II, p. 37.

Capt. H.W. Niven, DSO and Bar, MC, and uttered his final words: "You know Hughie, this is suicide." Talbot Papineau had been so dismayed by the conscription crisis that he gave up a safe staff job to go into the line with his regiment. Moments after he spoke, he was blown to bits by an artillery shell.

Also in the PPCLI's Roll of Honour:

> 411142 Riddell, J.R. Orig o/s unit—1st Univ.; joined PPCLI in the field—July 28, 1915; Reg't Record: Pte.—L/Cpl. Lieut., May 13, 1917. Died of wounds received at Passchendaele, Oct. 30, 1917.[12]

JAMES ROSS RIDDELL

Ross Riddell was the only son of Norman and Elizabeth Riddell of Carleton Place. He was born on June 9, 1892, and after schooling in Carleton Place went to Kingston to attend Queen's University. He became active in the university's Canadian Officer Training Corps in which he was promoted to the rank of lance corporal.

Ross was in his final year of Arts when he joined a special group of infantry replacements that went overseas during 1915 and 1916. The university companies were raised to reinforce the PPCLI. Originally, in January 1915, McGill University was authorized to provide a complete overseas company for the 38th Battalion which was being mobilized in Ottawa. Ross's records show that he joined on April 20, 1915, in Montreal, as a private in the 38th Battalion. The mobilization date of the company was deferred to allow the students to complete the university term. Early in May, they went to Niagara-on-the-Lake for summer training with the McGill and Toronto Canadian Officer Training Corps units.

 At this same time, the British were experiencing a shortage of officers.[13] The War Office suggested that the McGill Company of the 38th Battalion should be organized as an officers' training company. The Canadian government, having no difficulty obtaining officers, had an urgent demand for infantry reinforcements; so it designated the company as No. 1 University Company and sent it overseas as a reinforcing draft for the PPCLI. It had a strength of six officers and 250 men.[14]

[12] Ibid., p. 88.

[13] Junior officers (lieutenants and captains) had a very short life span as front-line officers in the trenches of France and Belgium.

[14] Col. G.W.L. Nicholson, *Canadian Expeditionary Force*, p. 228.

Although separated by 100 years, the battle tactics of World War I were not so far removed from those of the War of 1812. Victory went to the commander who threw the most bodies into the fray. Just as old battlefield tactics died hard, so did other customs and traditions, such as having their women follow them to war, if only as far as England. Quite often these women served there with a voluntary aid detachment in one of the British military hospitals. One such was the wife of Maj. Ian Sinclair who was with the 13th (Royal Highlanders—Montreal) Battalion. Mrs Sinclair recalled:

My hospital had a Canadian staff . . . near Folkestone . . . We were so close to the coast that when the casualties from the ships came in, we got them directly from the front line dressing stations . . . They were really a mess. The wounded were shipped out as fast as possible. We were one of the nearest hospitals. The wounds were terrific. Our surgeon was a Canadian, trained on Harley Street and came down once a week to operate . . . All we had for dressings was saline solution. Nothing else except a thing called P.C.A. [phenal, camphor and alcohol]. If the wound was simply filthy, we used to dress it, but after a few days the P.C.A. was so strong it would sluff everything away, so we used it to clean up with. Once the saline was used there was not one darn thing left. The chaps died of infection simply because there wasn't anything to stop it. We could not put iodine on a stump. That was too strong. The best treatment was saline. It was amazing how extraordinarily effective it was when you think that they got no injections or anything at all. Morphine was used, naturally, but no antibiotics. An awful lot of the fellows died of shock. Even after having blood tests and plasma they died of shock. There were a great deal of amputations.[15]

When Ross joined up, he gave his previous trade as student. He was described as twenty-two years old, standing 5' 9" tall, of a medium complexion with blue eyes and brown hair. He was found to have a scar of about three inches in diameter on his upper chest from a scald incurred during his childhood.

He was taken on the strength of the PPCLI in the field in France on July 17, 1915, and served in the ranks that winter as a rifleman. On June 24, 1916, he was appointed to the rank of lance corporal. In the *Carleton Place Herald* of June 20, 1916, was the following item:

Mr. W.M. Cameron received a cablegram from his son Donald, who expects shortly to cross the Channel, which incidentally stated that 'Sinclair and Riddell are all right.' As both these young men are with the Princess Patricia's and had not been heard from since

[15] Gordon Reid, *Poor Bloody Murder* (Oakville: Mosaic Press, 1980), p. 166.

the recent fight at Ypres considerable uneasiness was felt and this statement from Donald is glad news indeed. Mr. Riddell also received a confirmatory message.

This was most probably very welcome news indeed to Ross's mother who, with his sister Mary, left on July 5 for a trip to the old country.

Ross was reunited with his mother and sister on August 20, 1916. He was sent to Shorncliffe to attend cadet school in an effort to obtain his commission. He was given the rank of temporary lieutenant and attached to the Royal Canadian Regiment and PPCLI depot at Seaford for training. On April 25, 1917, as a new lieutenant, he was sent back to the PPCLI in France. However, on April 30, he was diverted to the 3rd Canadian Entrenching Battalion and stayed in the field with them for the summer. His pay was increased, from the soldier's salary of one dollar a day plus a field allowance of ten cents, to the officer's pay of $3.60 a day. He was granted ten days leave in England on September 7, 1917, and when he returned to France on September 19, he rejoined the Patricia's.

Previously reported killed in action, the record shows that Ross was in No.10 Canadian Field Ambulance when he died on October 30, 1917, of wounds received in action. Lt. Riddell was wounded in battle at Meetcheele, whilst advancing for an attack on Passchendaele on October 29–30, 1917. While being brought back, the ambulance was blown up and he was again wounded by a bomb or shell. He died at the Canadian Field Ambulance station a few hours later.

The Almonte Gazette, of November 9, 1917, copied this story from the *Carleton Place Herald*:

Makes the Supreme Sacrifice

Sad indeed was the message that reached Carleton Place yesterday that Lieut. James Ross Riddell, son of Mr. and Mrs. N.M. Riddell, has fallen in battle, at Meetcheele in Flanders, which was captured last week by the Princess Patricia's Canadian Light Infantry . . . The bereaved parents and only sister have the sympathy of the entire town in their bereavement. Lieut. Ross Riddell was born in Carleton Place 25 years ago and received his education here. Passing through the high school he entered Queen's University and whilst still in course enlisted in the spring of 1915 with a draft of the Princess Patricia's and went overseas. In one of the engagements he was buried by a shell and narrowly escaped suffocation, but was never wounded. He enlisted as a private, obtaining his commission in the field. He has made the supreme sacrifice for his country and his name will be inscribed upon the roll of honor with thousands of other brilliant young men of Canada who have given their lives in the cause of humanity.

In the edition of November 16 is this report:

A memorial service for the late Lieut. J. Ross Riddell and Private Frank Fumerton was held in St. Andrew's Church, Carleton Place, last Sunday night.

Last Sunday evening a large congregation assembled in St. Andrew's Church, the occasion being a memorial service for two members of the congregation who had fallen in battle, Pte. Frank Fumerton and Lieut. J. Ross Riddell. The church was decorated with flags and guns, whilst the seats the boys used to occupy were adorned with floral wreaths. The pastor, Rev. Mr. Monds, delivered an appropriate sermon, in which he made a plea for wider sympathy in the world. He made a touching reference to the heroism of the deceased, making special mention of Lieut. Riddell, who frequently offered to take the hazard of 'Listening Post' duty for those of his comrades who were not so free as he, who had those at home depending upon them. The service throughout was a most impressive one. There was special music by the choir.

The Commonwealth War Graves Commission record shows that James Ross Riddell, lieutenant, PPCLI (Eastern Ontario Regiment), who died on Tuesday, October 30, 1917, is buried in Brandhoek New Military Cemetery No. 3 in Vlamertinghe, Ieper, West-Vlaanderen, Belgium. Brandhoek, and the Vlamertinghe Church, was a comparatively safe area where field ambulances were continuously posted. As

A Father's Tribute

Harry Lauder was a famous singer and vaudeville performer in the United Kingdom. When on a concert tour to the British troops near the front lines, early in 1917, he was taken to the grave of his only son. Despite being overwrought during an emotional visit, he performed for the soldiers that night. When he returned to England he wrote the following poem:

To the memory of my beloved son, Captain John Lauder, First 8th Argyll and Sutherland Highlanders, killed in France, December 28th, 1916:

Oh, there's sometimes I am lonely
And I'm weary a' the day
To see the face and clasp the hand
Of him who is away.

The only one God gave me,
My one and only joy,
My life and love were centred on
My one and only boy.

I saw him in his infant days
Grow up from year to year
That he would some day be a man
I never had a fear.
His mother watched his every step
'Twas our united joy
To think that he might be one day
My one and only boy.

When war broke out he buckled on
His sword and said "Goodbye,
For I must do my duty, dad;
Tell mother not to cry,
Tell her that I'll come back again."
What happiness and joy,
But no, he died for liberty,
My one and only boy.

The days are long, the nights are drear,
The anguish breaks my heart,
But, oh! I'm proud my one and only
Laddie played his part.
For God knows best, His will be done,
His grace does me employ.
I do believe I'll meet again
My one and only boy.

two cemeteries became filled, the New Cemetery No. 3 was opened in August 1917 and closed in May 1918. There are nearly one thousand World War I casualties commemorated at this site.

About six weeks after the family received the news of Ross's death, his father received a letter from one of his son's comrades. It was printed in *The Almonte Gazette* of December 14, 1917:

Tribute to Fallen Officer from a Brother Officer

The following comforting letter has just been received by Mr. N.M. Riddell, of Carleton Place, from one of the officers in the same regiment as his son, Ross, when he met his death:

'You will no doubt have heard by this time of Ross' death, and I am writing to let you know a little of the sympathy that we all feel for you in your bereavement. Ross was one of the most gallant and bravest officers that the regiment has ever had, and was loved and respected by his men whom he used to think a great deal of. He got a slight wound at the start of operations, on the twenty-ninth, late at night, and refused to go out until ordered to do so. On the way out he was struck by a shell, and killed instantly. We, as soon as we heard of this, sent up a limber for his body, which was brought down here last night. This morning we had him buried in a good cemetery away behind the lines. Major Gordon, of Lethbridge, a chaplain of the 4th Division, preached his funeral sermon. His bearers were: Capt Pollard, 7th Bde. Veterinary Corps; Mr Ames, 49th Batt.; Mr. Lyall,[16] 49th Batt. and myself. Major Gordon preached a short but very appropriate sermon. A firing party of ours fired three volleys. The pipes played the Lament, and the bugle band sounded the Last Post. The Pioneers are erecting a cross over his grave, and you will get its location.—Lt. Wright.'

---

[16] The customary address for a lieutenant, used by all ranks including those junior to him, was the title "Mister."

Chapter Twenty-Three

THE GUNS!

As part of the organization of the Canadian Expeditionary Force in the summer of 1914, artillery units were mobilized at various local headquarters in Eastern Canada. They received most of their uniforms directly from the manufacturer, but it was not until they arrived in Valcartier at the end of August that khaki uniforms for war service were issued. They drew upon militia stores for equipment and purchased horses locally. By the time the artillery reached Valcartier, on August 29 and 30, 1914, they were reasonably well organized. They had three field artillery brigades, each with three batteries of eighteen-pounders and an ammunition column, a heavy sixty-pound battery with its ammunition column, and a divisional ammunition column.[1]

The 1st Canadian Artillery Brigade was mobilized on August 6, 1914, in Ottawa and trained in Valcartier. On the 26th of September 1914, the brigade embarked at Quebec City on the Cunard Line steam ship *Saxonia*.

> We left Quebec on morning of 29th and put into Gaspé Bay until morning of 3rd of October. During this time all ships in the convoy assembled and we formed into two long lines of fifteen ships each, our escort of three Cruisers then joined us and we put to sea. Weather was good during voyage and sea smooth.[2]

They arrived at Plymouth at noon on October 14 and by noon on October 16 were in their training camp.

> From date of arrival till January 5th/1915 we lived on Salisbury Plain. During this period we attempted to train in Battery Manoeuvres. Weather conditions hampered our work. On moving into the town of Devizes we spent our time in training gun crews and bringing our horses back to form again after their long period of exposure.
>
> Left Devizes midnight Feb 7th/1915 for Avonmouth. Embarked on HMT [His Majesty's Troopship] *African Prince*

[1] Col. G.W.L. Nicholson, *Canadian Expeditionary Force*, p. 22.
[2] Historical Record, 1st Battery, C.F.A., BEF, National Archives.

morning of 8th, left dock about 10 pm same evening and arrived St. Nazaire France Feb 12th via Bay of Biscay.[3]

In the field until March 19, 1917, each battery had four guns. Leading up the battle for Vimy Ridge, the artillery were reorganised so that each battery contained six guns. This provided much more fire-power and they kept the six guns until the end of the war.

The 1st Brigade and its gun batteries were constantly in action at the front in France and Belgium. They served at Fleubaix in March 1915, Ypres from April to early May 1915, Le Bizet from May 16 to 19, 1915, Festubert in early June 1915, Givenchy in late June 1915, Ploegsteert from July 1915 to March 1916, St Eloi in April 1916, Zillebeke in May, June and July 1916, the Somme from August 28 to November 18, 1916, the Lens front from January 4 to March 8, 1917; Vimy in March and April 1917 and the Third Ypres (Passchendaele) in the summer and autumn of 1917. With the 2nd Battery, until November at Passchendaele, was Norman McPhail from Carleton Place.

NORMAN R. MCPHAIL

Norman, born April 30, 1891, the son of Robert Allan and Matilda McPhail, was employed in the civil service when he joined the 2nd Battery of the 1st Brigade, Canadian Field Artillery (CFA) in Ottawa. With the entire complement of the 2nd Battery he entered into active service on September 22, 1914, at Valcartier. He had pre-vious militia service with the 42nd Regiment in Carleton Place and from August 12, 1914 to September 21, 1914, with the 2nd Battery of the 1st Brigade.

At enlistment, Norman McPhail was described as twenty-three years, five months old, weighing 145 pounds and standing 5' 9" tall. He had a medium complexion, grey eyes and brown hair and wore a neatly trimmed mustache. Scars were noted over his left eye-brow and on his left knee. He professed adher-ence to the Presbyterian Church.

Norman proceeded to Avonmouth with the battery on February 8, 1915, and directly into action in the Ypres Salient. His battery, the

[3] Historical Record, 1st Battery, C.F.A., BEF, National Archives..

2nd, worked in combination with the 3rd and the 10th, providing covering fire for the 1st Canadian Division in the battle at St. Julien on April 22–24. They were in close proximity to the Carleton Place men led by Capt. William Hooper in their abortive fight. In fact, by midnight on the 22nd, their guns were withdrawn to positions just to the rear of the farms being attacked. Unfortunately, the eight eighteen-pounders of the two batteries were not very effective in silencing fire from the enemy trenches. By April 26, with the 3rd Canadian Infantry Brigade placed in divisional reserve, the only active Canadian guns in the salient were those of the 1st Brigade, Canadian Field Artillery, west of the Yser Canal, firing in support of a French offensive.

At Givenchy-lez-la-Bassée, on June 15, the 1st Canadian Brigade, CFA, was employed supporting the 7th (British) Division while the 2nd and 3rd Brigades were covering the Canadian front. The task of the Canadian eighteen-pounders was to destroy the enemy's wire. But successive postponements of the assault prolonged the task and the Germans were able to repair breaches in the wire during the night. As a result, the artillery was to exceed the expenditure of ammunition prescribed by the British First Army (six rounds of shrapnel per yard of wire). However, after that action, the 1st Brigade commander reported that the wire on his front "was found to have been most satisfactorily dealt with."[4]

On November 17, 1915, the 1st Canadian Brigade was situated near La Petite Douve to support some of the initial trench raids carried out by the 2nd Canadian Infantry Brigade. Again, the job of their eighteen-pounders, and the thirteen-pounders of the Royal Canadian Horse Artillery, was to cut the enemy's wire so the raiders could get through more easily in the dark. The troops on both sides now settled down for winter in the fields of Flanders. Norman McPhail spent most of it, from December 30, 1915 to March 13, 1916, in No.18 General Hospital in Camiers with an infection. He was fortunate to be in out of the rain and the miserable living conditions. He rejoined his battery in the field on April 2, 1916, in time to man the guns at St. Eloi.

[4] Col. G.W.L. Nicholson, *Canadian Expeditionary Force*, p. 106.

When the 2nd Canadian Divisional Artillery relieved the gunners of the 3rd British Division it was the first time Canadian infantry divisions were supported by their own Canadian artillery. For two weeks, this area continued to be the scene of very heavy bombardment.

In June they were involved in a counterattack at Hooge which was to be carried out with few infantry but many guns. The British commanders were following the tactics so successfully employed by German artillery at St. Eloi. This brought together one of the greatest arrays of guns yet employed on so narrow a front. There were 218 artillery pieces ranging from 116 eighteen-pounders to two twelve-inch howitzers. Their main task was to pound the German front and support lines, hampering consolidation, and to find German artillery batteries to destroy. But bad weather caused the attack to be postponed, since aircraft could not fly and assist in registering the guns on their proposed targets.

Four intense bombardments of twenty to thirty minutes duration were carried out from June 9 to 12, when all German positions from Hill 60 to Sanctuary Wood were shelled unremittingly. Behind a thick smokescreen and in heavy rain the infantry was able to advance; the artillery bombardment meant the Württembergers could offer little resistance. The corps remained in the Ypres Salient through the summer to September.

On June 25, Norman was appointed acting bombardier and, on August 27, he was promoted to bombardier. The guns were active on the Somme from August to November 1916 and after another dreadful winter were employed on the Lens front from January to March 1917. Norm was granted leave from December 24, 1916, to February 10, 1917, which he spent in England. On March 18, he was promoted to the rank of corporal.

Infantry-artillery co-operation showed that a barrage could be followed very closely without incurring unnecessary casualties. This tactic was put to extremely effective use at Vimy Ridge when the four Canadian divisions advanced behind a perfectly timed artillery barrage.

On May 27, Cpl. McPhail was wounded by a gunshot wound to the right arm which was treated at No. 22 General Hospital in

Camiers. The *Carleton Place Herald* of June 12 reported the incident: "In yesterday's list of weekend casualties is the name of Bomb. Norman R. McPhail, of Carleton Place, appears under the head of wounded." It was considered a "slight" wound and by June 9 he had rejoined his unit. But from July 3 to 7, he was sent to the 3rd Canadian Field Ambulance unit because of severe contusions (bruising) of his right arm. Working with these fire-breathing monsters was always a hazardous task.

On July 3, Norm was posted from 2 CFA to 3 CFA. Then, from July 29 to August 1, he was again in hospital with an infection. On August 27, he was sent to the artillery school and returned to the battery on September 22.

On November 6, 1917, Norman McPhail was killed in action. His battery was putting up a barrage from a position about one thousand yards south east of St. Julien and in return they were being shelled by the enemy with 5.9 rounds. One exploded just behind Cpl. McPhail's gun position and a splinter from it struck him under his left shoulder penetrating his heart, causing instantaneous death.

After the Canadian successes of October 30–31, the Germans launched counterattacks. The artillery retaliated with methodical shelling, November 1–4. On November 5, the guns fired an all-out effort and, finally, on November 6, Passchendaele passed into Allied control. The infantry advanced behind another exactly timed creeping barrage that began at 6:00 a.m. The Germans fought hard to recover. When their infantry was not counterattacking, German artillery was shelling the newly won positions and the Canadian batteries behind them. Finally, with both sides exhausted, no further attacks developed. Seven hundred and thirty-four Canadians were killed or died of wounds during this assault.

Cpl. Norman R. McPhail, dead at age twenty-six, lies buried in Brandhoek New Military Cemetery No. 3, Vlamertinghe, Ieper, Belgium. In his will he left $50 to each of his brothers, Donald and John, and sisters, Kate, Nellie and Annabel. *The Almonte Gazette* published the following on December 14, 1917:

A memorial service was held in Carleton Place last Sunday for the late Pte. Norman McPhail, eldest son of Mr. and Mrs. Robert McPhail of Carleton Place, who was killed in action in France on Nov 6th. Pte. McPhail enlisted and went overseas shortly after the outbreak of the war and has since been doing his bit with the exception of a short time he was laid off duty suffering from wounds.

But this was not the last battle of Passchendaele. That occurred on November 10 when the 1st Canadian Division pushed the Germans back a further 500 yards north from the ridge. They handed over to British units later in the day. On November 20, Haig decided to close down the campaign in Flanders.

HERBERT DOWDALL

Herb Dowdall was born in Scotch Corners on July 9, 1897, the son the Mr. and Mrs. Robert Dowdall. As there is no mention of his mother, or her name, in his records, it is assumed that she died before he joined the army in 1916.

Herb was eighteen years, six months old when he was enlisted by the 8th Artillery Brigade Recruiting Depot in Ottawa, on January 17, 1916. He gave his civilian trade as a clerk. At his medical examination he was found fit for service and described as of a medium complexion with blue eyes and brown hair. He was 5' 3" tall, barely passing the minimum standard of 5' 2", and weighed 125 pounds. Clearly Herb was not a big lad. He listed his next of kin as his father, Robert, living at R.R. #1, Carleton Place, and his religious affiliation as Church of England. The *Carleton Place Herald* of January 18, 1916, noted Herb's enlistment and reported that he was in Company "C" of the 130th Battalion.

The new recruit was not long training in Canada before he was sent overseas. His unit left St. John, New Brunswick, on the troop-ship *Metagama* on March 11, 1916, and arrived in Liverpool on March 25. They went directly into Whitley Camp on the Salisbury Plain. There they spent most of their time in general training, specifically in learning how to handle and take care of their horses and mules, as well as equitation—how to ride the animals. About three weeks after he arrived in England, Herb was hospitalized with rubella, also known as German measles. From April 14 to 25, he was in the Isolation Hospital at Aldershot. He went overseas with the gunners to France, landing in Le Havre on July 15, 1916, where they joined the 3rd Division as the 3rd Divisional Ammunition Column.

Without the delivery of ammunition in great quantities and in a timely manner, the artillery was useless. Divisional ammunition columns were responsible for these supplies. In the case of Herb's unit, that meant keeping a steady flow of shells moving to the brigades of Canadian Field Artillery in support of the 8th Infantry Brigade. Each artillery brigade was composed of three field batteries of six guns each, and a Howitzer battery of four guns. Additionally, each of the three infantry brigades in a division had a trench mortar battery that the gunners had to keep supplied.

Herb Dowdall spent the winter of 1916–1917 and spring of 1917 following the 3rd Division gunners through France and Flanders. One of the first major actions he witnessed was October 21–25, 1916. The field artilleries of all three Canadian Divisions fired in support of the assault against Regina Trench at the Somme. More than 200 heavy guns and howitzers were in action. However, even this barrage from the 1st and 3rd Canadian Divisional Artilleries was deemed "woefully light and ineffective." Enemy machine guns were still allowed to sweep the advancing infantry, totally blunting their advance. Infantry battalion commanders called the barrage a "flat failure" because, as one of the artillery observers reported, the fire was "absolutely insufficient to keep down enemy machine gun fire, there being not enough guns on the zone and the rate of fire was too slow."[5]

On November 13, when the battle of the Ancre began, the artillery support from the Canadian divisions was on a grander scale than for any previous operation. It provided a forty-eight-hour intense bombardment of all German-held villages and trenches and all enemy approaches to the battle area.[6]

[5] Col. G.W.L. Nicholson, *Canadian Expeditionary Force*, p. 191.
[6] Ibid., p. 193.

During the fighting at Fresnoy, the Canadian attack on May 3, 1917, was given generous fire support by the Canadian Corps Heavy Artillery and the three divisional artilleries. In bright moonlight the thickly emplaced batteries opened fire along No Man's Land by the Arras-Lens railway. The heavy fire cut the wire and opened large gaps, greatly facilitating the infantry's rush to the enemy trench lines.

From September 16 to 22, Herb was sent to the rear on leave. He returned to his unit for the November assault on Passchendaele. Records of the ammunition column show that, in November 1917, it suffered seventeen casualties, six other ranks killed and eight wounded and three officers wounded.

They were operating in the Poperinghe-Brandhoek area. From the unit daily diary entries we learn:

7 Nov—Wx [weather] showery and cold, hail in aft.—200 pack animals each [made deliveries] to 9th and 10th Bdes CFA. 2 ORs killed, 3 wounded, 2 mules killed.

8 Nov—Fair day—from early morning E.A. [enemy aircraft] over our area about 3 AM but no bombing—rain from late aft onwards—German plane brought down by one of ours about 10:30 AM—40 pack animals [made deliveries] to 35th Bty CFA.

9 Nov—Wx fair—275 pack animals delivered ammo [ammunition] to guns, 125 to 9th and 10th Bdes CFA. 1 O.R. Died of Wounds, 4 ORs wounded, 9 animals killed.[7]

The one "O.R." that died of wounds was Driver Herb Dowdall.

Driver Dowdall received a gunshot wound to his right leg while in action on November 9, 1917. The bullet caused a compound fracture of the right leg. No penicillin or other antibiotics were available to No. 1 Canadian Field Ambulance. Herb died of his wound. His body lies buried in the Vlamertinghe New Military Cemetery, Ieper, Belgium.

November 14 signalled the beginning of the end of Canadian troop involvement at Passchendaele. British soldiers began to move into the Canadian trenches. Canada lost 15,654 dead and wounded, one thousand of them buried forever, anonymously, churned into the mud of Flanders.

[7] 3rd Division Ammunition Column War Diary, National Archives.

On January 4, 1918, *The Almonte Gazette* published the following letter:

Has Done His Duty

A comrade of the late Herb Dowdall's writes as follows to his brother in Almonte: "You will no doubt be somewhat surprised to hear from me. However, my position is this, that I was the last of Herbert Dowdall's comrades to speak to him but a few hours before his sad and regrettable, yet heroic passing away. I promised to write to his friends and tell them how he was. He thanked me, hence the reason I am taking the liberty of writing you. I wrote his sister, Maude, some time ago, giving her all details. I presume you will now be in possession of those, so I will not dwell further on the subject, than it was an honor to know a boy of his high moral principles. Besides, he was one of my very best men, and could always be relied upon to carry out his duties and showed great courage and coolness under heavy fire at all times. In addition he set an excellent example, though but a mite to the biggest and best of them. It may be a consolation to you and the other members of your family to know he died doing his duty and which is far finer still, I think, that he did his duty. A parcel arrived here some days ago for Herbert from you, so knowing that it would not be returned to you, we, some of the boys in his subsection, took the painful liberty of using its contents, which I am sure would be in accordance with Herbert's wishes and yours as well. That is where I found your name, though the others were invisible through some of the icing melting a bit. So trusting that our action meets with your approval, I would ask you to accept our very best thanks for the cake, which was thoroughly enjoyed and in excellent condition. By the way, I am Herbert's N.C.O., and I miss him ever so much, in fact, his place here will be hard to fill."

In December 1917, the local newspapers recorded that, "Much to the surprise of their friends was the sudden arrival home on Monday of Flight Commanders S.T. Edwards and A. Roy Brown, whose decoration we recorded last week. The boys have a month's leave of absence, and will be able to spend Christmastide with their ain folk. They look well and are receiving a cordial reception from their old time friends." Rumours remain that the two were sent home, and to Washington, on a secret mission to enlist American aid for the war.

Conscription in Canada had become a fact with the passing of the Military Service Act in August 1917 that required the registration of all eligible men. The first men to be "called to the colours" were drafted on January 3, 1918.

On December 21 the Gazette reported that:

> The National Hockey League of Canada, organized to take the place of the N.H.A. until the close of the war, will consist of the Ottawa, Wanderer, Canadian and Toronto clubs. Though the Quebec club has been enrolled it is not to exercise its franchise this year, and the Quebec players will be divided up to strengthen other clubs. Wednesday, December 19th, has been named as the opening date of the matches; the season to close on March 9th with world's series matches to follow.

The winter of 1917–1918 in Eastern Ontario was the coldest in the memory of that generation. Some schools and businesses had to close due to a scarcity of fuel; coal was the primary fuel and it was being used by the war industries. On February 15, the Almonte Gazette published the following items:

> The weather man is evidently out to break records this winter. Since the first of November there has fallen 74 [inches] of snow, and for eighteen successive days, during the latter part of January and the forepart of February, the temperature did not rise above zero [degrees Fahrenheit], and on many days was very much below.

> The Hawthorn Mills [in Carleton Place] are going to save fuel by running a portion of their machinery by electricity. They have made an agreement with Messrs. H. Brown & Sons for a certain amount of power, and the wires are being strung at present to supply the demand.

And on March 8:

> The Bates and Innes firm of Carleton Place did business last year aggregating one million dollars. The mills have been running twenty-three hours of the twenty-four each day, being chiefly engaged in war orders. U.S. war orders are being filled at present.

> Mack Farrell, a boy about 12 years of age, of Belleville, while looking into a window allowed his tongue to rest upon an iron bar impregnated with frost. the boy lost the end of his tongue through his thoughtless act.

Chapter Twenty-Four

AIRMEN

The achievements of Canadian airmen in the Great War are all the more remarkable for their humble beginnings. At war's outbreak there was no military flying in Canada; indeed, it had been only five years earlier that the first airplane flight occurred. On a cold February day in 1909, the Silver Dart soared over the ice of Cape Breton's Bras d'Or Lake. But Canadian politicians could see no need for experiment, development, or the training of pilots in aviation. No funds were made available. No aeroplanes or equipment purchased, and no flying fields were built.

In August 1914, Col. Sam Hughes sent with the First Contingent to England, three men—Ernest L. Janney, of Galt, Ontario (provisional commander of the Canadian Aviation Corps with the rank of captain); William Frederick Nelson Sharpe, of Prescott (to train as a pilot with the rank of lieutenant); Harry A. Farr of West Vancouver (an infantryman who was to be the mechanic with the rank of staff-sergeant)—and one biplane, a Burgess Dunne seaplane purchased from the United States. This was the Canadian Aviation Corps. Neither officer was ever paid. Janney returned to Canada on January 23, 1915, Lt. Sharpe was killed on his first solo flight on February 4, and Farr was discharged from the Canadian Expeditionary Force in May 1915, "in consequence of the Flying Corps being disbanded."[1] The aircraft never left the ground, ending up in a scrap heap on Salisbury Plain.

It was not until 1918, when the tremendous advances in aviation made it apparent that an air force would be essential to post-war military organization and also act as an incentive to the development of commercial aviation, that steps were taken to create a small air force for overseas and a naval air service for home defence—but not in time for either to become operational for service in the Great War.[2]

In almost every theatre of operations, Canadian pilots, observers and mechanics served in the Royal Naval Air Service and Royal Flying

[1] Sydney F. Wise, *Canadian Airmen and the First World War—The Official History of the Royal Canadian Air Force*, vol.I (Ottawa: University of Toronto Press et al, 1980), p. 29.

[2] Air Historian, "History of the R.C.A.F." (1962), Part 3, Sections 1 and 3, *Report of O.M.F.C.* (Overseas Military Forces of Canada), p. 349.

Corps. These two services amalgamated, on April 1, 1918, to form the Royal Air Force. In many cases, cadets were enlisted by the British authorities in Canada with the same status as if they had enrolled in the United Kingdom. Canadian military officers could be seconded while other ranks were first discharged from the Canadian forces and then enrolled as British airmen (either as cadets or non-flying personnel). There was also the opportunity for direct entry of Canadian civilians in England.[3] Most Canadian adventurers, desiring the life of an aviator, paid for their flying training at schools in Canada or the United States and then paid their own passage to England to join the air services.

COLIN DUNCAN P. SINCLAIR

Colin Sinclair died serving in the air force but he first paid his dues in the trenches.

He was scheduled to begin studying at Queen's University when he enlisted into the 3rd University Company in Montreal on July 15, 1915. He was one month past his eighteenth birthday and one of the first to enlist after the company was formed. The *Carleton Place Herald* of June 1, 1915, showed that he was still in secondary school with the report that "The High School cadets were on the ranges and C. Sinclair shot 17 out of a possible 20." He graduated with his Normal entrance and matriculation certificates in June 1915.

The university companies were raised to provide reinforcements for the Princess Patricia's Canadian Light Infantry (PPCLI). They were all mobilized at McGill, but students were recruited from other Canadian universities. All recruits were graduates or undergraduates of universities. Many enlisted with their friends.

Nos. 2 to 5 University Companies went overseas between June 1915 and April 1916. They joined the PPCLI in France before the heavy fighting in June 1916. The PPCLI's historian wrote: "They saved the Regiment from practical extinction . . . and they beat the Württembergers in Sanctuary Wood . . ." No. 5 Company arrived after the battle at Sanctuary Wood to rebuild the battalion's shattered strength.[4]

[1] Col. G.W.L. Nicholson, *Canadian Expeditionary Force*, pp. 503-504.
[2] Ibid., pp. 228-229.

Colin was the eldest son of Rev. R.C.H. Sinclair, a Presbyterian minister, and was born on June 2, 1897, at Oliver's Ferry, McCue PO, Lanark County (Rideau Ferry). Nothing is known of his mother. When he enlisted, he gave his trade as student. He was described as eighteen years old, standing 5' 5" tall and weighing 122 pounds. He was recorded as being clean-shaven, having a dark complexion with brown eyes and black hair. He stated his religious affiliation to be Presbyterian. There was a visible small scar on the back of his right hand.

After a short indoctrination training in Canada, Colin sailed to England, arriving on September 14, 1915. On November 30, he was transferred to the PPCLI overseas. He arrived in France on December 1 and joined the Patricia's in the trenches on February 12, 1916. The *Carleton Place Herald* of June 20, 1916, reported that:

> Mr. W.M. Cameron received a cablegram from his son, Donald, who expects shortly to cross the Channel, which incidentally stated that 'Sinclair and Riddell are all right.' As both these young men are with the Princess Patricia's and had not been heard from since the recent fight at Ypres considerable uneasiness was felt and the statement from Donald is glad news indeed.

This was the Battle of Mount Sorrel, which occurred in the Ypres Salient, June 2–13. In Sanctuary Wood, the Patricia's were facing the 157th Battalion of the 26th (Württemberg) Division. Early in the morning of June 2, the German bombardment, preliminary to an infantry attack, burst upon the Canadian lines. For four hours the Canadians endured a "veritable tornado of fire," the heaviest artillery barrage up to that time. Just before 1:00 p.m., the Württembergers exploded four mines just in front of the Canadian trenches, then rose to advance. They encountered small isolated groups of Canadians, survivors of the artillery fire who could offer very limited resistance. The first line of Germans arrived with fixed bayonets and carried hand grenades. There was brief hand-to-hand fighting with bomb and bayonet. Flame throwers were used when the sheer force of numbers could not overcome the Canadians.

Machine-gunners with the Patricia's inflicted substantial casualties but could not stem the advance. The enemy overran a section of the 5th Battery, Canadian Field Artillery, and after killing or wounding every gunner took two eighteen-pounder guns. This was the only time in World War I when Canadian guns fell to the enemy. They were recovered in later fighting.

The Germans pushed the line back 600 yards at Sanctuary Wood, but credit for checking the advance belongs to the Patricia's, and to the reinforcements from the university companies. One of the two companies in the firing line was overrun, but the other held out for eighteen hours, isolated from the rest of the battalion and with all officers either killed or wounded. The rear companies fought off the enemy's attempt to cut their supply line. Fighting in portions of the communication trenches, the German advance was over the dead bodies of each little garrison. Sanctuary Wood cost the Patricia's 400 casualties. One of the 150 killed in action was their commanding officer, Lt.-Col. H.C. Buller.[5] Colin Sinclair observed his nineteenth birthday the day the attack began; he spent it in the thick of the fighting.

The three Canadian divisions spent July and August in the always dangerous Ypres Salient; but no major actions developed. By September they were in the Somme. By September 15, the PPCLI had secured a foothold on Fabeck Graben, just west of the village of Courcelette during the battle for Flers-Courcelette. Here the British invention, the tank, was first used in warfare. On October 8, the Patricia's, with their sister battalion, the Royal Canadian Regiment, participated in the attack on Regina Trench. Initial success was fought back by determined German counterattacks and they ended the day in their original positions. This was the last action in which the Canadians participated on the Somme. On October 10, the 3rd Division was relieved by the 4th Canadian Division.

[5] Nicholson, op. cit., pp. 149-150.

The Canadian Corps moved to the relatively quiet sector between Arras and Lens where they hunkered down for the winter, free from any major operations, except for harassing raids on the enemy trenches. By March 1917, these raids were occurring nightly as the Canadians prepared for the assault on Vimy Ridge.

> We have just received orders for our future movements. We go into a piece of the line which is quite new to us. From accounts sent to us, it does not sound very inviting. We are on the low part of a slope, well over-looked by the Germans. No movement is permitted during the day. Relief will have to be made at night. The line is a long one. The immediate danger is mining.
>
> Agar Adamson, PPCLI[6]

The 3rd Division went into the line opposite La Folie Wood. Their objective was one kilometre away, the eastern side of the ridge. Six battalions, including the PPCLI, would make the attack. Their advance went quite well. They captured La Folie Farm and drove on to their planned objective, south of Hill 145. It was still in the hands of Germans who poured unrelenting machine-gun fire into the flanks of the 3rd Division. The hill was the 4th Division's target but their advance had faltered badly. Late in the day, the Nova Scotia Highlanders, who had been in France only a month, pushed through and took Hill 145, an audacious feat of arms. Colin Sinclair considered himself very lucky to have escaped with his life from this harrowing battle.

There is an oft-repeated myth about the Canadian infantryman. Fed up with mud, cold and lice and just war-weary, he looked up from his trench to the clear blue sky and a single soaring aircraft. That, he decided, was a better way to fight the war. Despite the legend, very few Canadians escaped trench warfare into the flying services. A shortage of experienced infantry officers led the Canadian Expeditionary Force senior officials, in 1916, to ban transfers.

But the legend could very well have been L/Cpl. Sinclair's tale; and he must have been one of the few who managed to leave the sticky muck for the clean cool air. After his toils with the Patricia's for a year and four months in France, he applied for his commission as an

[6] N.M. Christie, *Winning the Ridge: The Canadians at Vimy Ridge, 1917* (Nepean: CEF Books, 1998), p. 3.

infantry officer. The history of the battalion records his service as, "476021; orig—3rd Univ.; joined in field—Feb 9, 1916; record: Pte.—L/Cpl. sos [struck off strength] Apr. 18, 1917 (Lieut. R.A.F.)."[7]

On April 17, 1917, Colin was transferred to England to the Eastern Ontario Regiment depot in Seaford. The purpose of this transfer was for him to attend cadet school. Upon graduation he would be granted a commission in the Canadian Infantry Corps. He completed officer training on July 1, 1917, was made a temporary lieutenant and posted to the 7th Reserve Battalion where he awaited orders to a regiment fighting in the field.

The Almonte Gazette of June 1, 1917, reported:

Wins Commission on the Field

Lance Corpl. Colin Sinclair, son of Rev. R.C.H. Sinclair, has been given a commission in the field in acknowledgement of his conduct, and is at present in England qualifying for his lieutenancy. From what we gather from letters written by his comrades Colin was one of a dozen who went out by night to obtain information of a certain German stronghold. But the officers in charge of the squad fell wounded and to Corpl. Sinclair fell the duty of getting them and the men back to their own trenches. This he did most successfully, the object of the adventure also being attained. For his clever work the young corporal received a holiday in England. In the battle of Vimy Ridge Colin again distinguished himself, and for this last service received the commission.—*Herald.*

However, with his younger brother Huntley, a second lieutenant already flying in the Royal Air Force, Colin heard the siren call of flight. On October 30, he was sent to the Royal Flying Corps School of Aeronautics at Reading for flight training as a pilot. This also meant a raise in pay; and on November 21 his records were annotated to reflect the award of flying pay at $14.50 a month.

The usual flying instruction consisted of about one-and-a-half months of ground school, four weeks' basic flying training and another four

[7] Ralph Hodder-Williams, *Princess Patricia's Canadian Light Infantry, vol.II, The Roll of Honour and Appendices* (London: Hodder and Stroughton Ltd., 1923) p. 323.

weeks of advanced flying that would include manoeuvres such as loops, spins, stalls and figure-eights.

> A cadet first received dual flying instruction. As soon as he could handle the machine in the air, and make landings without bouncing too much, he was dispatched on his first solo. Here it may be pointed out that the most critical event in a learner's life was not so much the first take off and flight, but the first solo landing. It was indeed an achievement to bring your roaring Juggernaut back to Mother Earth, without splitting it and her wide open. Intermingled with solo flying was more dual flying, with stunting of every description. Later still came aerial photography, cross-country flying, and finally, a stiff course in aerial gunnery. By the time the young airman had passed his final tests he knew how to fly.[8]

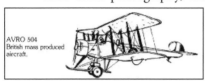

AVRO 504 British mass produced aircraft.

The most likely aircraft in which Colin learned to fly would have been the Avro 504J. This two-seater biplane, fitted with a 100-hp Gnôme Monosoupape engine, was first used as an advanced trainer, until it became apparent that it was ideal for ab initio training. It was a reliable aircraft with the handling characteristics of a single-seater fighter and thus could be used to carry out all the acrobatics in the syllabus. So impressive were the results using the 504J that the aircraft was selected as the standard trainer for the RFC.[9]

Lt. Sinclair reported to the advanced training school at Stamford on January 11, 1918.

Near the end of his training, when he was looking forward to a posting to an operational squadron in France, his career in the air ended. On March 17, 1918, Aero 5, the training squadron at Stamford, reported that Colin Sinclair had been accidentally killed at Bickers Fen, Donnington, Lincolnshire, as the result of an aeroplane crash.

In *The Almonte Gazette* appeared the following on March 29:

Lieut. C.D. Sinclair in Fatal Accident

Rev. R.C.H. Sinclair, of Kenmore, formerly of Carleton Place, has received official notification that his eldest son, Lieut. Colin

Duncan Sinclair, was accidentally killed on March 17th, as a result of an airplane accident. The young man was born nearly twenty-one years ago at Oliver's Ferry, on the Rideau, where his father was then minister of the Presbyterian church there. He was a graduate of the Carleton Place high school, getting his Normal entrance and matriculation certificates at the June examinations in 1914 [*sic*]. On the 13th of July, 1915, he enlisted with the 3rd Universities [*sic*] Company, being one of the first to enlist upon its formation, when he was just one month beyond his eighteenth birthday. He went over with his company to England in September, to France in December, and into the trenches in February of 1916. He was in all the heavy engagements, such as Ypres in June of that year, the Somme in September, taking part in a trench raid also in February, 1917. Through all of these he came out unscathed. He was in the battle of Vimy Ridge also, where he had one of the narrowest escapes of all his experiences. After that battle, he was ordered to England to train for his lieutenancy, and on the completion of his course, and while waiting in reserve, he applied for his transfer to the Flying Corps. It was near the end of his course of preparation, and when he was looking forward to soon getting over to France again in this capacity, that he met with the accident in which he lost his life, the particulars of which have not as yet come to hand.

The official commemoration in the Commonwealth War Graves Register reads:

COLIN DUNCAN P. SINCLAIR

(Lieutenant) son of Mr. R.C.H. Sinclair, Ottawa. Enlisted in Montreal, Princess Patricia's Canadian Light Infantry, Eastern Ontario Regiment, attached to the Royal Flying Corps. Killed accidentally in England March 17, 1918, age 20. Buried in Stamford Cemetery, Lincolnshire, United Kingdom.

ALLAN CLYDE MOFFATT

Allan Moffatt, born in 1890 to David and Mary Euphemia Moffatt, left his employment in Montreal to join the Royal Air Force. He enlisted as an air mechanic:

All operational recruits, irrespective of their trade categories, were classed as air mechanics, better known as A.M.'s, and unless they later earned the rank of corporal or higher, air mechanics they remained in name, whether they were clerks, cooks, policemen, truck drivers—or actual mechanics!

All those joining a mechanical branch were allowed to choose the work they considered themselves best fitted for, but budding 'ack emmas' (A.M.'s) had to undergo preliminary tests at the old Toronto Armouries under British R.F.C. experts, whose keen appraisals quickly determined if the recruit was really suited to the branch of work he had selected.

The test over, recruits were bundled off to the training camp at Leaside. There, for three weeks or so, they slept under canvas, suffered daily drill, with lots of 'physical jerks' and plenty of kitchen and sanitary fatigues. As rookies were licked into shape, they were sent off to various points to fill the hundreds of jobs that awaited them, and the Royal Flying Corps swelled towards its final training strength of well over 10,000 men. When the Corps was fully organized, the demand for air mechanics ceased, but the call for cadets for flying training went on unabated up to the last day of the war.[10]

Little could be learned of Allan's life in Carleton Place, but his name appeared several times in the columns of the *Carleton Place Herald* as a holiday visitor to his home:

September 7, 1915—Allan Moffatt of Quebec is spending a week's holidays at home.

September 5, 1916—Mr. Allan Moffatt of Quebec, was among the home-comers yesterday.

December 26, 1916—Mr. Allan Moffatt was a holiday visitor from Montreal.

On April 12, 1918, *The Almonte Gazette* printed the notice of his death: "In the Military Base Hospital, at Toronto, April 7th, Pte. Allan C. Moffatt, son of Mr. and Mrs. David Moffatt of Carleton Place, aged 27 years." And in the Carleton Place news section appeared:

[10] Ibid., p. 122.

After a heroic fight of about ten days Pte. Allan Clyde Moffatt, son of Mr. and Mrs. David Moffatt, passed away on Sunday night in the Military Hospital at Toronto, from pleuro-pneumonia. Pte. Moffatt was 27 years of age and a machinist by trade. Early last summer he enlisted with the Aviation Corps, and was placed in the mechanical department, Toronto, where he continued on duty until his fatal illness overtook him. His parents were with him at the last, as was also his brother Howard. The remains were brought home Tuesday morning, and the funeral took place Wednesday afternoon to St. Fillan's cemetery. It was under the auspices of the Oddfellows of which Order he was an enthusiastic member. The bereaved parents and sister and brothers have the deep sympathy of many friends in their hour of grief.

The Commonwealth War Graves Commission commemoration reads:

In Memory of
Air Mechanic 2nd Class ALLAN MOFFATT
72072

Royal Air Force
who died aged 28 on Sunday, 7th April 1918.
Air Mechanic 2nd Class MOFFATT was the son
of David and Euphemia Moffatt, of Carleton
Place, Ont.
Remembered with honour
CARLETON PLACE UNITED CEMETERIES, Ontario, Canada.

His grave is located in the St. Fillan's section of the cemetery beside those of his parents. His father, David, was a local contractor, living from 1849 to 1926. His mother, was Mary E. (Somerville) who lived from 1849 to 1922.

Chapter Twenty-Five

CANADA'S HUNDRED DAYS

Amiens

From May until mid-July 1918, the Canadians were mostly spared the rigours of the trench-line. But the war in the air never let up, and

in July the *Carleton Place Herald* reported that Murray Galbraith got the second Bar to his Distinguished Service Cross (DSC). He already had the Croix de Guerre from France and now had the DSC and two Bars from England. The second Bar was awarded for his action during a recent German raid over England.

The period of August 4 to November 11, 1918, has become known as Canada's Hundred Days because of the Canadian Corps' commitment to participation in the vanguard of the advance to Mons. The blackest day for the German Army came on August 8, when the Canadians spearheaded an attack near Amiens that completely surprised the enemy. With no preliminary bombardment in the days ahead of the attack to warn of the assault, the Canadians, flanked by Australian and French troops and led by tanks, advanced twelve miles in three days.

The secret to success was secrecy. The Australian commander specifically requested Canadian troops be on his flank, so the Canadians moved the entire corps, fresh from their "summer rest" thirty miles south, from the Arras area to southwest of Amiens by train and bus, without a hint to the Germans. All movement was done at night and each soldier was warned to "keep your mouth shut." In the air, planes patrolled to spot any movement that would breach security, and bombers buzzed the lines to cover the noise of tanks rolling up to position. To motivate the troops, they were reminded of the sinking, on June 27, of the Canadian Hospital Ship *Llandovery Castle*. It had been torpedoed and survivors in the water had been machine-gunned. Only twenty-four of the 224 men aboard, and none of the fourteen

Nursing Sisters, had been rescued. Aside from the fact that this ship had previously carried home many Carleton Place wounded and sick, the sinking itself was also significant to the community. As reported in the *Herald* of July 9, 1918:

> Nursing Sister A. McDiarmid, daughter of the late John McDiarmid, Beckwith, was lost with the sinking of the Canadian Hospital Ship Llandovery Castle, torpedoed by Germans. She had two sisters and a brother in Ashton.

The first week of August, in nightly marches, the Canadians moved from their billets into concentration areas. There was much congestion of wheeled and foot traffic through very dark nights over unfamiliar ground on very narrow roads. Finally, on August 7, they were as ready as they could be.[1] The next morning they would go in.

> The night was quiet. Save for the roll of heavy gunfire to the north, in the neighbourhood of Villers Bretonneux, scarcely a rifleshot disturbed the scene. From the rear came the first rumble of traffic as the light artillery took up positions, previously selected but by no means prepared. Like the infantry they were out in the open. The stillness of the night seemed to intensify the almost inaudible tramp of the attacking troops as they flitted to their assembly areas. Towards the German lines the flares lit up No Man's Land with a dazzling brilliance; but they disclosed nothing of the momentous preparations and industry now at their height. Three o'clock in the morning of 8th August saw a low mist rising. By that hour, however, there had been a great diminution of activity. From Gentelles Wood came the dull throb of the tanks as they 'tuned-up' for their journey forward.
>
> The rumble of the tanks as they commenced their journey over the hard ground sounded strangely hollow in the thick mist. By 4 o'clock they had passed the thin waves of men in the rearward area and were directed towards the front lines. Overhead, a loud drone told of contact aeroplanes already in action. To the infantry those few minutes before Zero Hour were fraught with anxiety. The noise of the tanks was magnified in their apprehensive ears to a deafening volume; it seemed too much to hope that the riot would escape the enemy's notice. But nothing happened.

[1] As each Division reached its assembly area it signalled headquarters that they had arrived with the words "Llandovery Castle."

Lying 1000 yards in rear of the 5th Battalion, the Second were at the outset somewhat nearer to the gun-line than to the front trenches. For that reason the sudden crash of the barrage at 4:20 a.m. seemed to make the whole earth tremble. Through the intense fog an avalanche of shells screamed overhead to descend in a torrent of bursting metal on the German lines. The smoke, mingling with the mist, enveloped the country in an almost impenetrable blanket.

It was calculated that in 50 minutes the attacking troops would be sufficiently advanced to allow the Second Battalion to move forward without engaging too closely to the 3rd Brigade reserves. Accordingly the Battalion set off from their assembly area at 5:10 a.m. Observation, even in the grey light of dawn, was limited to less than 50 yards; and in the valley of the Luce this distance was reduced to five. Platoons proceeded with their files closed, the officers marching entirely by compass.[2]

At exactly 4:20 a.m. the thunder of more than nine hundred guns of all calibres covered the assaulting infantry as they pressed forward. With the Australian 3rd Corps on their left and the 31st Corps of the 1st French Army on their right, the Canadian Corps threw their might against the 51st Corps of the German Second Army. The 1st Canadian Division was in the centre with the 2nd Division on its left and the 3rd

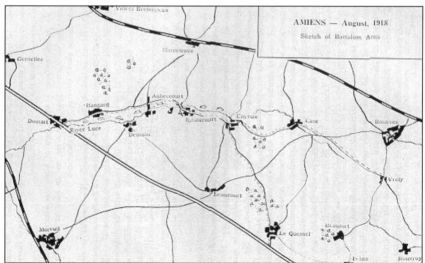

[2] Colonel W.W. Murray, *The History of the 2nd Canadian Battalion* (Ottawa: The Historical Committee, 2nd Battalion, C.E.F., 1947), pp. 260-261.

on the right. In reserve, the 4th Division prepared to follow. The previous secrecy was justified. The advance proceeded well and in most cases the Germans were taken by surprise, often surrendering without firing as the advancing Canadians overwhelmed them.

Both George Fanning and Archie McCaw participated, and lost their lives, in the attack at Amiens. George was with the 2nd Battalion of the 1st Brigade of the 1st Canadian Division, and Archie advanced with the 43rd Battalion of the 9th Brigade of the 3rd Division.

The 1st Division, in the centre of the corps, was given the job of breaking through the wooded area north of the river Luce. The battalions were well spread out to lessen casualties. Each infantryman welcomed the new "fighting order" that meant they carried less than they had in previous operations. For this advance each man was laden with a haversack, 250 rounds of ammunition, gas mask, water bottle, "iron rations" (corned beef and biscuits), an entrenching tool, two Mills bombs and two sandbags.

The mist and fog in the river valley slowed the 2nd Battalion's advance. By 8:20 a.m. they halted to wait for the tanks to catch up and assist in capturing the village of Ignaucourt. But many of the behemoths had become ditched in the swamps and they were unlikely to arrive in time. Unable to delay longer, and wanting to take advantage of the enemy before they had time to recover, the infantry advanced without the tanks. German resistance appeared crushed. Pushing through the valley to the next village of Cayeaux, the 2nd Battalion encountered machine-gunners but these nests were overcome with few Canadian casualties, due in no small part to the tactical training they had mastered that summer in reserve.

Reaching the ridge that was their day's objective, the infantrymen were treated to the spectacular sight of old-style cavalry mounted on horseback, and new-style tanks destined to replace the animals, operating in action together for one of the last times in history.

> The way was now open for exploitation of the victory . . . With the gradual receding of the machine-gun fire, indicative of the rapid progress being made by the assaulting infantry, the horsemen became more numerous . . . The ordinary noises of battle

became drowned in an unfamiliar sound, unfamiliar to soldiers who had become accustomed for years to seeing no quadruped on the field other than artillery horses. A loud drumming of hoofs resounded over the valley road. A short while before dotted with straggling bodies of infantry, the road back towards Domart and Hangaard became obscured in a swirl of dust. The rataplan of galloping horses, the jingle of accoutrements and the clash of swords ushered in the cavalry. Above the dust-cloud rose the glitter of lances, their bright pennants flying in the wind, the sheen of the weapons radiating flashes in the sunlight. Cheering wildly, a never-ending line of dragoons, hussars and lancers, galloped over the crossings of the Luce, mounted the slopes on the other side, and, extending, swept in a thunder of hoofs through the advanced lines of infantry. With a clear sweep and heedless of the fire that rained upon them, they breasted the face of the hills and disappeared into the blue.[3]

Small tanks, ungainly but speedy, rumbled along in the train of the horsemen. The faint rattle of machine-guns, swelling and dying away, borne over the ridges from Caix was all that told of the continuation of the battle. Long before midday the Second Battalion were resting comfortably on a general line that followed the easterly flank of the Beaucourt Valley. Amid the orchards of Cayeux-en-Santerre they bivouacked in an environment of pastoral beauty. They were six miles within enemy territory, four of which had been gained only after stiff fighting.[4]

As a result of this day's operations the Germans suffered their greatest defeat since the beginning of this war. German troops had been thrown back eight miles in the Canadian sector, seven miles by the Australians, five miles by the French and two miles by the British. General Erich Ludendorff wrote "August 8th was the black day of the German Army in the history of this war."[5] German morale would never recover and even the Kaiser was now convinced that the war could no longer be won. Canadian casualties were comparatively

[3] In fact, the very last cavalry charge into wartime action had occurred on March 30, 1918 at Moreuil Wood, 12 miles southeast of Amiens. A mounted squadron of Lord Strathcona's Horse, led by Lt. G.M. Flowerdew, charged the occupying German infantry. The enemy stoutly resisted and in the ensuing hand-to-hand fighting Flowerdew was mortally wounded. His gallant leadership resulted in the Germans being routed and in him receiving, posthumously, the Victoria Cross.

[4] Murray, op. cit., p. 265.

[5] Ibid. p. 407n.

light—3,868, with 1,036 killed, 2,803 wounded, and twenty-nine taken prisoner. The 2nd Battalion suffered one officer killed and two wounded and ten other ranks killed, sixty-two wounded and nine missing in action. One of the missing was George Fanning.

GEORGE DAVIS FANNING

George was born to Edward and Eliza Ann Fanning in Carleton Place on January 1, 1898. Following his education in town, he found employment as a clerk. He also found time to participate in the local militia unit, the 4nd Regiment, Lanark and Renfrew, from October 11, 1915 to May 11, 1916. George was employed as a guard at the Petawawa internment camp. He travelled to Ottawa to join the 207th (Ottawa and Carleton) Battalion of the Eastern Ontario Regiment on May 12, 1916.

When he attested into the Active Force he was eighteen years old. He was described, at his medical examination on May 12, as standing 5' 10" tall and weighing 152 pounds. He was of a medium complexion with blue eyes and brown hair. He was also seen to have a slight varicose vein in his left leg. George was a member of the Church of England.

Private Fanning took most of his basic training locally, at Lansdowne Park. The *Herald* of October 10, 1916, noted that, "Pte Geo. Fanning of the 207th has been spending a day or two at home." On May 28, 1917, he embarked aboard the S.S. *Olympic* for the long sail to England. He arrived at Liverpool on June 10. In the United Kingdom the battalion was absorbed into the 6th Reserve Battalion to provide reinforcements for the Canadian Corps in the field.

On January 18, 1918, George was posted to the 2nd Battalion and he arrived in France the next day. He was employed at general duties until February 2 when he joined the 2nd Battalion bivouacked in the field at Camblain Châtelain.

The battalion's duties that first quarter of 1918 were in the trenches, on relief, working parties and patrols. They shuttled between the

Hill 70 area and the village of Les Brebis. One of their main preoccupations, when out of the line, was lectures and demonstrations on the employment of the new tanks in action. Another was farming. The battalion was quartered in an agricultural area. With the prevalent shortage of food, and with many of the troops from rural areas of Eastern Ontario, they took to ploughing and sowing crops. Unfortunately they were far away, in the Amiens sector, when the results of their labour ripened.

World War I had an intriguing ability to seduce many male members of the same family to enlist. And the army had no predilection to turn any of them away. Like the McDiarmids, the Fanning family sent four brothers off to war. One, George, was killed in action; Lloyd and Harris, the youngest, survived; and the eldest, William, was invalided home wounded but later died—his wounds resulting in complications leading to his death.

The editor of *The Almonte Gazette* published the following article on February 15, 1918:

> Four Sons in Khaki, a Splendid Record
>
> With a quartet of her sons at the front, Mrs Edward Fanning, of Carleton Place, is certainly a proud woman. Few mothers have such a patriotic family, who are giving practically their all for King and country. One of her four sons, Cpl. W.A. Fanning, of the 87th (Grenadier Guards) Battalion, who fought in the battle of Vimy Ridge and other engagements, is on his way home to enjoy a well deserved rest. Another son, Gunner L.E. Fanning, of the 32nd Battery, is 'Somewhere in France,' on the firing line. For a time members of Ottawa's famous battalion, the 207th, her other sons, Pte. G.H. Fanning and Pte. H. Fanning, have since been transferred to the 154th Battalion, and are now doing duty on the firing line.[6]

On March 20, George and the 2nd Battalion had to fight off a surprise German attack on Hill 70. The battle of bombs and bayonets, rifles and light machine-guns raged furiously. Training with the Lewis

---

[6] This was probably a "standard issue" press release from the Militia Department after William was wounded and on his way home. The 154th (Stormont, Dundas and Glengarry Highlanders) provided reinforcements for the corps in the field until it was absorbed by the 6th Reserve Battalion on January 1, 1917. In fact, George and Harris had been posted to France, and were serving together in the 2nd Battalion.

guns and exercises in bomb-throwing paid off
and their enemies were repulsed with heavy losses. The battalion lost ten other ranks killed,
twenty-nine wounded, four missing and two
who later died of their wounds. One officer was
wounded.

In April and May, the battalion was in the trench lines near Arras.
The summer of 1918 found the troops in reserve and in billets in the
hamlet of Manin. Except for field training and musketry the men rest-
ed, finding time to engage in athletics. They won the brigade soccer
championship two to nil over the 1st Brigade Headquarters team. On
Dominion Day, 1918, there was a great celebration and sports carnival
at Tinques. Gen. Currie's guests for the event included Field Marshal
H.R.H. the Duke of Connaught, Prime Minister Sir Robert Borden and
Gen. John J. Pershing, the American commander-in-chief. But the 2nd
Battalion was moved that day from Anzin St. Aubin to the Fampoux
Sector and only sixteen officers and one hundred other ranks were
allowed to go to Tinques. Then, in July, the nine weeks of holiday from
the front lines came to an end. They moved into the line east of Arras.

On August 3, the battalion boarded trains at Petit Houvain for the
long, and secret, journey by boxcar to Aumatre where they disembarked on the morning of the 4th and marched seven miles toward
Amiens.

That same day, August 3, Capt. William Henry Vickers Hooper
gained his release. It was reported in the *Herald* of August 27 that his
wife Mabel had received a message to the effect that he ". . . previously reported prisoner of war, was repatriated August 3. He was wounded and taken prisoner at Langemarck [on April 24, 1915], got to
Switzerland a year or so ago and is only obtaining his freedom now."

On August 8, 1918, George Fanning went missing. No trace of
him was ever found. However, information later surfaced that, during
military operations at Ignaucourt and Cayeux-en-Santerre whilst
advancing with his platoon, Fanning was seen to have been struck by
a piece of enemy shrapnel and instantly killed.

The *Carleton Place Herald* of August 20 reported, under photographs of George Fanning and Archie McCaw:

Heavy Casualty Lists

Two Carleton Place Men Killed and Two Wounded

Killed: Pte George Fanning and Pte Arch. M. McCaw

The sad news of the death of Pte. George Fanning reached the parents here last evening by cable. George was one of the four sons of Mr. and Mrs. Ed. Fanning who enlisted with the 207th in Ottawa. The eldest, William, arrived home some time ago disabled. The youngest, Harris, is on the invalid list at present in England, and Lloyd is still in France. The presumption is that Pte. Fanning fell in the last big raid made by the Canadians, when they surprised the enemy by a brilliant attack and were so successful in gaining their objective. The sympathy of the whole town flows to the bereaved family.

William Fanning, a member of the 87th (Canadian Grenadier Guards) Battalion, was wounded on June 26, 1917, by shrapnel to the right thigh. He had been invalided home to Canada and was discharged in June 1918, with his right leg one inch shorter than the left. Harris also served in the 2nd Battalion and was wounded before George was killed. No doubt George was nearby when Harris was wounded. Harris and Lloyd both survived the war. William died, partly as a result of his wounds, in May 1931. The *Gazette* noted on March 8, 1918, that Pte. Jos. H. Fanning of Carleton Place had been wounded. This would have been his second wound.

In the *Herald* of September 3, 1918, the following card of thanks appeared:

The undersigned desire to return their most sincere thanks to the many friends who have by letter and otherwise expressed to them their sympathy in their hour of bereavement. These tokens have done much to assuage the pangs of sorrow and encourage us to look on the brighter side and will not soon be forgotten.

Mr. and Mrs. E. Fanning and family

The Commonwealth War Graves inscription reads:

GEORGE DAVIS FANNING

(246267 Private) born in Carleton Place, son of Edward and Eliza Ann Fanning of 544 Bronson Avenue, Ottawa. One of four brothers who served in France. 2nd Battalion, Eastern Ontario Regiment. Missing, presumed dead, August 8, 1918, age 20. No known grave, commemorated on the Vimy Memorial, Pas de Calais, France.

In that same battle on August 8, Archie McCaw was in action with the 43rd (Winnipeg, Cameron Highlanders) Battalion of the 9th Brigade in the 3rd Division. The 3rd was flanked on their left by the Canadian 1st Division,[7] and on their right by the 42nd Division of the French 31st Corps. Of the Canadian Corps' frontage of 7,000 yards the 3rd Division had about 2,500 yards. They were to advance 7,000 yards and then the 4th Division would pass through them into the attack. The river Luce neatly bisected the 3rd's area of operation.

The 3rd Division was in a most precarious position. The French on their right had no tanks and had to rely on an artillery barrage preceding their infantry. This meant a forty-five-minute delay in the French advance during which time the entire right flank of the Canadian division would be unprotected. Canadian machine-gunners were called upon to fill the breach, which they did most admirably and the attack went off without a hitch. The 3rd had the most treacherous ground to cross because the swamps on either side of the river made a formidable barrier. The 9th Brigade's three infantry battalions and fourteen tanks were ordered to break out with the 43rd Cameron Highlanders making a frontal assault along the Amiens-Roye road as a distraction while the other two battalions, the 58th Central Ontario and 116th Ontario County, outflanked the enemy at Demin village and Hanon Wood.

In the early fog, the tanks got lost. The 43rd Cameron Highlanders followed the creeping artillery barrage one thousand yards along the Amiens-Roye road, totally distracting the Germans who were unable to do anything about the Canadian presence. The Highlanders had reached a blind spot in the road which the enemy small arms fire could not reach. The 58th and the 116th, led by Lt.-

[7] This was the first time the Canadian divisions again worked together in action since the Battle of Vimy Ridge.

Col. George Pearkes, who had won the Victoria Cross at Passchendaele and who was destined to become a beloved lieutenant-governor of British Columbia, broke German resistance in their sector enabling the 43rd to sweep through to their primary objective at Dodo Wood. All this happened before eight in the morning.

It was then the cavalry's turn. At noon they galloped forward. Ironically, even the speedy Whippet tanks were unable to keep up with the horses they were destined to replace; and in the opening engagement all but fifty of the Royal Canadian Dragoons were wiped out. They were forced to dismount and continue the fight with lances and revolvers. The Fort Garry Horse eventually captured the village on foot. Clearly the days of the cavalry were numbered. They were relieved late that afternoon by the 4th Division's infantrymen who had passed through the 3rd Division at 12:40 p.m.[8]

ARCHIBALD MCMORINE MCCAW

Archie McCaw was born in Brockville on August 18, 1885, the son of Thomas and Mary McCaw. The family moved to Carleton Place when he was a youngster and it was there that he received his elementary education. While growing up, Archie enjoyed most sports, but he excelled at rowing. In 1905, he paddled in the open fours crew and in 1906 he was a prominent member of the war canoe team, successfully competing against teams from Smiths Falls and Ottawa. He and John Hockenhull belonged to the Carleton Place half-mile crew that won the Canadian championship in the 1907 regatta at Montreal. The team was welcomed home by a torchlight parade. They went on to win other war canoe championships.

Hockey was another favourite sport for most Carleton Place boys, and Archie was an avid skater. One Thursday evening in January 1906, while casually skating on the rink, he fell and broke his right arm. He was gliding along backwards, hands in his pockets, when the heel of his skate caught in the ice. He went down heavily, fracturing the arm just at the elbow.

[8] Arthur Bishop, *Canada's Glory: Battles that Forged a Nation* (Toronto: McGraw-Hill Ryerson Limited, 1996), pp. 154-155.

After high school Archie trained as a draughtsman. The pursuit of his career took him to Winnipeg with the Canadian Pacific Railroad. He was thirty years old when he joined the 179th (Cameron Highlanders of Canada) Battalion on October 21, 1915. At enlistment he was described at 5' 7" tall, with a fair complexion, hazel eyes and fair hair. The medical examiner recorded finding a scar on the shin of Archie's right leg. He was a member of the Presbyterian congregation.

After the best part of a year training in Canada, the battalion went by train to Halifax. The *Carleton Place Herald* reported on October 3, 1916, that, "Mr. Archie McCaw was among the western soldiers who passed through a few nights ago." They boarded the R.M.S. *Saxonia* on October 4, 1916, for the trip across the Atlantic. The ship docked in Liverpool on October 13. No further training was required in England and Archie went to France to the 43rd Battalion (Cameron Highlanders) on November 12, 1916.

The Cameron Highlanders, whose motto was *Ullamh* (Ready), served in France and Flanders with the 9th Brigade of the 3rd Canadian Division from February 20, 1916, until the armistice. Their dress uniform was a khaki cutaway tunic with a kilt of the Cameron of Erracht tartan. Headdress was a khaki Balmoral or a dark blue Glengarry with red and black dicing. The battalion is perpetuated by the Canadian Militia Regiment—The Queen's Own Cameron Highlanders of Canada.

Pte. McCaw joined the battalion just as it was recovering from operations at the Somme. He was in plenty of time for Arras, Vimy Ridge, Hill 70, Passchendaele and then Amiens, although he almost missed the action at Vimy Ridge. On March 22, 1917, he was admitted to No. 9 Canadian Field Ambulance with complaints of a general myalgia. On March 23 he was sent to No. 6 Canadian Field Ambulance with a diagnosis of acute bronchitis. His health improved and on April 3 he rejoined the battalion in training for the assault on Vimy.

The 43rd, with the entire 9th Brigade, was in reserve for the initial attack on April 9. The 3rd Division, advancing from the northern outskirts of Neuville St. Vaast, had a relatively easier task than the other divisions and they made their objective of La Folie Wood, across the ridge, in about two-and-a-half hours. Because of the division's rapid success, the 43rd was spared the worst of Vimy.

At Passchendaele, on October 25, the 3rd Division was ordered to capture Bellevue Spur, then advance 1,200 yards to the village of Passchendaele, located on the highest point of the ridge. The battalions plodded forward through thick mud, but any gains they made were lost when they were thrown back under heavy shelling by German artillery. The Cameron Highlanders refused to relinquish their hard-won gains and stubbornly held out. It was here that Lt. Robert Shankland won his Victoria Cross. He and his men repulsed enemy counterattacks even though they faced tremendous German advantages in manpower. The lieutenant went back for reinforcements and led the fresh troops through heavy fire to the isolated men of the 43rd. His courage so inspired the troops that they held Bellevue Spur that day. The 3rd Division could not make its objective, Passchendaele, and the men dug in as best they could in water-filled shell holes.

Throughout the rest of the battle in the following days, fighting ferociously, the division's exhausted soldiers continued their assault along the rest of the length of Bellevue Spur. The fighting dragged on with little progress. The night of October 30–31 was full of confusion. No one knew who held what front-line positions. The division paid a very heavy price and was still short of their objective. The depleted battalions were withdrawn and men of the 1st and 2nd Divisions took their place.

On January 31, 1918, Archie McCaw was appointed lance corporal, and on April 24 he was promoted to the rank of corporal and appointed armourer corporal. This meant a pay increase of $1.55 a month.

During the summer of 1918, the division was at Amiens. On August 8, three battalions of the 9th Brigade crowded into a narrow bridgehead south of the river Luce. Each battalion was dispersed in order to advance in five waves at one hundred yard intervals. The foremost two waves of skirmishers were to help guide the tanks, the next three consisted of well-separated sections in a single file. In little more than an hour, the 43rd Battalion had taken German opposition completely by surprise and occupied Rifle Wood. But it was not until 7:30 p.m. (the attack had gone in at 4:20 a.m.) that the wood was cleared of enemy soldiers. Forty machine-guns were captured along with some 250 prisoners. The success was exhilarating. New battalions of the 7th Brigade went through the 43rd's position to continue the rapid progress. That afternoon, the dug-in infantry witnessed the heartwarming and exhilarating sight of massed cavalry forming up to attack.

Archie McCaw never saw the dawn of this day. With the battalion's headquarters company taking part in an attack on enemy positions from the west of Hourges to Dodo Wood, he was killed by shell fire at the "jumping off" trench.

On August 20, 1918, the *Carleton Place Herald* printed Archie's photograph under the heading "Killed in Action—Pte. Arch. M. McCaw." The article contained this news:

> Mr. Thomas McCaw received a cablegram this morning from the Militia Department advising him with regret of the death in action of his son Pte. Archibald McMorran [sic] McCaw. The deceased was 33 years of age, and enlisted with the Royal Highlanders at Winnipeg in 1916. He was a machinist by trade and held many positions of trust with the C.P.R. in the West, having used his fine education to utilize his practical mechanical knowledge to the best advantage. He was most popular with his fellows, and his death will be deeply lamented. Our sympathy flows out to the bereaved parents and only sister, Mrs. W.J. Milne.

And in the issue of August 27:

> The flag on the Club House at the Park was placed at half mast three days last week in honor of Archie McCaw, who was one of our most enthusiastic paddlers in the days gone by.[9]

The Commonwealth War Graves Commission inscription reads:

[9] He had been a member of the 1907 winning half-mile crew at the Canadian Regatta. The Carleton Place Canoe Club was only formed in 1900.

ARCHIBALD (ARCHIE) MCMORINE MCCAW

(859148 Armament Corporal) son of Thomas and Mary McCaw, Carleton Place. 43rd Battalion, Manitoba Regiment. Killed in Action August 8, 1918, age 33. Buried in Hourges Orchard Cemetery, Dormart-sur-la-Luce, Somme, France."

Hourges Orchard Cemetery has 127 Canadian headstones, mostly men of the 43rd and 116th Battalions who led the 9th Brigade's assault along the Luce River. It was once only bare stumps in a scarred battlefield but now is a long narrow gravesite set in verdant woods. There are only two rows of granite stones in this small haven.

On Tuesday, September 17, 1918, the *Herald* reported on the memorial service for Archie:

> On Sunday evening a service in memory of the late Corp. Arch. M. McCaw was held in Zion church. It will be remembered Corp. McCaw was killed in action in the famous drive made by the Canadians at Amiens about the 8th of August. The service was a befitting tribute to one of the sons of the church and was a most impressive one. The preacher, Rev. Mr. Dobson, took for his text the words of the disciple who questioned the wisdom of the anointing of the Saviour's feet with the precious ointment and asked 'Why this great waste?' The question was answered by the Lord himself, which showed that the use of the ointment was justified and hence not a waste. The words were applied to the war and in justification of the tremendous human sacrifice the principle at stake was given. The preacher pointed out how essential sacrifice was to any great achievement, the salvation of man requiring the supreme sacrifice of the Son of God. The sermon was a lesson of resignation and comfort in these troublous days. A few words from the last letter of the deceased soldier, written whilst in the front trenches, and received only a few days ago, was full of love and affection for the home folk and contained these prophetic words: 'You will hear from the Canadians.' And we certainly did. The brave boys, God bless those who are left of them in that famous drive.

WALTER LEWIS

The third Carleton Place soldier to die at Amiens was Walter Lewis. He was serving with the 38th (Ottawa) Battalion in the 12th Brigade of the 4th Division. The 4th Division passed through the 3rd, on August 8, 1918, beginning at 12:40 p.m., about two hours behind the cavalry. The two leading brigades were the 11th and the 12th, both of which encountered considerable machine-gun fire that slowed their advance. The 12th faced considerably less opposition and made good progress over ground that had been swept by the cavalry. The 38th Battalion made such good time that, with the 85th Battalion, they reached their objective by half-past four in the afternoon, four hours from the start line.

The next day, the 9th, Fourth Army Headquarters had a change of mind and delayed further attack for five hours. The enemy made good use of this time to recuperate and reinforce their positions. The 4th Division was sent to clear an area along the Roye Road, but these revised orders meant that the division would be some four miles short of its intended objective.

On August 10, the 4th Division began again to advance at 8:00 a.m. They had been matched with a British division and ordered to attack and clear the old trench lines. The 38th Battalion, moving forward along a railway line, came under heavy fire from the village of Lihons on their left flank. Because they were so far ahead their left side remained uncovered by the Australians advancing beside them. Resistance was hardening considerably. By evening they had pushed their way into the German lines but at a very heavy cost. During the night the 4th Division beat off three counter attacks by the German Alpine Corps. Further advance was no longer possible and the division began consolidating. They had taken over the Canadian 2nd Division line during the night of August 11–12.

Walter was born to John and Ellen Jane Lewis of Carleton Place on July 20, 1898. At age eighteen years, one month, on August 22, 1916, he succumbed to the vigorous recruiting campaign and joined the 240th Overseas Battalion in Renfrew. He stated his trade as stove mounter. During his medical examination he was recorded as weighing 115 pounds, standing 5' 4" tall. He was of a ruddy complexion with brown eyes and black hair. The examining doctor also found a scar on Walter's right thigh over the patella. He stated that he regularly attended the Church of England. Walter was an enthusiastic Boy Scout in the original Carleton Place troop.

Following a winter of local training and further recruitment, the 240th embarked aboard the S.S. *Megantic* in Halifax on April 30, 1917, and set sail for the United Kingdom They arrived in Liverpool on May 14, 1917, and were immediately absorbed into the 6th Reserve Battalion to provide reinforcements for the Canadian Corps in France. After further training in England, Walter was transferred to the 38th Battalion on February 1, 1918. He joined them in the field in France on March 26, linking up with other Carleton Place members of the battalion, like Percy Hughes and Cornelious O'Donovan, none of whom would experience the armistice.

On the way across the channel, or travelling in France to find his unit, Walter had the bad luck to lose some of his kit. On his very first inspection with the 38th, on March 28, he was awarded a stoppage of pay of eleven shillings, nine pence. He was missing his cap; a comforter, which cost him 1/ 5d; his cardigan—9/; badges—2d; a comb—4d; a toothbrush—3d; a knife—4d and his fork—1d.

Three weeks later, on April 22, 1918, Walter was wounded in action. This was the second casualty in the family, his brother Robert having been previously reported wounded.

The German armies were on the rebound. In Picardy they had recaptured the Messines Ridge, seized Armentières and swept over the villages east of Hazebrouck to take Mount Kemmel. Counterattacks by British and French forces failed and the Germans solidified their gains. After a slight lull in the fighting during the last week of April, the Germans returned to the offensive in Flanders, known as the Battle of the Lys. They concentrated their efforts against the heights south of Ypres. After much bloodshed, the enemy advance was finally halted south of Ypres. With a gunshot wound to the left buttock and right heel, Walter was sent to the No. 11 Canadian Field Ambulance on April 22. He recovered and was returned to his unit on April 30. The *Carleton Place Herald* of April 24, 1917, reported:

> No less than five Carleton Place men were reported yesterday in the Casualties list . . . Pte Lewis, son of Mr. John Lewis, wounded.

After a fairly quiet summer, the Canadian Corps moved in early August to Amiens. The Historical Record of the 38th Battalion tells of their movement into battle:

> August 1918—Battle of Amiens.
>
> During the night of 9/10 the Bn moved to the high ground between the village of Caix and the Amiens-Nesle Railway. The 85th and 72nd Bn were to press forward at 10:15 am with the 38th and 78th Bns following in close support. Tanks were allotted to precede the infantry and clear up awkward obstructions.
>
> At a quarter past ten the men went forward again, the 38th following the 85th Bn at a distance of some 800 yards. For a time things went well, but when the regiment passed through Rosières-en-Santerre the advancing troops encountered severe machine-gun and light artillery fire . . . both battalions went on strongly . . . the 85th swung left to attack German gunners and Col. Edwards took the 38th through the 85th front to continue the advance and occupy both objectives alone.
>
> But this was impossible. Beyond the Méhericourt-Lihons Road our fellows plunged into the old trench system, a maze of barbed wire and pointless gulleys. All the time continued enfilading fire from the left flank. Gaining a yard here and there the men pressed forward, continually held up by heavily-armed strong points, and losing severely for every foot of progress. Tanks might have altered the situation considerably, but they could not operate effectively over such broken ground . . . by late afternoon the regiment occupied hasty positions close behind the Chilly-Lihons Road.
>
> Here the battalion remained for a time, subject to heavy artillery and machine-gun fire from the front and left flank, and

in addition undergoing two brisk bouts of shell-fire from our own guns at the rear . . .

It was difficult work. The regiment had suffered heavily . . . the men pressed forward again through the darkness, and during the night A and B Companies connected up with the 78th Bn in front of Hallu, with D Company holding a line of advance posts in the center of our position and C Company on the Chilly-Lihons Road . . . by 6am on the 11th the 12th Bde held a strong and connected front line.

Regimental losses were fairly heavy . . . Nearly two hundred men were killed or wounded.

In the Battle of Amiens the Canadians made an advance of 22,000 yards. They captured 167 heavy guns, over 1,000 machine-guns and 10,000 prisoners, a number in excess of the casualties of the Corps. They drove the enemy from twenty-five towns and villages—freeing the Paris-Amiens Railway—and rendered futile the whole German attempt to divide the French and British Armies. The regiment played a very good part in these amazing achievements.[10]

The Battalion's War Diary presents a good description of the battle as Walter experienced it:

Aug 7—Marched in bright starlight and fine weather from Bovilles to Gentilles Wood. Orders and instructions were fully explained to officers and men. All ranks showed great enthusiasm at the near prospect of having a smack at the Huns and proving their adaptability for open warfare.

3rd Battle of the Somme

At Zero Hour—4:20 barrage opened and at 5:20 12th Bde moved into position. 38th Bn was left leading battalion. Advance during morning carried out without opposition and the bn suffered only a few slight casualties.

12:10 began 2nd phase—long range machine-gun fire was encountered, taken on by Lewis guns and rifles. No serious opposition encountered proceeded to village of CAIX. Held positions during night of 8th/9th.

[10] Historical Records–38th Battalion, National Archives.

0500 am 10th— move to high ground to assembly positions between CAIX and AMIENS-NESLE railway to await further orders. Moved out at 10:15 am preceded by tanks. Advanced to ROSIERES carried out without incident but on emerging on the East of the Village came under machine-gun fire and light artillery fire.

Australians on left flank halted by opposing fire and 85th Bn unable to proceed—38th pushed through 85th and tried to go to own objective—proved impossible owing to increased fire being brought in enfilade from the left and great difficulty was experienced . . . owing to the presence of large quantities of old wire in good condition and network of trenches which retarded progress . . . subjected to enemy fire of artillery and machine-gun both from our front and left flanks and in addition two shoots by our own light artillery harassed us from the rear . . .

About 8:30 am on the 11th the enemy placed a heavy concentration of artillery on our right Companies A and B . . . and about 9 o'clock made an attack from the East and North East. A and B Companies withstood this attack gallantly but suffered many casualties, especially from their left flank where the enemy worked in behind them. After repelling this attack the forward companies were withdrawn a short distance to improve and straighten the line.[11]

The 4th Division, on August 10, gained two miles in the face of determined German opposition. The 12th Brigade, with the 11th, was confronted with three villages to capture before the labyrinth of trenches could be broached. Mancourt fell easily, Chilly by noon and Hallu by two o'clock. The 38th Ottawa and the 8th Nova Scotia battalions, advancing along the railway line, were halted under extremely heavy enemy machine-gun and artillery fire.

By the end of action on August 10, Pte. Walter Lewis was nowhere to be found. In the heavy fighting along the railway toward Rosières, he had vanished. He was never listed as a prisoner of war and no trace of him was ever found. Walter was last seen on a Lewis gun post in the village of Hallu, just before the enemy laid down a barrage and coun-

---

[11] War Diary, 38th Battalion, National Archives.

terattacked about 10:00 a.m. on August 10, 1918. No further information concerning him was ever received by his battalion commander.

The Commonwealth War Graves Commission commemorates Walter as follows:

WALTER LEWIS

(1042092 Private) son of Mr. J.E. and Mrs. E.S. Lewis, Carleton Place. 38th Battalion, Eastern Ontario Regiment. Missing, presumed dead, in France, August 10, 1918, age 17. No known grave, commemorated on the Vimy Memorial, Pas de Calais, France.

Over the next few days, Canadians and Australians held tenaciously to hard-won gains. A renewed offensive over this impassable, churned-up ground would only present totally unacceptable losses. Sir Arthur Currie wanted to leave Amiens which was by now considered a successful operation.

On August 14, Haig issued orders for the Canadian Corps to move north to the Arras Sector as part of the British First Army. The Canadians did not withdraw until the 16th and in the meantime were charged with straightening out and strengthening the front line. This was the last time they fought as a volunteer force: reinforcements in the form of conscripts had begun to arrive.[12]

[12] Arthur Bishop, *Canada's Glory: Battles that Forged a Nation* (Toronto: McGraw-Hill Ryerson Limited, 1996), p. 160.

Chapter Twenty-Six

ARRAS

During the night of August 19–20, 1918, French troops began to relieve the Canadian Corps. On the 19th, the 2nd Canadian Division was moved by motorbus and train northward to the Arras sector. They were followed on August 20 by the 3rd Division and, a few days later, the 1st and 4th Divisions joined the rest of the corps. The commander, Gen. Currie, had the satisfaction of reporting to his troops that Gen. Byng had called the Canadian performance at Amiens, "the finest operation of the war."[1]

The 1st Canadian Division arrived on August 25, not in time to participate with the 2nd and 3rd Division in the Canadian Corps' Battle of the Scarpe, which lasted from August 26 to 30. During the night of August 28–29, the 1st relieved the thoroughly tired 2nd Division near Cagnicourt. This was in the middle of the Battle for Arras which lasted from August 26 to September 5. The Canadian Corps was ordered to attack on September 2 toward Cambrai, along the Arras-Cambrai road. The 1st Division was concentrated south of the road. Lt. Frank Murphy was serving with the 15th Battalion (Toronto—48th Highlanders of Canada) in the 3rd Brigade of the 1st Division. And so we now follow their movements.

On the morning of September 1, the 2nd and 3rd Brigades captured the Crow's Nest, a German strong point on a high bluff overlooking a large section of the Canadian defences. This position made an excellent jumping-off point for the next day's attack. They now faced one of the most powerful and well-organized enemy defence systems, composed of abundant concrete shelters, machine-gun posts and dense masses of the hated barbed wire.

Currie intended to use the 1st Division as the main attacking troops. He planned to break the German defences along the Arras-Cambrai Road and proceed to within striking distance of the Canal du Nord. The 3rd Brigade, with the 2nd Brigade on the left, would lead the assault. The enemy sensed coming action and made several coun-

[1] General Currie's diary, August 22, 1918.

terattacks during the afternoon and evening of September 1. The Canadians had hard fighting just to maintain their positions for the main offensive.

Just before dawn, on a very dark night that fortunately was free of rainfall, the artillery barrage signalled the beginning of the attack. The 3rd Brigade met little resistance at first and pushed quickly up the slope. German defenders were surrendering in large numbers. But to the right, heavy machine-gun fire held up the infantry's advance. The 15th Battalion, pushing through the 16th, suffered crippling casualties and slowly fought their way to the Bois de Bouche, where they were halted until British forces arrived to strengthen their flank. By 6:00 p.m., artillery fire was called in and eased the situation enough to allow the tired Canadians to proceed and capture Buissey Switch at 11:00 p.m. The Canadians had succeeded by taking Buissey Switch and the villages of Villiers-de-Cagnicourt and Cagnicourt in the face of resolute opposition from the German 1st, 2nd and 3rd Guard Reserve Divisions. In the process, Lt. Frank Murphy suffered a devastating wound to the abdomen.

FRANCIS MICHAEL MURPHY, MiD

Frank was born on June 30, 1888, the youngest son of James and Elizabeth Magdalen Murphy, Carleton Place. After completing his education, he went to work for the Bank of Montreal, first at the Trafalgar Square Branch in London, England, and then in Toronto. It was there that he joined the 134th Battalion (48th Highlanders) of the Canadian Expeditionary Force.

The motto of this highland regiment was *Dileas Gu Brath*, gaelic for *"Faithful Forever."* They wore the Davidson tartan kilt and headdress of a dark blue Glengarry with black cock's feathers. Neatly coiffed, with a precisely timmed dark mustache, Lt Francis M. Murphy cut a fine figure of a Scottish officer in his regimental full dress uniform. In England, the regiment was first absorbed by the 12th Reserve Battalion to provide reinforcements for the Canadian Corps in France, but later restructured into the 5th Canadian Division where it served in England from October 27, 1916 until February 9, 1918, when it was again broken up to provide reinforcements.

Sir Sam Hughes had created the Overseas Battalions in Valcartier, giving most of them a regional identity. Canadians, a conservative people living in a new country, were used to creating instant traditions.

> Ideally, a soldier wore the same badge, shared the same traditions, gained promotion, and suffered punishment within one regimental family throughout his service. In the vast anonymity of the army, a battalion or battery was like a small town, full of remembered faces, shared experiences, and old friends and enemies.
>
> When most overseas battalions reached England, their privately purchased cap and collar badges, their expensive band instruments, and the "regimental colours" —banners neatly embroidered by the officers' wives—became superfluous. Those battalions already in France desperately needed junior officers and soldiers to preserve their own identity and contribute to their growing history.
>
> Most of the fresh soldiers were devastated. For a soldier, losing his own battalion was almost as traumatic as any family break-up . . . the colours found their way to some British or home-town church.
>
> Once over that blow, most soldiers soon made the transition to their new battalion. In fact, after the war, they usually identified themselves as part of their front-line unit.[2]

The dashingly handsome Frank Murphy joined the 134th Overseas Battalion (48th Highlanders) in Toronto on December 28, 1915. He remained in the militia and was appointed adjutant of the battalion. On March 7, 1916, he was promoted to the rank of captain. He transferred to the active force on January 18, 1916 and was a captain on the 134th Battalion staff when he embarked for overseas on H.M.T. *Scotian*. They left Halifax on August 8, 1916, arriving in Liverpool on August 18. Curiously, while he assigned a portion of his

[2] Desmond Morton, *When Your Number's Up: The Canadian Soldier in the First World War* (Toronto: Random House of Canada, 1993), pp. 76-77.

pay to his mother in care of his brother Peter, who worked with the Bank of Ottawa, he directed that in case of casualty his mother was not to be notified first, but the first to know should be a "Major Creighton, Local 15."

Capt. Murphy remained on headquarters staff until, at his own request, he was transferred on March 6, 1918, to the 12th Reserve Battalion in Whitley to prepare for action in France. On March 12 he was detached to the 16th (British Columbia—Canadian Scottish) Battalion and went to France with them on March 13. On April 3, Frank was listed as joining the 16th Battalion holding unit, awaiting further disposition to a unit in the line. On May 7, in order to get into action, Frank reverted from his position as a supernumerary officer in

the rank of captain with the 16th Battalion, to the rank of temporary lieutenant to be absorbed into the establishment of the 15th (Toronto—48th Highlanders of Canada) Battalion. It had no room for any more captains so in order to get into action he had to take the reduction in rank. This also put him back amongst friends from Toronto and the 48th Highlanders.

Frank joined the battalion, which was part of the 3rd Brigade of the 1st Division, as they went into reserve after holding a line stemming the German advance in the Arras Sector. Fortunately they were exposed to little action and could devote their time to strengthening their positions and replenishing their manpower and equipment. He witnessed the spectacular Dominion Day 1918 celebration which featured the corps' largest sports day. The 1st Canadian Division won top honours in the full programme of track and field events. The division also hosted the day's memorable "Concert Party."

The next day, Prime Minister Sir Robert Borden inspected units of the 1st and 4th Divisions. On the following Saturday, July 6, the 3rd Brigade, with its two Highland regiments (the 13th [Montreal—Royal Highlanders] and the 15th), hosted a Highland gathering at Tinques, which included Highland regiments of the British Army as well as all the Highland battalions of the Canadian Corps. The day of Highland games competition concluded with the playing of the Retreat by the massed pipe bands of the 3rd Brigade. This soul-stirring spectacle involved 284 pipers and 164 drummers.

The long period of rest and training came to an end on July 15, when the corps went back into the line. The end of July had them moving with the utmost secrecy into a concentration area west of Amiens.

For the attack on August 8, the 1st Division was in the centre of the corps' line with the 3rd Division on its left and the 2nd on its right. The primary objective of the 1st Division meant their 3rd Brigade had to attack down a slope, through Hangard Wood and the German front line and support trenches, and across a wooded valley known as Morgemont Wood to capture the enemy main line of resistance on the high ground. They had to fight through a sharp valley called Pantaloon Ravine in which there were many German gun positions and finally make their way onto the forward slope of the north bank of the Luce River. They were then ordered through the heavily wooded valley of the Luce, through the small village of Ignacourt and on to the large town of Caix.

The division was supported by a battalion of tanks and seven brigades of field artillery, which meant that each gun had a front of about forty yards.

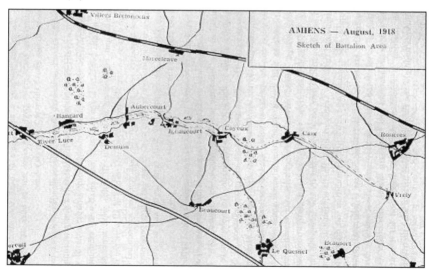

The 3rd Brigade used the 13th, 14th and 16th Battalions to attack, with the 5th and 15th in support. They met little resistance and by 11:00 a.m. had crossed the Luce and secured the village of Ignacourt. The 3rd Brigade rested while the 2nd pressed on, continuing the attack through the next day, August 9. This great Battle of Amiens was fought by infantry and tanks against machine-gun defences. Artillery provided a barrage for the first advance of 5,000 yards, but were little used thereafter. From August 10 to 20, opposition stiffened and the fighting was a series of bitter minor operations. On August 20, the corps moved north toward Arras, and the final battle.

The Battle of Arras, from August 26 to September 4, was intended to break through the enemy's line and push for Cambrai. The 1st Division was still moving north from Amiens when the operation opened. The last units moved by train and bus to the Neuville Vitasse-Telegraph Hill area on the 27th and the 1st Division was ordered to relieve the 2nd Division on the night of August 28–29. A major offensive was planned to begin on September 1 to break the German hold on the Drocourt-Quéant line, cross the Canal du Nord and seize Bourlon Wood and the high ground to the north. The assault was then slipped a day, to September 2, in order to give the artillery time to soften up the enemy and cut the concentrated mass of barbed wire.

On the night of August 31, the 3rd Brigade went into the line, with the 15th and 14th Battalions in the fore, taking over a trench from the 1st Battalion that bore the morbid name "Cemetery Avenue." The relief was hampered by shell-fire, the darkness of night, a cold rain that fell at intervals and the uncertainty as to where the 1st Battalion positions really were. They finally got into position at 3:30 a.m. At dawn the next day they were to begin their advance to secure a "jumping-off" position on the Crow's Nest for the great attack of September 2. There was no communication between the companies and battalion headquarters during the night except by runner. Lt. F.M. Murphy, the acting adjutant, now issued the CO's orders:

1. The attack will be made under a rolling barrage with 100-yard lifts every four minutes.

2. 4.5 Howitzers will bombard selected targets.

3. On the capture of the Crow's Nest the 15th Battalion will send up a rocket breaking green over green.

4. After the capture of the final objective, a succession of white Very lights will be fired.

5. Zero will be at 4:50 am.

So, the 15th Battalion once more moved forward to wait out the dripping night in order to commit sudden assault and battery upon their foemen from beyond the Rhine.[3]

The guns opened up and suddenly the Highlanders were off, stumbling and slipping across the shuddering ground before them. The plan of attack proved excellent, casualties were comparatively light and the Canadians overwhelmed the surprised defenders. By the time the sun rose and broad daylight appeared, all objectives had been taken. The battalion spent the rest of the day consolidating their gains. The first message back to headquarters read, "Crow's Nest taken. 50 prisoners, 1 officer. Casualties light. Germans want peace."[4] However, throughout the rest of the day they met determined enemy resistance as the Germans mounted four counterattacks in bitter fighting using stick grenades and mortars in the trenches.

The battalion was then ordered to attack the Drocourt-Quéant Line, the last obstacle looming between them and the Canal du Nord. The line was wire-belted, strongly manned and cluttered with machine-guns. It would be a major operation, fraught with difficulty and one of the hardest nuts the Canadian Corps had to crack. Long after midnight on September 1, with but a short time available for organization, the CO's operation order was issued by Capt Murphy.[5] They were the last documents this gallant officer signed.

Five a.m. marked Zero Hour on September 2. The infantry moved forward with the 15th and 14th Battalions of the 3rd Brigade leading the advance. The attack proceeded rapidly against a strong resistance that slowed but did not stop the determined Canadians. They took the

[3] Kim Beatty, *48th Highlanders of Canada* (Toronto: 48th Highlanders, 1932), p. 349.

[4] Ibid., p. 352.

[5] He had been promoted in the field but the official order was not implemented before he died.

line and then advanced again at 9:00 a.m.. German resistance stiffened and the attackers were stopped.

> It was to the immortal credit of the 15th Battalion and the leadership of the officers that the men had the individual courage to get up and face the fire. The 15th Battalion was now advancing into the machine guns. They leaned forward with grim faces like men facing a hurricane, their jaws twitching and flinching as if feeling a bullet crashing home. It took stark bravery . . .
>
> Men were crashing down along the broken, uneven line and during a rush forward under heavy fire Capt. F.M. Murphy fell at Major Girvan's [O.C. of the 15th] side, mortally wounded by machine gun bullets. He died shortly afterwards . . . Against rifle, bomb and flanking fire the men sweated and cursed and fought on.[6]

By 4:00 p.m. they had established their line east of Cagnicourt. The 3rd Brigade suffered heavy casualties during the day of intense hand to hand fighting. That night they were relieved by the 1st Brigade. They had the Drocourt-Quéant Line but had yet to cross the Canal du Nord. They had battled hard over shell-torn ground using artillery, infantry and machine-guns. It was stopped, not by enemy resistance, but by the natural obstacle of the Canal du Nord, reinforced by machine-guns. The 15th Battalion moved back for a well-earned rest.

Capt. Frank Murphy had been dealt a mortal wound. About 9:00 a.m., while with his battalion in the attack on the Drocourt-Quéant Line, he took a machine gun bullet to the stomach. He was taken back to No. 2 Canadian Field Ambulance, but medical help was to no avail and Frank died later that day, September 2, 1918. Under a photograph of the young man in uniform, his death was reported in the *Carleton Place Herald* on September 10:

> Lieut Frank Murphy Died of Wounds
>
> Mrs. Murphy received a message last Friday evening from her son Peter, manager of Bank of Ottawa, Montreal, advising her of the death of his brother Frank, who died of wounds in France September the 2nd. Frank was the youngest son of the

[6] Ibid., p. 361.

late James L. and Mrs. Murphy, and was born in Carleton Place. He was 30 years of age. He selected banking for his life work and made good rapidly, having held an important position in London, Eng., for some years. On his return he was stationed in Toronto where he enlisted with the 184th Gordon Highlanders, being made Captain and Adjutant, and went overseas two years ago. He spent a long term in Whitley Camp in England and went to France as a non comm. officer. The bereaved mother and other members of the family have our sympathy in their hour of grief.

On December 31, 1918, Lt. Murphy was awarded the honour "Mentioned in Dispatches." This entitled him to use the initials MiD following his name and wear a Palm Leaf on the right chest of his uniform. An MiD was one of only two gallantry awards in the British Commonwealth system that could be awarded posthumously, the other being the Victoria Cross. The MiD is not necessarily a gallantry award but it describes exactly how the soldier was recognized—a mention by name in official dispatches. It was awarded to officers and soldiers for service in an operational area in contact with the enemy, for an act of bravery, exceptional conduct, efficiency, or performances over and above the call of duty. It was awarded for gallantry in some cases, but the vast majority of awards were for meritorious service.

Lt. Frank Murphy is buried in France. The commemorative information reads:

In Memory of
F. M. MURPHY
Lieutenant [7]
15th Bn., Canadian Infantry (Central Ontario Regt.)
who died on
Monday, 2nd September 1918.

Frank's body lies in the Anzin-St Aubin British Cemetery, Pas de Calais, France. The village of Anzin-St. Aubin is on the northwestern outskirts of Arras. The red brick walled cemetery was begun by the

[7] Although Frank was promoted to captain in the field, the paperwork never got completed. It became superfluous after his death and thus the new rank never became substantive. Although he was a captain at the war's beginning, by taking a reduction in rank to get overseas, he died a lieutenant.

British Army's 51st (Highland) Division in April 1917. It was closed in September 1918, containing over 350 World War I casualties.

ARTHUR NORMAN HOUSTON

Field ambulance units operated close behind the fighting battalions. Regimental stretcher-bearers would take the wounded back to a regimental aid post where the field ambulance bearers would carry the injured to the dressing station. Rudimentary as it was, aid was never far away but getting to the stations in the Flanders mud more often than not proved an insurmountable barrier.

Shortly after he turned eighteen, Arthur Houston travelled to Kingston to join, with some of his friends, the Queen's University Ambulance Corps.

At enlistment, on May 26, 1916, Arthur was given regimental number 535964. He listed his next of kin as his father, S.B. Houston, of R.R. #2, Perth. His mother was a daughter of Mr. Brice McNeely of Ramsay. He claimed his birth date as October 7, 1898, and his previous occupation as a student. He was a member of the congregation of the Church of England. Arthur's medical examination revealed a young man fit for overseas service, eighteen years old, 5' 5" tall and weighing 120 pounds. He had a dark complexion, brown eyes and brown hair.

The Queen's University Ambulance Corps spent 1916 training at the Barriefield camp, which afforded the local men plenty of opportunity to visit home. And almost everyone was recorded in the *Carleton Place Herald*:

> August 15, 1916—Ptes. H. Menzies, A. McFarlane, W. Coyles, H. Sinclair, D. Emerson, W. Peevers, W. Morphy, A. Houston and S. Houston of the Queen's Ambulance Corps, Barriefield, spent a few days at their respective homes here last week.

> September 26, 1916—Lanark News—Four sons of Mr. & Mrs. Stewart [*sic*] Houston of Drummond are now wearing the khaki. Bruce, the eldest son, enlisted in the west with the 210th

Battalion and is training at Camp Hughes. Fred, Stewart and Arthur are at Kingston with Queen's Field Ambulance, the former holding rank as Captain.

December 26, 1916—Amongst our soldier boys home for the Yuletide are Arthur Houston of the Queen's Ambulance.

February 20, 1917—Sergt. S. Houston, Pte. H. Robertson & Signallers H. Umphrey and Houston, all of the Queen's Ambulance Corps are spending a few days at their respective homes here.

February 27, 1917—A dozen of our boys who are with The Queen's Ambulance Corps have been making their farewell home visit. Sergt. Houston, Ptes. McCullough, Sinclair, Robertson, Houston.

Officially designated the 15th Canadian Field Ambulance of the Canadian Expeditionary Force, the unit embarked from Canada aboard the S.S. *Saxonia* on March 28, 1917, arriving in England on April 7. They stayed for almost another year in Whitley camp providing medical services to the troops training and awaiting postings as reinforcements to the Canadian Corps in France. On March 3, 1918, Arthur was posted to the Canadian Army Medical Corps Depot in Shorncliffe and from there, on April 9, he went overseas as a reinforcement, landing at Le Havre in France.

In June 1918, while four Houston brothers were serving overseas, the fifth and youngest brother, Drummond, at age seventeen, was swept away by the spring currents of the Mississippi River and drowned. After eating their lunch at the high school, about a dozen boys wandered to the river for a quick dip at Manny's Point. Drummond's body was found six days later just below the falls in Appleton.

On April 23, Arthur was posted to the 12th Canadian Field Ambulance working with the 4th Canadian Division. The first week of May, the Canadian Corps (1st, 3rd and 4th Divisions) began a period in reserve and training. Dominion Day brought a welcome respite from the intensity of training. Nearly fifty thousand Canadians gathered in perfect weather at Tincques, a village fourteen miles west of

Arras. They competed in the corps' largest sports day and were entertained by battalion brass and pipe bands.

The corps' long period of rest ended on July 15 when they went back into the line. They then began preparing, in utmost secrecy, for the offensive at Amiens. The Canadian Corps' attack began at 4:20 a.m. on August 8, lead by the 1st, 2nd and 3rd Division. The 4th would leapfrog the 3rd as it advanced, to take over the 3rd's positions at Beaucourt village. Their orders were to attack German positions from Le Quesnel to Caix, but as the 4th Division followed the early successes of the day, German resistance strengthened considerably. The advance slowed and as darkness descended it was clear that the capture of Le Quesnel would have to wait until tomorrow.

The second day, the 1st, 2nd and 3rd attacked again, but it was not until day three that the 4th was given the unpleasant task of breaking into the old defences of the Somme. In front of these trenches, they had to advance across open ground raked by machine-gun fire. Grimly they fought their way through and by evening were firmly entrenched, holding on by the skin of their teeth as the enemy mounted fierce counterattacks. The last major assault was over on August 10. Once again the Canadian Corps had spearheaded a major British victory. Arthur Houston had his first taste of war and the human cost of battle. Canadian losses totalled 11,822 killed and wounded.

During a lull in the fighting at the end of August, the 4th Division moved north with the 1st to join the 2nd and 3rd back in the Arras sector. The Canadian Corps was ordered to attack on September 2 and seize crossings over the Canal du Nord. The 4th Division, advancing in the centre of the corps, had a particularly hard battle. The 12th Brigade had to contend with a German pocket along the Arras-Cambrai Road but with no supporting tanks to help. They found the opposing trenches on the Drocourt-Quéant Line heavily wired and strongly manned, but they pushed on in spite of mounting casualties. By midmorning they had captured the road.

The advance continued on September 3 with the 4th Division liberating several villages, only to find the east side of the canal strongly held and all bridges destroyed. The German defence crumbled and started to withdraw. Canadian forces suffered 297 officers and 5,325 other ranks listed as casualties. One was Pte. Arthur Houston.

On September 3, Arthur was carried to his own field ambulance dressing station with a gunshot wound in his left leg. He was treated and the same day evacuated wounded to the Casualty Clearing Station. On September 4, he was admitted to No. 56 General Hospital in Etaples. His wound healed sufficiently that on September 10 he was sent to the Brigade Depot classified as "ambulatory" with a medical category "A". On September 17, he left to rejoin the 12th Field Ambulance, catching up with them on September 21.

Arthur was back in the thick of battle during the Canadian advance toward Cambrai during the last days of September and early October. The enemy was badly shaken and the end was clearly in sight. But they would stubbornly not give up. On October 9, Canadians captured Cambrai in one of the bloodiest battles of the war. Then, advancing quickly, they fought through Valenciennes, Mont Huoy and, on November 11, reached the historic city of Mons.

The armistice was signed. The war was over.

Canadian troops remained in Europe as part of the occupation force. In 1919, they started for home.

On March 8, 1919, Arthur Houston was struck off strength of the 12th Field Ambulance to return to the Canadian Army Medical Casualty unit in Shorncliffe. He signed up for a course of study with Khaki University of Canada at the Central College in Ripon, Yorkshire, as a project of the Canadian YMCA. With military duties reduced to a mini-

mum the Khaki University undertook to prepare men for civilian life. Education, in many cases, had been interrupted by the war and the Khaki University helped individual battalion schools by preparing and printing textbooks on elementary subjects. In September 1918, Khaki University of Canada was formally authorized as a branch of the General Staff, with control over all educational organizations overseas. The Central College offered matriculation courses and the first two years of university arts courses.

On May 3, 1919, Arthur completed his studies and was returned to Canada for discharge which occurred on May 26, 1919. His medical examination for leaving the service described him as in good physique with a burn scar on his right side. Somewhere he had picked up twenty pounds and grown an inch—140 pounds, height 5' 6".

But recovery from such traumatic wounds is slow and never complete. Arthur Houston died April 4, 1922, at age twenty-four, leaving to mourn three brothers—Brice, Stuart, and Fred; two sisters— Elizabeth and Evelyn; and his parents—Stuart and Janie. His death was officially attributed to his military service.

1st Division

Marching toward Mons during Canada's Hundred Days, with the 2nd Battalion of the 1st Brigade of the 1st Canadian Division, was Charles Ross Simpson. In the winter months of 1917–1918, the 1st Division had been involved in dashing raids against the enemy at Avion, Lievin, St. Pierre and Hill 70. Stationed in the British First Army's sector, however, they were outside the area of heaviest German attacks. In March they made a sudden rush to Arras to help stem the Hun advance, but the following days were taken up mostly with outpost fighting and continuous raiding.

On August 8–9, the Battle of Amiens was the first of the great counteroffensives launched in 1918. The three Canadian Divisions attacked with the 1st Division in the centre, the 3rd Division on its left and the 2nd Division the right. The 1st Division had a front of 3,000 yards. They were ordered to attack down a slope, through the scrub and brush known as Hangard Wood, and across the wooded valley of the River Luce. They were to capture the high ground which held the main line of German resistance. But on August 1, the division was still in front of Arras. They were relieved during the night of August 2 and moved by bus and train to their assembly area southwest of Amiens. They arrived early on August 5. It was only on the night prior to battle that the 1st, 2nd and 3rd Brigades were in place in front of Gentelles Wood.

On the morning of August 8, at 5:10 a.m., three battalions in line, the 2nd, 3rd and 4th, moved forward. This was Ross Simpson's first major battle. He had joined the 2nd Battalion in the field in February.

CHARLES ROSS SIMPSON

The *Carleton Place Herald*, in the edition of May 23, 1916, reported that, "Five Carleton Place boys have united with the 207th Battalion viz., Clayton McMullen, Percy Hughes, Norman Morris, Ross Simpson and W. McEachen." Ross had enlisted in Ottawa with the 207th (Ottawa and Carleton) Canadian Infantry Battalion on May 12, 1916. Nine days earlier he had turned eighteen and become eligible to join the Canadian Expeditionary Force. He had been in the militia with the 42nd Regiment Guard detachment.

Ross was born on May 3, 1898, to William R. and Patterson (Minnie) Simpson. Both he and his brother, Ralph, attended Victoria School (the present museum), in Carleton Place. When Ross joined the army the family was living on Herriott Street and he was working as a butcher. He regularly attended the Presbyterian Church. His medical examiner found a young man with a ruddy complexion, blue eyes and fair hair who stood 5' 8" tall. He was obviously in very good health.

Pte. Simpson spent almost a year in training and performing guard duties locally and in Petawawa. This afforded him plenty of opportunities to visit home, as the *Herald* printed on December 26, 1916: "Amongst the soldier boys home for the Yuletide is . . . Ross Simpson of the 207th Battalion." The battalion, and Ross with it, embarked on the S.S. *Olympic* from Halifax on May 28, 1917. He disembarked in Liverpool on June 10. Percy Hughes, who had enlisted the same day and had been with Ross ever since, disembarked a day earlier.

The battalion went into a bivouac on the Salisbury Plain where it was absorbed by the 6th Reserve Battalion to provide reinforcements for the corps in France. Most, like Percy, went to the sister battalion, the 38th, but Ross was posted to the 2nd Battalion. He sailed to France on January 18, 1918, and, no doubt happy to be with his brother Ralph, joined the Battalion on February 3. This placed him in the line for the Battle of Amiens in August.

On August 8, Ross began to move forward at 5:10 a.m.; and everywhere the infantry was successful. They had no covering heavy artillery barrage but their advance was supported by eighteen tanks, three machine-gun batteries and the 2nd Brigade of Field Artillery. The 2nd Battalion secured its objective—the high ground east of Cayeaux—and crossed the Luce by 11:00 a.m. The brigade continued the attack on the 9th with the 2nd Battalion in support. The attacking battalions encountered intense machine-gun fire and had to divert southward. With the forward troops falling to the machine-guns, the 2nd Battalion was ordered into the gap. Without stopping they fought on through to the objective. At 9:00 p.m. they were relieved in the line by the 3rd Battalion. Conditions for these two days of fighting had been almost ideal for the tanks and infantry, which worked in close cooperation.

On August 20 the troops moved north again to their next great battle. From August 26 to September 8,they were in the line near Arras. The 1st Division was the last to leave Amiens and did not arrive in the Arras sector until the August 27, when the infantry moved into the Neuville Vitasse-Telegraph Hill area. On the night of August 28–29, they accomplished a difficult relief of the 2nd Division, which was pushing forward on attack.

The 1st Brigade was ordered, on August 30, to advance its line 3,000 yards in preparation for a larger attack the next day. At 4:40 a.m., the 2nd Battalion was along the Fresnes-Rouvoy Trench. They advanced well but heavy fighting continued all day. A German counterattack was stopped by 2nd Battalion men but they could not drive the enemy completely back until nightfall and only then with the help of other battalions. The 1st Brigade was relieved during the night of August 31. There remained the Canal du Nord to cross.

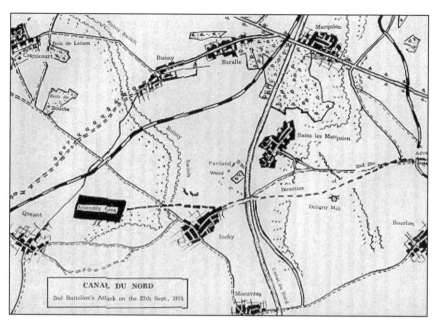

CANAL DU NORD
2nd Battalion's Attack on the 27th Sept., 1918

On September 1 and 2, the 1st Canadian Division turned in "one of the finest performances in all the war," according to General Currie, in their successful assault and capture of the Fresnes-Rouvoy and Droucourt-Quéant Lines. Canadian operations then experienced a lull in the fighting until the end of the month.

The last big "show" for the 2nd Battalion, before the war began to taper off, was the Canal du Nord operation that began on September 27. At 5:20 a.m. the attack opened under an intense shrapnel and smoke barrage. The horizon, as far as the eye could see, was a mass of billowing smoke—a dense white smoke shot through with the flicker of bursting shrapnel or the black smudge of high explosives. The 2nd Battalion, passing through the initial attack of the 1st Battalion, was held up almost at once in a railway cutting and embankment, succeeding only by heavy hand to hand combat. By 2:00 p.m., they held Bourlon Wood, the villages of Raillencourt and Haynecourt were only yards away.

Fighting on the succeeding days proved most costly to the Canadian divisions. The Engineers had to construct five traffic and four footbridge crossings over the Canal. All but one were completed by 6:00 p.m.; in the process they suffered many casualties from machine-gun fire. The Germans were pulling back toward Cambrai. Artillery caissons, motor-lorries (trucks) and men were milling about in a chaotic mess. The fight was far from finished. No. 4 Company, pushing forward to establish an outpost while the battalion rested, collided with a German unit doing the same thing. They encountered a lively fight but the enemy was dispersed and the Canadian line was established.

At 2:00 a.m. on September 28, the officers learned that the 4th Division would continue the advance. The 2nd Battalion had suffered one officer killed and fifteen wounded and twenty-four other ranks killed and 175 wounded. Seriously wounded was Ross Simpson.

According to Rosslyn Virtue, the last surviving direct descendent— a niece who is named for Ross, he was found on the battlefield by his brother Ralph, who carried him back to the 22nd Canadian Casualty Clearing Station. Ross was quickly diagnosed as suffering a gunshot wound to the right axilla (armpit). Closer examination revealed the wound was in his back and abdomen, causing some paralysis. On October 1, he was admitted to No. 20 Canadian General Hospital in Camiers, where he would spend the winter of 1918–19. It was not until March 1, 1919, that he was moved from the "dangerously ill" to the "seriously ill" sick list. The final diagnosis on his case sheet, covering the period January 19 to March 11, 1919, was as follows:

> Paraplegia—loss of use [of] legs. No bladder control and rectum. Entry bullet 8th interspace R post axillary line, no exit, x-ray bullet in left lung. Bullet at 11th rib of left side 3" from vertebral articulation—depth from posterior mark about 3/4". Permanent invalid. Slight reaction to electricity right foot.

On March 11, he was "invalided wounded" to the United Kingdom and after two months recuperation, Ross was taken aboard the Hospital Ship *Aragraya* for the trip home to Canada. He arrived at Kingston's Sydenham Military Hospital on June 6. On June 25, he was sent home for rehabilitation and discharged from the service.

On October 8, 1918, the *Carleton Place Herald* ran the notice: "Pte. Charles Ross Simpson, son of Mr. And Mrs. W. Simpson, Carleton Place, wounded." And on January 19, 1921, the newspaper reported on his funeral:

Pte. Ross Simpson

Close upon the announcement of the death of Mr. Peever[8] came the news of the death in the Hospital of Toronto of Pte. Ross Simpson, son of Mr. And Mrs. W.R. Simpson, which took place on Thursday evening. Ross had been an invalid for some time. He enlisted at Ottawa with the 207th, after spending some time at Petawawa, and went overseas in time to get into the fray receiving a bullet in his spine. This caused a partial paralysis, and although everything possible was done for him, he could not recover and after years of patient suffering he passed to rest—a hero. Ross was but 21 years of age, as was Wesley Peever. The body was brought here and the funeral took place on Sunday afternoon from the home of his parents on Herriott street to Maplewood cemetery, and was very largely attended,

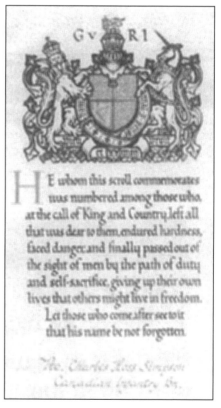

although the weather was desperately raw and cold. The pallbearers were all vets—Norman Morris, Geo. Horne, James McGill, Arthur Maguire, H. Fanning and E. McPherson. The services at the house and at the grave were conducted by Rev. Mr. Dobson . . . The bereaved parents and relatives have the sincere sympathy of hosts of friends in their hour of grief.

[8] Wesley Peever, who was gassed at Hill 70 in 1917 and died in January 1921.

World War I ended for Ross Simpson at the Euclid Hall Hospital in Toronto. At 8:30 p.m. on January 13, 1921, he died of pyelonephritis (kidney failure) caused by the paraplegia that resulted from the gunshot wound he took in the spine. For years his father William personally cared for the young veteran's grave in Maplewood Cemetery.

The Commonwealth War Graves Commission citation reads:

Charles Ross Simpson (246252 Private). Son of William and W.R. Simpson of Carleton Place. Enlisted 207th Ottawa-Carleton Overseas Battalion. Died 13 January 1921, age 22. Buried in Carleton Place United Cemeteries.

Chapter Twenty-Seven

CAMBRAI

4th Division

Many of the men from Carleton Place served overseas with the 38th (Ottawa) Battalion. The battalions into which they had enlisted were broken up in England to provide reinforcements for the decimated units in France. Two belonging to the 38th during the march to Mons, and specifically the battle for Cambrai, were Percy Hughes and Cornelious O'Donovan. Percy had enlisted and gone to England with the 207th (Ottawa-Carleton) Battalion, joining the 38th in September 1917, whereas O'Donovan had enlisted directly into "C" Company of the 38th at Kingston in May 1915. Both had seen a great deal of war by the time they reached the Canal du Nord and Cambrai. Both were killed on September 29, 1918.

The Canadian Corps was ordered, on September 24, 1918, to cross the Canal du Nord, break through the Canal du Nord and

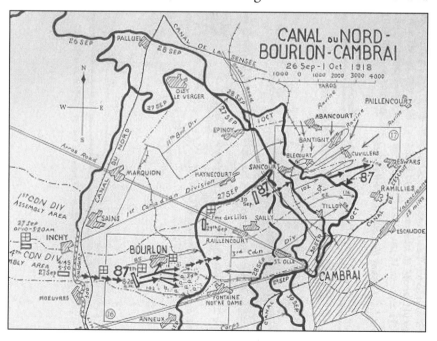

Marquion trench systems and push through the attack in the direction of Cambrai and beyond. The left attacking battalion was the 38th. All companies were in the attacking line.

The following account of the Battle of Cambrai is excerpted from the 38th Battalion historical record:

When the Cambrai fighting began in late September people at home were nodding their heads wisely, and remarking that the German resistance was undoubtedly beginning to crumble. Our fellows knew better and said nothing. The fighting was very terrible, and only such glorious victories could have justified such a roll of casualties.

The men of the 38th entrained at Arras on the 25th [September] and by 2 o'clock in the afternoon of the following day had arrived near their assembly position. They had passed a fairly quiet interval since the heavy fighting, at the beginning of the month, and were fatalistically ready for another scrap.

. . . The business of the regiment in the first phase—the Bourlon operation—was to capture the railway running northwest from the village and hold it . . . By 3 am . . . the men were assembled in the Slip trench west of Inchy . . . "A" and "B" Companies were to begin the good work. At 5:20 am, our barrage opened on the Canal du Nord, and our fellows went forward at once. They passed through Inchy and crossed the canal — there were casualties here . . .

The men passed through the 10th Bde and went forward to the Marquion Trench in good style, wiping out resistance in a few brief minutes of bayonet-work. They captured 25 machine guns and 150 prisoners. It was a good start, and things were going well.

. . . the fellows went forward to their objective at the railway line. The first half-mile was not so bad; long range machine gun fire formed the only opposition and casualties were light.

Things changed though, after that. Heavy fighting took place all along the front, and many earnest Germans were killed before "B" Company on the right reached the tracks. On the left "A" Company was having trouble. A strong machine gun nest before No. 1 platoon was making things uncomfortable for the attacking troops. Colonel Gardner and Lieutenant Trendell made a risky reconnaissance in the neighbourhood, and solved the situation by bringing up the reserve company to the objective at a suitable distance, leaving the first waves of men to deal with the strong point. This was done most satisfactorily. Sore at the delay, our fellows charged, reckless of losses, and bayoneted the gunners. Then they found the reason for the particularly stubborn resistance. Close behind the point a battery of 5.9s was situated, with the crews working frantically to get their weapons back out of danger. They were not successful, however, and a nice-looking lot of guns went to the rear with "38th" chalked on their muzzles.

That completed the day's work. When the survivors of No. 1 platoon got forward they found the railway line occupied by the rest of the regiment, with "D" Company holding a sunken road a couple of hundred yards ahead. Two company commanders had been killed—Captain Goodwin, M.C. ("B") and Capt. Starkings ("A") . . . A hundred other ranks were knocked out—killed or wounded. A pleasant total of souvenirs had been gathered, however, the 5.9 howitzers, a battery of 77 mm guns, 28 machine-guns, two anti-tank guns, and 200 prisoners. It was an excellent list. The battalion rested and prepared for the next day.[1]

The official history continues:

Throughout the rest of the day—the 27th—the regiment remained at the railway line, re-organizing and consolidating. In the evening information was received that the 10th Brigade was to attack in the morning from Marquion trench towards Raillencourt, Sailly, Sancourt, and that the battalion was to advance behind the attacking waves, but a mile to the rear. So the 38th men went forward again about 11 a.m. on the 28th,

[1] 38th Battalion History, National Archives.

and occupied the positions in and about Marcoing [*sic*] Trench. A distance ahead they could see 10th Brigade troops consolidating in front of the Douai-Cambrai Road. The Germans were fighting desperately, and there had been another check.

It is not fair to our soldiers to say the enemy fought lightly. In trench and strong-point he fought furiously and well, recklessly maintaining his fire until he was surrounded, and frequently until our bayonets were at his throat. Then he died like a man, he fought like hell, and—it may be—raised himself in the estimation of the Canadians. This is not a sentimental plea for Fritz, but bare justice to our fellows.

East of the Douai-Cambrai Road the Germans were moving troops in numbers. From a ruined mill away on the left the battalion observers covered the country-side, and realized something of the stiff job to be handled in the near future. Our Vickers guns began to shoot up the moving bodies of men, and battalion headquarters moved forward to some old gun-pits ahead. Things were brisk enough, and the enemy's shells were dropping all about.

. . . Orders were received for an attack the next morning.[2]

The task of the 38th was to cross the Douai-Cambrai road—where the check had occurred on the previous day—and capture a section of the Blecourt-Morenchies Road some distance ahead. At twenty minutes past eight in the morning of the 29th our barrage moved forward, and the men followed on behind it. "C" Company [O'Donovan's company], Captain Johnson, attacked in the centre of the battalion frontage, with "B" Company, Captain Menzies, on the left, and "D" Company, Lieutenant Anderson, on the right. "A" Company, now under Lieutenant Matthews, had experienced the stiffest fighting during the first phase, and was in support today. Our fellows reached the Douai Road, carried it in fine style, and came on into the open on the other side. Then the real business began.

A lone machine-gun is not the desperately deadly weapon that many men imagine it to be. An experienced officer or man can almost invariably detect its direction of fire by the particular

[2] Ibid., 38th History.

brand of infernal row it happens to be making. If the gun starts direct fire on a man in the open, then his number's up for a trip to Blighty or a somewhat longer journey; but when the gunner opens up to the right or left the anxious target can tell in the fraction of a second whether the muzzle of the gun is being swung towards or away from him, and usually has time to take the necessary steps. However, it is a very different thing to attack a number of machine-guns set in depth, with scientifically arranged zones of fire. That is a ghastly business, and that is what the regiment had to do.

Every foot of country beyond the road was swept by bullets. From flanks and front the fire was terrific. On the right the Third Division had failed to cross the road—the men couldn't see whether the assaulting troops on the left had made the grade or not. Some distance ahead there was a slightly sunken road with occasional earth-works, and the soldiers went forward gallantly and obtained a certain amount of cover after they had killed the Germans sheltering there. So many officers were gone that it was difficult to control the movements of the attacking force, and to maintain a definite purpose. But there was no chance of further progress without the support of heavy artillery. About noon, the survivors of "B" Company were shelled out of the earth-works and sought shelter with the rest of the battalion in the sunken road.

For many long hours the remains of the regiment held the precarious line, shooting whenever possible and taking every opportunity of killing Germans. It is to be feared that the Germans killed many more of our fellows that day, however. At half-past one the 78th Battalion came up to the attack, but though the soldiers reached the line of the 38th, they were unable to push on any further. In the meantime our guns were being brought up in the rear, and our men stuck to the position. Casualties mounted rapidly, for the machine-gun fire never ceased and the shelter was insufficient.

When it got dark the regiment was ordered to withdraw to a line west of the Douai-Cambrai Road. This was completed by

10 o'clock, and here the men stayed through the night, standing ready to meet any possible counter-attack. Now the battalion was reduced to the strength of a company. On the morning of the 30th, troops of the 11th Brigade passed through to the attack, crossed the Douai-Cambrai Road, seized the railway line, and pushed on ahead. That lessened the strain, and the regiment was relieved.

These days of fighting were the most severe in the history of the regiment. On September 26th the battalion went up to the attack 570 strong—on September 30th 96 men came back from the Douai-Cambrai Road. Figures like these were not uncommon in the Cambrai operation . . . Victory's a costly business.[3]

And this "costly business" cost the lives of two more youths from Carleton Place, Ontario.

PERCY GRENVILLE HUGHES

Percy Hughes was born on July 6, 1895, the son of Thomas and Jessie Hughes. He received his early education in Carleton Place and in 1913 was a member of the Carleton Place baseball team. When he joined the 207th (Ottawa-Carleton) Overseas Battalion on May 12, 1916, he claimed previous service with the 42nd (Militia) Regiment Guard Detachment. He gave his age as twenty-one years, his religion as Methodist and his employment up until he enrolled as butcher. At his medical examination, Percy was found to have a medium complexion, grey eyes and brown hair. He stood 5' 6" tall and weighed 147 pounds. The *Carleton Place Herald* of May 23, 1916, reported that, "Five Carleton Place boys have united with the 207th Battalion viz., Clayton McMullen, Percy Hughes, Norman Morris, Ross Simpson and W. McEachen."

Pte. Hughes embarked from Halifax on the S.S. *Olympic* on May 25, 1917. He had spent a year in training in Canada at Valcartier. The battalion arrived at Liverpool on June 9, 1917. In England the 207th was absorbed by the 6th Reserve Battalion to provide reinforcements

[3] Ibid., 38th Battalion History

for the Canadian Corps in the field in France. Shortly after arrival in England, Percy visited a field ambulance unit complaining of "shortness of breath on exertion." The minimal tests found his heart normal and he was returned to duty. On September 26, 1917, he went overseas to the 38th Battalion. After service in various holding units, he joined the 38th on November 28, 1917.

Percy paid several disciplinary fines while serving in the trenches of France. A week after he arrived, on December 6, 1917, he was penalized a stoppage of pay for the "loss of government property by neglect"—his helmet, which cost him 85 cents, and his greatcoat which was valued at $7.60. The total of $8.45 was more than a week's pay for an infantryman.

During the winter of 1917–1918, the Canadian Corps, recovering from Passchendaele, was in the relatively quiet sector near Lens. The 38th Battalion served in the 12th Brigade of the 4th Division. At the end of March, with the Germans pressing the British Army, the Canadians were ordered into support. The 4th Division took up positions along Hill 70. They were involved primarily in defensive battles throughout April 1918, and until the first week in May, when they were once again relieved in the line by British formations. They stayed in reserve for most of the summer, reorganizing, replenishing and training. After the Dominion Day corps-wide sports meet, units of the

4th Division were inspected by the prime minister, Sir Robert Borden.

On May 28, Percy was again awarded a stoppage of 2/2d[4] and one day's pay for having lost his table knife worth 4d; a fork—4d; a spoon—5d; and his mess tin cover worth one shilling. Had he lost these items while in the line, it would have been acceptable as part of being in action, but since they were in bivouac in reserve such lapses became offenses. In the middle of July, the corps

[4] Two shillings, two pence (tuppence)–Canadian dollars and English Sterling were used interchangeably by the Canadian Corps.

went back into the line, but first, on July 4, 1918, Percy was fined three days pay because he was absent from the 8:00 a.m. parade. The army could brook no deviance from its precisely regulated discipline.

Percy went into action on September 29 with the 38th Battalion moving toward Cambrai in bitter fighting. He fell while advancing on an enemy strong point 300 yards east of the Douai-Cambrai Road, west of Tilloy. He was struck in the chest and instantly killed by a bullet from an enemy rifle. After he was killed, an examination of his personal record revealed that he wanted notification of his casualty to be sent to Miss G. McEvoy, in New Edinburgh, Ottawa. The *Herald* of October 29, 1918, published Percy's death in the casualty list. He had lived for twenty-three years, two months and three weeks. The record of commemoration held by the Commonwealth War Graves Commission reads:

In Memory of
P G HUGHES
Private
246251
38th Bn., Canadian Infantry (Eastern Ontario Regt.)
who died on
Sunday, 29th September 1918

His body lies in the Bourlon Wood Cemetery near the Pas de Calais, France, just six kilometres west of Cambrai, close to where he fell. The cemetery was created by the Canadian Corps Burial Officer in October 1918. Enclosed by a rubble wall, there are nearly 250 Great War casualties buried here; more than ten are unidentified. Two hundred and twenty-one of the dead were members of the 3rd and 4th Canadian Divisions.

Percy Hughes lies in Plot II, Row B, Grave 12. His Carleton Place comrade, Cornelious O'Donovan, rests nearby in Plot II, Row A, Grave 18.

CORNELIOUS O'DONOVAN

Cornelious was born in Bedford, England, on September 4, 1898, the son of Mary Ann O'Donovan. At Cornelious' enlistment, she was listed as a widow and no information appears about his father. She had emigrated to Canada with her four sons and listed her address as a post office box in Carleton Place. Cornelious[5] was among the immigrants recruited by the Findlay Foundry where he worked as a machinist.

On May 11, 1915, at age sixteen, he joined the 38th Battalion at Barriefield, near Kingston. He was two years underage, and he had already served three months in the militia with the 42nd Regiment in Carleton Place. At his enrollment examination, he was recorded as having a fair complexion, blue eyes and light hair. He stood 5' 10" tall and weighed 142 lbs. He listed his religion as Roman Catholic.

Three months later, on August 12, 1915, he was with the battalion when it went as the Protective Garrison to Bermuda. They remained on the island until May 30, 1916. While there, Cornelious was twice examined by a civilian surgeon in St. Georges for overseas fitness, on April 30, and May 8, 1916. On both occasions he was found "fit with satisfactory marks of vaccination." On April 29 he boarded the S.S. *Grampian* for the trip across the Atlantic to Plymouth. They landed on June 9, 1916, and within two months were off to the battlefields.

On August 13–14 the battalion crossed the English Channel to Le Havre where they became part of the 12th Infantry Brigade of the 4th Canadian Division. Just before they went, they exchanged their Ross rifles for the British Lee-Enfield. The division spent the summer in the Ypres Salient learning the tricks of warfare in the front lines. On September 2, Cornelious took a grenade course while in bivouac in the field. On October 10, the 4th Division went into the line for the first time. They relieved first the 3rd Division and then the 1st Division, both of which had just experienced the fierce fighting at Regina Trench on the Somme. For the first month, from October 12 to November 9, 1916, Cornelious was employed as a "runner" for the 12th Brigade headquarters, carrying messages from headquarters to the battalion officers in the trenches.

The division's introduction to battle came on October 21, 1916, when they were ordered to secure a section of Regina Trench. The artillery had been effective and the infantry advanced fairly easily. On October 25 they attacked again, but this time the artillery had not been able to eliminate German opposition nor cut the barbed wire.

[5] Cornelious's name appears in the commemorative information as "Cornelius." However, on his enlistment papers that he completed himself, his name is spelled "Cornelious." On the assumption that he knew how to spell his name that must be presumed to be the correct version.

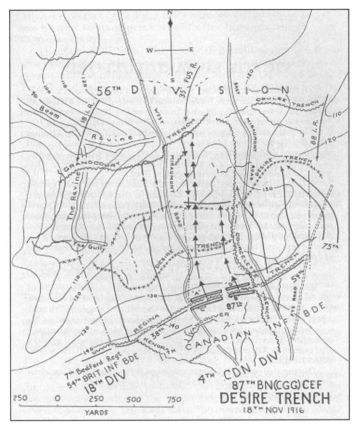

The ground and the weather were terrible and the infantry accomplished very little in the rain, mud and cold. On November 18, attention shifted to Desire Trench and the 38th advanced in the last action on the Somme front. The attack went well but this last battle still cost the Canadians 1,250 killed, wounded or missing. The Battle of the Somme, one of the bloodiest in World War I, which wasted 1.2 million killed or wounded, was over.

An entire generation lost its best and brightest. Entering this war, British officers and NCOs still hailed the bayonet as "Queen of the Battlefield." Commanders had completely lost sight of the lessons taught in the South African war concerning the effective use of the new mechanized army and especially the tactical advantage of the machine-gun. This frightful error resulted in the multitude of tombs. Thousands and thousands of lives were lost before senior officers real-

ized that infantry, however brave, cannot win a charge in close formation over open spaces against a concealed enemy armed with machine-
guns. To order fixed bayonets and sound the clarion call to charge created no magic recipe for victory.[6]

Between November 26 and 28, the 4th Division was relieved by a
British Division and proceeded to join the rest of the Canadian Corps
in the Lens-Arras area. Their next obstacle was Vimy Ridge. For the
first time, all four Canadian divisions were serving together under
Canadian command. For the attack, the 4th Division faced the highest
point on the ridge, Hill 145 and had as its assault battalions the 54th
and 102nd, both from British Columbia, the Grenadier Guards from
Montreal and the 38th of Eastern Ontario.

In that first wave of fifteen thousand
Canadians stood Cornelious O'Donovan.
From January 22, 1917, to February 13 he had
been at the 4th Division school taking the
NCO's course. He completed it successfully
and, on March 21st, was appointed to the rank
of lance corporal. Now he would help lead his section into battle.

The attack started well, and the 38th advanced according to plan.
But German machine-gun fire stopped the centre of the division's
advancing troops. The Eastern Ontario Battalion was suffering severely
and losing what little ground it had gained. Captain Thain MacDowell
won the battalion's first Victoria Cross by leading a small group to
destroy two machine-gun positions that were wreaking havoc with the
Canadian attackers. The 4th Division suffered huge losses but finally the
inexperienced Nova Scotia Highlanders (85th Battalion), in a brief and
bloody battle, captured Hill 145. April 12 dawned quietly. Canadians
had conquered Vimy Ridge and established a national identity on the
battlefield. On April 15, Cornelious O'Donovan was promoted to corporal. He was nineteen years, seven months old.

The 4th Division was back in action in August against Hill 70 in
the area west of Lens. It was tasked with mounting a diversionary operation but the simulated assault by the 12th Brigade drew more retalia-
tory artillery fire than the main attack.

[6] Edward Spears, Liaison 1914 (London: Eyre & Spottiswoode Ltd., 1930), pp. 33-36

They then moved back to Ypres and into the hellish shell-fire and quagmire of ooze that was Passchendaele. The 4th Division was ordered to ascend Passchendaele Ridge. The attack went according to plan, but the Nova Scotians, who had been so successful at Vimy, suffered their worst day of the war, losing 439 soldiers. After ferocious fighting on October 30, the 3rd and 4th Divisions were relieved by the 1st and 2nd. Cornelious O'Donovan had survived another battle.

The Canadian Corps spent the winter of 1917–1918 involved in what was termed "minor operations" that took 3,552 casualties from the corps, including 684 deaths. From March until July they were, mercifully, sent into reserve. On July 30, the corps began to move toward Amiens. Once concentrated, the 4th Division was placed in corps reserve.

The battalion's war diary provides a more precise movement of the troops, and the activities of Percy Hughes and Cornelious O'Donovan, who remained in "C" Company:

> 26 Sept—Moved by train from ARRAS to BULLECOURT. Wx [weather] fine—marched 3 km to area NW of Quéant—moved to Assembly position. "C" Company commander—Capt. A. Johnson.

> 27th—Attack opened with barrage on Canal du Nord at 5:20 am. Crossed canal at 0600, "A" and "B" Companies leading with "C" in support and "D" in reserve. Moved forward to attack through heavy enemy shell fire; at 11 am the objective [the railway running NW from Bourlon] was established.

From the Diary:

> 28th—Battalion moved forward at 6:30 am. "C" & "D" companies in front with "A" and "B" following at 500 yards. Reached Arras-Cambrai road without casualties. Several batteries of field guns were passed. . . The battalion was very heavily shelled all afternoon and had about 15 casualties. Munitions were issued and arrangements for the attack on AM of 29th made.

> 29th—In assembly at 5:40 am. The battalion attacked after a 20 minute barrage at 6:20 am. "B", "C" and "D" Companies in front and "A" Company in support. Battalion passed over

and crossed the Douai-Cambrai Road in face of intense shell and machine-gun fire and progressed some 250 yards when held up by very heavy machine-gun fire from railway embankment. We were unable to connect up on either of our flanks. Companies held their positions but were unable to advance. The 78th Canadian Infantry Battalion in support attempted to reinforce us but was unable to reach the Douai-Cambrai Road . . . During the night companies moved to west side of Douai-Cambrai Road.

30th—11th Bde passed through and attacked and 38th moved into support. Wx [weather] was fine throughout operation.[7]

The heavy machine-gun fire on September 29 cut down Cornelious O'Donovan. He was in charge of a Lewis gun crew, advancing with his company during the attack from Cantimpre to west of Tilloy. He was hit in the head and chest by enemy machine gun bullets and instantly killed. Strangely enough there is no mention of his death in the *Herald*. The Commonwealth War Graves inscription reads:

In Carleton Place, September 1918 heralded a new order for the work force. The Canadian Pacific Railway set new hours, calling its workers in by 7:30 a.m. and allowing them to quit at 5:00 p.m., except on Saturdays when they could leave at noon. This new schedule was in keeping with the forty-seven-hour work week.	*In Memory of* *CORNELIUS O'DONOVAN* *Corporal* *410569* *"C" Coy. 38th Bn., Canadian Infantry (Eastern Ontario Regt.)* *who died on* *Sunday, 29th September 1918.* *Age 19.*

In that record the next of kin is listed as William O'Donovan, a brother living at 1093.5 (*sic*) Wellington Street in Ottawa. Cornelious's body lies in the Bourlon Wood Cemetery, Pas de Calais, France, very near where he fell. At the top of a hill is the Bourlon Wood Memorial on ground donated by the Comte de Franqueville. On a great stone block is this message:

THE CANADIAN CORPS ON 27th SEPT. 1918 FORCED
THE CANAL DU NORD AND CAPTURED THIS HILL.
THEY TOOK CAMBRAI, DENAIN, VALENCIENNES
AND MONS; THEN MARCHED TO THE
RHINE WITH THE VICTORIOUS ALLIES.

[7] Ibid., 38th War Diary.

The autumn of 1918 brought the Spanish influenza epidemic that was also raging in Europe. In Carleton Place, there were few families untouched. The Herald reported on October 15, 1918, that, "the influenza epidemic has closed schools and churches and all public meeting places." In his diary George Findlay wrote on October 11, "Spanish influenza in full swing. Schools, churches and all public meetings banned and closed. Quite a few deaths." On November 3, a Sunday, he was able to write "Churches opened today after being closed four Sundays on account of the Spanish flu which has claimed a lot of victims. The wettest fall I can remember, very little sunshine."

The pandemic continued to claim victims well into 1919. In January, Sgt. George New's bride of a few months succumbed. He was captured in 1915 during the fight at Langemarck and had spent years as a German prisoner of war. He had been home less than a year. Then, in the first week of February, the Trotman family suffered the loss of five members in five days.

Standing guard are some of the original trees. Shattered by shell-fire during the battle they have been nursed back to health to stand as lonely sentinels.

A Carleton Place Boy in Germany

Tells of How the Canadians Fought before Reaching Mons

The *Carleton Place Herald* of February 4, 1919, printed a letter from one of the local men who had served with the 38th Battalion on the March to Mons. He remains anonymous but his bittersweet words bring a dreadful reality to the actions in which so many Carleton Place boys lost their lives so close to the end of the war.

Klon [*sic*—it should be Kôln], Germany, Dec. 28th, 1918

Dear Editor:

As we are having a few days to ourselves I thought I'd drop you a few lines and tell you of our experiences during the last three months. I have been in France since July, 1915, and never did I see such fighting as in the last two months, especially at Cambrai on September 27th. The air was full of shrapnel and machine gun bullets, and again on November 1st at Valenciennes we had a canal to cross and Fritz had his machine guns concealed in the houses on the other side. When our lads got down to the Canal, much to their surprise, they found the 1st Batt. Canadian Engineers already working there building a bridge across, in no man's land, which Jerry's shells blew away as fast as it was built, but after many long hours they succeeded in getting across and then came the infantry and machine gunners. There was only one man killed in our Batt. crossing the bridge, but believe me the Engineers were simply cut to bits by shrapnel. So far as I know they lost nearly two companies. Next morning we made our way up through the city, only to find thousands of civilians. They told us that Fritz took all the boys over eighteen and hundreds of girls with him, but when he had to get out of Thulin, it's the first town we got to in Belgium, he had to leave them all behind. We sure got some reception when we got into Mons. They were nearly crazy every place we stopped; they were right there with cups of coffee. We did no more fighting after we captured Mons. We stayed there for about 10 days, then we started on this so-called triumphant march to Germany. I hope I never have to make another trip like it was. But if we get back home we will soon forget all about this. We had a very good Xmas, only we have no snow, it's just real Canadian summer. All the troops were swimming in the Rhine on Xmas day.

So far as I can see old Jerry was pretty hard hit for provisions. They tell us they have had no meat for over four years and they sure look the part. Well my news is pretty near run done [sic], so I guess I'll close, hoping to be back in old Carleton Place soon again.

One of the 38th Batt.

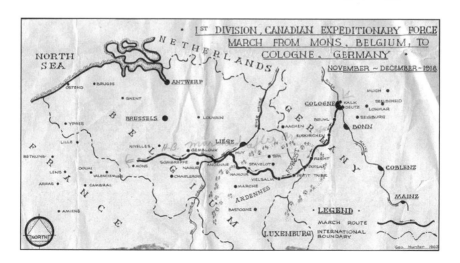

Chapter Twenty-Eight

ABOVE THE GROUND

In 1914, Canada had no organized military flying service. Therefore aspiring aviators, before they could be accepted by the Royal Flying Corps or the Royal Naval Air Service, had to produce a certificate attesting to at least elementary training in the air, acquired at their own expense. Although there was an abundance of young Canadians who were anxious to join either air service, few had the $400 that it would cost to obtain such a certificate.

The Curtiss School was established near Toronto early in the war, but most men of means travelled to Dayton, Ohio, to learn flying skills under the tutelage of the famous Wright brothers at their Wright Aviation School. Four from Carleton Place went to Dayton in 1915, to earn their U.S. Aero Club pilot's licence: A. Roy Brown, Murray Galbraith, Lloyd Breadner and Sterne Tighe Edwards. R. Franklyn Abbott graduated from the Curtiss School in 1916 and David Douglas Findlay graduated from the Stinson School in San Antonio, Texas, that same year.

However, there were many other avenues to a cockpit and many Carleton Place men found them. Officers could be seconded from the Canadian Expeditionary Force to the British air services, while other ranks were discharged from the Canadian services and re-enrolled as British airmen, receiving a commission in the Royal Flying Corps after successful completion of cadet training. In the United Kingdom, civilians could be directly enrolled. As pilots, observers and mechanics, Canadians were represented in almost every theatre of operations.

It required considerable manual skill and a great amount of raw courage and nerve to leave the earth sitting in a contraption put together with a few slats of hardwood, paper-thin skin and wings, some of which actually flapped, powered by a solitary motor that spewed cod-liver oil (the lubricant of choice), which could be taken out with a single random rifle shot. Pilots needed daring to throw such a flimsy apparatus all over the sky in a dogfight with an enemy intent upon their demise. Plus steely courage to fly straight and steady on a pre-planned bombing course with anti-aircraft shells bursting all around them, filling the air and their paths with shrapnel. But for those with adventure in their hearts, or those pilots and observers who were veterans of the infantry and so thankful to be out of the trenches, it was their single path to glory.

STERNE TIGHE EDWARDS, DSC AND BARS.

Sterne Edwards was born in Franktown, Beckwith Township, on February 13, 1893, the son of Dennis and Annie Edwards. He grew up and went to war with his lifelong friends—Roy Brown and Murray Galbraith. Roy and Sterne were especially close and the two starred on the local hockey team. As a youth, Sterne was self-reliant and quite serious for his age. He regularly attended church services with his family and was an outstanding athlete at school. He often took top honours at track meets, barely eclipsing Brown and Galbraith who were always close competitors. He graduated with honours from high school in 1912; the following year, 1913, his father died, and Sterne became the head of the family.

Sterne first got work as an engineer's assistant with the Algoma Central Railway in Hoban, Ontario. After his father's death, he went to Port Nelson where he worked with the Grand Trunk Pacific Railroad. He is reputed to have become very proficient at the game of poker, more often than not taking the lion's share of the winnings. However, he never took up the habits of either smoking or drinking.

When the First World War broke out, Sterne was working on a wilderness survey, two hundred miles north of the nearest railway station, located at The Pas, Manitoba. He set out through the forest on foot to walk the entire distance. En route he became quite lost, and was only saved by local natives who guided him on his way. In Carleton Place, he found an officer of the Royal Naval Air Service (RNAS) recruiting young men for that force, and Roy Brown who had returned from Edmonton. Brown, Edwards, Galbraith, and Walter Sussan decided to join the air services.

But first they had to learn to fly, as the RNAS was accepting only men who held a private pilot's licence. The nearest flying school, the Curtiss School in Toronto, was full so they applied to the Wright Aviation School at Dayton, Ohio. After a period of waiting, the four friends departed Carleton Place on August 30, 1915, travelling at their own expense to Dayton.

When he enlisted, Sterne submitted a record of his travel expenses. It shows that he went from Carleton Place to Dayton on the Canadian Pacific Railway, through Detroit, leaving at 5:45 a.m. on August 30, paying a fare of $16, plus $2.80 for a berth. He claimed a $2 subsistence allowance. He returned on October 11, arriving back in Carleton Place at 5:15 p.m. on the 12th. The cost was the same except that he claimed a subsistence of $3.

The Wright School was handling its largest class in history. Twenty-five Canadians were enrolled, and throughout the fall of 1915 the two Wright "B" pusher aircraft were in constant use. Most students slept in the hangar and walked to nearby farms for meals. The flying lessons cost $250 for 249 minutes of instruction. Total costs exceeded $600, all of which the students paid out of their own pockets.

> The aircraft would go up for a few minutes with an instructor and a student, then land, and a brief discussion of the flight would take place with the students grouped around the plane. Most of the instruction was carried out in this way on the ground, as little could be done in the air with the roar of the engine immediately behind the seats.
>
> The final tests consisted of three flights—two figure eights and one dead-stick [engine off] landing from 500 feet to a spot on the field. Edwards soloed after forty minutes. He finally obtained his licence—Aero Club of America Certificate Number 350—on 13 October, 1915. Galbraith won his on 3 November, and Brown on 13 November.
>
> Armed with their precious certificates, the three again approached the RNAS, and this time were signed on.[1]

Sterne's "RNAS Application from Civilian" listed his birth date as February 13, 1893, and that he was "of pure European descent, born

[1] Hugh A. Halliday, "Edwards, Stearne Tighe," *A Nursery of the Air Force* (Carleton Place: Forest Beauty Products, 1979), pp. 116-117.

of natural British subjects." His father's occupation was recorded as a railway timber inspector and he listed his own occupations for the last five years as "school 2 yrs, survey 1 yr, railway construction work 2 yrs. Kingston Public School. Carleton Place High School 1906–1912. Experience in connection with gasoline engines. Some experience in general mechanical work." His application was signed on August 10, 1915, and that same day he underwent a medical examination. The doctor recorded that he was twenty-two years, five months old, stood 5' 11" tall and weighed 163 pounds. Icing the cake was a letter of recommendation from his high school principal:

Carleton Place High School   August 18th, 1915
E.J. Wethey, M.A.
Principal
To Whom It May Concern

This is to certify that Mr. Sterne T. Edwards was a pupil in this school from Sept 1906–July 1912, during the last two years of which time I was principal. It gives me much pleasure to state that I found this young man an excellent student.

In June 1911 he won the school championship in Athletics and in July [of the same year] passed his Normal Entrance with Honours and his Junior Matriculation.

In 1912 he passed in Geometry and Trigonometry at Hon. Matric. McGill.

He was very fit both mentally and physically while his manners and morals seemed beyond reproach.

Edmund J. Wethey (M.A.)

Principal

Sterne was appointed a probationary sub-lieutenant on October 27, 1915, and sailed for England on the S.S. *Corinthian* on November 3, 1915. The other three—Galbraith, Brown and Sussan—followed on November 22. The friends were reunited at the training base at Chingford, and soon  became known among their fellow aviators as the "hobo quartet."

They trained on Maurice Farman Shorthorns, Avros and BE2c's, learning military flying and bomb-dropping. Sterne was a natural flier, although on March 31,1916, his log noted that he had made a "rather bad landing in a pond."

Edwards left Chingford for gunnery school at Eastchurch on April 9, 1916. He was unhappy with this move because he wanted to graduate with Roy Brown, who had been set back by illness. Writing to his sister, Mary, he told how it came about:

> I have been sneaking and hiding around the station so I would not be too far ahead of him [Brown]. However, was doing some bomb-dropping yesterday from 3000 feet and unbeknown to me the C.O. was watching. I had a wild streak of luck and made several hits and he told me when I came down it was very good and that he would report me at once as being ready to leave. If I had known he was watching I would have scattered those bombs for 40 miles.

Flight Sub-Lieutenant Sterne Edwards, with thirty-two hours and twenty-nine minutes in his logbook, arrived at Eastchurch on April 11, 1916. He mainly focussed on the airborne art of bomb-dropping, though on one occasion Sterne fired his machine guns at ground targets, and on another he shot at kites. One of his instructors was Flight Lieutenant Alcock, who later gained fame by flying across the Atlantic with Arthur Brown (no relation to Roy) in 1919.

On April 29, Sterne left Eastchurch and reported to 5 Wing at Detling, which moved to Manston on June 19. On July 1 it flew first to Dunkirk and then began a series of flights, interrupted by thunderstorms, which ended the following day at Luxieul, France.

The wing adapted itself to its new Sopwith One-and-a-Half Strutters aircraft with a month of training and formation flying. These were remarkable aircraft—the first British planes to employ synchronized machine guns. They were very stable machines and could adapt to two-seater fighters or single seat bombers. 3 Wing had two Sopwith fighters for each flight of five Sopwith bombers. Formation flying became a constant practice and a required skill, for they were about to embark upon a new adventure in warfare—strategic bombing.

But it was not all work and no play. The Canadians in the wing formed their own field hockey team and were especially pleased when they beat an English team at their own game. Sterne had also learned his poker lessons well when with the railroad in northern Canada. His prowess was described by Raymond Collishaw, another Canadian aviator who achieved fame in World War I. Collishaw thought the poker games even more dangerous than the hockey. He explained that there were usually three games in progress. One had a five franc limit, the second a limit of twenty francs and the third had no limit on bets. Players could work their way up, all too often suffering a serious loss that would plunge them back to the five franc game. Players would keep a roll of toilet paper beside them and after losing, when all their actual cash was gone, would rip off a piece and scribble their IOUs. Some had their finances for the next hundred years pledged.

SOPWITH PUP
Full aeorobatic reported the best to fly.

Collishaw later wrote "undoubted master of the no limit game was a Canadian who came from Carleton Place." Sterne was a shrewd player who owned a great wad of IOUs. They formed a big bulge in his tunic pocket which, had he survived the war, and collected, would have made him a wealthy young man.

The first operational flight entry in Sterne's logbook is dated September 1, 1916: "Chasing Huns . . . sounds good but have not been near enough to see one to date." Then, on October 12, a flight of sixty-one French and British aircraft from Luxieul and nearby fields attacked the Mauser small arms factory at Oberndorf. Sterne wrote home about the event which the *Carleton Place Herald*, in its edition of November 30, 1916, made note:

> Interesting notes gleaned from letters written home by another of our aviators:
>
> Mrs. E.D. Edwards had a cable from her son Sterne on Friday last from London, where he is now on a week's leave of absence after spending five months in France. Sterne's work is not individual, he is with a squadron, and they have to work as such.

Their business is dropping bombs on munitions factories and other important places in the enemy country. His letters are interesting:—

On the 13th of October he writes: "Well we have started business at last. Yesterday we raided a big munition factory 110 miles away, about 60 miles this side of the Rhine. It was the biggest raid we carried out, more than 60 machines taking part. I do not think there is much left of the munition factory to-day. Oberndorf is the name of the place. Nine of our machines did not come back, 6 French and 3 British. It is likely they were shot down by antiaircraft guns for they shelled us heavily and the sky was thick with bursts. However, on raid of that size and distance, one expects to lose some machines, and 8 of our boys each shot down a Hun, which helps some.[2] The shells came near me only once, and I dived a thousand feet to change the range. We have the fastest bombing aeroplane in the world. We were the only flight [A No.1 Topwith Squadron][3] to come back complete. B Flight had some of its pilots lose themselves as it was dark when we got back and they landed in fields some distance from our aerodrome. We were about three and a half hours in the air, those in the slower machines of course much longer. My engine was not too good coming back, and before I recrossed the lines I thought I would have to descend, but it held out, and took me over the Vosges to 55 instead of 80 miles and I got home. A Hun machine was over a few nights ago and startled us by dropping bombs near our hut. We lost no time in getting into our dugout which is only 20 feet from the door. The bombs did no harm, and when the searchlights picked him out and the guns started shooting he soon left."

On the 29th of October he wrote again: "We have been very busy lately and have moved twice in three days. We have done nothing in the way of raids for the past week, as there has been a continued gale blowing and plenty of rain. The day we flew over here it was very rough, the worst any of us had experienced. It took me 40 minutes to fly only 15 miles, and we should do it in 10. We are now at a little place about 18 miles from Nancy, and will probably stay some time. It is not very far

[2] Post-war records showed that no German aircraft were shot down.
[3] Perhaps "Sopwith."

from the lines. Think we will move further north soon. Of course it is very nice to be moving about so much for one sees so much of the country. Nancy is a very nice little city. Little Paris they call it. It is about the size of Ottawa and only seven miles behind the lines. That paper clipping I sent home some time ago had Murray (Galbraith) in it. He is hundreds of miles from us. I suppose you have heard that Murray got the D.S.C. [Distinguished Service Cross], for bringing down that German machine some time ago. I am glad for I think he deserves it."

On November 5, Sterne writes of not receiving any mail for over a week and is suffering with a cold: "Have been doing nothing on account of rough weather for some time. Have been down to Luxena and Epinal. There is some talk of leave soon, and if it does we go seven at a time for 10 days, and being out here first I expect to be in the first seven, and hope to see Bob before he comes to France. Had the officers of a French regiment billetted [sic] near by to dinner. The regiment is the Alpine Chausseurs, one of the crack regiments of France. We had a good time and they invited us to their mess to-morrow night. Our C.O. got a letter the other day from General Joffre, signed by himself, saying he was much pleased with 3 Wing, or something to that effect, and there is a rumor that we may be allowed to wear a decoration of some kind. We have just been supplied with plenty of good flying clothes, boots, headgear and seal gauntlets, and they are necessary as it is very cold up high now.

Will wire from England if I get leave.
Your loving son
Sterne"

The wing moved to Ochey to be close enough to bomb Volkinger on November 10 and 11 and St. Ingbert on November 12, 1916. Enemy aircraft rose to meet the first two attacks but the bombers returned safely. Then, on December 27, Dilengen was raided, but Sterne was forced to turn back four times with engine trouble and missed the actual attack. On January 23, 1917, the wing bombed Brebach and destroyed three German planes. However, in open cockpits, the pilots and gunners suffered freezing about the face and hands. One plane landed back at Ochey with a live bomb, which exploded, killing three mechanics. On February 25, Edwards flew in another raid on Brebach. In these operations he flew a total of fifteen hours and thirty-five minutes.

On March 9, Sterne was posted to 11 Squadron (RNAS) to begin a new activity—as a fighter pilot. He trained on Nieuport Babys and then was posted to Naval 6 Squadron on April 19. This squadron was attached to the Royal Flying Corps at Chipilly, and the new fighter pilot flew more patrols and escort missions than dedicated attacks. On June 6, he went to Dunkirk to pick up a new Camel aircraft and took off to learn the peculiar ways of this little scout aeroplane. While on a training flight, on June 22, the cowl came off at 3,000 feet. It severely damaged the engine, cracked the propeller, and damaged the centre sec-

tion and upper wing, before coming to rest on one of the wire supports. It is a testimony to Edwards' skill as a pilot that he was able to land the aircraft safely.

In Naval Squadron 6, he was given command of a flight and performed well, but did not get along with the commanding officer. Morale in the entire squadron was low and Edwards applied for a transfer. He was refused!

Numbers 9 and 10 (Naval) Squadrons, attached to the RFC, had taken heavy losses, so Naval 6 was broken up and the pilots sent to these units. Edwards got his posting three months after arriving on squadron, leaving Naval 6 on July 18. After taking some leave he reported to 9 (Naval) Squadron near Bray Dunnes on August 10, 1917. A member of this squadron was F/Sub-Lt. Arthur Roy Brown, and the two friends greeted each other enthusiastically. They were finally flying together.

GOTHA
German bomber.

Sterne's flying was now primarily "offensive patrols," airborne almost every day and sometimes going on two or three patrols a day. On one occasion, when trying to intercept some German Gotha bombers returning from a raid on London, he flew in vain as far as the Dutch frontier. Sterne flew eighty-five flights and nearly 160 hours during the last half of 1917. On August 8, 1917, he was appointed as a flight commander of 209 Squadron.

Yet strangely, he never once mentioned in his logbooks the fact that he was shooting down enemy aircraft.

It is on this point that one can get a deeper insight of the man. First he was modest. Even more important was his attitude to the war. Edwards regarded it as a job to be done, but he had a real horror of killing, even enemies. In his prayer book he once wrote a prayer asking forgiveness for taking the life of an enemy, and for the safe return of himself and his men. For him, Christianity was a vital thing. His last commanding officer was to say of him that 'he never judged a man by what he heard about him and . . . he always took the part of the weak.'

Yet one should not think that he was dour Puritan. He attended the London theatres on leave and enjoyed them immensely. His friendships were many and lasting. His letters home were warm with humour and vitality. The lad from the Ottawa Valley was now a dedicated young man, who still found life enjoyable amid the dangers of total war.

From the first day with Naval Nine he showed skill and determination. Edwards scored his first victory on 3 September when his flight attacked an Aviatick. He sent the plane down in a vertical dive with the observer crumpled up in the cockpit. On the 21st of that month he drove a two-seater down over Zarren after pouring 250 rounds into it and having both guns jam. The next day he and Flight Lieutenant Redgate shot a DKW down out of control, and on the 23rd he 'shot a double.'

On patrol that day he downed a [*sic*] Albatross out of a formation of five, which Belgian observers saw crash into the sea. He then attacked three more Albatross scouts. One was shooting up another Camel, so Edwards pounced. The German turned on its back and went down in a dive. At 8,000

feet the enemy's wings came off. That made four victories and one shared victory in three weeks, and he was recommended for the Distinguished Service Cross. The award was made on 7 October, but by then Edwards had made the citation out of date.[4]

The official citation for the award of the DSC to Sterne reads as follows:

Distinguished Service Cross to Acting Flight Commander Stearne [*sic*] Tighe Edwards, R.N.A.S.—In recognition of his services on the following occasions:—

On the 3rd September, 1917, with his flight he attacked a two-seater Aviatik. The enemy machine was observed to go down in a vertical nose dive, and the enemy observer was seen to collapse in the cockpit.

On the 21st September, 1917, he drove a two-seater enemy machine down out of control.

On the 23rd September, 1917, he attacked an Albatross scout, which crashed into the sea.

On the same date he attacked three Albatross scouts. One got on the tail of another officer's machine at very close range, shooting him up very badly. Flt. Cdr. Edwards attacked him from above, and the enemy machine turned on its back and went down in a vertical dive. He followed the enemy machine down to 8,000 feet, when its wings came off, and it fell to the ground. [5]

ALBATROS D-III
German Fighter 1917.

During September 1917, the army was pushing hard into Flanders and the fighting was especially bitter. Sterne became an air ace (five confirmed kills) when he brought down an enemy Aviatic on September 27 and a German Albatross on the 28th. At the end of September, RNAS Squadron 9 was detached from the Royal Flying Corps and sent to 4 (Naval) Wing. During that month, Canadians had destroyed at least twenty enemy aircraft.

On October 2, Edwards was leading his flight when he identified

[4] Halliday, op. cit., pp. 119, 122.
[5] Directorate of History Records, Canadian Forces Headquarters.

five enemy two-seaters over the town of Stype in France. He led his air-men to the attack, holding his fire until he was within 50 yards. One enemy airplane stalled and spun down out of sight, crashing to earth. On October 27, he attacked another Aviatik but this aircraft appeared to have armour plating. It seemed to sponge up hundreds of bullets before it crashed. That was his last victory in 1917.

On November 10, Sterne Edwards and Roy Brown went to England on leave. They booked passage on a ship to Canada and spent Christmas at Carleton Place.[6] Without doubt their tales of war in the air must have inspired Franklyn Abbott, who was also home for the holidays, having completed his basic pilot training, and was awaiting orders to proceed to England.

On January 30, 1918, Brown and Edwards returned to Naval Squadron 9, Brown to command 'B' Flight and Sterne Edwards to command 'C' Flight. The squadron was equipped with Camel aircraft with Bentley engines. They changed aircraft, for six weeks, to the French Clerget machines, then switched back to the Bentley Camels—newer and more powerful machines—in March, just as the Germans began their last, desperate offensive in Flanders. The squadron was attached to 11 Wing, Royal Flying Corps.

When the Royal Flying Corps merged with the Royal Naval Air Service to become the Royal Air Force (RAF), No. 9 Squadron was renumbered 209. The RAF system of ranks, at that time based upon army ranks, was adopted and Sterne became a captain. On April 7 the squadron was transferred from 11 Wing to 22 Wing to support army operations on the Somme.

[6] There is a story that Edwards and Brown were able to book passage so easily because they were in fact sent home on a secret mission that took them to Washington—a story that so far has yet to be confirmed. In 1917 the United States was still not a belligerent in World War I.

Between 21 March and 21 April, the squadron had to change airdromes seven times. On 21 and 29 March they were actually shelled out of their fields.

There were other problems as well. The Germans' use of large formations had forced the Allies to adopt similar tactics, but the change was hard to make, and flights were difficult to hold together and to co-ordinate.

In the meantime, Edwards continued to add to his score. On 2 April 1918 his flight was patrolling at 6,000 feet. Suddenly, six Albatross D-5's emerged from the clouds 300 feet below. The Camels attacked and Edwards opened fire on the rearmost machine from 30 yards. The enemy aircraft stalled and dived vertically. He followed for 3000 feet. When the Albatross pilot started to regain control, Edwards snapped off another burst. The German plane turned on its back, started another steep dive, and then blew up.

On 12 April, flak bursts led him to a two-seater reconnaissance aircraft, which he downed in one long burst.

Edwards was not flying the day his friend Brown shot down Richthofen's bright red triplane, but he obtained a piece of the fabric from the Fokker of the great ace and sent it home to his sister. Brown, however, was exhausted by weeks of hard fighting and duties as squadron commander when the CO was busy. On 25 April he landed very sick, and was posted to hospital. Edwards was now the 'old man' of the squadron.

His last month in action was marked by four more victories, several indecisive combats, and a bar to his DSC, awarded on 20 May.[7]

The official citation for the Bar reads:

Bar to the Distinguished Service Cross to Lieut. (tempy. Capt.) Stearne Tighe Edwards, D.S.C., R.A.F.—For conspicuous bravery and most brilliant leadership of fighting patrols against enemy aircraft.[8]

The news of the award did not get home until the following month. The *Herald* of June 25, 1918, reported:

[7] Halliday, op. cit., pp. 124-125.

[8] Directorate of History Records

More Honors for Carleton Place Boys
Lieuts Brown and Edwards Awarded Bar to D.S.C.

In the list of war honors to Canadians recently announced from London we notice with pleasure the names of two of our Carleton Place boys. The announcement is as follows:—

Lieut. Sterne Edwards, air force, belongs to Carleton Place, Ont., has destroyed or driven down many enemy machines and has always shown a fine offensive.

Lieut. Arthur Roy Brown, air force, Carleton Place engaged two Fokker machines and drove them down; dived at another and sent it crashing to the ground.

We congratulate the boys upon their splendid success.

On 2 May [Edwards] took off on an evening patrol. His flight first tried to catch ten Albatross D-5's, but could not get within firing range. Over Brie they dived down from 12,000 to 8,000 feet. A long burst sent one German into a slow spin until it  vanished into a haze at 1,000 feet, later to be confirmed. The first group of Albatrosses was diving to attack, so the Camels broke off and turned west. Over Cayeux they attacked six red-nosed D-5's. In a dive Edwards fired 100 rounds into the last enemy scout, which turned over into a dive and crashed.

PFALZ D-III
In use after the
Albatrol D-III.

Eight days later, Edwards attacked six Pfalz scouts, driving one down, but he was unable to get confirmation. On the 15th he again attacked six Pfalz scouts, and picked off the hapless 'tail end Charlie.' Sending him down out of control. His last victory came on 16 May when, with Lieutenants May (the same 'Wop' May) and Taylor, he escorted Breguet bombers. Ten Fokker triplanes tried to interfere, but the Camels headed them off and sent one down to force-land near Corbie.

The savage fighting was taking its toll of Edwards, however. Battle fatigue was then only dimly understood, and it had driven many a pilot to his death. Escort patrols, offensive patrols, bombing, dogfights–all these missions piled one on another had a cumulative effect until, on 23 May, he could take no more. He suffered a nervous breakdown and was sent to 24 General Hospital.[9]

Interestingly enough, Sterne was recommended on May 24, 1918, by his squadron commander, for promotion to the rank of major. The justification was his exceptional performance in action against the enemy in the air. But his illness, and the bureaucratic slowness of the Air Ministry, precluded the implementation of the promotion.

Recovery time and personal leave in Britain helped to restore Sterne's health. He was posted as an instructor to No. 2 School of Aerial Fighting and Gunnery. His days were now filled with imitation air battles and instructional flights. In July, Roy Brown collapsed at the controls of an airplane and was pulled from the wreckage more dead than alive. Sterne wrote a comforting note to Roy's parents that was printed in the *Herald* of July 23, 1918:

Capt Roy Brown Injured

A cable last week to Mr. And Mrs. J.M. Brown conveyed the sad intelligence that their son; Capt A. Roy Brown, had been seriously injured in an accident in England. A second message yesterday from his brother Horace, was reassuring, and a later despatch from Capt. Sterne Edwards last night reads as follows:

"Roy seriously injured seven days ago, condition now much improved, chances of recovery good, no permanent injuries likely to result. Everything possible being done."

This message was very gratifying not only to the family, but to all friends of the heroic young aviator whose record is so good, and to whose prowess and skill the noted German Baron Von Richthofen owes his downfall.

In August, Sterne reported to No. 38 Training Depot Station at Tadcaster as a flight commander. He was given command of a group of American fledgling aviators. He seemed to do very well as a flight instructor and on three different occasions was congratulated by senior officers.

[9] Halliday, op. cit., pp. 125-126.

In the ground war, Allied troops were advancing north. At Cambrai, and on the Hindenburg Line, the enemy was being defeated. An army of fresh American troops had arrived in France and entered the battle. Sterne Edwards concluded that he thoroughly enjoyed military flying and decided to apply for a permanent commission in the Royal Air Force. In the meantime, he still had a flock of students to teach, but often would find the time to take the little Sopwith Pup airborne to cruise the English skies for his own pure joy. German resistance totally collapsed. Turkey and Austria had capitulated and, on November 11, Germany signed an armistice. The days of killing were over; celebrations were exuberant. Sterne took the Pup up into the cool blue morning air.

He flipped the machine over and around, enjoying the freedom of aerobatics alone in the sky. In a spin the

SOPWITH PUP
Full aerobatic
reported the best to
fly.

ground revolved around him and started coming up fast. He tried to pull out of the sickening dive, to level off, and then his wing tip touched the field, dragging the fragile Pup to earth. Ground crews lifted his unconscious body from the wreckage. He was transported to York hospital where he began fighting his most difficult battle.

Each day he rallied and showed some improvement, but his mangled leg caused the doctors great concern. On November 20 Sterne Edwards was administered anaesthesia to have his leg amputated below the knee. He couldn't beat the shock. Two days later, in the early hours of Friday, November 22, he drew his last breath. Sterne Tighe Edwards was dead at age twenty-five.

Sterne Edwards was buried in Tadcaster Cemetery, Yorkshire. His personal effects were sent to his mother, including his poker chips, his dog-eared prayer book, and a photograph of a girl, but who she was and what she had meant to him has never been determined. In 1920 a memorial service was held at Carleton Place, and a tablet was unveiled. The inscription read simply:

IN PROUD AND LOVING MEMORY OF
CAPTAIN STERNE TIGHE EDWARDS, DSC
ROYAL AIR FORCE
WHO DIED ON NOVEMBER 22ND, 1918
OF INJURIES RECEIVED ON ARMISTICE DAY
WHILE IN THE SERVICE OF HIS COUNTRY
FAITHFUL EVEN UNTO DEATH

The man who drew the veil, as a last token of friendship and respect, was Arthur Roy Brown.[10]

The *Carleton Place Herald* reported news of Sterne's death in the edition of November 26, 1918:

DIED OF HIS INJURIES

Capt. Sterne Tighe Edwards

About ten days ago Mrs E.D. Edwards received a message from England that her son, Capt. Sterne Edwards, of the Royal Flying Corps, had been seriously injured on the 12th, the day after the armistice, by accident, presumably whilst engaged with others in celebrating the auspicious event. He had both limbs and skull fractured. On Saturday last another message came announcing his death.

The circumstances are particularly sad, just as the war was over, and the deepest sympathy goes out to his mother, the sister and brother.

Capt. Edwards enlisted three years ago in the aerial service and received his training in Dayton, Ohio. He went overseas the following spring, and made good in France. He won the D.S.O.[11] and later had a Bar added. A year ago he had a short furlough and came to Canada spending Christmas here. He left again in January, and on reaching England received his captaincy. He went again to the front but the strain of the arduous work got on his nerves and he was recalled to England where for some time he had been doing instructional work in a training camp. An effort will be made to bring his remains home for burial. Capt. Edwards was born in Franktown, being the eldest son of the late Denis and Mrs. Edwards, and was 25 years of age. He spent his boyhood and received his education in Carleton Place, and was one of our sterling young men.

[10] Ibid., pp, 126-128.
[11] An error–it was the D.S.C.

The Commonwealth War Graves Commission inscription, sadly, contains the wrong date of Sterne's death:

In Memory of
S. T. EDWARDS
1917, Royal Air Force
who died on Saturday, 2nd [sic] November 1918
Remembered with Honour
Tadcaster Cemetery, Yorkshire, United Kingdom.

The last mention of Sterne in the *Herald* appeared on January 17, 1919. It was a tribute from the Masonic Lodge for its veteran members:

Fifteen members of St. John's Lodge, No. 63, A.F. & A.M., Carleton Place, joined the overseas forces and participated in various conflicts. Every one escaped except Sterne Tighe Edwards. 'The noblest Roman of them all' might be written, only that each and every one wore the signet of the patent of nobility. All fifteen were young, loyal, stalwart and permeated through and through with the spirit of devotion and chivalry. This Masonic Lodge sparkles in Canadian history by the setting of these jewels in the crown of the empire.

JOHN HORACE BROWN

When Horace Brown's life ended he was serving in England as a pilot in the Royal Air Force. But before he joined the "Knights of the Air," he served as a serf on the ground, experiencing more than his share of trench warfare.

J. Horace Brown was in the very first contingent of soldiers to leave Carleton Place for service in World War I. He had been in the active militia, the 42nd Regiment of Canadian Volunteers, for about three years and when war broke out he was wearing sergeant's stripes. Horace recruited his younger brother, Howard, who was about eight or nine years old, to polish the brass buttons on his uniforms, for which he paid Howard one or two pennies. According to the *Carleton Place Herald* of August 18, 1914 "Among the first contingent of Company 'B', the 42nd Regiment, to go by train to Perth for reorganisation en route to Valcartier was Sgt. J.H. Brown."

At Horace's medical examination for entry into the active force he listed his age as eighteen years, four months. He was born on June 15, 1896, the son of John Morton and Mary Elizabeth (Flett) Brown. The ancestral home is a large red brick house at 146 Judson Street. He listed his previous occupation as student and recorded that he had been raised in the Presbyterian faith. The medical examiner found him to be 5' 5" tall with a fair complexion, blue eyes and light hair.

Horace was the second son in a rather well-off family. He was a quiet lad, of small to medium build, and quite fond of the outdoors. He was interested in photography, and liked to experiment with various cameras, developing his own prints. In 1913 he convinced his older brother Roy to buy boxing gloves. The two would slug it out with each other, in spite of the fact that Horace was prone to spontaneous nosebleeds. He was interested in stamp collecting and joined the literary club at school. However, that proved so boring that he exited one meeting via the window and never went back. Horace was intrigued by the variety of birds in the locality, keeping a record of his sightings. While he was in high school he worked evenings in his father's power generation plant.

In August, troops by the thousand poured into Valcartier—both militia regiments and civilians, the latter either attached themselves to various groups or just simply turned up to go to war. In spite of the chaos, the volunteers were organized into units, housed, uniformed, fed and equipped. When the 42nd Regiment arrived in Valcartier, the Carleton Place men were transferred to the 2nd Canadian Battalion (Eastern Ontario) and placed in "H" Company under the command of Capt. W.H.V. Hooper. Organization proceeded well enough that on September 22, 1914, the 2nd Battalion proceeded to Quebec and boarded the S.S. *Cassandra* of the Scottish Donaldson Line for the trans-Atlantic trip. After many delays in the St. Lawrence and the Gaspé Basin waiting for the convoy to form up with its Royal Navy escorts, they started the voyage on October 3. Early on the morning of October 14 the first ship entered Plymouth Sound.

However, it was not until 9:45 p.m. on October 25 that the battalion disembarked. "H" Company, with Capt. Hooper in the fore, a

Plymouth native who had not been home for nineteen years, led the "Second" through the streets of Devonport and Plymouth. At 1:45 a.m., they boarded the train for Amesbury a small town on the eastern edge of Salisbury Plain. A few miles march away were the rows of tents that would be their home for the next few months—Bustard Camp.

The winter of 1914–1915 was marked by England's heaviest rainfall in years. Most of the troops were relegated to the tents, and the mud, of Salisbury Plain. Somehow, Horace escaped for a short while by doing duty in Amesbury and taking a billet in a house. Letters he wrote home appeared in the *Carleton Place Herald*:

> *Nov. 13, 1914.*
> *Dear Mother:*
>
> *. . . We have a lovely place to stay at. It is a private house, loaned to the government by a Captain who went to the front. He has been killed lately, but they still have use of the place . . . there are ten men counting myself in my room. We have a clothes closet, a closet of shelves, a fire place; and there are two large windows. We leave the windows partially open at night.*
>
> *We are given two shillings per day for food allowance and are living like kings. I have rented a cot, mattress and pillow; it only costs a shilling a week for the three. Will put some gasoline on as a precaution, and will be very comfortable. I cleaned up all this morning, had a nice warm bath and an entire change of clothes, and am sending all my soiled ones off to the laundry. We have cleaned the house all over, scrubbed it, and are getting a little in the line of furniture such as tables and benches . . .*
>
> *You ask about my comfort when in camp. I bought a pair of knee rubber boots, a raincoat and an oil-stove. We bought cocoa, herring, and other things, and were fairly comfortable. We have had served out to us a sweater coat, a sleeping cap, a pair of socks and the Oliver equipment . . .*
>
> *Everyone from Carleton Place is well . . . I have my Carleton Place pennant and my silk Union Jack hung over the fireplace. Canada pennant got torn on the way across, I cut out the Maple Leaf and the printing and sewed it on my red sweater . . .*
>
> *With Love to all*
> *Horace* [12]

[12] The entire text of the letters quoted may be found in the Appendix.

In December and January the weather changed to sleet and snow. Horace missed "Teddy," his pet dog at home. He bought a whippet for $7 and named it after Teddy because of the similar appearance. The troops were occupied with physical training, musketry and route marches, some as long as 15 miles. On January 31, Horace wrote that he was "out of the Hospital and feeling fine," but his records are silent as to the nature of this illness. He did state:

> They are very particular about the health of the Canadians now, since there has been so much sickness among the troops . . . a great many of the Canadians have died. I have seen or heard about two dozen funerals since I went to the hospital, mostly all from spinal meningitis . . .

On February 4, King George V made a second inspection and the soldiers instinctively knew that it was their ticket to France. On the 7th, they squeezed aboard a freighter, the S.S. *Blackwell,* and after a furious night at sea, landed on February 8 in St. Nazaire. Once again they were delayed on board and did not reach dry land until noon on the 11th. They were loaded onto railway boxcars, marked "40 hommes ou 8 chevaux," and by a circuitous route set off for the Ypres area. On February 15 they reached the front near a little village named Merris, about two miles from Hazebrouck. The battalion had been reorganised and they were now in Capt. Hooper's No. 4 Company. Horace had managed to take Teddy with him and had even had a "dog-tag" (a military identification disc) made for the dog to wear on its collar.

The British troops they were to relieve took great pains to instruct the Canadians in the mysteries of trench warfare. On February 19, Nos. 1 and 3 Companies went into the line.

> Twenty-four hours were long enough for green troops starting out in this line of business. At 3 o'clock next morning the veterans of Nos. 1 and 3 Companies were relieved in the trenches by the tyros of Nos. 2 and 4. With the air of men who had been far and seen much, the trench-hardened troops turned over their area and trudged grimly back to Armentières.[13]

Before the battalion went into the line, Teddy disappeared and was left behind in the billet area. The little dog was never seen again.

[13] Col. W.W. Murray, O.B.E., M.C., the History of the 2nd Canadian Battalion in the Great War (Ottawa: The Historical Committee, 2nd Battalion, C.E.F., 1947), p. 27.

Horace wrote from the trenches in France on March 11, 1915:

Dear Mother:

Well, I am sorry I have not written sooner, but one keeps putting it off. There was mail came into the trenches last night. I got papers and we were mighty glad to get them as we get no news of anything. You know more of what is going on than we do except just near us.

I have a fine section of trenches and dug-out. It is pretty dry and I have built and fixed it up so it is quite good now. We stay in days and go back to rest for days in billets. We get more rest while in the trenches I think than when we are in our billets.

Yesterday we made a sham attack to draw up the German reserves, so an attack could be made by our left. Two of the old 42nd answered their final roll call in it. Two good lives for King and country. To-day we just kept the Germans guessing what we were going to do so they would not know whether we were going to attack or not.

We have been issued rubber boots for the trenches. Some of us turned in our fur coats. I did, as I have the lamb lined vest, one of those Mr. Fred McDiarmid sent us, and my pack is plenty heavy enough. I wish now I had a small kodak and if I can I will send my big one back as it is too heavy to carry around . . .

Those handkerchiefs and clothes you sent me come in very handy. I was glad to receive them as we do not have much chance to get things washed now. I have discarded quite a few things now and carry food instead because we did not get very good food in the trenches but it has improved this time, we had fresh meat to-day. We do all our own cooking in the trenches over open fires in old pails and have to hunt up the fuel. The worst of it is the hot fire melts the solder in our canteens and they leak. I wish we had the seamless ones. Do you think you could get one and send it to me. We have to carry the ones we have inside our packs and they are an awkward shape. I guess I will stop and make a cup of cocoa. The Germans fire at our parapet and knock mud into our food when we are cooking, but we do likewise.

The Germans and our side yell back and forth at each other, they speak perfect English and we often jolly each other. They ask are our jobs kept for us in Canada, how much pay are we drawing off our jobs, etc.

15 March 1915

Well I am back in billet to-day. It is the closest yet to our line. Everytime we come out we are in a different billet. We done nothing but rest yesterday and hold church in the afternoon. To-day we are going for a bath. Our bugler had a very narrow escape. He went into one of the bays and fired a couple of shots through a loophole when he got an answer that blew both front and rear sights off his rifle and knocked a couple of pieces into his face. He may lose the sight of his right eye but will likely live.

I guess you have seen in the papers how the British have advanced, right here we are well ahead and have to wait on the flanks.

I will close and hand it in.

With love, from
Horace

The 2nd moved to Vlamertinghe and into the front line near Ypres on April 20. Early on the 22nd, Horace was hospitalized at the Rouen hospital with a minor infection. It saved his life as many of the Carleton Place boys were lost over the next few days during the fight for "Hooper's House" when the Germans introduced poison gas. On April 25, he was evacuated as "slightly sick" to the hospital in Le Havre. There is no record of his reaction or inner feelings when he rejoined his company to find so many friends had simply disappeared.

The battalion moved out of their billets on May 3 and marched to the rear to the town of Bailleul. Here they were able to buy delicacies such as eggs and chips, coffee and French bread and indulge in their growing taste for *vin ordinaire* and the local grenadine. On May 8, on the Royal Flying Corps airfield outside Bailleul, the battalion held a memorial service for the officers and men who had fallen at Ypres.

On May 22 they moved back into the reserve trenches near Indian Village. In No Man's Land before them lay hundreds of bodies that had been there since the last winter. Attempts to bury them had been given up as the enemy continually swept the parapets with fire. On May 27, the troops prepared to move into the front lines the next day. Here, Horace received his first wound. The field medical card, dated May 27, describes a "GSW [gunshot wound] Rt Arm Slt [slight]." A notice in the *Herald* of June 8, 1915, stated that ". . . Mr. Jim Brown has received a wire to the effect that his son, Cpl Horace, has been wounded on May 28th." In a later letter, Horace wrote that he was back in the trenches again and that "the regiment is impatient to be at it again." He thanks Mrs. McPherson for a nice box of goods, one of many she had sent to the boys.

The 2nd moved again on June 10, to Givenchy and a sharp salient known as "Duck's Bill." Due to the closeness of the opposing forces— about fifty yards separated the trenches—every other man was detailed for sentry duty during the night, two hours on and two hours off. Horace spent his birthday, the third in uniform, under heavy bombardment. The original 2nd Battalion had been decimated at Ypres and the new drafts of men, snatched from their original battalions in England to fill the holes, needed much encouragement to overcome natural resentments. Fortunately a lull in the action that summer afforded the opportunity to reestablish a battalion "esprit de corps."

In October they moved into the line at Messines but apart from a few sham attacks little happened. Trench warfare had not yet assumed the character of later years. October and November pelted the troops with torrential rain, sleet, snow and blustery winds. There was no escape; in a trench there is no shelter. On December 19, Horace wrote home that he ". . . had a little smell of our friend's gas. I knew the smell but could not place it. It smelt somewhat like an old barrel of apples." The school auditorium of the ancient town of Bailleul was pressed into service to accommodate the entire unit for Christmas dinner. Company cook-wagons roasted meat and poultry; Christmas spirit was much in evidence this first year for Canadians at the front. By New Year's they were back in the cold, wet and muddy trench system of Flanders.

Marching north the last days of March, they occupied the trenches on Hill 60, back in the Ypres-Comines Canal sector. They were close to the PPCLI and Horace had the good fortune to meet Colin Sinclair. By the end of April there was no rest as the enemy launched an unusually violent shelling of the hill. On April 26, 4 Company was in the midst of a mine explosion, German bombardment and Allied counterbombardment, followed up by assaulting German infantry. The enemy was met with heavy fire and the Canadians maintained their hold on the lip of the crater. After three attempts, all repelled by 4 Company, the enemy artillery lifted and the attacking infantry withdrew. In May the Battalion was relieved. On May 4, 1916, Horace Brown was promoted in the field to the rank of corporal.

Bad weather continued throughout June and on the 11th the battalion moved into trenches near Observatory Ridge. On June 13 they played the role of observers as two other battalions attacked the ridge. At 3:30 a.m., 4 Company was ordered to move back to their positions in the forward lines. This presented a problem because three platoons remained in the support trenches unable to move due to heavy shelling. Many of the remainder were casualties. But the remnants of 4 Company held their position. Throughout the 14th, German artillery showered a deluge of shells on Observatory Ridge.

On June 13 Horace was wounded a second time. The best description of this wounding is contained in a letter written by Pte. Wm. J. Wright, dated July 1, 1916:

Before I forget, I want to tell you about Sergt. Horace Brown. He, Sergt. Lightfoot and myself had dug ourselves in a kind of trench and slept in the mud, rain and shells all night. His officer wanted someone to go up and see how things were in the front line and Horace, or Brownie, said he would go. He had just got up out of his dug in position and a shell was coming close to our line. There was a rifle with a fixed bayonet on it two feet away, and in his hurry to escape the shell he fell on the bayonet which pierced him just above the heart and about two inches deep. The officer and I bandaged him up and he was quite cool. I then took him down to the dressing station. He has a rather nasty wound, not serious in any case, but just a good 'Blighty' and he sure does deserve it. He is a good boy and a good N.C.O. and I will swear by him any time. If you see his mother or father you can tell them that they ought to be proud of their son's conduct. I can assure you it was a noble act if it had carried through, but [due to] the unfortunate beginning was never carried out. Brownie and I have been always good friends and I hope he returns before the 'finale' [and] that he is with me again. If there is any possible chance I want them to know of his heroic act. Although wounded in the attempt and game to the last he only fainted when I got him to the door of the dressing station 700 yards away. The ground was literally ploughed with shells but he kept his nerve all the way. The blood flowed fast and furious and I cannot really understand how he had the vitality to pull through.[14]

The official record states, in a medical case sheet dated June 13, 1916:

Bayonet wound left chest and knee—at Ypres while following up charge, jumped into a shell hole in which one of our men was concealed. He jumped onto the man's bayonet, wounding him in the knee (L) and L chest. Did not puncture the chest wall but lost a great deal of blood. Sent to 13 Sta. Balogne [*sic*] where dressings were applied. Does not remember much of what happened. Sent to Nottingham General Hospital on June 23 where wounds healed.

His fourth birthday in uniform was spent in hospital. The *Herald* of June 27 reported:

Mr. J.M. Brown received a message a few days ago from the Department at Ottawa advising him that his son Horace, who enlisted and went with the first contingent, had been wounded in the chest and was in hospital in France. As letters have been received from Horace since the big battle the first week of June it is thought he was with the Canadians when they recaptured their lost ground about the 13th instant. It is hoped that his wounds are not of a serious nature.

Later—

Since the above was in type Mrs Brown has received a letter from Horace, who is now Sergt. Brown, having received his stripes at the front, written on the 14th, in which he states that in entering the trench holes they leave for protection in advancing over dangerous ground that he fell upon a bayonet that penetrated his leg, and on getting it out received a second wound. He is convalescing in a French hospital. He adds that the Carleton Place boys are all well.

The healing process was stubbornly incomplete so, on September 4, Horace was discharged to Canada. He sailed on the S.S. *Olympic* on

[14] Costello, op. cit., pp. 95-96.

September 5 and arrived in Quebec on September 11. Coming home to Carleton Place, he was discharged from the 2nd Battalion to take a commission.

From the *Herald* of September 5:

The date of Sergt. Horace Brown's arrival is not yet known. Horace comes back to take a commission in the 240th, and incidentally to assist in recruiting for this counties [*sic*] battalion

And on September 19:

Sergt. J. Horace Brown arrived home on an early train Saturday morning having been detained longer than anticipated at Quebec. He has entirely recovered from his wounds and looks every inch a soldier. His two years service has developed him physically and he returns more of a man in appearance.

We understand he will receive a commission in the 240th Battalion, and hopes to return to the front again before the war is over.

The high and public school cadets, the Boy Scouts, headed by the Bugle band of the 240th from Renfrew, will assemble at the town hall at 2:30 and form in procession, to be followed by members of the Town Council, Speakers' League and citizens generally. They will proceed to the home of Mr. J.M. Brown, where Horace will be picked up, then across the river to William street, where Pte. H. Upton will be called for, and then return to the town hall, where an address and presentations will be made and a programme of music will be rendered.

On September 17, 1916, Horace made his "officer's declaration" to accept a commission as a lieutenant in the 240th Battalion. The medical examination found him fit for service and described a "scar above lt eye; large scar on lt thigh; mole 10 o'clock lt nipple and a 1" bayonet wound scar 4" above lt nipple."

Lt. J.H. Brown was transferred to Lanark in charge of the recruiting office. His father purchased his first automobile, a McLaughlin, which he made available to Horace for recruiting duties. On October 3, 1916, Lt. Brown was released from recruiting to be available for other duties and posted to Kingston.

Horace remained on training duties in Canada for almost a year while he sought a position in the air services. In September 1917 he was accepted by the Royal Naval Air Service as a pilot and sent to England for flying training. He embarked from Halifax on the S.S. *Justica* on October 8, 1917. His last army pay record shows he was discharged on September 22 and was receiving pay at the rate of $2 a day with a 60 cent field allowance.

Horace had been taken on strength in Ottawa as a provisional flight officer. He worked diligently at flight school at the Royal Naval College flight school in Greenwich. He then went to Vendôme, France, for flying training. He found flying "a cinch" and graduated on April 1, 1918, as a flight sub-lieutenant flying Sopwith Scouts "ready to meet the Hun." On April 27, he crashed a Camel, but "got off with a few bruises." He was posted to 93 Squadron on May 11, 1918.

SOPWITH DOLPHIN
A 1918 fighter.

In 1918 a move to establish a Canadian Air Force or a Royal Canadian Naval Air Service was being received deferentially by politicians and the press, but military leaders pressed on. On August 5, the British Air Ministry designated two RAF Squadrons, 93 and 123, to be manned entirely by Canadians. No. 93 would be a fighter squadron equipped with Sopwith Dolphins. The mobilization date was set as October 10, when they would begin preparations for service at the front. On October 19, 93 Squadron was redesignated as 81 Squadron, RAF, but from the outset it was known as 1 Squadron CAF (Canadian Air Force)[15]

Unfortunately Horace missed most of this due to an accident he suffered on August 18, 1918. He spent the entire fall and winter suffering the effects. On October 13, 1918, he wrote from Ilford Emergency Hospital:

[15] S.F. Wise, *Canadian Airmen and the First World War*, op. cit., p. 608.

Layed up in the hospital but nothing much. Met with an accident while cycling. Was wheeling from the drome to Ilford and a horse and cart standing on the wrong side of the road pulled out and blocked the road and one of the shafts hit me in the chest. It hit a book in my pocket and smashed my pen so some of the blow was taken up that way, but it sure bumped me up some anyway. It was on the left side over the heart . . . I have a touch of pleural pneumonia but am getting along fine now . . .

And on October 21:

You don't have to worry about me at all as I will be alright as soon as I get rid of the cold I have at present.

Horace recovered to spend Christmas holidaying with his brother Roy and another Carleton Place aviator, Douglas Findlay. In fact, Roy's health was a more serious concern as he had crashed and suffered serious injuries a few months earlier.

On February 10, 1919, Horace was admitted to the hospital with a severe respiratory problem. Complications set in; he was a victim of the worldwide influenza pandemic complicated by pneumonia. After surviving four-and-a-half years of the worst wartime conditions imaginable, Horace Brown, with brother Roy at his bedside, died in hospital on February 19, 1919. He was twenty-two years old. His father had the body brought home for burial, one of the few Canadian casualties who were returned. His father paid $600 for embalming, a sealed lead coffin and freight to an Atlantic port. Roy cabled his parents on March 8 that Horace was coming home on the S.S. *Minnedosa.*

The *Carleton Place Herald* reported, on March 18, 1919:

Capt Roy Brown has arrived at Montreal, and is expected home on the first train. The remains of his brother, Horace, were not sent by the air ministry on the same boat and will not arrive until later.

Then:

Capt Roy Brown arrived home last Wednesday morning.

And finally:

Lieut J. Horace Brown
Buried with Military Honors

The funeral of the late Lieut. J. Horace Brown, who died in the Eaton Hospital in London, England, on February 18th, of influenza, after spending four and a half years in military service, took place from his father's residence here on Saturday afternoon, the remains having arrived that morning by early train from overseas, and the local returned men assembled together and accorded him all the honors of a soldier's funeral. The weather was most unpropitious for an outdoor display, and yet there was a large turnout. The cortege left the home on Judson Street at 2 o'clock, headed by the soldiers, Major W.H. Hooper, with whom Lieut Brown enlisted in August 1914, being in charge with E.C. Reynolds, another of the same corps, as aide. On reaching Mill Street a band of about 20 men, under leadership of Mr. J.H. McFadden, organized voluntarily by the old players for the occasion, took the lead and played the Dead March whilst the procession proceeded to Zion Church, the bells of the Anglican and Methodist tolling as the cortege passed along. At the church the service was conducted by Rev. W.A. Dobson, assisted by Rev. J.J. Monds, and was most impressive. The pallbearers were Sergt. W.G. Bates, Sergt. Carleton Pattie, Ptes. Allan Chapman and W.G. Kirkpatrick, Cadet Harold Taber and Lieut Ernest McIntosh, the latter coming from Montreal to be present. The church would not accommodate all who sought admission and many took shelter in the school room whilst the service proceeded.

After the service the procession reformed and marched to the outskirts of town, where conveyances were waiting to take the soldiers to the cemetery. The firing party was composed of W. Andison, R. Lewis, W. McNabb, E. McDonald, W. Houston, J.R. McFadden, N. Williamson, Rex Sibbitt, Ross McFarlane, R.J. Graham, R.A. Giles, G.C. McMullen and Roy Dean, in charge of Sergt Major Long and Bugler R. Balfour, of Smith's Falls. At the grave three volleys were fired whilst the bugler sounded the Last Post.

Lieut Brown was one of our first boys to go overseas and his body is the only one that has come back to his native land for interment. As a consequence the citizens of the town turned out en masse to do honor to him and to show their appreciation of what the country owes to the brave soldiers as well as expressing their sympathy for the bereaved parents and friends.

The record of Lieut. Brown is well known to our readers, and need not be enlarged upon again. He enlisted at the outbreak of the war, went overseas with the first contingent, was wounded in France, and on recovering sufficiently was sent home on leave. Being physically unfit he received his discharge, but shortly after got into the service again and became recruiting officer in the 240th. On completing this work he joined the Royal Flying Corps and crossed the ocean again, later uniting with the Royal Air Force. He was still associated with this when taken down with the influenza that proved fatal. Horace was the second son of Mr. And Mrs. J.M. Brown and was in his 23rd year.

Words to a hymn for aircrew, sung to the music of a popular hymn written for sailors, had just been published. His mother copied it out by hand to be sung at Horace's funeral:

O God extend thy saving care
To those in peril in the air

The hymn is well-known to latter day airmen with the words rewritten to:

Hear Thou, O Lord,
a nation's prayer
For these thy children of the air!

The Commonwealth War Graves Commission annotation of his commemoration reads:

In Memory of
JOHN HORACE BROWN
Lieutenant
Royal Air Force
who died on
Thursday, 13 February 1919,
Age 22
son of James Morton Brown and
Mary Elizabeth Brown of
Carleton Place, Ontario
Carleton Place United Cemeteries,
St Fillan's Section

The War Medal

Victory Medal

WILLAM ROY KELLOUGH

Roy Kellough was born in Carleton Place on October 19, 1899, the youngest son of Mr. And Mrs. W.J. Kellough. Growing up he was known as a good athlete and "a relatively tough customer in a scrap."[16] He attended some of the 42nd Regiment's summer training camps and participated in locally organized fishing excursions. He was also a hunter, or at least he enjoyed shooting. The *Carleton Place Herald* reported on December 1, 1914, that "Roy Kellough, son of Mr. W.J. Kellough, while hunting placed his rifle against a fence. It fell, discharged and shot him in the arm below the shoulder." He belonged to the High School Cadet Corps. On June 1, 1915, he was a cadet sergeant and shot a mediocre thirteen out of a possible score of twenty on the rifle range.

Roy and his brother, Thorold McDiarmid Kellough, left Carleton Place in 1917 to go west to get harvest work on the Prairies. In Calgary they joined the Royal Flying Corps (RFC) together. They took their flying training in Camp Borden, Ontario, which had been established as an RFC school as early as 1916. By October 1917, both elementary and advanced flying skills were being taught at this school.

The two young fliers, now second lieutenants, were sent overseas in February 1918. By this time the RFC had become part of the RAF. Thorold went to No. 43 Temporary Duty Station on October 18 and Roy went to No. 33 Station on November 7. On February 25, 1919, Roy was in Europe flying DH9s with No. 88 Squadron. Another aviator from the area, Lt. K.B. Conn of Almonte, also belonged to this squadron.

Roy had a short-lived career in the air. He was killed in a flying accident on March 3, 1919. In the official inscription Roy's age is listed as twenty-three years, but if his birth date of 1899 is correct then he was barely twenty years old at the time of his death. The *Herald* made this report on March 11, 1919:

[16] Costello, op. cit., p. 154.

Airman Roy Kellough Meets Accidental Death

The sad news came to Mr. And Mrs. W.J. Kellough on Saturday that their son, Roy, who was with the Royal Air Force in England had been accidentally killed on the 3rd of March. Roy was the younger of the two brothers who enlisted with the air force and went overseas. Thorold, the elder, is still in the service. Further particulars are not yet to hand. The family have the deepest sympathy in their bereavement.

Roy's body was interred in Charleroi Communal Cemetery, Charleroi, Belgium. The town is near Mons. The cemetery holds 250 1914–1918 war casualties. The Commonwealth War Graves Commission commemoration reads:

In Memory of
Second Lieutenant WILLIAM ROY KELLOUGH
88th Sqdn., Royal Air Force
who died aged 23 on Monday, 3rd March 1919.
Second Lieutenant KELLOUGH was the son of Mr. And Mrs.
W.J. Kellough,
of Carleton Place, Ontario, Canada.
Remembered with honour
CHARLEROI COMMUNAL CEMETERY, Charleroi,
Hainaut, Belgium.

CHAPTER 29

PEACE—BUT THE MALADY LINGERS ON

On November 11, 1918, at 11:00 a.m., peace broke out in Europe. The *Carleton Place Herald* reported in its November 12 edition:

CANADA!
YPRES APRIL 22-24, 1915

A Day of Rejoicing

Shortly after the news reached Ottawa yesterday a few minutes before 3 o'clock in the morning, that the terms of armistice had been signed by the Germans, the tidings were flashed to Carleton Place, and Mayor Bates rushed out with his car, the siren shrieking to advise the neighbours. Before 4 o'clock he had the town bell clanging and in a few minutes every whistle and bell in town was on duty. People rose and dressed hurriedly, discharged firearms, sounded horns and demonstrated in one form or another, a spontaneous outburst of joy and gratitude that the awful war was at last at an end.

On the market square an immense bonfire was lighted and the reflection of the fire and the awful noise of the whistles and bells gave evidence for miles around of the momentous event.

By nine o'clock the streets were thronged with people from far and near, homes were decorated with flags, and everybody rejoiced. At the town hall the members of the council assembled, and most of the ministers. A prayer of thanksgiving was offered and the 'Praise God' &c was sung.

Then a procession was organized, with Lieut. McIntosh as marshal, on a white steed, followed by the mayor and council, the local clergymen and returned soldiers, the hook and ladder truck (with ladies clinging to the sides), the town and C.P.R.

fire brigades, a veteran band (led by Mr. Jos. McFadden and including such well known old timers as J.G. Steele, Townend, Gordon, Whitcher, Hockenhull, Lowe and others, Supt. Fogarty as driver, Major and W.J. Welsh with the bass drum), float from Hawthorne Mills, the war canoe and crew, Findlay Bros. Foundry and employees, the school children, and comiques, between 40 and 50 autos bringing up the rear.

A circuit of the town was made, and on return the procession disbursed, and the people assembled in the hall, where addresses were made by the Mayor, Canon Elliott, Revs. Dobson, Lawson and Monds, on behalf of the Victory Loan campaign, some $10,000. being subscribed on the spot.

All industries and stores were closed and the day was given up to noise and good fellowship. In the evening more bonfires and demonstrations of joy, until about 11 o'clock, when a very tired people sought the quiet of their home for a much needed and happy rest.

Although the war is over the list of casualties will come in for some weeks yet.

On February 4, 1919, the *Herald* published a poem written by David K. Findlay, which had previously appeared in St. Andrew's College Magazine in Toronto:

DAWN

Weeping may endure for a night, but joy cometh in the morning.
'Tis night, but still war's foaming flood
Rolls on in sacrificial blood;
Lurid flashes stab the dark;
Mortar answers Mortar's bark;
While afar the big guns bellow, and the dead lie huddled stark.

The shriek of high explosive and the bullet's sighing whine;
The deadly Maxim mutter as the foemen sweep our line;
The red lust of killing in the din of hellish wounds;
The grim frenzy of the fight, the madness of deep wounds,
And the Very's shuddering light shows the dead piled in mounds.

The dawn rose o'er torn trench and muddy rill;
The cold stars gaze in pale amaze to find the world so still.

Comes a whisper on the dawn wind to where the Crosses show,
To where the dead are dreaming dreams and Autumn flowers blow;

The flowers nod and bend to tell,
A whisper from each crimson bell—
To tell the dead that all is well;
That reason rules the minds of men,
That peace on earth has come again.

REBECCA ELLEN MCEACHEN

Rebecca McEachen was born in Drummond Township of Lanark County on May 7, 1886, the daughter of John E. and Elizabeth (Cunningham) McEachen. Rebecca was a trained nurse who served with the Canadian Army Medical Corps (Active Militia) from April 22, 1918, to June 21, 1918. She then enrolled at Carleton Place into the Canadian Expeditionary Force as a nurse.

The Nursing Sisters of Canada enlisted 3,141 young women; 2,504 served overseas and forty died. Fifteen were killed when the clearly marked hospital ship *Llandovery Castle* was torpedoed by a German submarine off the south coast of Ireland. The U-boat shelled survivors who had taken to the lifeboats.

Nursing Sister McEachen[1] was posted to the Ontario Military Hospital in Cobourg. She was assigned to a ward caring for soldiers, many of whom had been wounded in France, and were now suffering from the Spanish influenza. In 1918, an epidemic swept the world, killing an estimated 40 million people in less than twelve months.[2] This pandemic is one of the greatest medical mysteries of this century. In one year, it swept over the Earth in a wave of death, baffling doctors because it disappeared almost as quickly as it appeared. Within days, victims' lungs would overflow with fluid, drowning them. It was not until 1998 that a team of scientists, headed by a Canadian, collected samples of the killer virus from the frozen graves of six Norwegian miners. It is hoped that analysis of these specimens will

---

[1] Nurses were addressed as "Nursing Sisters" or "Sisters," no matter what their military rank. All were commissioned with an officer's rank but the term Sister formed a closer and easier bond with their enlisted patients.

[2] By comparison, AIDS had killed 11.7 million people by 1997.

yield the information required for scientists to develop a vaccine which so far has resisted research efforts. A vaccine could save millions of lives when the predicted influenza pandemic strikes again.

Pneumonia may be caused by either viruses or bacteria. The latter, called *streptococcus pneumoniae*, invade the lungs causing bacterial pneumonia. These can attack different parts of the body resulting in various afflictions. For example, in the brain, the bacteria cause meningitis.

Carleton Place did not escape. Schools and churches were closed and meetings banned for several weeks. Many men who survived the war were felled by this vicious killer, as were their families. The disease demonstrated no discrimination.

During this pandemic the military hospitals in Canada were overwhelmed coping with serious illnesses and accidents, and returned injured soldiers on top of the influenza. As well, a number of nursing sisters took ill, demanding drastic measures be taken. They began to recruit nurses to serve only on hospital influenza wards and only for the duration of the epidemic. They would retain their civilian status and be paid $3.50 a day if a graduate nurse, or $3 a day if an undergraduate, and $1.70 a day subsistence allowance. Many nurses were needed and many took the offer with hopes of a future permanent position.

While on duty at the Ontario Military Hospital, Toronto, Nursing Sister McEachen developed a middle ear infection on October 7, 1918, and had to be transferred for treatment to Hôtel Dieu Hospital. She recovered satisfactorily and on October 17 was transferred to duty at the Queen's Military Hospital in Kingston. On November 10, symptoms of the middle ear disease reappeared and she was admitted to the Kingston General Hospital on November 11. All of the signs of meningitis developed and, on November 15, a lumbar puncture was administered that showed the bacteria *streptococcus mucosus*. According to her medical history, "She gradually sank and died [during the] evening of November 16th, 1918." She was thirty-three years old.

Rebecca's father had predeceased her leaving her widowed mother to mourn. The *Carleton Place Herald* of November 18, 1918, reported her death and funeral:

Nursing Sister Rebecca Ellen McEachean [*sic*], daughter of the late John McEachean of Carleton Place, died on Saturday evening at Kingston, of spinal meningitis, succeeding an attack of Spanish influenza. The deceased had done excellent service during the recent epidemic and at last fell victim herself to the disease. The remains were brought on here yesterday, and the funeral took place this morning to St. Mary's church and thence to the cemetery. The aged mother and other bereaved relatives have the sympathy of many friends in their sorrow.

The Five Sisters window in York Minster, England, is dedicated to the more than 3,000 women who served the Empire and died doing their duties in the Great War. Their names are recorded on ten nearby Gothic panels; Canadian names are on the sixth panel.

The commemorative information of the Commonwealth War Graves Commission is as follows:

In Memory of
REBECCA McEACHEN
Sister
Canadian Army Medical Corps
who died on
Saturday, 16th November 1918, age 33.
Sister McEachen was the daughter of Mrs. McEachen, of
Carleton Place, Ont., and the late John McEachen.
Remembered with Honour
Carleton Place (St Marys) Cemetery, Ontario, Canada.

DAVID CHARLES HUMPHREY

Charles Humphrey was nineteen when he joined the 7th Canadian Engineers on May 29, 1918. He had been working as a locomotive fireman with the Canadian Pacific Railway. Charles was born on January 10, 1899, the son of Daniel and Rebecca Humphrey, attended Carleton Place schools and was raised as an adherent to the Church of England.

He enlisted at Toronto and gave his age as nineteen years, four months. He named, as his next of kin, his sister, Laura. Charles' medical examiner found him fit at 5' 7" inches tall and weighing 146 lbs. He was described as of a medium complexion with grey eyes and brown hair. He had several scars down the back of his right leg and on the outside of his left leg.

CONST.R

En route to his ship for overseas, Charles was halted in Montreal. He was hospitalized from July 4 to 13 in the Isolation Hospital because, while on duty in Brockville, he had been in contact with measles. When he demonstrated no manifestation of the disease he was released and proceeded to Halifax. He embarked aboard the S.S. *Nankin* on August 2, 1918, and arrived in Liverpool on August 15. In England, he was sent to the 3rd Canadian Engineers Reserve Battalion at Frensham Pond.

From April 1917 to the end of 1918, Canadian Railway units laid 1,169 miles of broad-gauge track and 1,404 miles of light track. The number of soldiers employed in this construction work in 1918 averaged nearly 8,000 per day with another 4,000 employed in maintaining lines already built. But as the war wound down there was less need to send reinforcements to France and Belgium. Sapper Humphrey spent the rest of the war in railroad operations in Britain.

On June 23, 1919, Charles boarded the S.S. *Belgic* and sailed for home. He arrived in Halifax on July 1, 1919 and on July 3, he was discharged in Kingston.

Although he was recorded as physically fit on discharge, having gained some ten pounds in the army, Charles soon began having respiratory and pulmonary problems. On May 1, 1921, Charles Humphrey, at age 21, died of pulmonary tuberculosis.

In the *Herald* of May 4, 1921:

> Death of D. Charles Humphrey
>
> After an illness of many months Pte. David Charles Humphrey, eldest son of the late Daniel and Mrs. Humphrey, passed away on Sunday at the Mowat Sanatorium at Kingston. Deceased was in his 23rd year. He enlisted when quite young, spending one year overseas. On his return he caught cold which devel-

oped into la grippe, and although he died everything possible [was done] to overcome the trouble [but] he was unable to stay the disease. At Kingston the young soldier was accorded a military funeral and received the full honours on one who served his country in time of need. The remains were sent on home for interment, arriving yesterday morning, the funeral taking place this afternoon from the home of his grandmother, Mrs. Wm. Williams, Charles St., to St. James Church and cemetery . . . One brother and one sister, William and Laura, survive.

The Commonwealth War Graves Commemorative Registry records:

In Memory of
DAVID CHARLES HUMPHREY
Sapper
2009204
Canadian Engineers
who died on
Sunday, 1st May 1921. Age 21.
Son of the late Daniel and Rebecca Humphrey,
of Carleton Place, Ont.
Remembered with honour
Carleton Place (St. James) Anglican Cemetery, Ontario, Canada.

Chapter Thirty

AFTERMATH

The "Maple Leaf" To The Fore
The placid Somme, on left and right
Was witness to a stirring sight
As onward rolled an eager band
Of soldiers from a foreign land,
Who little knew of arts of war—
Had never heard the cannons roar—
But at command they showed their worth,
'The land of maple gave them birth.'

St. Julien with its vine-clad hills,
Well nurtured by the brooks and rills,
Now holds in safety those who died
To stem the Huns' onrushing tide.
The foe adopted hellish aid,
And on the field our sons were laid.
We murmured not, for such a deed
Must rest upon a broken reed;
The day will come—a reckoning day—
In God's own time, in God's own way.

On Flanders' fields and in the vale
Of Ypres and of Passchendaele
The 'Maple Leaf' joined in the fray,
And won fresh laurels day by day.
Its sons were fighting for a cause
That aimed to uphold freedom's laws,
To help oppressed in every land,
And give the world a righteous stand.

The 'Khaki boys' of Vimy Heights,
Showed to the world their tact and might;
They forward pushed in serried ranks,
Supported by the deadly tanks,
And little thought of trials endured,
Since gains they made were well secured;
With cheerful song and spirits high
They hear the foe's retreating cry.

Again the 'Maple' stood the test,
Its praises ring from East to West,
From North to South the word has come,
Canadian boys, Well done! Well done!"

J.B. Rittenhouse

Memories of the tremendous toll are today diminishing. Many people now, if they think of the Great War at all, consider the slaughter to have been without purpose. They would have it purged from our recollection. But the volunteers who went overseas believed in the cause that placed their very lives in peril. They fought and died, lost limbs and nerves, to preserve a way of life ill-defined in 1914. It is only in our remembering that we can banish the dimming of their sacrifice and recognize the importance to this nation of their actions.

In the Great War of 1914–1918, a total of 626,636 Canadian men and women served in uniform for the nation and the Empire, 619,636 enlisted in the Canadian Expeditionary Force and 59,544 were killed. An additional 138,166 returned home wounded. Approximately 7,000 people joined the Royal Canadian Navy, 225 lost their lives and 543 were wounded. It is estimated that about 18,000 Canadians joined either the Royal Flying Corps or the Royal Naval Air Service and 1,563 of them died as a result. Those suffering wounds totalled 1,130. There were also 14,590 Allied reservists living in Canada who left to join their own national forces (British,

Department of Veterans Affairs

Belgians, Serbs, Montenegrins, etc.), but there are no statistics available for those of Eastern European descent who may have served with the Triple Alliance forces (Germany, Austria-Hungary, Italy).

The 1911 Canadian census recorded a population of 7,206,643. The total casualty count adds up to 61,332 killed and 174,623 wounded in World War I. That is nearly one in ten, an entire generation lost.

In Carleton Place, with a population of approximately 4,200, volunteers for military service numbered 287. There are forty-seven names engraved on the town's cenotaph in Memorial Park. Most left as boys or young men and were never seen again.

Canadians, as a rule, are slow to recognize their veterans. After the "Welcome Home" and parades, the mystique disappears quickly. Certainly no one at home can even imagine the horror of just trying to survive in the muddy ooze and cold sleet of Flanders, let alone dodge the bullets that someone is aiming at your head. Honour and glory are intangibles that quickly fade.

Preaching at memorial services as early as 1917, the Rev. W. Gould Henderson, pastor of Carleton Place Methodist Church, was calling for a continuing memorial day as a reminder of the sacrifice paid by the fallen. Yet it was not until 1931, after continued representations by the Royal Canadian Legion, that parliament amended the Armistice Day Act to set aside November 11 as a day upon which the nation could pay special tribute to those "who gave their lives that freedom might prevail." It was not until 1970 that the Holidays Act was passed which included Remembrance Day as a national holiday.

The design for a National War Memorial was approved in 1925. The competition was won by Vernon Marsh, an Englishman who died in 1930. His family completed the work and displayed it in Hyde Park, London, in 1932, before it was disassembled, packed into thirty-five wooden cases and shipped to Canada. In May 1939, His Majesty King George VI unveiled it at its present location in Ottawa. Prior to this, annual remembrance services had been held on the lawn in front of the Parliament Buildings, a site reverted to in 1998 and 1999 when the National Memorial area was undergoing rehabilitation.

In December 1918, the Carleton Place Canadian suggested that the mayor call a meeting to "talk over the matter of a suitable memorial for the Carleton Place boys who have fallen during the war. More than 300 enlisted and thirty or more sleep in Flanders Fields." A letter to the editor of the Carleton Place Herald, printed on January 28, 1919, following nineteen-year-old Arthur McDiarmid's funeral, made the following plea:

A Call To Duty by an Elderly Veteran of '66

Now that our beautiful winter is passing, and budding spring at hand with its rumblings of new industries: banks, mills, hydro electric, C.P.R. depot and street and water improvement, yet one of vital importance [is] not mentioned. That is of our returned Veterans. A few years ago we saw them leave our shores, the picture of physical manhood, and many of them came back to us, the empty shells of their former selves: to sit around in sorry meditation of the terrible nightmare after playing conspicuous parts in the most colossal struggle known to humanity.

When some of our boys came home on leave, and others incapacitated for further service, great crowds gathered to look after them and do them honor but even that is past and gone.

So now strong men of C[arleton] Place, rise in might, to your rightful place in the front ranks of Ottawa Valley towns, and make suitable recognition of our returned heroes. This might take the form of a monument of any of our local granites, suitably inscribed, and placed in that splendid lot facing the Post Office, at present the property of the sore-hearted and loving parent who has just lost his third son as a result of the terrible drama, and to whom the heartfelt sympathy of the community goes out at this time.

Get busy, men of C[arleton] Place, call a public meeting, that this may be thoroughly discussed, before it is too late. Many projects are in the air, whilst our boys are scattering rapidly and how soothing to the many sorrowful hearts, to drop into that cool, shady spot, made beautiful by the Horticultural and other capable hands, and view the names of our fallen heroes and of veterans, who may have left for other parts of our expansive country.

A Fenian Raid Veteran

Most of the town churches commissioned honour rolls early in 1919 listing all of the names of those from the congregations who had enlisted for service and held remembrance services for those who "had given their lives for Empire, Justice and Freedom." The Great War Veterans Association began to collect members from across the country as veterans continued to trickle home by ship and train.

Plans for the memorial in Carleton Place began in 1920 when town council passed By-Law 829 on September 20 establishing the Memorial Park Commission to choose a memorial and a location:

> Whereas it is desirable that a Memorial, in honour of those who paid the supreme sacrifice in the late great war and also of those who risked their lives to preserve our present great liberty, should be erected in Carleton Place.
>
> And Whereas the Heirs of the late James Gillies have presented this Corporation with that portion of his real estate adjacent to the Market Square for such a purpose.
>
> And Whereas it is thought a fitting and lasting Memorial in this regard would be the making of a park by joining the Gillies property with the Market Square to be called "The Memorial Park."
>
> And Whereas it will be necessary to appoint a Commission.
>
> Therefore the Municipal Council of the Town of Carleton Place hereby nominates and appoints the following persons to be called the Carleton Place Memorial Park Commission. The said Commissioners to be as follows. viz. The Mayor by virtue of his office and Wm. Findlay, Mr. M. Riddell, Robt Patterson, C.W. Bates, John Walsh, Mrs H.W. Drummond, Mrs Alf McNealy & Mrs Thos Armstrong.
>
> The said Commissioners to procure a suitable plan. To take such steps as they deem advisable to procure the necessary funds to have said plan carried to completion and to have full control in the making of rules and regulations re use of the Park and of enforcing the same.
>
> R.W. Bates, Mayor

The council minutes of April 11, 1921, reveal that the Gillies Estate gave the adjoining land to the Market Square for the park but council wanted to hold a public meeting to get the input of town citizens before proceeding too far. On May 9, 1921, council amended By-Law 829 to strike out the names of the commissioners and to replace them with the mayor, property commissioner, Regal of

Independent Order of the Daughters of the Empire, and the presidents of the Horticultural Society, the Red Cross Society and the Women's Institute. It was at this May meeting that council also made a motion to attempt to receive suitable "war trophies"[162] for the town. Throughout the summer and following winter the IODE regularly had the use of the fire hall in which to hold dances, the proceeds going toward the Memorial Park.

The question of a suitable location for the Memorial Park, on Market Square or on the corner of Lansdowne and Lake Avenues, was directed by council on November 28, 1921, to be put on the next municipal election ballot for the people's decision. The cenotaph now rests at their choice, on the old Market Square. At their meeting on June 9, 1924, Mayor W.H. Hooper and his council passed a motion:

> [A] vote of thanks to the Memorial Park Association, I.O.D.E., Women's Institute and other organizational bodies for the beautiful park they have created and also the soldiers' memorial, both of which we consider a work of beauty and a great credit to the donors.

On May 24, 1924, Mary McDiarmid, on the arm of her only surviving veteran son Leo, slowly but proudly walked up the path to unveil Carleton Place's solitary stone plinth memorial to the town's

Photo: B. Wilson

World War I dead. Mary lost three sons to this dreadful war—Victor and Harold on Vimy Ridge, and Arthur, who was gassed on Vimy Ridge but came home to endure hospitals and sanatoria, before dying on January 20, 1919, at age nineteen. Every November 11 thereafter, Leo's child, Martha, accompanied her grandmother Mary up the lonely path. After the latter's death, a gracefully aging granddaughter took complete responsibility for the yearly laying of the McDiarmid wreath. This family has never forgotten! Martha Knox still attends and participates at the Carleton Place War Memorial on Remembrance Day.

The Anxious Dead

O Guns, fall silent till the dead men hear
Above their heads the legions pressing on:
(Those fought their fight in time of bitter fear,
And died not knowing how the day had gone.)

O flashing muzzles, pause, and let them see
The coming dawn that streaks the sky afar;
Then let your mighty chorus witness be
To them, and Caesar, that we still make war.

Tell them, O guns, that we have not heard their call,
That we have sworn and will not turn aside,
That we will onward till we win or fall,
That we will keep the faith for which they died.

Bid them be patient, and some day, anon,
They shall feel earth enwrapt in silence deep;
Shall greet, in wonderment, the quiet dawn,
And in content may turn them to their sleep.

John McCrae[1]

[1]Brian Gardner, ed., *Up the Line to Death, The War Poets 1914-1918* (Oxford, Eng., Meuthen & Co. Ltd., 1964), p. 54.

Chapter Thirty-One

LOST SOULS

"A. McPhee"

This name appears on the Carleton Place cenotaph, but has successfully eluded all research. Every file at the National Archives Personnel Records Centre with a first or second initial "A" for Canadian Expeditionary Force members with the last name of McPhee has been checked. None has been found with a Carleton Place, or area, connection. Similarly, the card files at the Directorate of History for Canadians who served in the British air service have been searched with no success.

A ray of hope occurred when a notice was found in the *Herald* of October 1, 1918, that "Mr. Angus McPhee has just received word from his son, Angus, from whom he had no communication for 17 years. He is fighting with the allied troops in Palestine." This trail quickly evaporated. The nearest was Angus McPhee, regimental number 3323522, who enlisted from Alexandria but he went immediately on farm leave and never served in uniform. He was discharged on December 10, 1918.

There are seven Angus McPhees with Canadian Expeditionary Force records but none with any connection to Carleton Place. The only Angus McPhee living in the town was the elderly father of Neil John McPhee who was killed near Ypres in 1915. His wife, Jane (Hyland), died on May 4, 1919. They had another son, Archibald, who was a prominent paddler with the Canoe Club but who did not serve in the war. He moved to Smiths Falls in 1902 to work as a foreman in Mr. Gould's foundry. Angus was living at Archibald's home when he died on July 15, 1920. Angus and Jane McPhee of Carleton Place, also had two daughters. Elizabeth married a Dr. Charlebois and moved to Alexandria. She died during the night of August 26–27, 1918. The second daughter has also disappeared from the records.

Some sources thought the name "A. McPhee" referred to an "Archie McPhee" and they may be thinking of Angus' son. There are two Archibald McPhees in the Canadian Expeditionary Force (CEF) records. One Archibald McPhee, service number 326900 served in the 1st Brigade, Canadian Field Artillery, and, according to CEF records, hailed from Sydney, Nova Scotia. The other, number 408167 Archibald Neil McPhee, served in the 13th Battalion (Quebec Regiment) and listed his next of kin as his brother, Rev. D.A. McPhee of Alexandria, Ontario. This Archibald McPhee was listed in Angus's obituary in the Smiths Falls' newspaper as a brother of Angus's wife, Jane, which has to be in error because her maiden name was Hyland.

There are no records of a Carleton Place A. McPhee in the Commonwealth War Graves Commission (CWGC) records. The lack of mention in CEF or CWGC records simply means that the man was not killed in the war, did not die as a result of the war, or did not serve with the Canadian Forces. He could, however, have served with any of the allied forces, most probably British, and his death could have occurred after the war and was never reported to the CWGC.

Town council minutes were searched in an effort to determine the criteria and the reason for the names on the monument. It was hoped that a list would be found that would shed light on the names and why they are there. No such information appears to exist. The IODE was primarily responsible for the erection of the war memorial, but a request for a search of their records also yielded no information. It is truly unfortunate that a soldier of the Great War has disappeared from the Carleton Place memory.

Errors and Omissions

There are several errors on the monument, including misspelled names and incorrect initials. Following is a list of names, first as they appear on the stone and then the name as it is in their CEF personnel records:

R. Borland	Robert Boreland
R. Flegg	Thomas R. Flegg
A. Tuft	Arthur Tufts
W. Tyre	William Tyrie
Hamilton (initial missing)	Sydney Hamilton

Research by this writer revealed the following Carleton Place men whose names do not appear on the monument but who did die as a result of their war wounds or injuries and should be considered for inclusion with their comrades-in-arms:

ROBERT FRANKLYN PRESTON ABBOTT

Franklyn was born the only son of Mr. And Mrs. Charles H. Abbott, in Carleton Place, on May 14, 1897. At age nineteen in June 1916, he went to Toronto to the Curtiss Flying School where he gained his Royal Aero Club pilot's certificate (# 3856) on November 7, 1916. The same day he was enrolled in the Royal Naval Air Service as a probationary flight officer. He listed his previous occupation as student. While still in school he had the unfortunate experience, as reported in the *Herald* of November 24, 1914, of being at home when his parents' house on Neil's Lane caught fire and burned. With him was young Victor McDiarmid. Both escaped unscathed.

The *Herald* of November 28, 1916, carried this notice:

> Flight Officer R.F.P. Abbott, son of our townsman, Mr. C.H. Abbott, who recently completed his course at the Curtiss Aviation School, left for Montreal last week after a brief holiday at home. He will leave shortly for overseas to join the aviation corps of the British Navy.

AVRO 504
British mass produced aircraft.

On November 25, Franklyn sailed for England and by January 14, 1917, he was in training at Chingford. The most common training aircraft in England was the Avro 504, a biplane with a distinguishing long wooden skid projecting forward between the landing wheels. This prevented "nose-overs" during landings by student pilots, an all too common occurrence. His advanced training, probably on the Sopwith Pup, took

SOPWITH PUP
Full aeorobatic reported the best to fly.

him to Cranwell on April 25 and Freiston on June 11 where he joined the base at Dover. On June 21 he went to France and joined No. 3 Squadron at Dunkirk. As a front line fighter, the Pup was called a Scout. Most pilots found it a delight to fly, light and extremely sensitive to the controls. It had good speed and a high rate of climb.

Canadian naval airmen fought on every front but most of them were stationed in the British Isles or the large fighter base at Dunkirk, which it was forced to share, from time to time, with the Royal Flying Corps. Never content to just be an auxiliary service to the navy, the RNAS sought an offensive role. Canadians played an especially prominent role in the pioneer development of long-range bombing and the formation of fighter squadrons at Dunkirk. A flight consisted of ten aircraft and six pilots; a squadron had two flights and a wing two or more squadrons.[1]

During July and August Franklyn flew patrols in support of the ground war. The squadron was now equipped with the Sopwith Camel, the big brother to the Pup, with lightning manoeuverability but it could be somewhat unpredictable. Slightly larger than the Pup, it had a wing span of 28' a length of 18' 8", and a height of 8'. The wings were staggered and two Vickers machine guns were mounted on the engine hump that gave the aircraft its name. It was remarkably swift and sensitive but demanded constant pilot attention. It weighed 889 pounds and carried thirty-seven gallons of fuel, enough for two hours and forty-five minutes flying time. It could climb to 15,000 feet in seventeen minutes. This aircraft was regarded as one of the most deadly weapons of air warfare. From June 1917 to the armistice, the Camel accounted for 1,300 enemy aircraft downed in midair combat.[2]

On August 8, 1917, a formation of German Gotha bombers was winging its way toward London on a bombing mission. They were

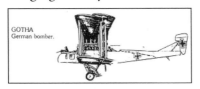

GOTHA
German bomber.

spotted by a patrol of five aircraft from 3 (Naval) Squadron at Dunkirk who were airborne on a fleet protection sweep. The patrol included

[1] Sydney F. Wise, *Canadian Airmen and the First World War: The Official History of the Royal Canadian Air Force*, vol. I (Toronto: University of Toronto Press, 1980), p. 147n.

[2] Curtis Kinney, *I Flew A Camel* (Philadelphia: Dorrance & Company, 1972), pp. 40-41.

Lieutenant R.P.F. Abbott of Carleton Place. They pursued the Gothas at 15, 000 feet over the English Channel almost to Harwich, England. One of the RNAS fliers emptied his guns into the last Gotha without any evident result then all the pilots had to land at English airfields to refuel. The battle was taken up by the RNAS Home Defence Flight which downed six of the enemy marauders.[3]

August 16 found Franklyn flying on patrol when he came across a tempting target, the German airdrome at Uytkerke. Diving down, Sub-Lt. Abbott levelled off at fifty feet and sprayed five hundred rounds from his machine guns into the hangars of the field. Pilots would often initiate such individual strafing attacks on enemy airfields. The next day Abbott's personal file was annotated:

> August 17, 1917—Carried out Fleet Patrol. Visibility was very fair. Just before landing he was attacked by 3 E.A. [enemy aircraft] and he spun down through the clouds with the E.A. following. Although wounded, he made a very good landing. He was taken to hospital immediately.[4]

The Almonte Gazette of October 5, 1917, printed the following report:

Our Splendid Aviators

> Flight Lieutenant Franklyn Abbott, who was wounded in the upper thigh, is having the very best treatment in the world. He hopes to be soon in England with his uncle. He received his wound in the air, after despatching some Hun planes. He was thankful to be able to land on home soil but it was nip and tuck—a hair's breadth margin. He was greatly elated at a visit to his cot of the beautiful and charming Queen of the Belgians. She was just able to say in shattered English that she was short on his tongue, as he was able to say in broken Belgian that he was short on hers. But the exchange of looks was the basis of a loving language and their communication was exhilarating. Franklyn says that Murray Galbraith deserves all the honors that have been showered on him. He was a daring, dashing, decimating aviator, and the Huns must have learned to shiver when they saw his curly hair in the clouds.

[3] S.F. Wise, op. cit., p. 250.
[4] Records held by the Directorate of History, Canadian Forces Headquarters.

Franklyn progressed through several hospitals and spent considerable time in the Royal Navy Hospital in Chatham, England, before being repatriated to Canada for rehabilitation.

On January 25, 1918, the *Carleton Place Herald* reported:

> Sub. Flight Lieut. Franklin [*sic*] Abbott arrived home on Saturday evening, much to the surprise of his friends. Franklin has had some experience. With other aviators he was across the enemy's lines when they were met by the Hun fliers and a fight ensued. A bullet penetrated the gas tank of his machine and passed through his thigh, from which wound he is still quite lame. He at once turned on his emergency tank and soared for
>
>
>
> the clouds, then made for his home drome, landing in safety, but when the machinist reached him he found him unconscious in his seat. He has been in hospital in France and in England and is now home on leave to recuperate, and is being heartily welcomed by his friends.

By April 5, 1918, Franklyn had returned to the war and was with No. 4 Squadron in Dunkirk. Nearby, Capt. Roy Brown was flying from a field at Bertangles with 209 Squadron, Royal Air Force. On April 21, Brown caught Baron von Richthofen who was concentrating on chasing a new pilot in Brown's flight, Lieutenant "Wop" May.

> There has been a bitter controversy . . . for it cannot be known whether Richthofen was mortally wounded or killed instantly. His plane continued to fly for some distance after Brown's attack until it made a crash landing, and Richthofen was found with his hand on the control column and his feet on the rudders. In the final moments of his flight he had passed low over several Australian machine gun posts and riflemen.[5]

Franklyn's flying now consisted of ground support and antisubmarine defence patrols. Early in August, co-operating in the Canadian Corps' offensive at Amiens, No. 3 Squadron Camels flew in support of the 3rd Division's operations.

---

[5] Curtis Kinney, op. cit., p. 60.

By September war had taken its toll; Franklyn was sent back to England and admitted to hospital suffering from tuberculosis. On October 25, he relinquished his commission due to ill health and went back to Canada to recuperate. The *Herald* reported on his homecoming in the edition of April 15, 1919:

> Lieut Franklin [*sic*] Abbott, of the Royal Air Force, arrived home last Wednesday evening, having received his discharge after spending two years in the service, being once wounded by the enemy and afterwards laid aside by illness succeeding a severe attack of influenza. Franklin looks very well after his trip and hopes shortly to be fully restored to health.

Franklyn Abbott died in the Kingston, Ontario, isolation hospital on March 25, 1932, from tuberculous meningitis, the effect of war service.

The Carleton Place Canadian reported Franklyn's death and funeral:

Franklyn Abbott Veteran Aviator Hears Last Post
Was Wounded in Action in 1917—
A Highly Esteemed Citizen

The angel of death has of late been hovering over homes in this community leaving sorrowing friends and relatives. To some it came to call away the young, to others the aged from the infirmites [*sic*] of age. On Friday, March 25th, there departed this life at the Kingston hospital, Flight Lieutenant Robert Franklyn Preston Abbott, only son and child of Mr. And Mrs. Charles H. Abbott, McArthur Avenue, who was called to his eternal rest following a long illness. The late Lieutenant Abbott was born in Carleton Place 34 years ago and was a life long resident. He was educated in the public and high schools here and was a general favourite. Early in the spring of 1916 he enlisted in the R.N.A.S. and early in the fall of the same year he went overseas. On August 17th, 1917, Franklyn was seriously wounded in an aerial combat and has been in failing health ever since. Following his return to Canada the young man spent much of his time at the sanitarium at Muskoka and also in the hospitals. He went to California in 1922 in hope that the change would benefit his health and returned home in the fall of 1925. He had engaged in contracting and building for a time and located at Franktown where he followed agricultural pursuits until his fatal illness. On September 29th, 1931, he entered a hospital in Kingston where he has been confined until he passed away, his death resulting from strictly war effects.

The late Mr. Abbott was one of the town's most popular and energetic young men, highly respected and dearly beloved. Always bright and happy with a kind word for all, he was welcomed wherever he went, and his death is an irreparable loss, not only to the town in which he resided, but to the whole community. Of a jovial disposition he was always ready to take part in any enjoyment and his witty humor always added to the program. Always the same, kindly to all, and with a great respect for the aged, he made friends wherever he went and his early passing is keenly regretted. During his long illness, Franklyn, as he was known to all, was tenderly nursed and cared for and everything that medical skill and loving care could do was done for him. Never was he known to complain about his sufferings but patiently and with great fortitude bore the heavy cross he was called to bear. A fine type of young Canadian manhood he was of honest and upright character, loved in life and honored in death.

The late Mr. Abbott was married in Monrovia, California, on October 29th, 1925, to Miss Eleanor Ann Slipp, who survives, with his grief stricken and sorrowing parents.

In fraternal circles he was a member of St. John's Lodge, A.F. & A.M., Carleton Place, L.O.L., Franktown, and the local branch of the Canadian Legion, No. 192. The funeral took place from his parents' residence on McArthur Avenue, on Monday afternoon to St. James church thence to St. James vault. The service in the church was conducted by Rev. Mr. Bruce, assisted by Rev. Canon Elliott, Rev. Canon Waterman, of Ottawa, and Rev. R.H. Waterman, of Pembroke, the latter being a great friend of deceased as well as a Great War Veteran. A full choir, under the direction of Mr. F.J. Tighe, was in attendance and three favorite hymns of deceased were sung. The pallbearers were Col. R.B. Smith, Oshawa; Messrs. L.R.A. Patchell,

Douglas Findlay, Leo J. McDiarmid, W.H. Hooper and Harry Umphrey, all veterans of the Great War. On Sunday afternoon the members of the local branch of the Canadian Legion paraded to the home of deceased and paid their respects in a body.

Beautiful and numerous floral tributes were received and included a wreath from his widow . . .

The Canadian joins with the host of friends in extending deepest sympathy to the bereaved wife and parents.[6]

WILLIAM ANDREW FANNING

William Fanning, son of Edward and Eliza Ann Fanning, was born in Carleton Place on November 23, 1889. He had been working as a "drug clerk" in Ottawa and had had six months' service, from August to December 1914, in the Composite Battalion of the 1st Regiment, Grenadier Guards of Canada, when he transferred to the Active Force. With this background he considered himself a "soldier" when he enlisted on December 15, 1915.

At enrolment William was described as having a dark complexion, grey eyes and dark hair. He stated that he belonged to the Church of England. William was twenty-six years old and stood 5' 10" tall. He was just a half inch over the minimum height requirement for the Canadian Grenadier Guards. The historical records of the battalion tells of this special requirement:

> . . . on consideration of the fact that a special standard of physique was specified for all recruits, permission was obtained from the Department of Militia to carry on recruiting throughout the Province of Quebec and Ontario and as a result, approximately a third of the battalion was made up of men from the mining districts of Quebec and Ontario, Gaspé, the 'Eastern Townships', Pembroke and Dundas County. The minimum height was at first placed at five feet six inches; two weeks after the recruiting campaign began, this was raised to five feet eight inches and finally to five feet, ten inches. When the bat-

[6] W. Brian Costello, A Nursery of the Air Force (Carleton Place: Forest Beauty Products, 1979), pp. 87-88.

talion left Canada the average height of its men was five feet, eight and one half inches . . . On October 23, 1915, the active recruiting campaign began and six weeks later the battalion was up to strength and was moved to winter training quarters in the barracks at St. Johns, Que.

The battalion became officially known as the 87th Canadian Infantry Battalion (St John, Quebec) and the motto was *Nulli Secundus* (Second to None). It served in France and Flanders with the 11th Infantry Brigade of the 4th Canadian Division from August 13, 1916, until the armistice. It is perpetuated by the Canadian Grenadier Guards.

On April 22, the battalion entrained for Halifax and sailed on the 23rd aboard the *Empress of Britain.* They arrived in Liverpool on May 5 and proceeded to Bramshott Camp, where it was first a part of the 12th Brigade and later was transferred to the 11th Brigade. The battalion embarked on August 10 and landed at Le Havre in France on August 12.

On September 30, Fanning was appointed a lance corporal. On November 10, he was admitted to the No. 11 Canadian Field Ambulance with influenza and remained in the aid station until December 12 when he was discharged back to duty.

The War Diary of the 87th Battalion has the following entries for the month of June 1917:

6 June—Battalion moved into front line.

8 June—Carried out attacks at Culotte Trench and Fosse trench. Enemy aircraft active. Fired on one low flyer with rifles and Lewis Gun.

12 June—Moved to Chateau de la Haie to rest (in Lens area by the Lens/Arras road).

15 to 19 June—On working parties in Zouave Valley on Cobourg Street Trench on construction of Canadian Corps Light Railway near the Lens Junction and La Culotte.

26 June—Battalion on working parties. Casualties—1 officer
[Lt. C.H. Edgley] wounded, 23 Other Ranks, near Electric
Generating station at La Culotte.

1 July—Moved to Zouave Valley for 4 weeks rest.

The infantryman in a rest area rarely got much rest. While rudimentary recreation facilities were sometimes provided by the Red Cross, YMCA or Salvation Army, more often than not the infantry soldier was put to work, repairing or building roads, buildings for quarters, carrying and stockpiling ammunition, artillery shells and equipment of all types, taking the rare opportunity for "bath parades," delousing, darning socks, laundering or exchanging uniforms and, in their spare moments, cleaning the mud from weapons, shining their leather equipment and polishing their brass buttons and badges. This was also a fine opportunity for senior officers to inspect the troops and offer morale-building words of wisdom and encouragement.

On June 26, William Fanning was confirmed in the permanent rank of lance corporal, and that same day was wounded by artillery shrapnel. He was sent back through the medical units and on June 29 arrived at No. 35 General Hospital in Calais. He was admitted with a gunshot wound (shrapnel) to the right thigh causing a compound fracture of the lower third of the femur (just above the knee). As soon as his condition allowed, he was further invalided back to England for treatment.

With a severely injured right leg, L/Cpl. Fanning was sent back to Canada aboard the Hospital Ship *Araguaya.* He boarded in Liverpool on March 11, 1918, and arrived in Kingston at the Queen's Military Hospital on March 26. He was treated and declared "medically unfit for further service arising from wounds." A case history prepared by the Kingston Convalescent Home for William's discharge, on June 17, 1918, recorded his disability as "for discharge from service, wounded June 26 ,1917, at Lens by a bursting shell. 1" shortening (of right leg), walks with a limp. He had a scar 2" long on his right thigh, and 3 FB's (foreign bodies—pieces of shrapnel) in the tissue 7" above knee joint."

William took those reminders of World War I with him to his grave. He died on May 12, 1931, at age forty-one-and-a-half-years.

His death was deemed, by the government, as "attributable to military service."

The *Herald* of May 13, 1931, carried this article:

Death of William A. Fanning

The sad news has reached Carleton Place of the death this morning at London, Ont. of William A. Fanning, son of the late Edward Fanning. The deceased was born in Carleton Place and was overseas during the war. He was 41 years of age.

And on May 20, the paper ran the following report of Fanning's funeral:

The death occurred on Wednesday last at London, Ont. of William Andrew Fanning son of the late Edward Fanning of Carleton Place aged 41 years and the funeral took place from the home of his mother, Mrs. Fanning, Bronson Avenue, Ottawa, on Saturday to St. James Anglican Church here for service. Internment being made in the family plot in St. James cemetery.

The chief mourners were his mother, Mrs. Edward Fanning, three brothers, Lloyd, Horace and Gordon Fanning, and one sister Mrs. R.C. Gilmour all of Ottawa.

Mr. Fanning died in London, after an illness of several years. He was born in Carleton Place and had lived in Detroit, as well as in Ottawa and London. While in Ottawa he was employed as a civil servant. He was a returned man and his experience in war caused the failure of his health. The veterans of Carleton Place turned out to do honour to their deceased comrade and the flag on the town hall was flown at half mast out of respect.

THOMAS JAMES GORROD

While much is made of the boys who added a few years to their age to get into the army and overseas before they were eligible, there were also those recruits who subtracted a few years because they were too old to serve. One such was Thomas Gorrod.

Thomas was born in London, England, and was educated and married there, before emigrating to Canada. He worked as a labourer in the Findlay Foundry. Thomas gave his date of birth on enlistment as 1870, on discharge as 1867, but it is more likely that the real date, as recorded in his obituary, was about 1865. That would make him fifty-three years old in 1918.

When his approximate true age was discovered, he revealed that he went to Canada "16 years ago" which would have made the date of emigration 1902. He also stated that he had thirteen years British Army service, with the 16th Lancers, and left for Canada after discharge. That would make his date of enlistment 1888 or 1889. If he was born in 1865 he would have been twenty-three or twenty-four years old at the time of that enlistment.

But Thomas was by far not the oldest Canadian to serve. That honour belongs to a Pte. Boucher of Gananoque. He was returned to England from the front lines when it was discovered that he was seventy-three years old. He had been in France, in action, for eight months. The king asked to meet "the oldest man in khaki" and Boucher was presented at Buckingham Palace. Boucher was a veteran of the United States Civil War.

Thomas Gorrod enlisted into the Canadian Expeditionary Force on October 19, 1915, at Barriefield (Kingston). With the war winding into high gear no one was checking ages too closely. He said he was born on March 18, 1870, which would have made him forty-five years, seven months old. He gave as his next of kin his wife Evelyn, who was residing on High Street in Carleton Place. He claimed to have served in the 42nd (Lanark and Renfrew) Regimental Guard since August 3, 1915, and to have been on a nine-week detachment with the Guard to Petawawa. He professed a religious affiliation with the Church of England. He was also barely over the height limit at 5' 4" tall, but he was found "fit for service" and sent to the 80th Battalion, which was recruiting in the Kingston area at the time. He was described as of a fair complexion with grey eyes and brown hair. Visible marks consisted of a tattoo of the letter "T" with dots along his left arm.

The 80th Battalion continued to recruit and train troops during the winter of 1915–1916. On May 16, 1916, they embarked aboard the S.S. *Baltic* for England and arrived in Liverpool on May 29th. In

England the 80th Battalion was absorbed by the 51st Battalion to provide reinforcements to the corps in France. But Thomas's trip to the front lines was further delayed when, on July 23, 1916, the 51st Battalion was designated as the Garrison Duty Battalion in Bramshott. In due course the 51st was broken up also to provide reinforcements in the field.

On May 23, Thomas was transferred to the Canadian Railway Troops at Purfleet in Essex, and, finally, on June 19, 1917, he landed in France with the 10th Battalion, Canadian Railway Troops. They had plenty to do from the moment of their arrival in France. They laboured under the dreadful conditions of the Ypres Salient before Passchendaele, and carried out their work with remarkable speed. The 10th Railway Battalion was in the Ypres Salient and was never out of the range of shellfire from the time of the Messines action in June 1917 until the end of the Passchendaele fighting. From April 1, 1917, to the end of the war, the Corps of Canadian Railway troops suffered 1,977 casualties.

On August 17, 1917, Thomas Gorrod was promoted to the rank of corporal. But he was beginning to have trouble with his eyesight and on April 3, 1918, he was returned to England to the Westcliff Canadian Eye and Ear Hospital near Folkestone. On April 24 he was diagnosed as having a corneal ulcer in his left eye. It was during this hospitalization that his age was discovered. The army decided to discharge Cpl. Gorrod and on June 5, 1918, he was processed through a Discharge Medical Board. The examining medical officer elicited the following history:

> . . . was 10 months in France. Returned on account of age. Was 13 years in Imperial Service. Discharged, time expired, went to Canada 16 years ago after discharge and found his eyes troublesome and weak especially in winter when the brightness from the snow affected them . . .

He was assigned a temporary medical category of D1, which meant his immediate return to Canada. On June 25 he was discharged from the hospital and on September 22, Thomas Gorrod sailed from England for Canada, aboard the Hospital Ship *Llanstephen Castle*. He arrived in Montreal on October 8, 1918. He was transferred to the Canadian Corps District Depot in Kingston on October 8 and discharged from the Canadian Expeditionary Force as overage and medically unfit on November 8, 1918. At his last medical examination, in Kingston on October 30, he was described as age forty-eight years, eight months (he now gave his birth date as March 17, 1867), medically unfit and possibly suffering from arteriosclerosis.

Thomas died on December 16, 1933. In the edition of December 20, the *Herald* reported:

Thomas Gorrod Passes

Thomas Gorrod, for many years an employee of the Findlay Stove foundry died in the hospital in Ottawa on Saturday, following a lengthy illness. Born in London, England in 1865, he received his education there. His marriage took place in England to the former Eveling [*sic*] Taylor about 45 years ago. Coming to Canada in 1906, he settled in Carleton Place where he resided till the time of his death. Mr. Gorrod served overseas in the 80th Battalion. He was a member of St. James Church and was held in high esteem by all who came in contact. Surviving besides his widow are three daughters, Mrs. T.J. McCleland and Mrs. Fred Brennan of Ottawa and Mrs. A. Tucker of Westboro. Two sons predeceased him . . .

Card of Thanks

Mrs. Gorrod and family desire to express to their neighbours and friends their sincere thanks for the kindness shown them and the sympathy extended in their recent bereavement, also to Findlay Ltd. and to the members of the Canadian Legion for courtesy extended.

Lest We Forget

War kills! War maims! Both bodies and minds are ruptured. What was the experience like? An oft-asked question from those who stayed behind but seldom answered. Witnesses of war rarely choose to remember. Today there is almost no one left to answer. Children and grandchildren comment that their fathers and grandfathers never talked about the war. They feel a part of their heritage is empty because of this deficiency.

Knowledge may salve the soul. Now, only remembrance brings such knowledge. Names on war memorials represent more than a surname and initial of some long-forgotten ancestor. They represent the flesh and blood of young men and women that, in most cases, lie scattered on foreign fields. They have lost their opportunity to study in hushed halls of higher learning; to find and marry the girl of their dreams; to be employed in their career of choice, experience pure joy at the birth of their firstborn or bounce a grandchild on their knee.

Old soldiers never die—but most choose to forget! Therefore it remains for the youth of the nation to remember their contribution to the well-being of succeeding generations. It was for today's youth that yesterday's soldiers fought and died. Two minutes' silence on Remembrance Day is a time to imagine the sacrifices that were made on our behalf, and to thank God that we must use imagination. The horrors of war have never been visited upon Canadian children. But they must appreciate and understand their country's military past and the role their forebears played. Commemorate the peace—and don't break faith with those who died.

If this work inspires one grandchild, or great-grandchild, to discover the service of a forebear who answered a nation's call, and perhaps never returned, then its purpose has been achieved.

At a recent remembrance ceremony in a Canadian cemetery in Europe Protestant Chaplain, Col. George G. Davidson intoned:

Did you see him when he fell O God?

Did you know that he would never again see the flash of a salmon on his travel in the warm blue water of the Miramichi; ride his horse into the foothills of Alberta on a soft spring evening; stook wheat with his father on a blazing hot Saskatchewan afternoon; stand freezing at the corner of Portage and Main; sweat in the heat of a Hamilton forge or watch the ice break up on the St. Lawrence from the bastion of Quebec? Did you see him walk his gal in the moonlight on the banks of the Saint John; plough the rich red soil of Prince Edward Island; smell the fog rolling in from Chebucto Head; put on his oil skins and jig squid in the bay or listen to the howl of the Arctic wolf?

Did you see him pay the price, O God?

Did you see his broken body so that we here could live as one?

Do you feel our sense of shame, O God, for the things we say and do that break our nations in pieces and mock the men who fell?

Amen.

EPILOGUE

Since this book has been restricted to include only those who names appear on the cenotaph, in the normal course of events, David Douglas Findlay would not be included. Through the courtesy of family members David and William Findlay, a copy of Douglas' diary and  flying logbook was made available. Findlay, an active participant in the war, was an impotent spectator to the deaths of many friends whose names do appear in this work. In that light it becomes appropriate to include the events in Flight Lieutenant D. D. Findlay's life and times from April 1918 to his return to Canada a year later. The effects of such momentous events on such a young man, as seen through his diary, are very moving. Douglas Findlay's life in the flying service at war's end truly is representative of the motto of the Royal Canadian Air Force: *Per Ardua ad Astra* (Through Adversity to the Stars). He was a survivor of the Great War, World War I, and went on to serve with the Royal Canadian Air Force in World War II.

Doug Findlay grew up in Carleton Place and had a young life similar to all the other aviators. He was an exemplary student, a very good athlete (they all played hockey together) and loved the outdoor life in his native Ottawa Valley town. His flying career, however, took a slightly different tack. Instead of learning to fly at the Wright Brothers School in Ohio, or the Curtiss School in Toronto, he went to San Antonio, Texas. Instead of going overseas to the battlefields of France, he went overseas to the dust and heat of the Middle East, flying for the Royal Naval Air Service in Mesopotamia.

In the Middle East, Findlay contracted malaria and was invalided home to recover. The ship on which he sailed from Britain to Canada was torpedoed off the Irish coast. Douglas escaped in a lifeboat with only his greatcoat over his pyjamas. He lost all personal effects, such as his flying log book, his diary and letters. On his return trip to England, while awaiting his ship in Halifax, he bought a little pocket-sized booklet from L. Clyde, Davidson & Co., stationers. It was April 9, 1918. That book is the diary to which reference is now made.

After two days and a night on the train from Carleton Place, Douglas was booked for passage on the S.S. *Metagama*. While waiting in Halifax he toured the northern part of the city that had been virtually destroyed on December 6, 1917, when two ships collided in the harbour. The *Mont Blanc*, loaded with 2,652 tonnes of munitions, exploded and blew most of the city to smithereens. Eighteen hundred people were killed and 9,000 injured in the greatest man-made blast ever to occur up until the nuclear bombing of Hiroshima. At 6:00 p.m. on April 9, Doug stood on the afterdeck of the *Metagama* and watched the sun set over the entrance to Halifax harbour. He could only think that it would be a long, long, very long time before he would again see Canada.

Disembarking at Liverpool on April 20, he took a train to London and checked into the Strand Palace Hotel to wait for further posting instructions from the Air Ministry. He learned the fate of friends. Hackman was a prisoner of war in Turkey; Palmer and Moore had been killed and "Bunny" Abbott was also gone. His new Royal Air Force uniform was in his opinion "an awful mess" and just typical of the way he thought the whole war was being conducted. He found conditions and attitudes in England greatly changed. His recurring malaria kept him weak and ill. For the first time he expressed his wish for the war to be over. Yet he still badgered senior officers for a posting to a front line squadron in France.

On April 25, Douglas presented himself before an Air Force Medical Board, which declared him fit for general service. He made the point that he would not relish any thought of returning to fly in the East, to the extent that he would resign his commission first. He spent the rest of his day with friends, such as "Horry" Brown (J. Horace), who returned that evening to his training at Manston, and Sinclair (likely Huntley, brother of Colin Sinclair), who was off to Cramwell en route for France to fly "HPs" (Handley Page bombers). Of Horace, Doug wrote in his diary, "He is a good lad and is keeping to the straight and narrow path."

Disappointed at being left out of action, Douglas reluctantly accepted an appointment as a flying instructor, and went to Redcar for training. The base was close enough to London that he could attend concerts and have luncheon meetings with friends at the Royal Aero Club. He found Murray Galbraith back in England and "large as life," and spent pleasant afternoons with Roy Brown at the Savoy. Getting back to flying was easy, "like a duck to water," and he once again started to enjoy the Avro flying machine and the freedom of flight. His instructional duties were with the DH6 and BE2e aeroplanes.

At the end of May, Findlay met Roy Brown and Sterne Edwards for an afternoon of rowing on the Thames River followed by dinner at the Savoy. He observed that, "Roy hasn't changed much and is just as white as ever. Not a bit swelled headed. Stearne [sic] expects leave soon." But his fill of the war was about complete. He expected to be posted to France soon, but was confident, "I won't be afraid of being afraid again and I hope that my trust in God is just as complete as it was in the East." On June 5 many of the aviators were in London for an impromptu squadron holiday. Celebrating with Doug in the Savoy was Sterne Edwards, Roy Brown, Huntley Sinclair, and several others. That summer, as they travelled around to various aerodromes on flight training duties, Sterne, Roy and Douglas saw quite a bit of each other.

On July 1, one of his best friends on the station at Huntingdon, a pilot named Candell, crashed while trying to emulate one of Doug's stunts in the air, spinning into an Immelman turn. Candell died from a fractured skull. On July 17, Doug returned from an RAF garden party to find a telegram from Sterne advising him that Roy had been seriously injured and asking Doug to contact "Horry" to have him go to Roy at Marske. Horace himself was still hospitalized in St. Albans, but managed to get away to see Roy. "Poor tough luck Roy."

Douglas left Huntington by train to spend the August 1st holiday with Horace. They went to the "Colliseum" to see a show and had dinner together. Horry had to go to Gieves, the military tailor, so Doug went with him and then Horry left on the 7:00 p.m. train. On August 16, Doug received a letter from "Sinc" in which he learned that, "Mellings was missing and Gilmour was badly crashed." Cynicism, and reality, were taking hold! Prophetically, Doug wrote, "I am fed up with this war. It's just weeding out the best and leaving the worst in positions of authority."

In September, after recovering from a very bad cold, Doug flew to Tadcaster to see Sterne Edwards and on the 12th he wrote the following:

> . . . saw Roy Brown for the first time since his crash. He is pretty well done up but has not much to show for it except a couple of scars on his face. I believe his back is badly hurt or broken again in another place but after a year or more's careful treatment he should be O.K. again. His head is also bothering him but is slowly improving . . . My third application for Active Service has gone in again . . .

He was still hoping to go to France to fly Camels. Instead he was posted to 56 T.D.S. (another training squadron) to instruct on Sopwith Scouts, although he was told to get as much practice air fighting and flying Camels as possible because he was in reserve for France.

The first student pilot Douglas had trained, a young Englishman named Richardson, was reported missing on October 7. With considerable relief, Doug learned three days later that Richardson was safe and a prisoner of war in Karlsruhe. On October 12, Sterne wrote that, "Roy's head had gone bad on him again and he may never be right." And that, "Horry Brown had crashed seriously and was in a hospital at Ilford." Douglas wired to the hospital for permission to visit Horace but was told that he could not until Monday the 14th. He arrived in London by the morning train but it was not until evening that he made his way to the Ilford Emergency Hospital. On October 16 he wrote:

> . . . I saw Horry. He had received a bad knock in the chest from the shaft of a cart and was looking like death and coughing very badly. I think I cheered him up some but he is very far from well. Saw the Matron [head nurse] there. She said that she thought there was no grave danger but that it was still doubtful.

> Next day I saw Roy at the Horton War Hospital Epsom. He is still in a room by himself and apparently pretty bad though he told me that he had been without a headache for three days and that he was feeling ever so much better . . . He swears that if the war lasts long enough he'll fly again.

> Then I went to see Horry and take him a Fountain Pen, his having been broken, and found him ever so much better than the previous day.

When Douglas arrived back on base he found that a Camel in which he had flown and "stunted" had mysteriously folded up in the air for no obvious reason, crashed and killed the pilot. On November 11, Douglas was en route by train to take another flying course at Frieston when he learned the armistice had been signed. He thought, "still enough has not been sacrificed by many yet. It's tough on those who have lost all they live for. I wonder when I shall go home."

On the morning of November 25, a telegram signed "Brown" caught up to Doug. It advised that Sterne Edwards was dead and the funeral was that day. Douglas couldn't make a train connection and the weather was so bad it was impossible to fly to Tadcaster. The wire did not state the circumstances of Sterne's death and Douglas was left to wonder if it was by accident or from the flu epidemic that raged throughout the world. "I can't realize that he is dead . . . I can't realize that Stearne is dead."

At the very first opportunity, when the weather cleared, Douglas flew to Tadcaster. He wired Sterne's mother offering to do anything he could to ease her pain. She accepted and Douglas spent much of his time over the next months fighting the bureaucracy at the Air Ministry. They would accept only a handwritten letter from Mrs. Edwards as authority to allow him access to Sterne's effects and to initiate any financial settlement. His flight to Tadcaster on Wednesday, November 27:

> I flew up here in a Camel, landing at Canwell for maps on the way . . . and found out details of Stearne's death. He crashed in a Sopwith Pup, No. 4181 on Nov 12th, the day after the Armistice was signed. All agreed that it was due to a spin and an error in judgement on his part in thinking he was higher than he really was. He was badly injured, chief being fractured base of the skull and compound fracture of one leg which later necessitated amputation. He died Saturday, Nov 23 at 5:15 a.m. All these details I got from a friend of his called Redgate.

On December 6, Douglas had Mrs Edwards' authority and he spent the day packing and checking Sterne's belongings, storing them safely away. He spent many more days haunting the Air Ministry to discover what pay, gratuity or pension benefits would be made available for Mrs. Edwards. It was looking less and less likely that Doug would be home for Christmas and he was getting increasingly fed up with the officials in charge of demobilization. Twelve days Christmas leave allowed him time to spend with Roy and Horry "at some out of the way place."

The three met at the Savoy on December 20 and tried to make hotel reservations for anywhere on the South Coast. But there was no room at the inns either there or in Wales when they tried there. Then the guardian angel of wayward fliers sent Mr. Edgar Morris to the rescue. He was a colleague of one of Roy's friends. By hospitable command, and brooking no argument, he crammed all three of them into a little Sunbeam automobile, and drove to his home in Ashurst near Tunbridge Wells. The airmen stayed until December 30 when they returned to London and took quarters in the Palace Hotel in Bloomsbury. The three went back to their respective stations on the 31st, Douglas returning to Stamford. New Year's Eve 1918 was spent at a "merry party" with RNAS comrades, including Roy Kellough. By January 10, Douglas had sent Sterne's effects and the money left at Tadcaster off to Canada; now he could devote more of his energies to demobilization and repatriation.

Douglas joined Huntley Sinclair in London on January 22 to visit Colin Sinclair's grave. Then, on the 24th, a dinner at the Savoy reunited Douglas with Horry, Roy, Musty (?) Abbott, Darnell and Jack Keane. As repatriation orders trickled in for other pilots Douglas felt encouraged. He had been given a Snipe to fly and found its speed and power so impressive that he flew this "real aeroplane" quite recklessly, stunting at every opportunity. He flew around the countryside, visiting with Abbott, Sinclair and dropping in on many of his other aviator friends. Finally, on February 12, his demobilization authority was issued; but he still had no news on repatriation. It became imperative that he wrap up Sterne's affairs.

On Sunday the 16th of February news arrived that both Horry and Roy were in the RAF Hospital at Eaton Square with influenza. Horry was reported to have "nearly died." On the 18th, Douglas returned at 7:00 p.m. from a long walk around the Stamford aerodrome to find a message waiting from Roy announcing Horry's death. Douglas could not locate his major to get leave and had to wait for the next train out in the morning. "Poor old Horry and Roy."

His diary entry for February 22:

> Have just got back from London, Went up there Thursday [20th] and saw Roy next day. He is taking Horry's death wonderfully well. Helped him scuttle around yesterday and we both went out to Epsom to see about his being sent to Canada to convalesce. Roy was with Horry when he died and he told me that poor old Horry's last intelligible sentence was something about seeing Doug.
>
> It's funny how all my friends have gone. Old Horry.
>
> I expect I'll just have to wait here for demobilization and transport to Canada now. Roy expects to get back pretty soon.

Douglas was now "marking time," waiting to go home. Sterne's estate was cleared early in March and Roy had sailed for Canada. But fate wasn't finished with David Douglas Findlay yet. On March 12, he received a cable asking him to advise Thorold Kellough that his brother Roy had been reported killed. Douglas had difficulty locating Thorold because the last he knew Thorold was in a hospital. The military signals service (communications and post office) eventually found him.

Douglas mused in his writings about a couple of friends who were getting married, which he found "Very funny because both are real kids . . . "

Findlay was finally demobilized and authorized to go home on April 5. He went on his last mission for Sterne Edwards on April 1, when he visited Tadcaster to photograph Sterne's grave. Doug's last night in London before he sailed for Canada was on April 8. He spent many of his final hours in England, including Easter, with Huntley Sinclair. They enjoyed an evening of English theatre at the Drury Lane watching The Magic Flute.

Douglas Findlay's diary entry on his birthday, March 21, 1919, sums a survivor's story:

> "Getting old and hoary, 22 today."

BIBLIOGRAPHY

Beatty, Kim. *48th Highlanders of Canada 1891–1928*. Toronto: 48th Highlanders of Canada,1932.

Benedict, Michael, ed. *Canada at War*, Toronto: Penguin Books Canada Ltd., 1997.

Bennett, Capt. S.G. (Stewart Gordon), M.C.. *The 4th Canadian Mounted Rifles, 1914–1919*, Toronto: Murray Printing Co., 1926.

Berton, Pierre. *Vimy*. Toronto: McClelland and Stewart,1986.

Bishop, Arthur. *Canada's Glory: Battles that Forged a Nation*. Whitby: McGraw-Hill Ryerson Limited, 1996.

Breckenridge, William. *From Vimy to Mons*. Sherbrooke, Que.: private, 1919.

Brown, Dave. *Faces of War*. Burnstown: General Store Publishing House, 1998.

Brown, Howard Morton. *Carleton Place: Founded Upon A Rock*. Renfrew: Juniper Books, 1984.

Christie, Norm. *Access to History; The Canadian History Series, Number 1 to 4*. Nepean: CEF Books, 1998.

Christie, Norm M. *For King and Empire*, vols I to III. Winnipeg: Bunker to Bunker Books, 1996; vols IV to VII. Nepean: CEF Books, 1997 & 1999.

Costello, W. Brian. *A Nursery of the Air Force*. Forest Beauty Products, 1979.

Craig, Capt. J.D., MC. *The 1st Canadian Division in the Battles of 1918*. London: Barrs & Co., 1919.

Currie, Col. J.A., MP. *"The Red Watch" With the First Canadian Division in Flanders*. Toronto: McClelland, Goodchild & Stewart, 1916.

Dancocks, Daniel George. *Welcome to Flanders Fields*, Toronto: McClelland and Stewart, 1988.

De Wolfe, J.H. (compiled by) *Our Heroes in the Great World War*, Ottawa: The Patriotic Publishing Co., 1919

Dorling, Capt. H. Taprell, DSO, RN. *Ribbons and Medals: Naval, Military, Air Force and Civil*. London: George Phillip & Son, Ltd., 1956.

Duguid, Col. A. Fortesque, DSO, RCA. "Canada on Vimy Ridge," The *Canada Year Book*. Ottawa: Queen's Printer, 1936.

Ellis, Frank H. *Canada's Flying Heritage*. Toronto: University of Toronto Press, Second Edition, 1961.

Findlay, George Hossack. *Unpublished Diaries*. 1884 to 1945.

Gardner, Brian., *Up the Line to Death—The War Poets 1914–1918*, Oxford, England: Methuen & Co, Ltd., 1964.

Giesler, Patricia. *Valour Remembered—Canada and the First World War*. Ottawa: Queen's Printer, 1982.

Grafton, Lt.-Col. C.S. *The Canadian "Emma Gees," A History of the Canadian Machine Gun Corps*. London, Ontario: The Canadian Machine Gun Corps Association, 1938.

Historical Calendar, 21st Canadian Infantry Battalion (Eastern Ontario Regiment) Belgium —France—Germany, 1915–1919, Aldershot, England: Gale & Polden Ltd., 1919.

Hutchinson, Lt.-Col. Graham Seton. *Pilgrimage*, London: Rich & Cowan, Ltd., 1935

Kinney, Curtis, with Dale M. Titler. *I Flew a Camel*. Philadelphia: Dorrance & Company, 1972.

Kostenuk, Samuel and John Griffin. RCAF—*Squadron Histories and Aircraft, 1924–1968*. Toronto: Hakkert & Company, 1977.

Lotz, Jim. *Canadians at War*. London: Bison Books Ltd., 1990.

Macdonald, Lyn. *To the Last Man—Spring 1918*. London, Eng: Penguin Books, 1998.

Macksey, Maj. Kenneth, MC. *The Shadow of Vimy Ridge.*, Toronto: The Ryerson Press, 1965.

Marteinson, John. *We Stand on Guard—An Illustrated History of the Canadian Army*. Montreal: Ovale Publications, 1992.

McKee, Alexander. *Vimy Ridge*. London: Souvenir Press Ltd., 1966.

Morton, Desmond. *Silent Battle: Canadian prisoners of war in Germany, 1914–1919*. Toronto: Lester Publishing Limited, 1992.

Morton, Desmond. *When Your Number's Up, The Canadian Soldier in the First World War*. Toronto: Random House of Canada, 1993.

Morton, Desmond and J.L. Granatstein. *Marching to Armageddon*. Toronto: Lester & Orpen Dennys Limited, 1989.

Murray, Col. W.W., OBE, MC. *The History of the 2nd Canadian Battalion (East Ontario Regiment) Canadian Expeditionary Force in the Great War, 1914–1919*. Ottawa: The Historical Committee, 2nd Canadian Battalion, CEF, 1947.

Nicholson, Col. G.W.L.,CD. *Canadian Expeditionary Force 1914–1919, Official History of the Canadian Army in the First World War*. Ottawa: Queen's Printer, 1962.

Plewman, W.R. *My Diary of the Great War*. Toronto: The Ontario Press, 1918.

Prior, Robin and Trevor Wilson. *Passchendaele: The Untold Story*. New Haven: Yale University Press, 1996.

Randall, Barry. *Recruiting and Conscription in Carleton Place in World War I*. An unpublished paper, 1985.

Reid, Gordon. *Poor Bloody Murder—Personal Memoirs of the First World War*. Oakville: Mosaic Press, 1980.

Roberts, Leslie. *There Shall Be Wings—A History of the Royal Canadian Air Force*. Toronto: Clarke, Irwin & Company, 1959.

Spears, Maj.-Gen. Sir Edward. *Liaison 1914*. London: Eyre & Spottiswoode (Publishers) Ltd., 1930.

Stewart, Charles H. *"Overseas" The Lineages and Insignia of the Canadian Expeditionary Force 1914–1919*. Toronto: Little & Stewart, 1971.

The Regiments and Corps of The Canadian Army. Ottawa: Minister of National Defence, 1964.

The Vimy Memorial. Ottawa: Veterans Affairs Canada, 1982.

The War of the Nations—Portfolio in Rotogravure Etchings. New York: The New York Times Company, 1919.

Topp, Lt.-Col. C. Beresford, DSO, MC., *The 42nd Battalion, C.E.F., Royal Highlanders of Canada, in the Great War*. Montreal: Gazette Printing, 1931.

Vachon, Georgette. *Goggles, Helmets and Airmail Stamps*. translated by Mary Downey, Toronto: Clarke, Irwin & Company, 1974.

Warner, Philip. Passchendaele, *The Tragic Victory of 1917*. New York, Atheneum, 1988.

Wise, Sydney F. *Canadian Airmen and the First World War—The Official History of the Royal Canadian Air Force*, vol. I. Ottawa, University of Toronto Press in co-operation with the Department of National Defence and the Canadian Government Publishing Centre, Supply and Services Canada, 1980.

Wood, Herbert Fairlie and John Swettenham. *Silent Witnesses*. Toronto, Hakkert, 1974.

3rd Divisional Ammunition Column: Nominal roll of officers, non commissioned officers and men. 1916.

207th Battalion: Nominal roll of officers, non-commissioned officers and men. 1917.

The Almonte Gazette

The Carleton Place Herald

The Ottawa Citizen

LETTERS HOME FROM "THE BOYS"

J. Horace Brown

Amesbury, Eng.
Nov. 13th, 1914

Dear Mother:

You may be surprised at the change of address, but I am now in Amesbury on picket, will likely be here about a week or longer. We have a lovely place to stay at. It is a private house, loaned to the government by a Captain who went to the front. He has been killed lately, but they still have the use of the place. It is a large house set back in lovely well kept grounds. There is a vegetable garden and a nice flower garden around the house, and lovely hedges and trees. There is an open fire place in nearly every room, including the bath room; there are ten men counting myself in my room. We have a clothes closet, a closet of shelves, a fire place; and there are two large windows. We leave the windows partially open at night.

The picket we relieved had been here three weeks. We have a good bunch of fellows. I do not know them personally, but I have been on fatigues or something with some of them at times and knew a few of them by sight.

We are given two shillings per day for food allowance and are living like kings. I have rented a cot, mattress and pillow; it only costs a shilling a week for the three. Will put some gasoline on as a precaution, and will be very comfortable. I cleaned all up this morning, had a nice warm bath and an entire change of clothes, and am sending all my soiled ones off to the laundry. We have cleaned the house all over, scrubbed it, and are getting a little in the line of furniture such as tables and benches. The officers have outfitted their rooms. It seems too good to last.

Our duty is to be at the station to see that everyone travelling has his pass, and that it is not over due; that is Canadians, we have nothing to do with others. We also have a town picket to keep the Canadians out of the saloons, and those without passes out of town. One day I was on fatigue loading trucks in Amesbury; that night I was put on main guard at 12:15 and was on till 8 p.m. next evening, without any meals, but that was an oversight. I was Battalion Orderly Corporal one day. You ask about my comfort when in camp. I bought a pair of knee rubber boots, a raincoat and an oil-stove. We bought cocoa, herring, and other things, and were fairly comfortable. We have had served out to us a sweater coat, a sleeping cap, a pair of socks and the Oliver equipment. It is rumoured we are to have our rifles changed for the short Lee-Enfield with the long bayonet. It is a better rifle and the magazine holds ten rounds.

Everyone from Carleton Place is well. None of the Canadians have left for anywhere; they are in different camps on the Plain. We get our pay twice a month, and have plenty, but when we go across we will just draw as we need it and the balance will be kept until we come back or sent to our next of kin. I do not like the idea of the wet canteen any better than you do. The lads were away from it in Valcartier, and now to have it and have plenty of money is the worst thing possible, but they are making punishments so strict they are cooling down some, several are being sent back to Canada. Needless to say the boys from Carleton Place are all well behaved. I have not received all the papers you sent. We have no trouble getting stamps, but when we can not get them we can mark them "Active service, no stamps available," and it will still go. Amesbury is a nice quiet little village. The name of the house we are in is the "Amesbury House," but put the old address on my letters. I have my Carleton Place pennant and my silk Union Jack hung over the fireplace. Canada pennant got torn on the way across, I cut out the Maple Leaf and the printing and sewed it on my red sweater. Now that I have more time I will write oftener to you and others

With Love to all
Horace

Bustard Camp, Salisbury Plain
31 Jan 1915

Dear Mother:

Well I am out of the Hospital and feeling fine. We are leaving for the south of France soon to complete our training there. The medical authorities say we have to get out of here as it is unhealthy, so we will soon be in Sunny France. That does not mean that we will be in the big scrap right away, but will just take up camp there in a healthier climate.

They are very particular about the health of the Canadians now, since there has been so much sickness among the troops. I do not know whether the censors keep it back, but a great many of the Canadians have died. I have seen or heard of about two dozen funerals since I went to the hospital, mostly all from spinal meningitis. We have heard that it has broken out at the front.

We are getting the Web equipment, but I guess we are keeping the same rifle. Some of the Canadians have the Lee-Enfield, but if we cannot get it we can get along quite well with what we have. Although we have all run down the Ross it is not a bad rifle, at least not as bad as some try to make out.

I have got all my clothes washed and got well cleaned up while in the hospital. We get dirty very quickly here.

I hope you received my big registered letter by this time which I sent while I was in the hospital. Do they ever censor my letters.

I got two letters from you. I also got the last scarf you sent. I gave away the two I had and kept one for myself. Thank you very much, we will be glad of them sometime.

We are drilling hard now. Yesterday we had an inspection by the King, Lord Roberts and some others. We went out in the morning and formed up. Nearly all of the contingent were present. After being inspected we marched past, then lined the R.R. where the King passed. I think the King was favourably impressed with what Canada is doing for the Empire, because just when he was passing near where I was the lads raised an extra loud cheer. The King saluted. He looked worried and more than one of us thought there were tears in his eyes. We all thought the troops marched past as good as any regular every did. Everyone was satisfied and the King and those who were with him seemed very much pleased with the bearing of the Canadians and their outfit. We like the Web equipment very much. There is the Knapsack, haversack, water bottle, sidearms, ball pouches and intrenching tool and yet it is not heavy. We will have sailed I think by the time this reaches you.

With love to all
from Horace

In the Trenches in France
Mar 11, 1915

Dear Mother:

Well. I am sorry I have not written sooner, but one keeps putting it off. There was mail came into the trenches last night. I got papers and we were mighty glad to get them as we get no news of anything. You know more of what is going on than we do except just near us.

I have a fine section of trenches and dug-out. It is pretty dry and I have built and fixed it up so it is quite good now. We stay in days and go back to rest for days in billets. We get more rest while in the trenches I think than when we are in our billets.

Yesterday we made a sham attack to draw up the German reserves, so an attack could be made by our left. Two of the old 42nd answered their final roll call in it. Two good lives for King and country. To-day we just kept the Germans guessing what we were going to do so they would not know whether we were going to attack or not.

The last billet we were at it was snowing when we left. I met one of the Artillery men there that used to go up to camp from Carleton Place with the 42nd. Minchin is his name. At that time he ran a pool room in the Mississippi Hotel.

We have been issued rubber boots for the trenches. Some of us turned in our fur coats. I did, as I have the lamb lined vest, one of those Mr. Fred McDiarmid sent us, and my pack is plenty heavy enough. I wish now I had a small kodak and if I can I will send my big one back as it is too heavy to carry around. If you meet anyone I owe a letter to, tell them I am o.k. and will try to write when the rush is over.

Those handkerchiefs and clothes you sent me come in very handy. I was glad to receive them as we do not have much chance to get things washed now. I have discarded quite a few things now and carry food instead because we did not get very good food in the trenches but it has improved this time, we had fresh meat to-day. We do all our own cooking in the trenches over open fires in old pails and have to hunt up the fuel. The worst of it is the hot fire melts the solder in our canteens and they leak. I wish we had the seamless ones. Do you think you could get one and send it to me. We have to carry the ones we have inside our packs and they are an awkward shape. I guess I will stop and make a cup of cocoa. The Germans fire at our parapet and knock mud into our food when we are cooking, but we do likewise.

The Germans and our side yell back and forth at each other. They speak perfect English and we often jolly each other. They ask are our jobs kept for us in Canada, how much pay are we drawing off our jobs, etc.

15 March 1915

Well, I am back in billet to-day. It is the closest yet to our line. Everytime we come out we are in a different billet. We done nothing but rest yesterday and hold church in the afternoon. To-day we are going for a bath. Our bugler had a very narrow escape. He went into one of the bays and fired a couple of shots through a loophole when he got an answer that blew both front and rear sights off his rifle and knocked a couple of pieces into his face. He may lose the sight of his right eye but will likely live.

I guess you will have seen in the papers how the British have advanced, right here we are well ahead and have to wait on the flanks.

I guess I will close and hand it in.

With love, from
Horace

Sterne T. Edwards

28 November 1916 (printed in the *Carleton Place Herald*)

Sterne Edwards with the Allied Airmen

Interesting notes gleaned from letters written home by another of our aviators:

Mrs. E.D. Edwards had a cable from her son Sterne on Friday last from London, where he is now on a week's leave of absence after spending five months in France. Sterne's work is not individual, he is with a squadron, and they have to work as such. Their business is dropping bombs on munition factories and other important places in the enemy country. His letters are interesting:—

On the 13th October he writes: "Well we have started business at last. Yesterday we raided a big munition factory 110 miles away, about 60 miles this side of the Rhine. It was the biggest raid we carried out, more than 60 machines taking part. I do not think there is much left of the munition factory to-day. Oberndorf is the name of the place. Nine of our machines did not come back, 6 French and 3 British. It is likely they were shot down by anti-aircraft guns for they shelled us very heavily and the sky was thick with bursts. However, on a raid of that size and distance, one expects to lose some machines, and 8 of the boys each shot down a Hun, which helps some. The shells came near me only once, and I dived a thousand feet to change the range. We have the fastest bombing aeroplane in the world. We were the only flight (A No.1 Topwith squadron) [perhaps Sopwith] to come back complete. B Flight had some of its pilots lose themselves as it was dark when we got back and they landed in fields some distance from our aerodrome. We were about three and a half hours in the air, those in the slower machines of course much longer. My engine was not any too good coming back, and before I recrossed the lines I thought I would have to descend, but it held out, and took me over the Vosges to 55 instead of 80 miles and I got home. A Hun machine was over a few nights ago and startled us by dropping bombs near our hut. We lost no time in getting into our dugout which is only 20 feet from the door. The bombs did no harm, and when the searchlights picked him out and the guns started shooting he soon left."

On the 29th October he wrote again: "We have been very busy lately and have moved twice in three days. We have done nothing in the way of raids for the past week, as there has been a continued gale blowing and plenty of rain. The day we flew over here it was very rough, the worst any of us had experienced. It took me 40 minutes to fly only 15 miles, and we should do it in 10. We are now at a little place about 18 miles from Nancy, and will probably stay some time. It is not very far from the lines. Think we will move further north soon. Of course it is very nice to be moving about so much for one sees so much of the country. Nancy is a very nice little city. Little Paris they call it. It is about the size of Ottawa and only seven miles behind the lines. That paper clipping I sent home some time ago had Murray [Galbraith] in it. He is hundreds of miles from us. I suppose you have heard that Murray got the D.S.C. [Distinguished Service Cross], for bringing down that German machine some time ago. I am glad for I think he deserves it."

On November 5th Sterne writes of not receiving any mail for over a week and is suffering with a cold: "Have been doing nothing on account of rough weather for some time. Have been down to Luxena and Epinal. There is some talk of leave soon, and if it does we go seven at a time for 10 days, and being out here first I expect to be in the first seven, and hope to see Bob before he comes to France. Had the officers of a French regiment billeted near by to dinner. The regiment is the Alpine Chausseurs, one of the crack regiments of France. We had a good time and they invited us to their mess tomorrow night. Our C.O. got a letter the other day from General Joffre, signed by himself, saying he was much pleased with No. 3 Wing, or something to that effect, and there is a rumor that we may be allowed to wear a decoration of some kind. We have just been supplied with plenty of good flying clothes, boots, headgear and seal gauntlets, and they are necessary as it is very cold up high now.

Will wire from England if I get leave.

Your loving son
Sterne"

Lockhart Campbell

Pte. Campbell's Last Letter

Published May 18, 1915

The following letter from Lockhard Campbell was written the day before the Battle of Langemarck and received the same day as the report of his death.

France, April 21st, 1915

Dear Mother:

I am writing you again to let you know I am still alive and well, hoping every one at home is the same. Well mother, we are just beginning to realize what this war means to the Belgium people. There have been scores of people coming through this place this morning who have been chased out of house and home just this last week back. You see old women, who have no other way of transporting their belongings, carrying larger and heavier packs than we carry on the march. Some of the farmers have had to get out and you see them coming along with their horses and waggons loaded to the limit. I don't suppose any of them know where they are going to get a house of any kind to sleep in again. It makes a person vow vengeance on those who are causing their suffering. The last week back we have been through a part of Belgium which has not been touched by the Germans and it certainly is a nice country. But still it isn't like it would be in peace time for there are refugees all through the country. There has been a lot of heavy fighting this last few days. There are loads of wounded coming through here all the time. It won't be long before we are at them, the Germans I mean, again, and there won't be any fun in it this time either, for the Germans seem to be determined to break through now or never. I have just read Olive's letter this evening of March the 1st so I will have to close this and write her a little spiel. I also had a letter from grandma, and one from Muriel. I have 4 letters to answer now all together so I better get busy.

From your son
Lockhard

James W. McGill

Belgium, May 5th, 1915

Dear Mother:

Just a few lines to let you know that I am still in good health, but my nerves had a pretty bad shaking up in the last big fight at [deleted by censor]. We were ordered up to relieve an English regiment who were holding the trenches near St. Julien and we happened to be the battalion to go into the first line. In going into them we had to cross a great deal of open country so they kept us under a heavy fire all the time which cost a number of lives. While we were getting into our trenches they got our Lieutenant and two sergeants, but theirs were only flesh wounds so were sent to the hospital. A few of the other boys got wounded about the same time. The rest of us got under cover by digging holes in the ground deep enough to cover our bodies from rifle fire, but all the time shells were bursting over our heads.

The men of the first brigade were holding the first line of trenches so Capt Hooper took 25 of his own boys ahead into a house at the right of the bush along with a machine-gun for the purpose of sniping at the enemy. It was a brick building, so was bullet proof, and we made holes through the walls to shoot through.

The enemy's artillery placed shells on every side of us but could not get the right range so we were left there for two days without any person being hurt and in the meantime we had messengers taking orders to headquarters and returning with others all the time. We also had men placed out in front of the house at night to report back in case the enemy crept up under cover of the darkness, which they did quite often, but we always caught them in time and our heavy fire drove them back. A machine gun shoots about 300 shots to a minute, so it has an awful effect, as they always advanced in masses and it was like mowing hay to see them go down.

On the second night our men out in front captured a German spy who had crawled up too far. We brought him into the house and searched him, finding he had four packets of ammunition for rocket purpose to light up the sky. He also had 2 revolvers to use these shells with, along with a swell iron cross presented to him by the Kaiser for acts of bravery, I suppose. We took him back to headquarters to let them deal with him. The men at headquarters said it was a fine capture as they wanted to get some of those rockets to analyze them as ours had proved a failure. When they shot those up in the sky it made it seem like day and one could distinguish any person moving, so the Captain kept one of the revolvers and a package of shells for our use at night to shoot over their lines, giving us a chance to pop them off as soon as they moved.

On the third day we ran short of our own ammunition, so I and another boy had to go back to headquarters and bring some up, both for the machine gun and ourselves, and in the meantime the boys had to fill the belts for the machine gun from their own pouches. In the afternoon of the third day I was sent out again for ammunition when the enemy broke through the French lines on our right leaving us open to a heavy flank fire, so we had to retire to keep in contact with the French. In the meantime the enemy flocked into the bush on our left in great numbers almost cutting us off in this house. While I was coming up through the reserve trenches with ammunition the Major gave me an order for Capt Hooper to retire. I got through with it, to him and he sent me back again to tell the Major to hold the trenches till we got into them, which he did, but the enemy was too close to us so as soon as the boys came out of the house they cut them down leaving only seven out of the bunch that went in. Of course a great many only wounded, but the officers in the rear said they [censored] them. I was lucky enough to get back to the Major with the message, so returned with his men, but I heard afterwards that he never left the trench.

L. Halsey and E. Reynolds from home were with the stretcher-bearers taking care of the wounded, so they never came any nearer than the dressing station, but it was almost as bad there as they were exposed to shell fire all the time, the enemy shelled this house and our headquarters setting both afire but I think they got all the wounded out alright as it seemed that every man you met was helping a wounded comrade back to safety. L. Halsey afterwards got wounded with a piece of shrapnel. Harry McLaren was in the house, but he says he was one of the first to leave it, so he got through all right. I cannot account for the rest, as we were not sure of what happened to them. Some think they were taken prisoners or were suffocated by that awful gas. I lost my company for two days and was with one of the English regiments who advised me to return to the billet I had left, which I did, but in the meantime the Canadians had mostly all formed up again and drove the enemy back.

It was a great day for the Canadians, but it cost a great many lives. I don't know how I got through, but I never got a scratch, but had to throw away all my personal property and kit bag as it was too heavy, and my life was more valuable.

When we returned to our billet they shelled us out of that, so they sent up a relief for us and we are at present back out of the danger zone and out of hearing of the guns, which is a great relief as the boys' nerves were in a bad shape from the awful din of battle. I think we will be here for quite a while as the enemy are very quiet at present. They are giving us fresh equipment in place of what we lost.

Well mother I must close hoping for an early reply.

Your loving son
James

(Published on July 27, 1915)
How Lockhart Campbell Died
Pte. McGill Gives Some Details of the Bad Incident

Princess Club Hospital
104 Jamaica Rd.
Bermondsey
London, Eng,

Mr. Samuel Crampton
Carleton Place, Ontario

Dear Sir:

In reference to your letter of June 9th I am sorry to state that poor Lockhard is gone to a better land; dying the death of a brave soldier without stain on his conscience.

He was always a good soldier and did all this work willingly and few ever heard him grumble.

I have been with him all the time since we left home and always found him ready to obey any command.

As he was counted a good shot, with nerve enough to obey all orders, he was one of the picked men to go into this house between the two firing lines for sniping purposes, or in other words to shoot off all stray Germans who were inclined to creep up for to study our positions. We held this house for three days till the enemy made his big advance on April 25th.

By advancing on the French on our right and driving them back by the use of that murderous gas part of our contingent were obliged to counter attack the advance of the enemy which caused a great deal of anxiety. In the meantime they also advanced on our left in an angling position completely cutting us off in this house. A number of the boys being wounded we were obliged to get back to our trenches as quickly and quietly as possible so the Captain sent six of us out at first and watched results. That was where Lockhard met his death by a bullet in the head. It was instant death, causing no pain, which was a blessing when we think of what some of the boys suffered on account of not being able to be moved. I cannot get any trace of many of the other boys, but expect they are prisoners along with the Captain.

I am in a lovely hospital in England getting the best of care and expect to get out again before long.

If there is any other information that you may want don't delay in writing me and I will do all I can to ease the wound it has caused to his kind parents whom I know well.

Please give my sincerest sympathy to his parents as his was a death to be proud of, dying for the honor of his country. Closing with sincere regards.

I am yours truly
James W. McGill
Regt No 8476

Capt. W.H. Hooper:

A card from France:[place deleted by censor]
France, Feb 14, 1915

Dear J.M.

All in billet here. Horace is happy in a hayloft. All C.P. boys are here and well. Neither as cold or wet as in England, but we're used to it now. Respects to Mrs. B. and yourself.

Capt. Hooper

Letter received by Mr. A.C. Mackay of Renfrew from Capt. Will Hooper.

France, March 14th, 1915

Dear Mrs. Mackay

It is with deepest sorrow I write you to notify you of the death of Cameron. My heart is indeed heavy and yet it should not be, for the boy died a hero's death. By direction of superior orders, we were making a very heavy showing in force on the morning of March 10th, when poor Ferguson Bremner was hit. Thank God he never knew what hit him. The Renfrew section, Cameron among them, at once opened heavy fire on the German trenches in order to keep down the enemy's heads while the stretcher bearers and myself hastened across the stretch to Bremner, and while nobly doing this Cameron was also hit. As Bremner had gone, I hastened back to Cameron, and am glad to say that I feel that it soothed his feelings as I talked to him of the mother he so dearly loved, and just as the end seemed near, I told him to "sleep, sleep, sleep and dream, dream, dream of dear mother, Cameron." Thus dreaming he passed away in less than half an hour from the time he was hit. It was all over painlessly, and the spirit of one of the cleanest living boys I ever knew had answered the Last Roll Call. Weep not, mother, but be proud that your boy so nobly died and so well followed out the teaching of Him who stood for all that was good and true. Your boy was true; true to mother and true to country. By this mail I am registering to Capt. Barnet a small box of trinkets. These I trust, you will receive in due course. I laid with him a photo of yourself [a full length one]. This, I know he would have liked. The enclosed cross marked his resting place until the boys make a more suitable and lasting one. This, I thought you would care for. The text is suitable—"He had faith in God." Nothing I can say further would in any way convey to you my feeling of sorrow so I will close now, and may God in his mercy help you all.

Yours respectfully
Will Hooper
Captain

News from Capt. Hooper (a POW in Germany) in a letter to his wife:

June 7, 1916

I got parcels containing cereals, just what I wanted. All arrived o.k. Remember me to Mort. Brown. I'm glad Horace and McLaren are still o.k. Send them good luck for me.

Oh say, a Lieut. O'Grady, from Edmonton, who up to three months ago was in hospital with Clyde Scott, tells me there is no doubt in the world but Clyde will be sent to Switzerland. I'm so glad, for O'Grady says that with special attention and in time he will suffer only a stiff knee. He says the brothers in the hospital all think the world of Clyde, and that they cannot do too much for him. O'Grady is here to appear before the Swiss Commission. I tell him he is a lucky beggar. Three months ago I'm sure I could have passed easily, but now I am so well finished that it's out of the question; only the muscles of my left leg still cause me anxiety. I am indeed lucky, for had one of the wounds gone an inch deeper into the stomach it would have been fatal.

I had a good walk on Saturday, along up the Rhine this time, and not too long with a good chance to sit down and rest. I'm in a new room now. Artillery Leech and I from the old room and six others are here; it is crowded, but the view from the window makes up for any discomforts. It looks right up the Rhine and up the junction of it and the Main, also on the station at Mainz Sud. I'm afraid I'll do little French this week, most of my time will be spent looking out of the window. I got copy of McClure's and Cosmopolitan; also canned goods.

P.S.—7pm, just changed from room 36 to 30, view is not so good, but we have more room.

Will

ABOUT THE AUTHOR

Larry Gray served twenty-four years in the Royal Canadian Air Force as a navigator. He went on to serve veterans as an advocate and adjudicator of pension claims.

During a posting to Europe, he became interested in the World War I battlefields, dragging his wife and two sons through muddy trenches one rainy April in 1969. His interest never waned. In 1986, he developed and led a veterans' organization tour of Flanders that culminated in their attendance at the Vimy Ridge Memorial on July 26, fifty years to the day from its unveiling.

Larry lives in Carleton Place with his wife, Gloria.

To order more copies of

We Are The Dead

send $29.95 plus $5.50 to cover GST,
shipping and handling to:

GENERAL STORE PUBLISHING HOUSE

Box 28, 1694B Burnstown Road

Burnstown, Ontario

K0J 1G0

(613) 432-7697 or **1-800-465-6072**

Fax 613-432-7184

URL – http://www.gsph.com